FUNDAMENTALS OF SHOP OPERATIONS MANAGEMENT

WORK STATION DYNAMICS

D1046829

Daniel T. Koenig, P.E.

Consultant on Manufacturing Technologies,
Systems, and Organization
Lake Worth, Florida

CENTRAL MISSOURI
STATE UNIVERSITY
Warrensburg

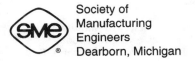

Society of
Manufacturing
Engineers
Dearborn, Michigan

ASME Press
The American Society of
Mechanical Engineers
New York, New York

Additional copies may be obtained by contacting:

American Society of Mechanical Engineers
Customer Service
22 Law Drive, P.O. Box 2900
Fairfield, New Jersey 07007-2900
1-800-843-2763
www.asme.org

Society of Manufacturing Engineers
Customer Service
One SME Drive, P.O. Box 930
Dearborn, Michigan 48121
313-271-1500
www.sme.org

Library of Congress Catalog Card Number: 99-052975
International Standard Book Number: 0-7918-0094-6

The American Society of Mechanical Engineers and the Society of Manufacturing Engineers would like to thank the following people for reviewing this book:
Sathyan Tivakaran, William Spurgeon, John York, Keith Thayer and Richard Suhar.

To Marilyn, Alan, and Michael for going through it again
by showing understanding and tolerance of my behavior
during the creation of this manuscript;
and to Deb and Cindy for learning fast and
supporting me in my quest.

Contents

Preface

The idea of writing this book had been working its way in my mind toward conscious thought over many years. But perhaps its true inception took place at the fall 1995 meeting of American Society of Mechanical Engineers Industry Advisory Board. At that meeting, which I was attending as President of ASME, we were engaged in a lively discussion about productivity problems and potential solutions, and it dawned on me that we were talking *around* the problem but not about its root cause. The proverbial light bulb went on and I realized that the true solution to the quest for improved productivity had to be sought where the action is: the factory floor, and our management of it. We needed to bring cutting-edge methodologies to floor managers, and they had to know how to use them. If factory operations cannot be optimized, productivity certainly will not improve. I quickly jotted down what was to become Figure 1-1 of this book, showing the relationship between the work that is performed at the work station and all the inputs, positive and negative, that determine how it unfolds. I made these points at the meeting, but later that day I felt I hadn't shown that to solve the problem, the focus of management efforts had to be primarily on the source, the shop operations task. Also, talking to colleagues only reinforced what I know to be true: most managers learn shop management techniques by trial and error and there is very little literature on the subject. That, combined with my desire to keep ASME a valuable asset to its industrial members, led me to write this book.

In general, engineers are taught to employ the scientific method in solving technical problems. By and large, we do that well. However, for some mysterious reason we fail to seriously apply its dictates to shop operations management. We seem to think that those populating the floors of our factories do not need this attention—that it was all done many decades ago by the likes of Taylor, Gantt, and the Gilbreths. But what about manufacturing resources planning, just-in-time, total quality management, and the quest for enlightened participator management (to say nothing of the overall information explosion and the complexity of processes shop supervisors have to deal with directly)? These methodologies, none of which were around decades ago, are enormous opportunities to improve profits if harnessed correctly. Unfortunately, nowhere near enough is being done to train engineers working as shop operations managers in how to apply those technologies, and even less to train nonengineers in supervisory roles. We engineers, who invent the majority of the technologies and methodologies to make our products, need to see our inventions to completeness by explaining them and giving the necessary instructions to those who will use them. Those who *run* factories need to be well taught in the effective methods, so that they can improve outputs and thereby make ever-improving living standards available to more and more people.

In this book I have written about the management processes and techniques that are proven winners for improving productivity and, thus, profits. My goal is to show how these techniques extend to factory management by explaining their application on the factory floor. I've tried to do this in a manner that would give the reader—a practicing shop floor engineer or manager, or an engineering student exploring careers in manufacturing—a practical, how-to-do-it slant, I want to give the reader specific ideas to try, with reasons for and ways to employ them. I know they all work because I, or associates of mine, have used them successfully. Also, by delineating these how-to-do-it recipes, I hope I will save new users the onerous task of learning by trial and error. This way they can build on my experiences and postulate even better, more advance methodologies in the future. This is the way to progress. This is the way we continue our journey toward making the world a better place for our children and grandchildren.

Daniel T. Koenig
Lake Worth, Florida
March 21, 1999

Chapter 1

An Overview of Work Station Dynamics

A SHORT HISTORY

Manufacturing is the process of transforming raw materials into useful products by way of engineered processes conducted at work stations. The methodology of optimizing work stations is a systematic approach I call *work station dynamics (WSD)*. This book is about the *processes* of work station dynamics, which are used to maximize factory output. It is about the techniques that need to be employed at the work station to reap the full benefit of the engineered processes. We will explore techniques that allow practitioners to realize the full potential for profit from their factories.

Let's look at the fundamental theories forming the basis of work station dynamics. They are commonly known as the *two basic tenets of manufacturing* (over the years I've shortened the title to the "Two Knows"):

1. Know how to make the product.
2. Know how long it should take to make the product.

and the *seven steps of the manufacturing system:*

1. Obtain product specification.
2. Design a method for producing the product, including design and purchase of equipment and processes to produce, if required.
3. Schedule to produce.
4. Purchase raw materials in accordance with the schedule.
5. Produce in the factory.
6. Monitor results for technical compliance and cost control.
7. Ship the completed product to the customer.

I introduced both of these concepts in the early 1980s after extensive trial and error. As a design engineer and manufacturing engineer, and later in various roles as a manufacturing function manager within the General Electric Company starting in the mid-1960s, I've been fortunate to be associated with some of the greatest minds dealing with the pragmatic necessities of manufacturing management theory. Because of my many years in world class manufacturing environments, where the intensive challenge to always do better prevailed, I can assert that the theories I am about to explain are not hypothetical. They are the reality of successful manufacturing practices. I call them theories because I have no strict way of proving them scientifically. I do know, however, that they work, and every person and organization that

1

I've taught them to and that has applied them has experienced considerably improved manufacturing results.

The Two Knows are the basis of manufacturing. All too often businesses brazenly go off to produce a product without a thorough understanding of how to go about it or how their new undertaking will affect their ability to show a profit. There is nothing more fundamental than knowing how to make the product and knowing how long it should take. Understanding how to make the product allows the organization to tool up, to train people, and to assess the risk. Knowing how long the task will take is fundamental in determining the quantity that can be delivered over time. These are such fundamental and essential first steps in deciding on a manufacturing venture that I am astonished at the frequency with which otherwise bright and logical people will plunge in head first without the necessary understanding.

The seven steps in the manufacturing system are the logical approach to producing any product or service. They are the codification of applying the basic tenets of manufacturing, or the Two Knows. When you analyze what any firm goes through in bringing any product from concept to reality, you see that the seven steps are indeed followed. Obviously, those who are conscious of this natural sequence will bring their products to realization with fewer inefficiencies and doublebacks than those who are oblivious to it.

Proper application of the Two Knows leads to optimal manufacturing practice. It is absolutely essential that we, as manufacturing engineers and managers, have a keen grasp of the techniques involved in optimizing the Two Knows. This is tantamount to operational success. Throughout this book we will investigate how application of the details of the Two Knows leads to logical control and planning of work stations, the results being success in overall manufacturing activity. I cannot overemphasize that every manufacturing action needs to be analyzed in terms of its relevance to optimizing the Two Knows, because everything we do at a work station should be guided by one or both of the Two Knows. Understanding this and the synergistic linkages between the various action steps of the manufacturing system leads to successful, profitable manufacturing. What I have set out to do is to examine all the actions derived from the Two Knows and the seven steps, which we'll call "inputs"; to describe each input; and then to show the optimization techniques available to get the best linkage between inputs for the best outcome. With that done, I'll then show and describe the process of implementing work station dynamics. This is sometimes called the *productivity improvement program*, commonly referred to as *short interval scheduling* or *factory floor control*.

THE WORK STATION DYNAMIC SCHEMATIC

For an idea of what work station dynamics is all about, let's look at a schematic diagram of the process and a brief description of each component (see Figure 1-1). In succeeding chapters I will describe in depth the steps of WSD and how to optimize for manufacturing—and thus business—success.

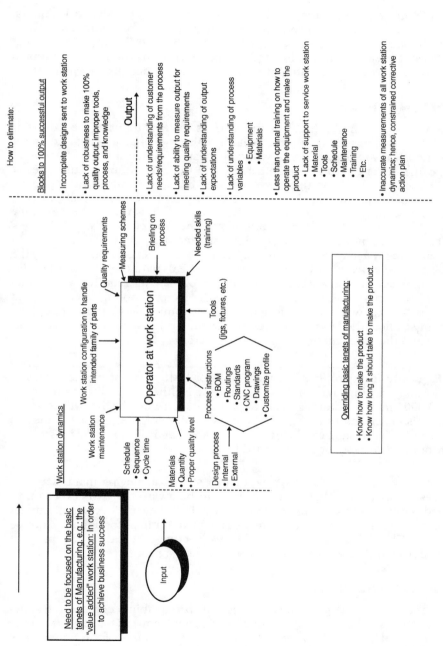

Figure 1-1. Work station dynamics: the ability to produce in accordance with a plan.

As Figure 1-1 shows, the work station operator is responsive to 11 inputs, described in the following sections, that are necessary for optimizing manufacturing activity and make up the specifics of the Two Knows; 10 are direct inputs and one (design) is indirect. By correctly applying the 11 specific inputs we go a long way toward eliminating the reasons for subpar performance.

The Design Process

The one indirect input, the *design process*, is the first input to the work station. This involves the creation of what is called a *workable design* and a set of supporting *tooling designs*. A workable design is one that is producible in a specific factory with reasonable skills and the current, or planned, set of equipment. This means there is some sort of compatibility with the proposed design and the capability of the factory proposed to actually carry it out. Supporting tooling design is a necessary follow-up to the workable design that allows the factory's equipment to be used efficiently.

The process by which we design for manufacturability is formally known as *concurrent engineering*. The major factors for consideration are, first, the subset called *producibility engineering*, which deals with the process of evaluating materials to be worked with and the tolerancing required versus factory capabilities; and, second, designing the factory tooling, methods, and fixtures. We know that good design is a compromise between ideal application of science (the laws of physics and chemistry) to achieve a desired outcome and the practical limitations of the factory.

Example: A microfinish on aluminum of RMS 8 is not possible with normal turning and milling machines. Neither is a dimension of ±0.0001 in. If a factory is asked to produce such a finish without special precision machines and grinders in its set of equipment, it is doomed to fail. The design would not be workable, and all good designs are workable designs for the intended factory.

Creating a producible design is the first step in achieving manufacturing success. This means that engineers have to be aware that whatever is proposed outwardly to customers is relevant only if their factory can manufacture it economically. Once this hurdle is passed, optimal tooling needs to be defined. This is as important a design objective as creating the product design itself and is the second factor in the design process.

Process Instructions

With the product design, refined through the producibility engineering activity, we have set the stage for optimizing the Two Knows. This leads us to the second input, *process instructions*. This gets down to the very fundamentals of making the product, the instructions to the various factory work stations explaining what has to be done, how it is to be done, and how long it should take to achieve the desired outcome.

Process instructions are the routings, method instructions, computer numerical control (CNC) programs, applications of time standards, and specific engineering instructions developed by engineers as they analyze the intents of the workable designs. Instructions for manufacturing have to be very product-specific. The main features are the routings, which are the sequenced listings of events to be carried out at various work stations and the engineered times to accomplish; and the method instructions, which specifically describe the process to be followed. CNC programs are subsets of method instruction but intended for computer controllers instead of human operators.

Note that the *bill of materials (BOM)* is not part of process instructions, even though it is often linked to routings. Specifically, the BOM is a listing of materials with quantities, often shown in sequence of use or assembly, that does not impart knowledge of how to accomplish the tasks or the time it should take to do so.

Quality Requirements

The third input is *quality requirements*. This is a close companion to process instructions. It needs to be planned concurrently with process instructions because factory management often makes the mistake of implying quality actions but not specifying them. Hence, the result is often failure.

For every process step there should be a quality step. Quite frequently quality steps are built into the process and monitored through statistical process control (SPC) or other means However, they need to be consciously planned.

Examples:
(a) *Process instruction:* Machine to a specific dimension, ± tolerance.
   Quality requirement: Operator measure each piece to assure compliance; *or,* Operator audit one of X pieces to assure compliance and enter into SPC database.
(b) *Process instruction:* Preheat material to specified temperature before applying epoxy bonding agent.
   Quality requirement: Preset oven to alarm at low or high temperature.

The key philosophy of total success—whether quality defect levels are measured in parts per million or parts per billion or any other index—is the cognizant awareness of the need to plan the quality step in parallel and compatible with the process step.

Schedule Sequence and Cycle Time

The fourth input is *schedule sequence and cycle time*. Work has to be done in accordance with a planned routing sequence among work stations on a micro as well as a macro basis. This means that each step of the sequence has to fit into the time planned for it, across all the various work stations required to translate raw material to finished product. This includes making the individual parts as well as the various sub- and final assemblies.

A major aspect of the second of the Two Knows is that the sequence time has to be planned. This is necessary so that each work station can be loaded in proper sequence, neither overloaded nor underloaded with work to be done during a specific time period. Remember, time is one-directional only; it cannot be reversed, so we can never recover wasted time. However, we can optimally load each work station in a manner that assures that we make the best possible use of time before we waste it.

There are many ways to load work stations. The most commonly used to optimize output per time period tend to be combinations of scheduling algorithms called *manufacturing resources planning (MRP II)* and *group technology (GT)* sorting techniques. MRP II systems by themselves do a good job in macroscheduling once a cycle time for each work station is known. However, MRP II does not deliver fully optimal loading, because it considers setups to be part of the cycle. Therefore, other means have to be found to group parts through work stations to minimize non-value-added work (setups, primarily). One such tool is GT classification and coding schemes, sometimes also associated with GT layouts; but regardless of the method, it is always necessary to sequence work to minimize cycle time beyond the capabilities of MRP II. This means that first in, first out scheduling is often nonoptimal and it is much better to hold parts back until they are grouped with similar parts, in order to gain more value-added time while reducing non-value-added time.

Also involved in optimizing the schedule and reducing the over all cycle time is the concept of *pull versus push* production control systems. A push system concentrates on starts and adds planned sequenced cycle times to get to the calculated finish date. Pull systems, on the other hand, concentrate on demands from the final assembly operation to have all components arrive only when needed and in proper quantities. There are pros and cons to both philosophies, and determining the best practice for each circumstance depends on the type of factory involved and the business criteria to be met. But there are some broad areas of advice on choosing between push and pull production control systems:

Push systems:

1. Are sufficient for simple routings with no or minimal assemblies.
2. Are insufficient for parts consisting of one or more assemblies; they create waste because most often the parts arrive at assembly points before they're needed to assure availability. Hence:
3. Can create excess work-in-process (WIP) inventory on hand. A push system is thus frequently called a *just-in-case* system, or even, contemptibly, "pushing on a rope," which may be no less effective.

Pull systems:

1. May amount to overkill for simple routings with no or minimal assemblies.
2. Use backward scheduling from the planned ship date, based on planned cycle times.

Scheduling to produce is the most intensely mathematical activity associated with work station dynamics. We can say this because optimizing it depends on formulas linking work stations in proper sequences to produce multiple products through the same machines and processes. Linear programming and matrix algebra may be used effectively in solving the generic optimization problem.

Tools, Jigs, and Fixtures

The fifth input is *tools, jigs, and fixtures.* The process and quality requirements based on the defined workable design will dictate the tools, jigs, and fixtures necessary to achieve the overall intent of that design. There is also a definite iterative process between tool and jig selection and the quantity to be produced. For example, the selection of a single-station punch press as opposed to a multiple-punch setup or a high-speed progressive punch press will depend on quantity to be produced and the time frame allowed for completion.

In the choice of tools, jigs, and fixtures, we are optimizing the first of the Two Knows based on quantity and delivery requirements. As Figure 1-2 shows, a greater investment in such equipment can result in faster time to produce and lowered cost per part.

Example: If 100,000 stamped parts are required in two years, the process selected and the corresponding jigs and fixtures would be very different from those indicated if 100 million are required in two years. The former would require a simple die that would be assigned to a sin-

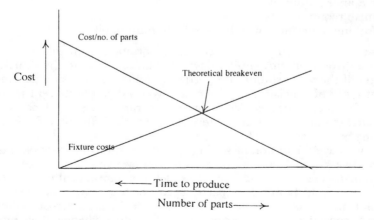

Figure 1-2. Cost versus time per part. As fixture costs increase, both time to produce and cost per part decrease.

gle-stage press and most likely be set up as needed. The press would probably run slower than a progressive press with a compound die, which would be used in the latter scenario. Also, the compound die solution would most likely be fed by coil stock instead of individual pieces and most likely be an automatic feed instead of a one-at-a-time hand feed.

Although we usually think of the design process as being for a part only, the truth is that designing the tools to produce the part is equally as important. Logically we can't have one without the other. This leads to the concept of *value engineering:* the theory of cost optimization of a design versus its intended value. Value engineering is the topic of the last sections of Chapter 6.

Work Station Configuration to Handle the Intended Family of Parts

The sixth input is *work station configuration to handle the intended family of parts.* There is no universal work station (except perhaps in science fiction novels) that can do all things for all products; if there were, no manufacturing company could afford it. However, that doesn't say we don't strive to do as diverse a number of jobs per work station as possible. Typically, this means reserving a work station for parts that share some type(s) of characteristics. They may have a basic process in common—for example, turning, milling, drilling; or welding, brazing—or they may share other defining commonalities, such as:

1. Length to width relationships
2. Length to diameter relationships
3. Flat shape relationships
4. Maximum and minimum sizes
5. Tolerance requirements
6. Finish requirements
7. Working materials—whether steel, aluminum, plastic, etc.

Characteristics 1 through 4 are geometric parameters, in that they define shapes that would employ similar devices to attach them to the value-added surface(s) of the work station. Properties 5 and 6 are precision parameters; different types of precision requirements would dictate different manufacturing techniques. Number 7 is a process parameter: several parts might have a similar shape, but if the materials used were different, different manufacturing processes would be dictated.

Thus, we have the option of setting up work stations to work on multiple parts that we group in accordance with whatever similarities we identify. Even so, many engineers and managers feel it is impractical to set up work stations for whole families of parts, because, they say, they operate job shops, not mass production facilities. This is really a false assumption. All companies specialize in only certain lines of products; hence, their universe is already truncated considerably. It is highly unlikely that a company would make printed circuit boards and also transmission gears, at least in the same factory facilities. Any number of methods can be used to define families of parts, ranging from empirical decision to GT classification and coding. We will explore these methods in a separate chapter.

The work station, then, is designed to have all the equipment necessary to handle the intended family (or selected families) of parts. We divide this equipment into a primary and a secondary set. The primary set consists of equipment the company uses to transform raw material into finished product; also, if appropriate, the equipment necessary for assembly. The secondary set consists of the auxiliary equipment necessary for supporting the work at the work station. This would normally be the jigs and fixtures to hold and position the work, as well as the computer information terminals and workbenches. Secondary set components are used to indirectly transform raw material to the finished material output designated for the work station. Contrast this with a CNC machine that is an example of a primary piece of equipment. Secondary equipment is necessary to make sure the primary equipment runs optimally.

Example: If a process calls for spacing between drilled holes centerline to centerline to be accurate within ±0.0001 in., then a *coordinate measuring machine (CMM)* is probably required as a secondary piece of equipment. This would be especially true if the volume is high. Without the CMM, the danger of making out-of-tolerance parts would be higher, or even unacceptable.

Material Quantity and Quality Levels

The seventh input is *material quantity and quality levels*. The impact here is on optimization of the second of the Two Knows (know how long it takes to make the product). This input is the necessary function of making sure that the correct material in the proper quantity and at the necessary quality level is received at the work station, when it is required.

Input in sufficient quantities and output in sufficient quantities to meet customer needs are paramount to success. Not only is quantity important, but quality is equally important. We can't have one absent the other. If 100 parts are required, 100 *good* parts need to be received at the end of the cycle. The start of the manufacturing process requires that the material be of sufficient quality not to frustrate the goal of making the required number of parts via the selected process.

Work Station Maintenance

The eighth input is *work station maintenance*. Recall the advertisement for FRAM filters, "Pay me now or pay me later." This refers to the lower cost of

preventive maintenance versus the higher cost of fix-when-broken maintenance—to say nothing of the severe inconvenience. Work stations involving
equipment of any kind are self-destructing devices. Where moving parts are
involved, there will inevitably be failure—sooner or later. The purpose of
work station maintenance is to minimize down time, thus optimizing production output.

Think of preventive maintenance (PM) as being like medicine: it has to be
taken when needed, to prevent catastrophic illness later on. PM significantly
reduces the likelihood that catastrophic failure will occur. Thus, it needs to
be part of the overall cycle time. It is a factor in understanding the second of
the Two Knows.

Needed Skills and Training

The ninth input is *needed skills and training*. First of all, be assured that there
is no such thing as a fully automated process. There never has been one, nor
is there ever likely to be one. Nor does fully automated equipment exist.
Although machines and other equipment may be reliable and seldom require
human intervention, at some time in their life they will. So the success of a
manufacturing process depends on the skills of the *people*.

Some machines and processes are ill defined and hence require continuous monitoring and working by the operator. We tend to call processes that
require more intervention skilled operations; an example would be hand
grinding to get a required surface finish. On the other hand, some machines
and processes are well defined and rarely require intervention by the operator. But when they do, inept intervention could spell catastrophic failure for
the company.

Example: A grinding error in the CNC program to manufacture the
mirror in the Hubbell Space Telescope not diagnosed by the operator
led to a very costly and embarrassing failure for NASA. This points out
the need for having appropriate skills for working the work station.

Usually, the more complex a machine or process is, the more technical are
the skills required. Either the necessary skills are imparted by company
training, or the operator possesses them when he or she is assigned to the
job (and more than likely was hired for having them).

It is absolutely wrong, both logically and morally, to put people on any job
without the necessary skills. Such mismatches cause great frustration for the
individual and economic failure for the company. Mismatches allowed in a
cavalier fashion are akin to allowing a novice to be the pilot of a 747 airliner.
It is management's responsibility to ascertain that the necessary skill sets are
matched with each work station. To do otherwise is to settle for less than
optimum performance.

Remember, operators are really line managers of the process and must be
vigorously trained to handle a wide variety of potential calamities.

Briefing on Processes

The tenth input is *briefing on processes*. Just as an airline pilot briefs him- or herself on the flight path, the weather, the peculiarities of the specific aircraft, and other important factors of the flight from departure to destination, operators have to be briefed on the part they are making as to quantity, design requirements, quality checks, and information on their jigs and fixtures.

We can't expect that the operator will simply read the routing and review the drawing and know exactly what to do, especially if this is the first time the part is being made or the first time the operator is attempting the job. Since most work is job shop–oriented, there will always be differences, major or minor, from shop order to shop order. Literally thousands of changes are implemented daily in an average 100-employee facility. Hence, there has to be a comprehensive methodology on how to get change information to work stations, on time. The best method is to use combinations ranging from written instructions for minor changes to full briefings for new products.

Work Station Dynamics Measurement Schemes

The eleventh input is *work station dynamics measurement schemes*. In addition to traditional industrial engineering (IE) measurements of effectiveness, efficiency, and quality levels, it is necessary to measure how well a company can discern the proper method for making its product. We must determine:

1. How well do we understand the process?
2. How close are we coming to targeted prices, and what is causing the variances?
3. How well do we measure the effectiveness of changes?
4. How well do we measure creativity toward doing the process better?
5. How do we determine if the process is optimized?

These types of measurements define the intellectual quotient of the company. It defines how well the company can act as a cohesive team in making its products. Companies that consistently challenge their own ability to quantify these attributes tend to be the best companies. These are firms that we call world class.

THE BLOCKS TO OPTIMUM MANUFACTURING PERFORMANCE

By understanding the inputs of the Two Knows, we have a head start in actually optimizing manufacturing. Another way to look at it would be to try to conceive of things that block our ability to gain an optimum output. The goal is to have zero *waste*. (Waste is defined graphically in Figure 1-3.) To strive for this goal means we have to have a mind-set and desire to achieve

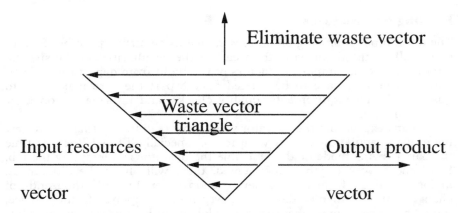

Figure 1-3. Output = input – waste. Process improvements move the waste triangle up, so that the waste vector is shortened and more of the input resources vector is translated to the output product vector.

perfect quality (e.g., zero ppm defective). There are many blocks to 100% successful output. Let's look at the major ones.

Incomplete Designs Sent to Work Stations

For all practical purposes, incomplete designs mean that the work station becomes a development center—the design engineers are using the work station as a means for developing the design. This is prototype development, not standard manufacturing operations, and is not conducive to optimum performance. Incomplete design means that the work station cannot perform the intended job in its entirety. Typically this occurs when a design is insufficient for the part to be made within the necessary tolerance band and ends up creating unacceptably high reject rates. When a tolerance is needed to support a future assembly operation and the process cannot deliver a satisfactory outcome, we have an example of an incomplete design. Designers always need to consider the ability of manufacturing processes to deliver the required results as part of the design process.

Incomplete design is a productivity deflator. At best, only productivity suffers as the process is stopped often to decide what to do next. At worst, the design is unsuccessful and attempts to fix it fail, wasting labor and material as well as manufacturing resources.

Lack of Robustness to Make 100% Quality Output

A lack of robustness is usually caused by lack of producibility engineering efforts to make a design workable for the intended factory. Lack of robustness in design often occurs when the design doesn't consider the methodology of manufacture and simply assumes that what is called for can be complied with via the common capabilities of the firm. This can be a grievous error that simply ties the factory in knots through poor yields, resulting in inability to make deliveries on schedule. When this happens, objectivity in analyzing manufacturing problems suffers and a spiral of confusion and frustration occurs.

The solution to the problem is not difficult to find. It involves going back to basics and recognizing that manufacturing capabilities need to be matched with specification requirements before a design can be considered complete. If the capabilities do not exist to meet the desired outcomes, then the design cannot be considered ready for implementation. To do so will inevitably cause high costs, late deliveries, and probably quality problems that will damage the company's reputation.

Lack of Understanding of the Customer's Needs and/or Requirements from the Process

Misunderstandings with the customer are closely related to incomplete design. But whereas sending incomplete designs to the workstation is usually an internal matter, failing to understand the customer's needs is typically associated with a product that the *customer* has designed without specifying the complete requirements. This is a malady that tends to afflict job shops contracting to build their customer's products rather than designing a specific product and offering it for sale to a range of customers. In this case design and manufacture are independent rather than mutually dependent.

To correct this problem it is necessary for manufacturing engineers to query customers on all unclear items. Also, it is important for the manufacturing engineer to spell out in detail the capabilities his or her factory possesses vis-à-vis the customer's request for quote (RFQ).

Sometimes specifications required by the customer are defined only in industry standard specifications and codes. In this case, manufacturing engineering, during the RFQ process, needs to discern all applicable codes and standards that the customer says applies.

Lack of Ability to Measure Output for Meeting Quality Requirements

Sometimes a company fails to build in quality requirements along with process instructions. The design is then incomplete and can never be fully satisfied unless the company finds a way to measure quality of output. The firm must be able to evaluate whether it is meeting its commitments to customers in both delivery on schedule and quality of the product. The best way to get objective evaluations is through sources not directly associated with producing the product. That is why manufacturing companies often rely on independent quality organizations.

650675

Lack of Understanding of Output Expectations

When operators misunderstand what output is expected, the reason could be either lack of skills on their part or insufficient briefings on expectations. The two together or separately will result in unsatisfactory outcomes.

Frequently, operators are not truly conversant with the skills needed to accomplish all the tasks necessary at the work station and management blithely ignores this fact. The results are that some work is done satisfactorily, while other work is not. The ratio of good work to bad, however, tends to change with the overall experience and skill levels of the individuals. This means that training is "the way" to teach individuals how to achieve the expected results.

Sometimes briefings are incomplete, and reasons for doing things a certain way are not sufficiently explained to operators. The result of incomplete information is usually a product that is not in compliance with customer specifications. Confidence wanes, and this causes operators to reject briefing materials and revert to doing things as they are accustomed. People do not like to make changes from comfortable situations to unknown ones. Surprisingly, this is so even if the old way is known to produce unsatisfactory results.

The corrective action is simple: train well and completely. Brief workers thoroughly about all items pertaining to the product they are expected to produce. To do less is analogous to fielding a football team that uses only vaguely defined plays and has players who are not skilled in their positions.

Lack of Understanding of Process Variables

Failure to understand process variables is typically an engineering failure. It occurs when the process is not thoroughly investigated and so is not understood by design engineering, and, hence, contingencies are not properly planned. Most often it is the result of a design or process that has not been investigated thoroughly for the proper level of robustness. The failure may be in either materials or equipment or both.

Another way process variable ignorance occurs is through less than optimal training in how to operate the equipment. This results in a catch-as-catch-can situation where outcomes are almost always very bad. The root cause is a breakdown of shop operations management's obligation to provide trained personnel at the work stations. The people in engineering and quality control are also at fault for not blowing the whistle and seeing to it that proper training occurs.

Lack of Support Service to the Work Station

Lack of support could include a whole host of items such as late deliveries of material, or wrong type or quantity; failure to supply tooling to do the job properly; schedule foulups; or lack of preventive maintenance. The cure is to pay attention to work station dynamics. At the very least, construct a checklist to go with every job to assure that all relevant items are attended to. (See Fig. 1-4)

Lack of Accurate Measurements of All Work Station Dynamics Activities

Measurements are the key to success. Goals have to be set, and we have to know whether we are achieving them. To find out, we take measurements of the specific "measurables" for the goals, which need to be defined and developed.

Example: A factory's setup time goal is 7.5% of run time for December 2001. The measurement is value-added time versus non-value-added time attributed to setups. The measurements are analyzed for root cause of meeting or not meeting the goals. With an understanding of root cause, corrective actions can be planned and carried out. We then iterate with more measurements to see if corrective actions are appropriate. The iteration process goes through as many cycles as necessary to obtain the desired outcome.

Work station dynamics is the conscious application of the Two Knows and is a very pragmatic approach. In all instances, understanding how the product is to be made at the work station and how long it should take to do so is vital if we are to minimize production costs and optimize quality and output. To be able to do this, we need to actively support the needs of the work station.

JOB CHECKLIST

Job identification: _____
Due date: _____

Process engineer: _____

Description of job to be performed: _____
_____
_____

	YES	NO	EXPLANATION
1. Process instructions received:			
a. Drawings	——	——	_____
b. BOM	——	——	_____
c. Routings	——	——	_____
d. Methods instructions	——	——	_____
e. CNC program (if required)	——	——	_____
2. Quality requirements defined	——	——	_____
3. Tools, jigs, and fixtures available for use	——	——	_____
4. Process briefing conducted	——	——	_____
5. Training needs determined	——	——	_____
6. Training conducted as required	——	——	_____
7. Work station equipment maintenance performed	——	——	_____
8. Materials available in sufficient quantities	——	——	_____

Figure 1-4. Work station dynamics checklist.

Since virtually all work follows the dictates of the seven steps of the manufacturing system, it is reasonable to expect that optimization occurs when we diligently apply the best processes in carrying out those steps. We also know that all activities of work in companies producing a manufactured product are focused on servicing the value-added activities, e.g., the factory floor work station. That's where the product takes form and eventually evolves into something marketable—where the "rubber meets the road." How we make that happen is the topic of work station dynamics. It is a set of techniques that, when applied properly, yields outstanding productivity improvement results.

Many books are written about activities that support manufacturing. My reason for writing this book is to get at the core of the action, the work station. Most theorists bypass this intuitively obvious fact. If we want productivity improvement, we need to make it happen where the work happens, at the work station. As I've stated earlier, there is a certain set of inputs and blockages that occur at work stations. I will show how care for and attention to these inputs and blockages are the most direct way to achieve the desired productivity improvements. I call this *work station dynamics*, and it provides results. Everyone who has learned these techniques agrees. Let's explore how you, too, can do it. Let's begin the process of detailed exploration of those techniques.

Chapter 2

The Design Process

The design step is the only indirect step in the work station dynamics process. We call it indirect because the result of the design effort is not inputted to the work station without going through some sort of filtering process. Instead, the results are received at the work station only after an evaluation for suitability for the intended factory. The design then has to pass through the process planning steps of being interpreted for each and every work station.

In this chapter we will explore how designs are conceived, particularly with respect to the process of validating design for production. We will also look at aspects of design once not considered to be design at all. These are the design concepts that deal with how a factory can be set up to achieve the intent of the design's purpose in an optimal manner. Combining all this, we call the process *concurrent engineering*, a term that is relatively new to the lexicon of manufacturing practices. It's beneficial for us to delve deeply into concurrent engineering, because the philosophy it champions is paramount for work station dynamics success.

WHAT IS THIS DESIGN ENABLER CALLED CONCURRENT ENGINEERING?

The design process does not take place in a vacuum separate from the manufacturing process. We know it is the prime precursor to manufacturing. Without design there can be no product at all. Therefore, we say that the design process, the only indirect input in the work station dynamics concept, is the vital first step. In this chapter we will explore the design process, done in the concurrent manner, to learn how the best, most producible design can be inputted as planning for product creation.

In successful companies, design is an iterative process involving virtually all functions. It is this synergistic process that is known as concurrent engineering. Concurrent engineering is an ever expanding concept of integrating creative concepts with the pragmatic realities of factories to solve customer requests for satisfactory (totally functional) products. We will focus our exploration of design on concurrent engineering from the viewpoint of the work station. Specifically, we will look at the entire process of developing designs from the standpoint of optimizing the Two Knows.

My definition of concurrent engineering is very straightforward:

Concurrent engineering is the synergistic process of doing all the pre-production, production, and postproduction development work in a manner such that efforts are scheduled and done in a parallel, interactive fashion, rather than in a series, singular manner.

Concurrent engineering is also the structured search for the best way to serve customers by matching the company's best capabilities with the customer's needs. Concurrent engineering unites an organization's functions by creating synergy between those functions. Synergism is established by setting up parallel efforts between the functions, usually via cross-functional teams. By doing so, the output becomes greater than the sum of the parts.

Concurrent engineering theory embraces the principle of allowing the functions to do their jobs with the active and real-time advice of the other functions. It works by shortening the product cycle time. This parallel effort greatly reduces the cycle from conceptualization of the product through delivery to the customer. In this chapter we will take a look at the mechanism for forming the parallel interactive actions, always focusing back on its ultimate impact on shop floor productivity, the improvement of which is the goal of all work station dynamics efforts. Along the way we will also investigate some of the powerful techniques employed within the umbrella of concurrent engineering that allow companies to achieve design excellence and develop products customers really want.

CONCURRENT ENGINEERING STRUCTURE: AN EXAMPLE FOR THE NEED

The design process—and therefore concurrent engineering—is not a precise and bounded body of knowledge such as thermodynamics or strength of materials. It is a concept, or, perhaps, some would call it a theory, of how a manufacturing company ought to structure its front-end process for delivering its products to the customer. Parallel-effort techniques are applied in carrying out the process. Some are internally directed techniques, and some are external. The internal category is mainly design engineering and manufacturing engineering based techniques, while external techniques deal primarily with marketing principles.

Here's an example about parallel-effort teamwork—an example that I'm familiar with because I was right in the middle of it as it happened—that demonstrates the superiority of the parallel interactive method approach. It occurred in 1978, prior to the popular conceptualization of concurrent engineering. Twenty to twenty-five years ago, it was thought that teamwork was important only among groups of people whose activities were adjacent or closely related in the spectrum of work. This meant walls were up and people did their work within a very narrow universe. The order of work was as follows:

1. Marketing defined a need.
2. Design engineering developed a concept to meet that need.
3. Manufacturing took the concept and made a real product out of it.
4. All did their work mostly independently of each other.

By allowing this thought process to dominate, organizations added significantly greater costs and time to the process of creating and delivering products to customers. Costs were not optimized. Why? Because the process was wasteful. The left hand did not know what the right hand was doing. In many cases the instructions from marketing to engineering, or from engineering to manufacturing, were incomplete or just plain wrong. This was primarily due to unfamiliarity with what the other function(s) had to do to complete their portion of the job. Most likely, *none* of the functions knew the others' capabilities. Hence, instructions were usually incomplete or based on incorrect assumptions. The laws of probability came into play and stated that the vast majority of outcomes would be considerably less than optimum, and they were. A humorous depiction of this problem can be seen in Figure 2-1.

Returning to my own example, during the latter half of the 1970s the large motor producer I was involved with was making large synchronous generators and induction motors for complex industrial operations. Though there were several products, these devices had numerous characteristics in common. All delivered power of 500 kW (about 700hp) and larger and had high rotating velocity, 1800 to 3600 rpm. The manufacturing process included making 2- to 8-ft-long rotors made up of machined forgings with silicon steel laminations shrunk onto the shafts. Then poles or windings were attached, depending on whether the devices were to be motors or generators. Because of the size of the units, journal bearings were required, which meant that very precise machining of the rotors was needed. Also, because of the mass

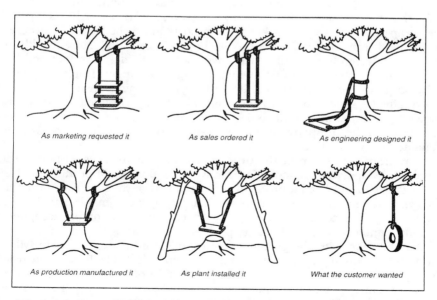

As marketing requested it   As sales ordered it   As engineering designed it

As production manufactured it   As plant installed it   What the customer wanted

Figure 2-1. Satisfying the customer—a perspective on the problem.

and rotational energy involved, vibrations were limited to amplitudes within the 0.0001- to 0.002-in. range. As you can see, the precision required of the manufacturing processes was significant.

The problem we were experiencing was that motors were failing at an alarming rate due to high vibrations at operating speeds. This was causing potentially high losses in profits and, even worse, in market share.

In order to achieve the design requirements for vibratory characteristics, the designers felt it was absolutely necessary to machine to very tight tolerances. Good engineering judgment would concur that tight tolerances to assure concentricity are necessary for balancing the spinning rotor. Therefore dimensional tolerances and RMS finish requirements were set very tight. Surface finish requirements were 4 to 8 RMS, sometimes relaxed to 16 RMS and occasionally all the way to 32 RMS. I say this sarcastically, because even a 32 RMS finish is considered a tight-tolerance machined surface.

Surface finishes of this magnitude can be obtained only via grinding processes. This is several orders of magnitude more expensive than simple lathe turning, because grinding requires a precursor lathe step: first, one precision-machines the part to near finish dimensions on a lathe, and then one sets up the work on a grinder to get to the final dimension.

Grinding is a very high-stress abrasive process. Therefore it can induce high bending stresses in cylindrical shafts and, hence, distortion, in the form of bowing. The greater the surface area ground, the greater the probability of bowed shafts. Lathe turning would create the dimensional tolerance requirements, but the best RMS finish would be only about 64 RMS. So grinding was required. The results were a consistent 10–25% scrap rate.

The problem was that the factory had to make a product on a consistent basis that was outside of its capability to produce satisfactorily. As a result, the scrap rate was wreaking havoc with costs and schedules. Was there a problem with the design concept as well as its execution? Quite frankly, no one knew. Design for manufacturing was not a consideration factored into the creation of the design by the engineering department. Engineering was oblivious of the need, and the manufacturing department wasn't conditioned to explain the need. Both struggled in their strictly confined domains and were unaware that they could assist each other on a formal (or even an informal) basis to the company's overall benefit. Working together in cross-functional teams was an unheard-of process.

Conventional wisdom of the time stated manufacturing should solve its problems by applying technologies that were the domain of production. Neither side realized it had a problem that extended beyond its own domains. This existed because there was no real contact between manufacturing and engineering. There was no *synergism*. There was no common acceptance that the company's cost and quality problem was everyone's problem.

After battling with the problem for several months, we came up with a solution for reducing motor vibrations to acceptable levels. First, we learned through experimentation that surface finish did not have much to do with shaft concentricity and bowing resistance. We found that proper stress-free machining does. Second, only the journal bearing area required a 4 to 8

RMS surface finish. This represented only about 5% of the total surface area. Surface finish also has much less significance for achieving a good shrink fit. In fact, it turned out that a surface finish of about 64 RMS is optimal for surface friction for a good shrink fit. The fear of imbalance by not having a very fine surface finish was unfounded when evaluated against the large inconsistencies possible between individual laminations. Since rotors of this size have thousands of laminations, approximately 30 per inch, the laws of probability take over and it is correct to conclude that the inconsistencies will balance out and there will be no imbalance due to surface finish. Surface finish, as long as its reasonable (e.g., a 64 to 125 RMS machined finish) is not sufficient to cause imbalance during shrink fit of the laminations.

The main problem was to keep the induced stress level in the shaft relatively low before shrinking on the stack of laminations. Minimizing grinding minimizes induced stresses. This fact worked in favor of the solution. This information was known to manufacturing engineering through experience and empirical practice but not normally known to design engineering, which had little knowledge of actual machining operations. The company got into this embarrassing situation because design engineering was ignorant of manufacturing processes in reverse proportion to its expert knowledge of the conceptual design process. The manufacturing engineers had little knowledge of the fear of losing shrink fit and the potential for causing disastrous vibrations because they didn't deal with external complaint situations and it was unlikely they would be aware of them until the problem reached crisis proportions.

Both functions had pieces of the solution, but the walls were up and little formal communications existed. Information was virtually one way down the chain from conception to realization. Both sides were working hard but independently and couldn't solve the problem by themselves. Neither had enough information to solve the problem. When both engineering and manufacturing realized that minimizing vibration was really a mutual problem, the solution came as if by magic. Both understood that the straighter the shaft, the less chance there was for unacceptable levels of vibration to occur. We set up joint teams to investigate causes of bending and found that grinding was the culprit. The teams found that journal bearings did indeed need 4 to 8 RMS finishes to minimize vibrations. At the same time, engineering experiments carried out with manufacturing assistance confirmed that a rougher surface than initially called for made for better shrink fits, and did not have any effect on shaft symmetry. As a result the teams restricted grinding to journal bearing areas. This was the only area where it was really needed. This significantly reduced the induced stresses, and the incidence of bowed shafts went down by about two-thirds.

After this incident, senior management, seeing the benefits that ensued from cross-functional teamwork, authorized the creation of *producibility engineering*. This is one of the subfunctions of manufacturing engineering and one of the internal technologies employed in the concurrent engineering process (although management didn't know it at the time). Senior management learned very emphatically that parallel-effort teamwork is much more effective in solving problems than going it alone.

ATTRIBUTES OF GOOD DESIGN*

Before exploring concurrent engineering techniques, it is desirable to understand the design process. It's surprising how many companies have difficulty understanding the attributes of good design and its relationship to satisfactory quality and lowest manufacturing costs.

Design is absolutely critical to success. It results in the plan for producing at the work station. If our plan is good, most likely we will succeed and be profitable. If our plan is bad, no amount of Herculean and heroic effort is sufficient for us to succeed, and we won't be profitable.

We need to have a definition of a design. A design is a combination of many things. First of all it's a plan to achieve a *goal*, and a goal can be anything. To give an unrelated but totally illustrative example, to successfully stage Mozart's opera "The Magic Flute" would be a goal. The producer and director would need to conceive how to do it. This would be the design, how to achieve the desired artistic interpretation. When engineers think of a design, they narrow the definition to mean mostly physical things, e.g., machines, vehicles, electronic devices, and virtually all the amenities of life. So, from an engineering viewpoint, a design is a plan to make a physical thing, and if the plan is properly followed it will result in the desired outcome. This would not just be a random outcome but a physical thing that performs a function the designer intended it to do. In its most common form, the design is recorded in an electronic database, or, more traditionally, in a set of drawings and explanatory notes.

A design is also an expression of creativity. Designers are given a goal to meet, and they use their experiences, intuition, education, and creative abilities to achieve the goal.

Example. If we ask several people to move a 5-lb block from point A to point B, we'd probably find as many unique solutions as there are people. Within the imposed constraints, there will be many "correct" solutions in achieving the desired goal. A designer with a mechanical background might offer a solution based on principles of hydraulics. Perhaps an electrical engineer would opt to move the block using an electric motor geared to a rack-and-pinion screw lift. Both would be correct solutions. The common denominator for both solutions is their uniqueness drawn from the proposers' inherent creativity.

When we talk about constraints, that's the time the practicality of the approach has to be recognized. Here, we begin to think of producibility. There are designs extolled for their simplicity and beauty. There are others we berate as horrible "Rube Goldbergs" because they are too complicated

---

*Note: This section was originally printed in the author's previous book: "Manufacturing Engineering: Principles for Optimization," 2nd Edition, Taylor & Francis, Washington DC, 1994.

and not pleasing to our eye or psyche. We usually praise simplicity because it is makeable in the specific factory, i.e., it is producible. We hear terms such as functional, esthetic, pleasing to the eye. These can be thought of as ways of saying the designer has achieved the goal of making it easy for those who have to produce the product to do so. In that case manufacturing can make the product with only reasonable application of their skills. This we judge to be a good producible design.

THE SET OF DESIGN ATTRIBUTES*

A design has a set of attributes, and all designs share these same attributes. There are five recognized attributes of design:

1. Producibility
2. Simplicity
3. Lowest feasible cost
4. Esthetics
5. Ability to meets quality requirements

Producibility

A design has to be producible in the intended factory. If the design cannot be produced, all other attributes have no meaning.

Simplicity

This is the common sense attribute. Good design dictates that it be as uncomplicated as the physics of the situation allow. The KISS principle (*keep it simple, stupid*) applies at all times. This is an admonition to bright people not to demonstrate their technological mastery, but to deliver designs that meet the intended purpose, and no more. The need is for straightforward, understandable instructions (via the drawing or other communications medium) that make use of the factory's capabilities.

Lowest Feasible Cost

The cost attribute must be met. We must meet the targeted cost of producing to assure that the required profit margin can be achieved. If the design results in a product that is beyond the means of the intended purchaser, then it is a failure. For example, if the basic, "plain Jane" automobile a company produces cost $100,000, then the market for that product would be very limited indeed! It would be considered a failed design. It must be understood that taking cost out of a product is not just a nice thing to do, but a necessary thing to do.

---

*Note: This section was originally printed in the author's previous book: "Manufacturing Engineering: Principles for Optimization," 2nd Edition, Taylor & Francis, Washington DC, 1994.

Esthetics

Esthetics are important. We do not live by bread alone. This is an admittedly difficult attribute for some engineers to comprehend because there is no absolute here. It requires a sense of the market. Some products can safely ignore the need to consider esthetics, some cannot. An example: Esthetics are not important for screwdrivers, but certainly are for grand pianos. These are examples at the extremes. But the point is that most products fall somewhere in between, and the question must be asked, How important are esthetics to design success? Unfortunately, this is a subjective question, and the answer will vary with the particular situation. But ignoring the question could court disaster.

Ability to Meet Quality Requirements

This attribute sounds deceptively simple, but it isn't. The design *must* meet quality requirements. But what are they? How are they defined, and how are they met? Is it the meeting by manufacturing of the design specification? Is it the pleasing appearance of the product? Is it achieving an undefined goal the customer may have? Is it meeting some industrial or government-imposed standard? Even though the customer doesn't care or is oblivious of the requirement? It can be all or some of the above. Quality attributes vary depending on the viewpoints championed by various constituencies the designer and manufacturing have to contend with.

THE PROCESS OF CREATING A DESIGN

The process of creating a design is very much a multifunctional task, and this is something we're just coming to recognize. As recently as 15 years ago this statement would have been vigorously disputed in many quarters. No more. Fifteen years ago we would have said that design is simply applying scientific principles to form and function, thus defining what should be produced at the work station. This is no longer a valid definition.

There are three components of design.

1. Predesign
2. Engineering phase
3. Postdesign

Predesign is the definition of the customer's needs and desires and is coordinated by marketing. The engineering phase is the traditional applying of scientific principles to achieve a workable plan for making the product, in accordance with the predesign requirements. Postdesign is dominated by the customer service component of marketing, and it involves helping customers understand and properly use the product they've purchased.

The first and last phases of design are sales- and marketing-driven and while they do impact on the work station, they do so in a tangential manner. Predesign sets the stage for how the designer will solve the presented problem and impacts the work station only insofar as the results need to be producible with normal effort. The postdesign phase only affects the work station if modifications are required as discovered through actual use of the product. This is a common occurrence and leads to modifications and improvements in the manufacturing processes. Coincidentally, this is how progress is made, and fortunately it is usually an evolutionary and not a revolutionary process. The middle phase, the engineering phase, is the one most important to work station dynamics, because it is the direct predecessor to the specific manufacturing instructions given to the operator. Let's look in detail at this process.

THE ENGINEERING PHASE OF CREATING A DESIGN*

The engineering phase consists of three components, carried out in chronological order, and concurrently iterated after the preliminary work, or first pass, is done:

1. Concept design
2. Producibility design
3. Manufacturing facilities design

Keep in mind that all phases of design, to be successful, must be compatible with the five attributes.

Concept Design

The process starts with concept design, which consists of ideas for product offerings. The concept design is the rationalization of an idea in terms of science. The idea can be new, such as when Sony introduced the commercially viable VCR. Or the idea can be an extension of or an improvement on an existing idea. The introduction of the automatic transmission by Oldsmobile would be an example, in that transmissions already existed but they required human intervention to up- and downshift. The VCR introduced an entirely new product into the marketplace, while the automatic transmission was simply an improvement to an existing product.

In the concept design stage we have to face the reality of scientific facts: we must define the product in accordance with the laws of science. For example, when designing a ship, Archimedes' principle of buoyancy must be complied with. The task is to make sure that the concept has been well conceived and thoroughly evaluated to make sure the goals of the design are achievable. Once a concept becomes a science-based design and is well established, we can begin to consider producibility.

---

*Note: This section was originally printed in the author's previous book: "Manufacturing Engineering: Principles for Optimization," 2nd Edition, Taylor & Francis, Washington DC, 1994.

Producibility Design

To evaluate the design properly for manufacturability, the prime question that has to be answered is, Where will the product be built, and what are the capabilities of that source? The designers and the entire concurrent engineering team must make sure that whatever information is transmitted to the source factory, it is understandable and within the source factory's "normal" capabilities. If not, the probability of the design being faithfully executed is severely deteriorated.

The producibility design phase is the process of customizing the design for the production source. If a company happens to be strong in machining and assembling with fasteners but has no experience in welding, then proposing a design with a welded joint instead of an equally acceptable bolted joint would be a disregard of the customizing that is necessary for ultimate success. Not doing customization more than likely leads to substandard production results.

Manufacturing Facilities Design

The producibility design is not the end of the engineering phase of the design. We now have to be concerned with the product within the factory. Even if we know that the factory has the capability to make the intended design within its normal constraints, this still does not guarantee it will be the lowest-cost production arena. The next phase is design of the facilities, sometimes called *methods engineering*.

Through the producible design development, the concept design is tested to see whether it fits within the envelope of practicality, to see if it can be made in the factory it is intended for. In the facilities design, we need to do the detailed work of tooling up the factory. The tooling, while it could be very creative, does not have to be heroic, provided that the design is producible. It just has to be serviceable and cost-effective. For example, if a surface finish of 64 RMS is required and the factory possesses a normal array of machine tools, then it is producible; and designing sufficient holding devices is something that can be achieved without extraordinary effort. It is, however, very necessary that we not allow the design process to stop until those holding devices are designed for the product slated to be produced in this specific factory and on the specified machines. It is these details of pragmatic and detailed design that can make or break a profitable situation. This is often forgotten or simply brushed aside as a given to be taken care of by factory personnel. This is an error that besets many companies and is a prime reason why costs are never optimized or even approach optimization. Here also is the area where many companies are penny smart and dollar foolish by not employing enough qualified engineers to do this phase of design. The manufacturing facilities design is the specific designs for jigs, fixtures, and sometimes processes that are necessary to implement the producibility design so that costs are optimized.

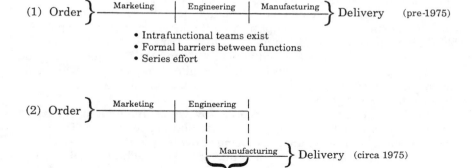

(1) Order } — Marketing | Engineering | Manufacturing } Delivery (pre-1975)

- Intrafunctional teams exist
- Formal barriers between functions
- Series effort

(2) Order } — Marketing | Engineering | | Manufacturing } Delivery (circa 1975)

Producibility engineering

- Same as (1), plus
- Manufacturing provides on site consulting/data to Engineering
- Series and some parallel efforts

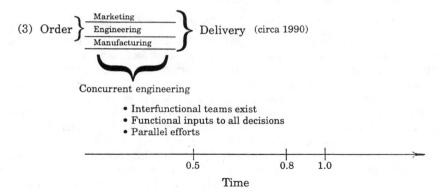

(3) Order } Marketing / Engineering / Manufacturing } Delivery (circa 1990)

Concurrent engineering

- Interfunctional teams exist
- Functional inputs to all decisions
- Parallel efforts

0.5   0.8 1.0

Time

Figure 2-2. Evolution of concurrent engineering. (From Daniel T. Koenig, "Manufacturing Engineering: Principles for Optimization," 2nd ed., Taylor & Francis, Washington, 1994.)

TECHNIQUES OF PRODUCIBILITY ENGINEERING USED IN THE CONCURRENT ENGINEERING PROCESS

Figure 2-2 shows, in graphic form, the power of concurrent engineering. Note that product development time is theoretically reduced by a whopping 50%. In fact, many companies have reported results of this magnitude and even larger. Concurrent engineering does produce significant results. Let's see how by investigating the methodology of concurrent engineering. We'll start at the beginning, with producibility engineering.

Producibility engineering is the discipline responsible for creating producible designs. It was created as a checking mechanism to make sure that factories were not asked to attempt making products beyond their capability. The original concept was not intended to foster parallel efforts to meet customer needs. It had a very focused approach to minimizing manufacturing losses by imparting information to design engineering vis-à-vis the specific drawing and determine whether or not the factory would have difficulty in achieving the design goals.

Producibility engineering is a process by which manufacturing based engineers are assigned as liaison personnel to design engineering. Their purpose is primarily to impart manufacturing know-how to the designer as part of the design process. One way of thinking of producibility engineering's place in the concurrent engineering continuum is to regard it as manufacturing engineering's technical contribution to the concurrent engineering team. Likewise the designer would be design engineering's technical contribution to the concurrent engineering team.

The Producibility Engineering Process*

When It Is Improper to Accept a Design for Manufacturing

The producibility engineer is expected to tell the design engineer how to make the design producible. You may already have heard of an activity similar to this commonly referred to as *design for manufacturability*. The difference is that DFM doesn't specify a role for ownership of making sure the shop operations viewpoint is heard. The producibility engineer's job is to critique the design from the viewpoint of how to optimize manufacturing process costs, consisting of cycle time (labor) and material utilization. The producibility engineer must also keep in mind that cost reduction must be bounded so that it does not interfere with proper product performance to design specifications. Therefore, the producibility engineer has to be knowledgeable of the theory of design and the intent of the specific design before a credible critique can be made. Also, as the factory representative, it is absolutely essential that the producibility engineer understand the factory's limitations.

To assure that a design is capable of being produced in the factory, the producibility engineer has to master two tasks:

1. Understand the intent of the design.
2. Understand the factory's capabilities relative to the design.

Once these are mastered, then the producibility engineer can offer cogent criticism to the designer. Suppose the producibility engineer found that the intent of the design simply did not match the capability of the factory. Suppose, also, that the producibility engineer was certain that the intent must be met for the product to be successful.

---

*Note: This section was originally printed in the author's previous book: "Manufacturing Engineering: Principles for Optimization," 2nd Edition, Taylor & Francis, Washington DC, 1994.

What are the choices? There are two:

1. Reject the design for production.
2. Recommend major changes in the factory to accommodate the design.

Choice number one, at first glance, appears to be a stonewalling strategy. But really it's not. Telling design engineering that it must reject what it's proposing because it would be folly for the manufacturing group to attempt it is a sufficient answer, when true. The last thing the company could tolerate would be for manufacturing to try to do something outside its realm of competency. The second choice is a reasonable compromise when there's hope for the design. If the possibility exists for the company to take on the manufacturing task with some modifications to make it "doable" without high risk of failure and high costs, then the producibility engineer needs to convey this information to the designers. This way producibility engineering is positioning the company to be in a win-win situation. Manufacturing can do the job with reasonable chances of success, and the designer has created a solution to the customer's problem, again with a reasonable chance of success.

Let me give an example of the logic stream leading to rejecting a design for production. Situations such as this typically occur when companies try to redefine what type of company they are without taking their true capabilities into account and, much to their chagrin, they find they can't manufacture their products any longer. In such cases, the company will usually be much better off if manufacturing is allowed to reject the design in the first place.

In this example, Company A, a piano maker, was trying to redefine itself as a musical instrument maker. As we shall see, such a change in direction could lead to serious mismatches if it were based on a faulty manufacturing capability strategy. As it turned out, there were problems in Company A's desire to serve the new market versus its capability of doing so. Let's look at the details.

When the opportunity occurred to expand its horizons as a musical instrument maker instead of only a piano maker, Company A was tempted to offer a line of electronic organs. Pianos and organs are both keyboard instruments, and both require fine furniture fabrication; but there the similarity ends. Pianos are more than 90% mechanical in design, and their manufacture is dominated by mechanical engineering. Organs, on the other hand, are more than 50% electronic. Thus, there was no synergy. Regardless of the apparent lack of synergism between the products, design engineering responded approvingly. But design can always move in new directions much more quickly and easily than manufacturing. New design skills can be acquired much faster than physical capability and experience to make new products.

Company A decided to go ahead with the expansion. The following outcome unfolded. Design engineering acquired the necessary technological expertise by hiring some electronics engineers with organ design background. The engineering team then produced designs for building organs. Manufacturing, having no in-house expertise to even critique the design, had no choice but to contract out the electronics components to the point of purchasing complete subassemblies. It then planned to assemble, test, package, and ship.

How confident was manufacturing in its ability to produce organs at the same quality level as pianos? Not very. Manufacturing needed to rely on newly hired engineers in design who were relatively unfamiliar with the company or the factory. And because the new engineers came from a discipline that was new to the company (electrical versus mechanical) and had little time to integrate into the company culture, the probability that either design or manufacturing would understand the other's needs was very low to nonexistent. This was a surefire recipe for failure.

The company received the subassemblies from vendors but had virtually no in-house capability of performing the receiving inspections and completing the assemblies. It needed to rely on the newly hired electronics design engineers to do manufacturing engineering work as well as design work. Since these design engineers were unfamiliar with the ways of a mechanically structured factory, they made mistakes, and frustration abounded. This was a classic case of the technical leaders' having no understanding of the factory's capabilities and being pressed to do two jobs at the same time. Manufacturing management responded by hiring another new group of engineers who understood the design engineers' intent but found themselves trying to set up an electronics assembly factory with scant technological resources to do so.

The ultimate results were failure to deliver organs on time and at the required quality level. This led to loss of reputation in the musical instrument world. The company then put more financial resources into organ manufacturing to gain back reputation, basically by downgrading improvements in its own field of piano manufacturing. Ultimately what happened was that the company damaged its own marketing position for pianos and never gained the results it strove for in organs. The company would have to go through a long and arduous learning cycle, while at the same time placating irate customers—all in all, a very unsuccessful experience that could have been avoided if producibility engineering had existed and done its job to demonstrate that the situation was lose-lose to start with.

The postmortem is very clear. It was unrealistic all along to predict a successful business outcome. Failure being the probable outcome, the proper choice of the management segment responsible for producibility engineering was to reject the design, even if it agreed in principle with the technical intent of the design. The company simply did not possess the manufacturing capability, and therefore the design was not producible. If the company had really wanted to get into the organ business, its best choice would have been to purchase an organ company or enter into some sort of business arrangement, perhaps a joint venture, with another company with the proper skills match.

When It Is Proper to Accept a Design for Manufacturing Even Though Capability to Do So Does Not Exist

The compromise choice of action puts the onus on *manufacturing:* the producibility engineer *agrees* with the design intent, manufacturing *doesn't* have the capability to adequately produce it, but even so the producibility engineer doesn't reject it. This choice is appropriate where there is enough synergism between past experience and current requirements that through either obtaining the next generation of equipment or some advanced training for current personnel there can be a successful outcome.

Here, the producibility engineer is saying manufacturing has no choice but to acquire the capability to produce, or the company will suffer the consequences of lost business opportunities and profits. If the producibility engineer is convinced that the design is proper and within the range of products the company must offer, then the producibility engineer should recommend that manufacturing take on the challenge of tooling up to make it.

Where is the line of demarcation? How does the producibility engineer determine whether the company should be urged to invest capital and human resources to make the product depicted in the design? Sometimes the choice is obvious. For example, in the silicon chip business, the ability to crowd more and more electronic circuits on a silicon wafer is the difference between staying in business and permanent decline. So, if a new chip design requires improvement in photoetching capability, the producibility engineer will probably recommend that his or her manufacturing colleagues develop the necessary equipment. The need to meet the design requirement, in this case, is obvious to all.

Sometimes the choice is not so obvious. A choice to accept the design commits the company to spend funds to gain capability to produce. Here are some guidelines for making the choice:

- If compatibility exists between the proposed design and previous designs, then accept.
- If tooling requirements to produce are within the realm of state-of-the-art equipment, then accept.
- If employee experiences are similar to those required for successful manufacture of the proposed design, then accept.
- If training requirements are extensions of current skills, then accept.

Let's expand a bit on the acceptance guidelines.

When compatibility exists, we know that the new design, while not within the current capability of the factory, still requires processes similar to what presently exists. In the chip maker example it boils down to getting equipment that can do the same as current equipment but with higher density capability. It is probably an extension of current concepts, unless the theoretical constraints have been reached. In that case all bets are off, and to accept the design will require a more intensive look based on the technology required to do the job. If the technology is too alien, then the company will probably pass on the opportunity.

When we consider tooling to be within the "current state of the art," we mean no new technology needs to be developed in order for the factory to comply. No new invention is required. For example, if the design called for an electric car with a 100-mile range, the technology already exists. On the other hand, if the range required were 1000 miles, then, as of this time in our technological development, the edge of practicality as we know it has been breached. A new invention is required, and therefore we cannot accept the proposal to proceed. We must wait for the invention to catch up with our desires.

We must also consider employee and training issues when we make the go, no-go decision. These are people issues—e.g., their current capabilities and their ability to learn new technologies—and are the hardest to evaluate.

We are dealing with many levels of experiences and capabilities. With human resources guidance, manufacturing management's goal is to determine the median experience level and compare that with the tasks that will have to be accomplished to produce the intended design. If it is felt that the differences are not too great, then the design can be accepted. Likewise, whether training can be accomplished successfully depends on how close the new skills levels are to the current levels.

A guideline for the producibility engineer's job performance can be shown in what's called the *producibility engineer's decision tree* (see Figure 2-3). This is a self-explanatory flow diagram/checklist to assist in determining whether or not a design can be accepted for manufacturing. Using this aid focuses the decision on pertinent factors the company must come to terms with before a product can be slated for production. The most frequent use of this tool comes into play during the producibility design review exercise. I strongly recommend that all companies make use of the producibility engineer's decision tree a routine part of introducing new orders to the shop floor.

The Producibility Design Review*

The producibility design review is not the normal design review for functionality and meeting of the customer's specifications. It is a review for discovering whether or not a producible design exists.

A producible design is defined as a design that can be manufactured correctly and economically in the factory for which it was intended. The producibility design review, sometimes called the design for manufacturability design review, starts with a look at the basics. Can the design be produced while the status quo is maintained in the factory? If so, end of review—the design is producible. From here on it becomes more difficult, the degree of difficulty increasing as the requirements of the design become less compatible with the factory's capability. The trick is to determine how much the factory's ability can be stretched to meet the design requirements.

The practitioners of producibility design reviews do this by considering all five items listed under the design review segment of the decision tree:

1. Produce in a routine manner?
2. Requirements essential?
3. Cost trade-offs evaluated?
4. Are "specials" being minimized?
5. Are improved facilities required?

The secret is to list the reasons for incompatibility and then see what can be done to overcome these deficiencies. At the same time we're looking at the manufacturing side of the equation, the design side also has to be looked at with equal intensity. Creating a producible design is a systems integration activity and one which optimizes the process for the entire company.

---

*Note: This section was originally printed in the author's previous book: "Manufacturing Engineering: Principles for Optimization," 2nd Edition, Taylor & Francis, Washington DC, 1994.

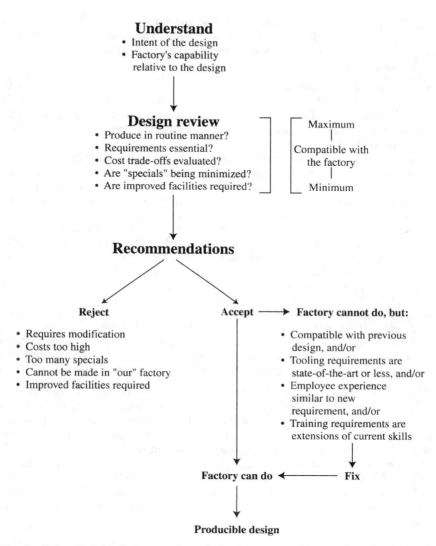

Figure 2-3. Producibility engineer's decision tree. (From Daniel T. Koenig, "Manufacturing Engineering: Principles for Optimization," 2nd ed., Taylor & Francis, Washington, 1994.)

One of the most important aspects of the producibility design review process is the evaluation of tolerances the designers are proposing. As in the large-motor example, it is easy to see that this can be a make-or-break issue. Proper setting of tolerances is a concurrent approach between manufacturing engineering and design engineering. Design engineering has the responsibility for creating tolerances that will assure that the intent of the design is not compromised, while manufacturing engineering needs to evaluate the pragmatic ability to hold such tolerances. Here are some simple working rules for setting tolerances:

- *Understand the materials you are working with.* It is absolutely vital to understand the physical and chemical properties of the materials one is working with to know the process limitations vis-à-vis dimensions. For example, it makes no sense to require tolerances tighter than ±0.015 in. for hardwoods, on account of their hygroscopic nature. Since hardwoods absorb and give off moisture as local relative humidity varies, it's normal for wood structures to grow and contract as much as 0.015 in. within hours. It is technically absurd to set tolerances tighter than nature will allow. The rule, then, is to understand the limitations of the chosen materials and set tolerances accordingly.
- *Use the statistics approach to setting tolerances.* Absolute dimensioning never occurs in the real world. In practical terms, that means we must understand that we cannot design for either the maximum or minimum side of the dimension. We need to design to the given dimension and use statistics and probabilities to set the tolerances. This will give the most realistic vales for the tolerance ranges.
- *Avoid the need for setting tolerances as much as possible by simplifying designs.* Use such techniques as chamfered holes and fastening devices, gaskets, and tapered pins in assemblies to avoid precision assembly requirements whenever possible. Consciously design for ease of assembly, thereby minimizing the need to set tolerances.

The overall message I wish to convey with the producibility design review is that, used correctly, it sets the stage to achieve pragmatic compatibility between the designers and manufacturing engineering. It is a team approach that is searching for the win-win position. If design needs something that is beyond the realm of manufacturing capability and design gets its way, has it really won? Perhaps it has, for the short term, but the company certainly hasn't, and we all know that. I believe that the producibility design review breeds team building in its finest sense. It requires the engineers on both sides of the issue to truly search for ways to solve customers' problems, and this is the way to optimize profits.

DEFINING CUSTOMER NEEDS WITH CONCURRENT ENGINEERING PHILOSOPHY

In order to have a producible design at the work station, we need more than a design that can be successfully manufactured. It also has to meet customer expectations and needs. An important segment of service to customers is understanding the nature of customers' desires—which are sometimes hard to determine and can be very abstract and thus elusive—and then planning how to provide for them. Producibility engineering theory took a tentative step in this direction but stopped short. It did two things. It created the producibility design review, which is a constructive critique and problem resolution technique. Second, the liaison role of the producibility engineer often led to more effective cooperation between engineering and manufacturing. However, these are primarily internal activities.

Concurrent engineering is both an internal and an external activity. It melds internal and external activities into one team to optimize both for the benefit of the customer. To complete the job we need to focus on external needs as well as internal. While work station dynamics, the major benefactor of successful concurrent engineering practice, is an internally focused activity, it, like, any other process does not exist in isolation. External processes will affect how internal processes are applied, so it behooves us to be aware of the external world as we apply all the techniques of work station dynamics. The major way concurrent engineering approaches the external world is through a methodology called *quality functional deployment.*

QUALITY FUNCTIONAL DEPLOYMENT

There are many ways to serve customers' needs, to find what they want and then do it for them. But the company has to do it in a manner that satisfies the customer and at the same time meets the profit goals. An excellent way (in my opinion, the best way) for concurrent engineering teams to discern customer needs is through practical quality functional deployment, commonly known as QFD.

QFD is a process whereby a company attempts to match its strong points with the desires and needs of its customers. Why do this? Simply because most companies do not possess enough resources to be all things for all customers. It is inconceivable to think that a firm, no matter how large, that dominates an industrial sector can easily dominate another sector, even if both sectors are considered similar. The piano/organ manufacturing example is an example of this. The point is, it makes no sense to try to sell into markets in which the company has no manufacturing expertise or capability. QFD presents a methodology for a company to match its capability with a customer's needs. If the match is strong, as it would be for an automobile maker to migrate to sport-utility vehicles, then it makes sense to expend effort selling into that market.

The theoretical process of applying QFD consists of five steps:

The Theoretical QFD Process:
1. Identify customer desires
2. Rank these desires
3. Based on the ranking, assign a weight for each of these desires.
4. Develop measurable parameters for each of these desires in direct relationship with your factory's capability, both design and manufacturing processes.
5. Include the highest measurement parameter into the product design being offered to the customer.

This seems to be a straightforward approach. In practice, theoretical QFD is very difficult to apply, as will become apparent shortly. However, a pragmatic variant can be used to gain useful approximations of customers needs:

The Practical Process of Applying QFD:
1. Identify customers' desires by customer visitations and discussions.
2. Have the customer rank these desires.
3. Rank the company's design and manufacturing capabilities, using "ask the experts" techniques.
4. Match the company's highest capability in both design and manufacturing with the highest customer desires.
5. By subjective evaluation, determine if the match of step 4 is high enough to warrant a concurrent engineering product development project. If yes, proceed.

The difference between the theoretical and practical approaches to using QFD is trying to be exact versus making pragmatic guesses. The pragmatic approach is how business works best and therefore is the only way to apply QFD. We have experienced people making decisions based on the facts available and levels of risks deemed acceptable. The benefit is quick action, which is very compatible with concurrent engineering theory. By being compatible, I mean that various functions are teamed together to solve customer problems in a parallel effort instead of the historical series chain approach. QFD asks questions to determine whether company capabilities are matched well with customer needs. The only way to do this in any reasonable time frame is to do it concurrently.

Notice the questions that the practical version of QFD asks. They are investigatory in nature but never require an exact answer—because in the real world exact answers are extremely rare. If we had to wait for exact answers, we would never make any progress in making decisions. To make profits requires some degree of risk. With practical QFD we are in essence categorizing risks so decisions can be made to either enter a market or not (also to either stay in or get out of a market if parameters change). From the viewpoint of manufacturing, this exercise is crucial for success. The last thing manufacturing wants is to have to pursue an "impossible dream." Therefore, the QFD technique that allows matches of strengths or lack of matches to be identified beforehand will be an important precursor of future manufacturing success.

We've now explored the design process, the only indirect input in the work station dynamics concept, but have seen it is the vital first step. We explored the design process to learn how the best, most producible designs can be inputted to planning for product creation. We examined the concurrent engineering process from the viewpoint of the work station. Specifically, we have looked at the entire process of developing designs from the viewpoint of how we will use the results to optimize the Two Knows. Finally, we have looked at the various rules of design to understand the iterative nature of the process, both internal and external. This indirect input to work station dynamics sets the table for successful manufacturing operations. The next chapters of the book will illustrate how we build on good design to create good manufacturing.

Chapter 3

The Ins and Outs
of Process Instructions

The question we ask immediately after receiving a design is, How do we translate it into useful data the factory can use to make the intended product? This may sound like a contradiction. After all, it is reasonable to expect that a design should contain all the information necessary to make the product. And in fact it does. But it is not work station–specific. The subcategory of planning called *process instruction development* makes it work station–specific.

Factory instruction sets are known in their entirety as *process instructions*. Process instructions deal primarily with the methodology of manufacturing from a producible design in the specific factory it is intended for, and then determining how long the manufacture should take. Therefore, process instructions are generally nontransferable from factory to factory unless the factories have substantially similar manufacturing equipment.

Creating process instructions is like selecting items from a computer program menu. With menus we select certain segments of the program to make it specific to the task at hand. Similarly, in this case we extract the information that is necessary for a specific work station to do its job and exclude the rest. Our task is to ultimately use all the information presented by the design, but at the appropriate work stations. So we are going through a detailed sorting procedure. We are further refining the Two Knows—know how to make the product, and know how long it should take to do so—for relevance to the specific work stations. When we finish the task, we will have created process instructions for all work stations involved in manufacturing the product. In this chapter we will explore optimizing the Two Knows from the viewpoint of creating the manufacturing instruction set for the factory.

The development of process instructions is normally an iterative process between design engineering, manufacturing engineering, and the customer (usually represented by sales, or by marketing if it is for a product development project). However, we will examine it as a linear process, for ease of investigation. We'll look at the methodology, stopping to consider appropriate examples as we go.

PROCESS INSTRUCTION FLOW SEQUENCE

The second input for work station dynamics is the development of process instructions. I consider this to be the key step in defining how a product will be manufactured. If done right, it will result in the lowest cost and shortest time to make the product. Not surprisingly, this is a major contributing factor to a company's profitability.

The process instruction flow sequence can best be demonstrated with the schematic diagram shown in Figure 3-1. Notice that it is fully integrated

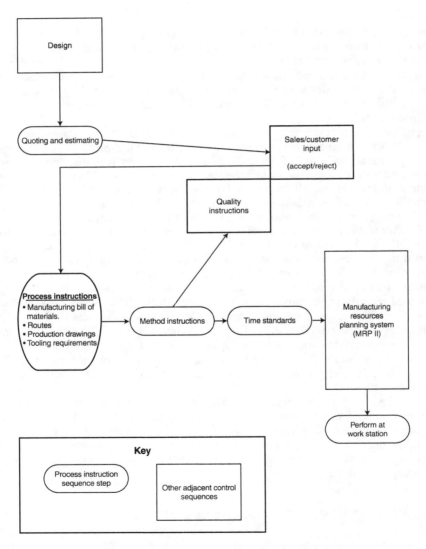

Figure 3-1. Process instruction flow.

with the design step and the companion quality instruction step and leads to the execution of the process at the work station. The process instruction flow sequence is also very closely aligned with the manufacturing resource planning system, also shown in the figure. Finally, the process instruction flow sequence is associated with marketing's interaction with the customer, in that many features of the proposed methodology will have potential impact on the customer's use of the product. Therefore, it always makes good sense to require customer consultation and consent for all process instructions. This is another example of the benefits of concurrent engineering. By getting customer consent, we are creating a partnership with the customer, thereby placing some of the responsibility for the final outcome on the buyer.

A typical example of such interaction with the customer could involve surface finishes or coatings. Sometimes surface finishes or coatings may cause the customer to alter accustomed uses of the product or subsequent manufacturing processes. In that case, if a new process costs more than an earlier one, the customer will be more willing to go along with it, having participated in the decision that resulted in this change rather than being forced into it without a choice. We say that the customer has taken ownership of the process as well as future ownership of the resultant product. Thereby the customer will tend to be less critical of the final results.

Another reason to get the customer involved in process planning is the regulation issue. Sometimes customer quality requirements or documentation needs may dictate the process the supplier must follow. If this is the case, then the process being followed will need to be approved by the customer beforehand.

Process instructions are the how-to step where the manufacturing engineer defines the specific methodology for making the part, then determines the sequence, and finally integrates the procedures with estimated times to complete each step. The methods, sequence, and timings are presented in sufficient detail for the receiving factory to understand the process to be followed. The amount of detail required will depend on the product, the knowledge and skill of the operators, and the degree of deviation from the norm of the usual jobs done by the factory.

Example. A piano factory that makes a line of standard grand pianos and nothing else and has been in the business for many decades hardly needs detailed process instructions for its operators. However, if that same factory decided to introduce furniture-style piano benches to complement its pianos, these would be a new product, one that is unfamiliar to the workforce. In this case the need for detailed instructions is much greater. As time goes by and the workforce becomes familiar with the process of making piano benches, the need for detailed process instructions is reduced until eventually they become archival records only.

Some categories of factories will always require process instructions of significant content—particularly, what are known as "job shops," factories in which the products are always changing and the only constant is the use of similar equipment in the manufacturing process. An example of a typical job shop would be a general-purpose weld shop. The techniques are the same from job to job, but the product design changes. Therefore, say, TIG (tungsten inert gas) welding may be employed from job to job, but the weld preps, the amount of weld required, and the size of the welded connection may vary considerably. This means that detailed instructions are required to be successful.

There is one preferred sequence to follow in the creation of a process instruction set (also known as process planning). Keep in mind that this description is for a full set of process instructions where the workforce has no familiarity with the product and its related process that we can take advantage of. The steps are:

1. Understand the intent of the design.
2. Determine the material alternatives available to make the product. Make a materials selection based on familiarity of use and the economics of the situation.
3. Conceptualize the manufacturing processes to be used.
4. Determine whether special tooling will be required. If so, conduct the necessary design process to create it.
5. List the process steps in sequence with information on how each is to be performed. The list is called the routing.
6. Select the work stations to perform each process step.
7. Using industrial engineering techniques, establish, or have established, the time it takes to accomplish each process sequence step at the selected work stations.
8. Create an indented bill of materials that will instruct manufacturing on what material will be used at what process step and in what quantity.
9. Input the indented bill of materials, the routing with cycle times, and tooling requirements to the scheduling system—preferably an MRP system, though for low-volume operations a manual system can be acceptable.

APPLYING THE FLOW SEQUENCE TO CREATE A PROCESS INSTRUCTION SET

Let's look at how we can apply the flow sequence to develop a process instruction set for an intended factory to make a specific product. In the example we will be conservative and say that the workforce needs full instructions because of unfamiliarity with the product. The product we will plan for is a claw hammer with a metal head and shank, and a rubber grip on the shank.

The order calls for making 10,000 hammers. We'll go through the nine steps of process instruction development to demonstrate the thought processes and considerations to be factored into the decisions. While this

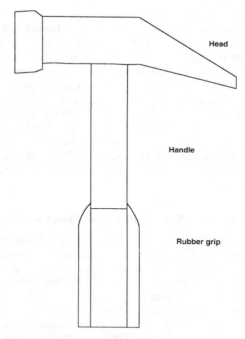

Figure 3-2. Hammer process instruction example.

may seem to be a trivial problem, and the solution mundane, it does illuminate the procedure.

1. Understand the Intent of the Design

The intent is very straightforward: to manufacture a device for driving nails and also removing them. The hammer head must withstand a high impact stress, and the shaft needs to withstand bending stresses and cracking at the connection of the head to the shaft. The handle and the shaft must be constructed in such a way that they cannot be parted in normal use. In addition, the feel of the tool must be comfortable to the user. There is also an esthetic consideration: the hammer must look like and be a high-quality product.

2. Determine the Material Alternatives Available to Make the Product. Make a Materials Selection Based on Familiarity of Use and the Economics of the Situation

While selecting the materials is normally a design engineering responsibility (based on the conceived functionality of the product), the manufacturing engineer must be satisfied that the materials selection makes sense for the factory. The specific manufacturing engineer involved will probably be the producibility engineer on the concurrent engineering team.

A hammer may be made of several hard-impact, brittle-fracture–resistant materials such as steel, stainless steel, or perhaps even very hard rubber. However, if the factory is to make the hammer, the material selected should be one that is common to the specific factory's experience. This insures the highest probability of success. Manufacturing engineering will rarely, if ever, have full veto power over selection of materials for the product to be fabricated. It will have a responsibility to inform the designers of the manufacturing pros and cons of the materials selected. The goal is to work as a team in creating a product that optimally achieves the goals of the design and is economically viable as well.

3. Conceptualize the Manufacturing Processes to Be Used

There are many conceivable methods that would create the desired end product. However, there is usually only one that is "the" economic choice. The manufacturing engineer must find that one. Usually, it is based on the processes that the factory has available or has easy access to. These processes have typically come into being on the basis of previous production opportunities, or were put into place as part of the company's original strategic plan for getting into the business of producing the product in question or similar products.

For the hammer example we will assume that the basic processes already exist in the specific factory. The task is to select the most efficient of those processes for the product at hand. The manufacturing engineer will select methods on the basis of knowledge of the capability of the process alternatives. If the manufacturing engineer has doubts regarding the capabilities of processes, they can be resolved through experimentation or by searching reference manuals for documentation. For the hammer example, a likely methods sequence choice for the volume of production required would be as follows:

- *Forge the head.* The complex shape of the head would make it very impractical to machine from bar material. Likewise, using a casting process would probably not provide the volume necessary without multiple investment in molds. Forging, on the other hand, would require only a die and perhaps a backup. Forging would also allow some control of grain formation, so that the proper tensile (and compressive) strength could be achieved in the desired orientation. By contrast, casting would result in an isotropic grain orientation, which is not maximized for the impact strength that a hammer requires. Thus, forging is the choice. We can assume the company has a forging capability; otherwise, that portion of the manufacturing would have to be sourced at another location.
- *Machine, drill, and tap the underside of the head to accept the handle.* This would typically be done on a CNC drill or perhaps a hard-fixtured drill if the repetition rate of the drill and tap operation is large enough.
- *Machine bar material to form the handle. Thread one end to attach to the hammer head.* This type of operation is usually performed on a special

type of lathe that accepts bars, called round stock, of near net shape diameter in 8- to 12-ft lengths. Often, the regime is to feed the bars through a hollow headstock and to cut them to length before securing (chucking) them in the headstock and tailstock of the lathe.

- *Assemble the head to the handle.* For a production run of 10,000 hammers, the cost of an automated assembly machine would not be justified. Instead, we would probably construct a fixture to hold the handle and spin tighten the head to the handle. Perhaps a torque wrench–type device would be used to assure correct tightness. Then, a procedure for keeping the head from becoming loose is required. A logical procedure would be to spot-weld in four places, 90 degrees apart, to equalize any induced stresses. This would be accomplished in the same fixture used to join the handle and head. Finally, a cosmetic grind operation would be added to create an acceptable appearance.

- *Put the grip on the handle.* The final manufacturing step is to attach the grip, a rubberized sleeve that fits over the handle at the opposite end from the head. Since we are depending on a shrink-type fit, we will require a device to stretch the sleeve and then slip it over the handle. This can be done with an expandable split sleeve approximately one-third to one-half the length of the handle. The expandable split sleeve is inserted into the rubber grip and expanded. Then this assembly is slipped over the hammer handle. The expandable split sleeve is relaxed and withdrawn, and the rubber sleeve then press fits onto the handle. Since the expandable split sleeve is reusable, the number of these assembly devices will depend on the rate of production required; this would be determined by a time standard evaluation.

- *Package the hammer for shipment.* The manufacturing method has been defined but the process is not yet complete. It's now necessary to prescribe a packaging method. With a relatively modest build plan of 10,000 hammers, it would be prudent to use simplified processes that are as low-cost as possible. Two methods are possible: simple corrugated paper cartons with partition sleeves, and perhaps shrink wrap. The former requires only specifying carton and sleeve sizes, and then ordering. The latter requires a shrink wrap machine and the necessary wrapping material. Both options need to be economically evaluated, and the lower-cost option adopted. Both methods would fulfill the packaging requirements.

4. Determine Whether Special Tooling Will Be Required. If So, Conduct the Necessary Design Process to Create It

Notice that many steps involved in the process plan required use of specialized tools, fixtures, and jigs in order to make the hammer efficiently. It is no secret that successful completion of any manufacturing process requires a well-thought-out plan for going about the work, and not simply a sketchy sequence under which the operators are left to their own creativity to accomplish what the planner requires. The planner must very specifically define the individual steps and must anticipate all possible "what if" scenarios. You may also recognize this step in creating the process instruction set as corresponding to one of the steps in creating a product design—specifically, the manufacturing facilities design.

Let's assume we need to produce an RMS finish on the hammer handle of 16 or less to achieve the esthetic appearance the marketing members of the concurrent engineering team say is required to sell the hammer. What are the options? Lathe-turn, or cylindrical-grind. Cylindrical grinding can produce the surface finish needed, but at greater cost. Lathe turning is definitely the less expensive way to proceed. However, can it produce the desired results? The manufacturing engineer must determine whether it can before the lathe alternative can be used. This will be accomplished first by theoretical and then by experimental methods. In this example we would investigate various combinations of feeds, speeds, and tooling options. Perhaps we would calculate chip size and consistency, utilizing the finite-element method. Probably—and more realistically, for the size of the project and the expected constraints on time and funding for tooling design—the research would be more pragmatic in approach. We would use reference sources relating materials, tooling, and feeds and speeds to determine the probable optimal settings. We would try several alternatives to see whether any gave the needed results. This way, we could develop specific instructions for the operators that would get satisfactory results. The point is, we would be telling the operators what specific tools to use so that the process would be robust enough to give satisfactory and repeatable results.

When a process is proven to be effective, special tools or fixtures are sometimes required to be able to perform it correctly. This may mean that the manufacturing engineer will have to design those tools and have them built, and then supply the tools to the operators along with instructions on their use. Even if the tools can be purchased from commercial sources, the engineer will still have to provide instructions on their proper use.

In the hammer example, there are many areas where special tools are necessary for manufacturing. Let's look at one of these areas and see how the tooling could be designed to fit the circumstances of the task. Keep in mind that the order is for 10,000 pieces, a modest sum. Therefore, the solution used also needs to be of modest cost to design. Conversely, the speed to develop has to be fast, since the production time will also be limited, again by the relatively small production run. We'll look at the device used to expand the rubberized grip for assembly.

The rubberized grip on the handle is assembled by using an expandable split sleeve. The expandable sleeve is inserted into the rubber grip and expanded. Then the combined assembly of the rubber grip and sleeve is slipped over the hammer handle. The expandable split sleeve is relaxed and withdrawn, and the rubber grip becomes press-fitted onto the handle. The design problem is to create a simple, quickly constructed device, or series of devices, that will work repeatedly for the duration of the production run. Let's see how the design problem can be solved.

The design consists of five devices making up a series of simple tools that have as their sole purpose the installation of the rubber grip on the hammer

A.

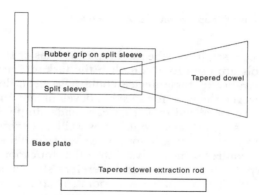

Rubber grip on split sleeve

Split sleeve

Tapered dowel

Base plate

Tapered dowel extraction rod

B.

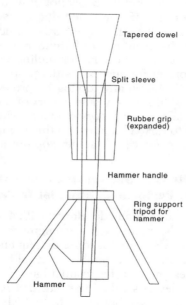

Tapered dowel

Split sleeve

Rubber grip (expanded)

Hammer handle

Ring support tripod for hammer

Hammer

Method:
1. Insert rubber grip over split sleeve.
2. Tap tapered dowel into split sleeve, to 2/3 the length of the split sleeve (use base plate as backstop).
3. Put ring support tripod over hammer (head down). Ring support acts as a position stopper for rubber grip placement.
4. Put rubber grip/split sleeve/tapered dowel assembly over hammer handle so that 1/3 the length of the split sleeve is engaged over the hammer handle. Abut to ring support of tripod.
5. Slide rubber grip off split sleeve, while simultaneously extracting split sleeve from hammer handle.
6. Rubber grip adheres to handle from location of ring support on tripod upward to end of hammer handle.
7. Insert tapered dowel extraction rod into split sleeve at opposite end from tapered dowel. Use hammer to tap end of rod to drive tapered dowel out of split sleeve.
8. Repeat process for next hammer and rubber grip.

Figure 3-3. Method and tools for inserting rubber grip on hammer handle. *(a)* Assembly fixture for placing rubber grip on split sleeve; *(b)* assembly of rubber grip on hammer handle.

handle. The process sequence (the method) is a series of steps that describes how the five tools are used to accomplish the task and are set up again to repeat it. Conceivably, a single device could have been designed to do the same thing. However, the need for speed in development and ease of use dictates a set of less specialized tools that can made simply and applied with minimal training. Anything else would be overkill and probably not cost-justified. As simple as the set of tools appears to be, we can see that the expandable split sleeve requires some analysis; the other four tools do not. The split sleeve has to expand and contract, and therefore stress analysis is required to assure that it will not exceed the yield point. There may also be a need for a low cycle fatigue evaluation, but probably not. It would be simpler to make a few spare split sleeves and, if one failed due to cyclic fatigue (which is highly unlikely), to replace it with a spare. Also, since we are required to make only 10,000 parts, the likelihood of fatigue failure is remote.

The point is, the evaluation of design for tooling to make the company's products is just as important for success as the proper execution of the primary product design. Whenever any tooling or procedure goes beyond an ordinary tool set or the skill set we would expect of a qualified operator, we need to design the unusual tools or processes and provide detailed use instructions. For management to turn a blind eye to this requirement, as often happens, means that the company will not achieve optimum profitability.

5. List the Process Steps in Sequence Order with Information on How Each Is to Be Performed. The List Is Called the Routing

Manufacturing methods are usually developed with a sequence in mind. For our hammer example, the manufacturing engineer, while conceiving the *method*, would also have visualized a route or sequence that allows for the natural flow of manufacture and assembly. Natural flow is simply the "goes into" pattern that the designers of the product have in mind when laying out the product. This is sometimes called the *indented bill of materials*, which works backward from the assembly level through the manufacture of discrete parts in the order of need.

The natural order is used as a matter of preference. However, this does not mean that the sequence needs to be linear. Nonlinked parts or assemblies are and should be made in parallel.

The "goes into" pattern is an inverted tree diagram starting with the branches and progressing to the trunk. Figure 3-4 displays the independent and dependent relationships with respect to sequence of operations. A dependent operation can start only when a preceding operation is complete, while an independent operation can commence at any time in the cycle, within reason, given the ultimate need to finish the job. The manufacturing engineer will construct a tree diagram, similar in principle to the one shown in Figure 3-4.

Using the tree diagram, the manufacturing engineer can now begin to create a routing. By definition, a routing is a sequence of events to be performed by properly equipped operators to manufacture the product. It's not uncommon for the work station to also be selected during this step (however, in our

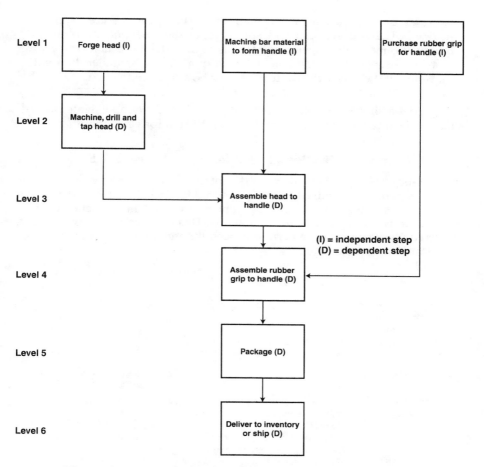

Figure 3-4. Sequence of manufacture (hammer example).

example, we will not show work station selection). The amount of detail listed in the routing will depend on the workforce's familiarity with the product.

Example: For the hammer head, the routing will call for the forging operation to be first. It will list the material to be used, the engineering drawing reference number, the die to be used, the number of units to be produced, and the cycle time per unit quantity (in this case, the number of units per hour). It will not state the specific process of operating the forge press. Nor will it call out the temperature necessary to properly forge the hammer head. It is presumed, and rightly so, that the basic work station operations are available and the operators are properly trained. The routing step will specify only the *essential* information about the individual operation. This is akin to telling a taxi driver to take a passenger from the hotel to the airport. The dispatcher does not have to tell the driver the route to take or how to drive the taxi.

Figure 3-5 shows the route sheet for the hammer example. Note the balance between brevity and the essential information for each operation.

6. Select the Work Stations to Perform Each Process Step

Work station selection is made with the intent of having the tooling and the process capability available to do the required job. Most of the time, this is a given, because most manufacturing concerns do not have a choice: their work stations do not have equal capability. Usually a company will have a preferred work station for a certain procedure and a backup of lesser capability for doing the same job.

ROUTING SHEET

Date: 01/22/00

Hammer
Drwg No. 123E456
Material: 316 stainless steel

Operation No.	Work Station	Description	Unit of Measure	Quantity per Queue	Run Time	Setup Time
10	Forge press*	a. Use die no. 16 b. Use std. forge practice, make 123E456Pt3	100	10,000	100 hours	10 hours
15	CNC lathe Open headstock	a. Use 1.125 in. round stock, 12 ft length b. Feed round stock into lathe, use program 1212, make handles per drwg 123E456Pt2	30	10,000	333.33 hours	2 hours
18	Purchasing	a. Purchase rubber grip, 123E456Pt1	10,000	10,000	N/A	N/A
20	CNC drill	a. Use fixture 1 b. Use program 1213, make 123E456Pt3	240	10,000	41.67 hours	1 hour
30	Assembly station 1	a. Assemble 123E456 Pt2 to Pt3 b. Thread hammer head onto shaft c. Spot weld per process A123	45	10,000	222.22 hours	1 hour
40	Assembly station 2	a. Assemble 123E456 Pt1 to Pt2 b. Fit 123E456PT1 on fixture 2, expand c. Fit fixture 2 onto 123E456Pt2 d. Slide 123E456Pt1 onto Pt2 e. Use process B123	60	10,000	166.67 hours	1 hour
50	Pack station	a. Pack 123E456 assembly per process C123	180	10,000	55.56 hours	0.5 hours
60	Warehouse	a. Deliver 123E456 assembly to warehouse	180	10,000	55.56	N/A

*Routing sheets normally refer to work stations by a filing number, but for illustrative purposes names are used here instead of numbers.

Figure 3-5. Route sheet (hammer example).

The manufacturing engineer will always specify the preferred work station. Also, if there is a possibility that the backup work station will need to be pressed into service, then the engineer will list it as an alternative. This means that a second set of tooling, jigs, and fixtures needs to be called for if the primaries cannot be used on the alternate work station. A second consideration will be the cycle time differences between the primary work station and the alternate(s).

7. Using Industrial Engineering Techniques, Establish, or Have Established, the Times It Takes to Accomplish Each Process Sequence Step at the Selected Work Stations

Notice that the routing sheet contains run time and setup time. While this is not necessary from the purely focused viewpoint of figuring out how the product will be made, it is absolutely necessary as one of the major factors of determining whether or not the procedure selected is acceptable. As we know, manufacturing needs to produce the products so they meet all design specifications with the utmost consistency and at the lowest possible cost. The second "Know"—know how long it should take to make the product—comes into play to determine plant capacity and, ultimately, profitability. If the product takes too long to make with respect to competitive products, its labor costs will be proportionally higher, and thus it will be less competitive.

Another reason why time to do the job is on the routing sheet is that it can be used to evaluate the organization's performance in making the product. Obviously, it is a standard to measure operator performance against. But perhaps not so obvious is the ability to measure the effectiveness of the support functions getting materials to the work stations, the effectiveness of the process tools selected, and how well the organization has prepped and trained the workforce to do their jobs.

For the above reasons, it is very important that the times put on the routing sheet be as accurate as possible. They must correctly reflect the time it should take adequately trained personnel to perform the various steps of the process, using the prescribed method. Accurate times are found by evaluating the process, the intended workplace, and the tooling to be used and applying associated time standards found in reference manuals. These are called *scientific time standards* and have an advantage over *estimated time standards*.

Scientific time standards apply the principles of motion economy to measure the expended energy necessary to do work. The less energy applied to do a specific task, the faster work can be done. Thus it is possible to equate effort with time to do a task, and hence we can measure time to do work.

Estimated time standards encompass every other method of assigning times to specific operations. These range from stopwatch measurements of the specific jobs to outright guesses based on past experience. Stopwatch measurement is the best of the estimated versions. It actually measures increments of jobs the way time is measured in a sporting event. It does this over a relatively short period of time, perhaps through a series of repetitive timings. Since this is a single measurement or a short series of measurements in a noncontrolled situation (because there is no way to tell how the operators would perform if not being observed), the results are only a crude estimate of what the timing would be under most normal circumstances. It is also presumptuous to expect that the stopwatch method can be fine enough to pick up all the nuances of wasted motions; hence, an optimum estimate is rarely approached.

Estimation of time to perform tasks based on past experience is a non-starter altogether. It is akin to trying to predict the future turns of an infrequently traveled road by staring out the rearview mirror. Rarely is experience with a past product an accurate predictor of a new product's cycle time. The method works only if the earlier product is truly very similar, perhaps falling into the same family of parts according to the group technology concept. But it does work to the extent that it gives us a ballpark version of the real optimal time. Perhaps this is useful as a reality check on the scientific time standard, to assure that it was reached by a sound method. But in no way is it a pragmatic solution in a truly competitive situation. Estimated time standards are in all cases less accurate than scientific time standards, and so they cannot be depended upon in a tight, competitive situation.

Scientific time standards for specific jobs are based on the study of incremental motions needed to do specific elemental tasks, such as reaches, grasps, lifts, transports (rotational and linear), and placements. Times for a large majority of the subsets of these incremental or fundamental motions have been cataloged by industrial engineers over many decades. This means that if a process can be defined in terms of all of its constituent incremental motions, it is possible to accurately determine the amount of time to accomplish the job. Obviously, the task is not trivial; however, a large body of knowledge is readily available via texts and engineering journals. There are, as well, many commercially available software programs to enable reasonably trained personnel to do the time setting tasks adequately well, after a week or two of training. It is the commercially available software that most methods engineers use to apply times to the selected methods.

With scientific time standards available for each operation, the methods engineer inserts the times into the routing as shown in Figure 3-5. Note that time is listed on the routing sheet in three areas: units processed per hour, time to set up the work station, and run time at the work station. Run time is dependent on the number of discrete parts to be produced. For example, if we want to make 1000 parts and the rate is 100 parts per hour, then the run time will be 10 hours. However, setup time is independent of the number of parts to be made. Setup time is strictly dependent on the work station and the specifics necessary to make it perform. This means that setup falls into the realm of an engineering creativity exercise. It also portrays a glimpse of manufacturing cost containment strategy. If setups are complex and long, then there is a strong desire to have large production runs. We would want to mitigate the cost of the setup over a larger number of parts, since setup cannot in any way be construed to be a value-added operation. If a company has large production runs, then it will have base-loaded, perhaps hard-automation equipment. On the other hand, if the company depends on many different types of orders over a relatively short period of time, it will require very flexible facilities. This in turn means that in our example we cannot afford long setup times.

The subject of setup time reduction is as old as industrial engineering itself. Many consulting companies earn their livelihood selling setup reduction methodology. Some techniques are valid, some not. The good ones all look at setup as a non-value-added task that should be minimized to the highest degree possible. Their basic technique is to look at all steps in a setup. First, they eliminate all redundant, repeat, and unnecessary steps. Second, they find out what steps can be done prior to actually performing the setup on the machine or work station, thus doing things in parallel rather than in series. And third, they establish special tools to enhance setup effectiveness much like an Indy car pit stop operation. These three steps are time-honored industrial engineering efficiency improvement evaluations, and they do work. It is a matter of application and logical thinking on the part of all participants to make them successful.

8. Create an Indented Bill of Materials That Will Instruct Manufacturing on What Material Will Be Used at What Process Step and in What Quantity

The indented bill of materials (BOM) is simply a "goes into" pattern, from incremental parts to subassemblies to final assembly of the shipped product, with the quantities of materials required for each operation. Figure 3-6 shows an example of a BOM.

The bill of materials is a concise summary of the sequence of manufacturing along with the materials required, in the required quantities. Let's look at Figure 3-6 to see how it is organized and to understand how it relates to the task of creating a process instruction.

- The *header* is essentially the same as what's found on the route sheet: a description of the part and the material, or materials, used for manufacture. There are eight columns. Each gives information necessary for engineers and purchasing agents to do their job in coordinated manner. Starting at the far left, let's look at each column.
- The *level number* is the hierarchy of the manufacturing profile. The lower the number, the closer the item is toward the final configuration of the assembly. The product, itself, is always designated as zero (0). The designation "indented bill of materials" comes from the fact that originally the BOM was laid out like an essay outline, with different indentation levels to indicate major points and supporting subpoints; hence, the term "indented." Now we use numbers in place of the traditional indentation levels. For the hammer example, we have two major subassemblies designated as level 2 and then one final assembly designated as level 1. Level 0 is always the finished product after completion of the final assembly.

Indented Bill of Materials

Date: 01/22/00

Hammer
Drwg No. 123E456
Material: 316 stainless stell

Level No.	Part No.	Quantity Per	Unit of Measure	Make/Buy Volume	Description	Make/Buy	Phantom
0	123E456ASM	1	each	10,000	hammer assembly	M	Y
1	123E456ASM	1	each	10,000	hammer head to handle assembly; thread/weld	M	Y
2	123E456PT1/2	1	each	10,000	hammer handle assembly	M	Y
3	123E456PT2	1	each	10,000	hammer handle machining	M	Y
4	123E456PT2	1	each	840	316 stainless steel 12 ft x 1.125 in. dia. bar stock	B	N
4	123E456PT1	1	each	10,000	hammer handle rubber grip	B	N
2	123E456PT3	1	each	10,000	hammer head machining	M	Y
3	123E456PT3	1	each	10,000	hammer head forge	M	Y
4	123E456PT3	1	each	3,500	316 stainless steel 4.00 in. dia. round forge stock; 1/3 lb. per	B	N

Figure 3-6. Indented bill of materials (hammer example).

- The *part number* column shows the drawing numbers associated with the product design. In the example, I've shown numbers referencing different parts of the same drawing. However, it is conceivable that there could be many drawings and part numbers in a BOM. This would probably be the case for a more complex part.
- *Quantity per*, the next column, specifies the number or amount of each line item used in the makeup of the product. Since this is a simplified example, the quantity is 1. However, consider an assembly that has fasteners such as sheet metal screws. In that case the quantity would be the number of screws required for the assembly to be finished.
- *Unit of measure* tells the user how the line item is accounted for. For example, if paint had been required, the unit of measure would be a liquid measure of appropriate magnitude—perhaps quart or gallon.
- The *make or buy volume* is the total number of units of measure needed to fulfill the order quantity.
- The *description* explains the line item. For make items it shows the process—e.g., assemble, machine, weld. For buy items it specifies what to buy, even though the specifics are also found on the drawings. This is a summary useful for tying in to the manufacturing resources planning (MRP II) system.
- The *make/buy* column designates whether the line item is a purchase item (B), or a fabricate item (M). In no case is one line item both. It's always an either/or situation.

- To explain the *phantom* classification in the far right column, we revert back to the original purpose of a bill of materials, which is to list all the components a purchasing agent has to gather together for the company to make its product. A line item is a phantom if it doesn't directly involve a purchase activity. For example, the hammer handle assembly is made up of two direct purchase items: the steel, and the rubber grip. These are not phantoms. In the machining and assembly, however, no direct purchasing activity has to occur. These are phantoms from the purchasing agent's viewpoint.

The indented BOM is a useful tool for structuring the manufacturing process and is vital for providing process information to the work station. It, along with the routings, provides the basis for all instructions to the work station for a particular work order. This, combined with general instructions common for all jobs, makes up the standard instruction package provided to shop operations.

9. Input the Indented Bill of Materials, the Routing with Cycle Times, and Tooling Requirements to the Scheduling System— Preferably, an MRP System

We've now completed all the tasks of process planning except integrating it with the production control system. The effort of process planning provides the controlling factor for the production schedule. We have defined the Two Knows of the manufacturing process. We know how to make the product, and we know how long it should take to do so. Now it's necessary to transmit that information in a coordinated manner, so that we can direct traffic through the factory, linking jobs in sequential order. We do this by inputting the process planning information into the scheduling system. With process planning, the scheduling system will have the cycle time integrity necessary to optimize production. This happens because we know with a high degree of certainty how to make the product and the time to do so; thus, we have a tight schedule that is also practical.

Manufacturing resources planning systems are integrated scheduling systems that allocate time in accordance with both schedule and continuous feedback of actual accomplishments. The feedback will most likely differ from the schedule, because even the most meticulously laid out plans can never cover every conceivable contingency. But we do know that even though our schedule can never be 100% certain, the actual results will be well within any reasonable parameters. The parameter variances will be based on the accuracy of the planning and the effectiveness of carrying it out. Obviously, if the accuracy portion is done well, then the management challenge for running an effective shop has one less variable to contend with. We will review MRP II systems in Chapter 5. However, it is important at this juncture to understand that no scheduling system is any good unless it is supported by accurate data. The process planning we have just described is the best way possible to provide the accurate data needed for accurate manufacturing.

Chapter 4

Quality Control at the Work Station

In this chapter we will investigate the quality aspects of work station dynamics. An essential part of the information delivered to the work station consists of process checks. Checks are done to assure that the products are being manufactured in accordance with the design requirements. Quality aspects are woven into execution of the process plan; in fact, a case can be made that quality planning is a subset of traditional process planning. With modern CIM (computer-integrated manufacturing) systems, as in the earlier CAPP (computer-aided process planning) system, quality planning is part of the common database. We will see that quality planning does not exist as an independent entity, but rather there is synergism between it and other mechanisms for optimizing the output of work stations. We will focus on the theory of quality control and the procedures for carrying out the quality control operations at the work station.

In order to properly execute the Two Knows, we need to have a well-thought-out process plan. We must select the work station where the work will be performed. With the particulars of that work station defined, the process plan will include sequences of events choreographed to assure that raw material is transformed into finished products in the most optimal and logical manner. We need to vigorously pursue the design of the best jigs and fixtures for bringing the product design into existence with its intended form and function. We require a thorough understanding of how long each stage of manufacture will take, thus gaining necessary insight into production costs. These topics, which we investigated in Chapter 3, are vital and necessary for a manufacturing company's business success, but they are not entirely sufficient.

To complete the loop, to make the planning process complete, the other, lesser known component of the second "Know"—know how long it should take to make the product—is required. This is the quality aspect. To *really* understand plant capacity, we need to know the time it takes to do the necessary quality checks. In addition to the physical time needed to make the product, time has to be allowed to verify that the process is being performed correctly. It takes a conscious effort to understand quality requirements and to make sure the process allows time for quality checks. Sometimes the physical work is straightforward but the checking procedure is difficult and time-consuming.

Example. The manufacture of printheads for high-capacity and fine-detail printing involves laser drilling of very-small-diameter and precise-dimensioned holes. The process is well within current technologies, and relatively fast to perform. But the testing—the quality control step—may require elaborate printing tests with measurement down to angstrom units for line width variations on various grades of papers and on other surfaces. This process has fairly high failure rates. The design is not terribly robust, because many variables have not yet been wholly accounted for. This means testing has to be severe and very critical, the result being that the time for in-process testing far exceeds the actual physical processing time. Thus, for factory capacity to be known, the computation of cycle time needs to include process time, which is well defined; and testing time, which is not. Here, we have a not too uncommon situation where the time to produce is significantly less than the test time.

The requirement for testing goes back to meeting the customer's design requirements. It is an integral part of the cost of the process and of the capacity of the plant. Quality requirements are not something separate from the specifications for intended use and robustness in the product design. They are simply a way of demonstrating that the product being offered to the customer does, indeed, meet the specifications of the design. In many ways, quality requirements are simply a certification process with sufficient proof (data) to convince the buyer that the product is what it portends to be.

Let's see how the second "Know" is affected by an all-encompassing certification schema. We will see that a good quality program actually reduces time, and thus costs, to make a product, with one proviso: the quality plan must be compatible with the true needs of the customer. If quality cycle time is properly included in total cycle time, the customer should always favor bearing some extra expense, for it is what ensures getting it right the first time and giving the customer a reliable delivery schedule.

THE CONCEPT OF QUALITY

The place to start is by reviewing what's called the *concept of quality*. Quality performance of a company goes far beyond the activity taking place at the work station. But the work station is the focal point, and if it doesn't happen at the work station we have failed. Therefore, while concepts of quality are all-encompassing for the entire company, performance at the work station is their reason for being.

Concepts evolve over time. The concept of quality up until the mid to late 1970s was very different from what it is today.

Concept of Quality circa 1975

Around 1975, the spotlight was on achieving a quality level that was acceptable to and agreed upon by the customer. It had to be accepted that there would inevitably be out-of-compliance parts or products slipping through and ending up in the customer's inventory. The strategy was one of containment, not prevention. It was expected that the process used would make a percentage of bad products and some of those bad products would not be discovered before shipment. The quality strategy featured probabilistic schemes under which some bad parts would be accepted as good and end up in the customer's inventory and—conversely—some good parts would be rejected by the customer and sent back to the producer. Several specific concerns and procedures grew out of this approach to quality:

- Yield measurements
- Scrap and rework accounting
- Customer claims administration
- Customer service cost administration, involved with weeding out the out-of-spec parts that reached the customer
- Burden of proof issues to be faced by both producer and customer
- An autocratic management function that assumed full responsibility for resolution of problems and rarely involved shop operations, except in a punitive fashion

Quality management was very much akin to the cop on the beat. The quality overseers were there to assure that those "recalcitrants," the shop operations people, didn't cheat and did what they were suppose to. The mental set was far from a team approach. Internally, the measurements showed how well the managers of quality controlled the process versus how much the shop was able to slip past. With customers and vendors it was a struggle to see who got the upper hand. Naturally, this type of system bred suspicion, discontent, and absolutely no teamwork to produce the best product possible.

The Modern Concept of Quality

We contrast the law-and-order style of quality management with the modern approach, which revolves about teamwork and respect for all members of the infrastructure. The concurrent engineering philosophy of teamwork is the best way to deliver a suitable product to the functions that need to use it. With this concept governing the supply chain, all participants, both internal and external to the company, are equally important for success. Optimization occurs only when all supply chain members are doing their job to the best of their abilities. There are no monitors to enforce compliance, other than group dynamics and the urge not to let fellow team members down.

The new, modern quality strategy highlights:

- Perfect quality as a driver of market share—a profitability enhancer
- Perfect quality as a key assurance to the customer that delivery needs can be met
- The understanding that perfect quality of product and/or service drives repeat sales

- A self-imposed quest for excellence
- A striving for continuous improvement as a constant of business life
- Achieving perfect quality as a team approach
- Measurement as an aid for self and group improvement, not a punitive technique designed to keep operators in line

We see here the emphasis on striving for perfection in whatever one's individual role may be in the supply chain.

The modern quality strategy emphasizes continuous improvement. Therefore it is a people-focused strategy. It proclaims that we can have perfect quality only when everyone performs perfectly. This is like a football team executing a play perfectly. All 11 members of the team successfully carry out their assigned task and with confidence that the other team members will do likewise.

We know that we cannot inspect quality into a product. Quality starts with designing the product so that each segment is "vetted" to be as robust as possible. The design is followed up with a manufacturing plan based on thorough understanding of the product design and compatible with it. The manufacturing plan encompasses the proper work stations, with the correct jigs and fixtures. The plan has adequate methodology documentation, and has assigned preparation time to school the workforce in the nuances of its execution.

The manufacturing plan has a logically thought out measurement schema to assure the team that the process is producing the product to its required parameters. It has factored in the training time to assure that the workforce can perform the measurements and interpret the resultant data. The workforce is also trained on how to take corrective action, as required by the measurement results.

The plan regards the procurement of materials and other purchased components in the same fashion and devotion to excellence as it does with internally made parts. Outside sources are treated as part of the team. In fact, there is no distinction between the expectations placed on vendors to produce perfect quality and those placed on the internal work stations. All work stations, be they internal or external, are treated equally.

The Cost of Poor Quality

The modern quality strategy also makes good business sense from an economic viewpoint. If all we had in mind were to increase profits for the short term without regard for the longevity of the enterprise, we would still employ the supply-line quality mentality for one very significant reason: to reduce the cost of errors. We all know instinctively that the time required to fix errors erodes profit dollars: in a poor quality operation, some of the earnings that could be earmarked for improvements or dividends are going instead toward correcting errors. Numerous evaluations have been put on the cost of errors, sometimes known as the cost of quality. In my General Electric consulting days, we used the "7 factor" multiplier for determining the cost of errors. I believe the cost factor could be even higher for complex assemblies. Be that as it may, the 7 factor multiplier is an excellent order-of-magnitude estimator for predicting the cost of quality. To show how that works, let's look at an example.

Recall the hammer manufacturing example from Chapter 3. In Figure 3-4 there were six levels of manufacturing, from raw material to finished product. The cost of error correction among these steps is variable. How extensive a fix is needed would depend on where the error occurred. Let's assume an error is discovered at the CNC lathe where the bar stock is machined to size to form the handle. In this case we are at level 1, and therefore there are no preceding steps to be undone. But even in this case the cost will be substantial. Suppose the handles are over size. (If they were under size they would have to be scrapped, because adding material and then remachining would be prohibitive and ludicrous. The only choice would be scrapping out the defective parts.) Then we would have to find all the over-size parts, disrupt production, re-set up the machine, and remachine to an acceptable shaft profile.

Now consider the costs if we discovered the error at a later stage of production. Let us assume the error is discovered at the assembly of the rubber grip to the handle. Imagine that the machining of the handle was deficient in that even though the shaft threaded into the hammer head, the diameter was too large to accept the rubber grip. To fix this error we first have to remove the shaft from the hammer head, and then repeat the fix as described previously. This means that the tack weld of the shaft to the head has to be removed and the surface re-dressed before the shaft and the head can be reassembled. Thus we have level 3 and level 1 work to be done over again on the handle. In addition, the re-dressing will probably require redoing some significant portion of the level 2 work of retapping the hole in the hammer head.

With the complexities involved, I found by experimentation that the true cost can be approximated by the following equation; I call this the rule of 7:

$$\text{Repair cost} = (7)(L_3) + (7)(7)(L_2) + (7)(7)(7)(L_1)$$

where: L_3 = original level 3 costs
L_2 = original level 2 costs
L_1 = original level 1 costs

We can see that we have a geometric progression whereby the further the down the line the error is discovered, the cost rises as 7 raised to the power 1, 2, 3, ... , n. In this case n would be 6, because there are 6 levels of production to make the hammer.

This can get very expensive. Therefore it is often a better choice to scrap instead of repairing once the power factor gets above 2. The mitigating circumstances forcing a contrary decision could, for example, be a delivery promise constraint or nonavailability of replacement material.

In addition to the cost of repairing poor quality, we must consider the associated losses of resources and capacity. Even if we can absorb the cost of fixing poor quality, think what it does to resources and capacity. Every time we devote factory capacity to repairing parts that have already been through the manufacturing cycle, we are robbing ourselves of capability to make more sellable goods and thus reducing our ability to make a profit. In the same manner, every time we need to devote resources—human, machines, and materials—to fixing mistakes, we are reducing our ability to focus on additional business opportunities.

These silent wastes cut into a company's ability to maintain its commitments to its customers. For example, scheduled delivery dates are based on the planned method and associated cycle time. However, if a part has to be fixed or even scrapped and entirely redone, we are distorting the schedule. We have not planned for scrap and rework when we laid out our plans to manufacture the product. We based our delivery time on a carefully choreographed scheme and made promises to the customer based on that scheme. Now, with unintended delays due to poor quality performance, we find that our product will be delivered later than expected. This is bad enough for the specific customer of the affected product, but the delay also extends to other customers' orders dependent on the same manufacturing facilities. So we have a detrimental snowballing effect. Think of what happens when a major hub airport has delays, such as Chicago's O'Hare during a winter snowstorm. Think about the backups and cancellations that occur literally around the world due to late arrivals of airplanes or blockages at gates because a flight that should have left didn't. The results is a form of controlled chaos. This is exactly the same as what happens when a factory's schedule is distorted because of poor quality.

QUALITY PLANNING TECHNIQUES

We can begin to mitigate the deleterious effects of poor quality by understanding the modern concepts of quality and by using them in our integrated planning processes. Let's take a look and see how that is accomplished.

There is no secret formula. It is simply good planning. Just as we developed a design and then planned precisely how we would transform raw materials into a finished product to accomplish its intent, we need to plan how we will make sure that we are accomplishing it effectively. As a corollary, we need to plan how we will assure ourselves after the fact that we did it correctly.

Quality planning is accomplished in two phases. The first is a generic procedure we can follow to "keep book" on what we need to do. The second is a specific set of action steps related to a specific product's methods, planning, and routing documents.

The first phase is often called a *quality plan*, but is actually a process control system for measuring the organization's effectiveness in producing perfect products, with a schema for generic corrective actions. A sample process control system is shown in Figure 4-1. The recent surge of ISO 9000 certification events within thousands of companies is an example of the authentication of process control systems. Many companies have come to the realization that the quest for perfect quality is a legitimate and successful strategy. ISO 9000 is a certification by an unbiased source that tells the world that Company X has a workable process control system. Keep in mind that it does not validate a company's capability of making a product to customer specifications and needs, but rather certifies that the company has a good system for measuring its ability to do its work in a planned and structured quality environment. Only a specific set of quality-oriented action steps linked to the specific process plan can have a real effect on product quality.

The second phase of quality planning, specific action steps, consists of focused plans that emanate out of the quality plans block of the process control system (see Figure 4-1). Here we set up specific certification and measurement steps for each operation to evaluate whether or not we have achieved the intent of the design at that intermediate phase of manufacturing.

Example. If we were doing pressure vessel welding, we would definitely want to insure the integrity of the weld. After all, we are certainly depending on the weld to be 100% perfect, because the strength called for by the design is essential. The size, shape, material, and welding process have been selected to meet the design criteria; therefore, it is reasonable that we should be required to measure the end results to see if we have met them. Thus, the process plan and method instruct the operator on how to make the weld, and the corresponding quality plan delineates how to measure the results to see whether the welding was done right.

We need to examine the process control system in some depth and then see how it will guide the development of a specific quality plan. There are many forms of process control systems. The one shown in Figure 4-1 is a generic system that works well for job shop operations and is adequate for flow production. It is also the simplest, bare-bones system with no frills, and thus excellent for illustrative purposes.

As we can see from Figure 4-1, the process control system is a closed-loop system designed for continuous improvement. Its major components are:

- Quality plans
- Measurements
- Data collection, recording, and classifying
- Corrective action (short term)
- Corrective action (long term)
- Reports

The expected results from a well-executed process control system are a significant reduction in scrap and rework, a minimization of production delays, and an obvious improvement in product quality. While the process control system is compatible with all these goals, we should not think that it and it alone is responsible for these improvements. It is a significant factor in making business optimization come to be, but it is certainly not the only factor.

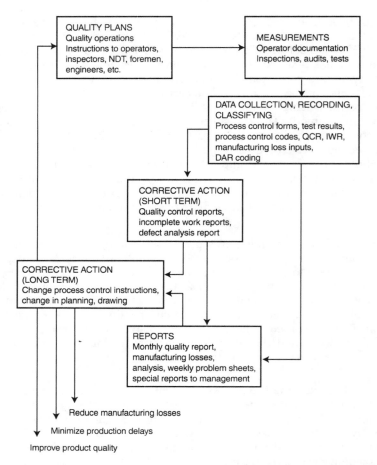

Figure 4-1. Process control system. (From Daniel T. Koenig, "Manufacturing Engineering: Principles for Optimization," 2nd ed., Taylor & Francis, Washington, 1994.)

In fact, all inputs to work station dynamics have to be executed properly for the optimum results to occur. The process control system does not operate in a vacuum. Too many companies try to compartmentalize segments of work station dynamics as if they were islands unto themselves, neither affecting nor affected by other factors that influence business control. To do this is to suboptimize. We need it all to be successful. We need to be careful not to become such advocates for one segment of business improvement that we think it is the sole key to success. The truth is that process control is a part of a synergistic whole.

Let's look at the components of the process control system

Quality Plans

Quality plans are the specifics of the direct actions of people and machines for obtaining an output within the design specifications. Later on in this chapter, I will describe how to develop a quality plan.

Measurements

Measurements are the initial indicators of how shop operations is doing with respect to the required outcome. They consist of:

- Operator documentation
- Inspections
- Audits
- Tests

Operator documentation is anything that the quality plan deems important to satisfy verification needs. Whatever is necessary to assure that the intent of the product design is being met at a particular phase of the manufacturing process should be required. It may be something as simple as the operator's recording a temperature at a set time interval, or as elaborate as measuring critical dimensions as part of a statistical process control (SPC) routine.

Inspections are the same as operator documentation except they are done by a member of the quality control department instead of the operator. They are going out of favor now, because we believe that good quality cannot be inspected into a product. We do not want to set up the false situation where the inspector tells the operator whether or not it is OK to proceed. Rather, the operator needs to take ownership and pride in the work he or she does. We expect that the operator not only will have the responsibility to follow the method or process precisely, but will also be a member of the team that determines whether the process is capable of delivering satisfactory quality as promised. The operator may now be considered analogous to a test pilot who not only flies the aircraft but at the same time is responsible for the product's quality just like any other member of the design and manufacturing team.

Audits are periodic reviews of measurements, or taking of actual measurements, by persons other than operators or inspectors, typically, cognizant management and engineering personnel who have overall authority for the particular segment of manufacturing. Audits may be formal or informal.

A formal audit, when it occurs, is probably contractually required by a customer, or perhaps a regulatory agency. An example would be a specified number of measurements to assure a customer that the process for making the purchased item is under control. Another example might be a procedure to assure that the final product will meet all safety requirements, as required by law; manufacture of automobile air bags would be subject to such an audit. Typically, complex products such as gas turbines require formal audits with corresponding documentation, whereas simple products such as cut-to-length aluminum bars would not.

An informal audit is nothing more than the engineer's, the foreman's, or the manager's simply observing the workings of the area and conversing with operators. The purpose is to take the pulse of the operation to make sure that the process is working as it is supposed to and good product is being produced. The term "managing by walking around," popularized by Tom Peters, is apropos here. This is just good common sense for those with the authority and major accountability to understand how the work is progressing as measured against schedule and compliance with design criteria. Tests are more elaborate measurements designed to definitively determine whether a product during the course of production complies with the design and specifications. Tests are much rarer than measurements and are more elaborate, and hence more costly. Tests are specified only to prove that a particular product, or segment of a product, is worthy of a perfect quality pedigree. They are done because there is no other analytical way to assure the pedigree. A new airplane requires extensive testing for this purpose. A new water glass may not require any testing at all. With the surge to perfect quality, we are finding that products once considered obscure and not worthy of test evaluation are now being tested. To aid in testing, organizations such as the American Society of Mechanical Engineers (ASME International) and Underwriters Laboratory (UL) have developed standards for hosts of products to be compared against. The ASME Boiler and Pressure Vessel Code and Fastener Standards are two quite widely used criteria. UL standards are quite common for electrical fittings and hence can be used as test benchmarks. We know that the purchasing public will feel more assured if a product has an ASME or a UL stamp on it signifying that the product has passed a level of acceptability testing.

Data Collection, Recording, and Classifying

Data collection, recording, and classifying is the procedural part of the process control system specifying how measurement results will be stored and sorted for future use. Measurements give us immediate indications of how a process is performing. But being able to discern the nuances of whether or not a process is optimum requires analysis of pertinent data. This step in the process control system provides the readily accessible library of data to be used in ad hoc as well as preconceived analysis plans.

The type of data collection technique selected will depend on the product and process involved. If we are working in a chemical factory the data will probably relate to fluid measurement methods. If we are making discrete parts, then proximity to a desired geometric shape is probably the kind of data called for. The point is that there are many methodologies to contend with, with no one correct solution. For this reason, we select a data collection method only after a BOM and route sheet are decided upon and the specific quality plan has been selected.

Corrective Action (Short Term)

Corrective action comes in two versions: short-term and long-term. Short-term corrective action is like first aid, an emergency procedure to stop an injury from becoming worse, like stopping the bleeding before suturing the wound. In manufacturing, the first aid consists of stopping a process from making out-of-tolerance products and dealing with the immediate fix requirements.

Example. Suppose we find, through a specified inspection procedure and resultant data collection and analysis, that the weld of the hammer head to the shaft has a crack in it. We would want to first make sure all assemblies with cracked heads were found and isolated. Then we would determine whether the immediate problem of defective welds can be fixed. If so, we would set out to devise instructions to do so. If not, we would scrap.

This is an example of short-term corrective action. We have stopped the bleeding but haven't found the root cause that allowed the error to occur in the first place. Getting to root cause and making permanent fixes is long-term corrective action.

Corrective Action (Long Term)

Long-term corrective action consists of making permanent change so that the defect attended to via the short-term corrective action step cannot reoccur. In the hammer assembly example, it means understanding the root cause of why the crack occurred and taking action to eliminate that cause. If we are successful, weld cracks will never again be a concern. Usually, to prevent reoccurrence, we revert back to the process planning stage and make changes in drawings, process instructions, and other communicating devices used to portray what we wish to manufacture. You may think of this as the clarification procedure necessary to make the process producible with no variance from specification, and if you do you are correct.

Reports

The process control system requires dissemination of information in order for corrective action to occur. Reports are the vehicles used to inform all persons needing to know of the status of manufacturing with respect to the posted desired results. The rule of thumb here is that the further up the organization hierarchy the report is intended to go, the more general in scope the information is and the more strategic in nature it becomes. With the hammer weld failure example, senior management would not need to know the specific reason for failure unless the long-term corrective action would entail significant changes in process and hence affect cost, delivery, and capacity. On the other hand, the engineers responsible for designing the manufacturing process need to have specific data regarding the failure so they can find the root cause.

The most common process control system reports are scrap and rework frequency. They are a bellwether for judging the effectiveness of the process. However, they do not tell why the process is at the state it is in. We can approach root cause by using Pareto techniques to rank categories of scrap and rework.

In the hammer assembly example, our Pareto analysis may show rework occasioned by cracked welds, X%; handle diameter over size, Y%; rubber sleeve not engaged high enough up the handle, Z%. The Pareto analysis tells us the frequency of events and is useful in focusing an investigation to generate solutions that have a large impact on overall performance. Obviously, solving a problem that accounts for 25% percent of all rejections is worth more to the company than solving a problem resulting in 5% of all rejections.

There is another factor to consider in choosing what problem to solve first, second, and so forth: that of understanding the manufacturing process relationships, particularly, knowing which situations are independent and which are dependent. Knowing how the hammer is made, we would look for any cause-and-effect relationship. If the rubber sleeve is not engaging high enough, that failure is not an independent event. It is directly related to the over-size shaft problem. If we fix the root cause, the over-size handle diameter, then the sleeve problem will be eliminated completely.

There are many additional items that could be found in a report glossary. Most are specific to the product. Only scrap and rework reports and customer satisfaction level reports are just about universal. A customer satisfaction report can be very elaborate, using subjective as well as objective measurements and evaluations. One of the most common is one that records returns for manufacturing errors discovered by the customer. This is a useful document in that it allows trend documentation to be monitored, quantified, and compared from reporting period to reporting period. This is one of the reports that senior members of management are interested in because it takes little technical know-how to interpret.

DRAFTING THE QUALITY PLAN

We have seen how a process control system is put into place to set a company's policy for all of its quality evaluation actions. We can obtain further insight into process control operations by investigating how a quality plan is drafted. Remember, the process control system is a schematic for living in a zero-defects world. It contains the generic rules and regulations for assuring that the methodology used in manufacturing has the best chance possible of producing a product that meets design specifications. The quality plan will comprise the specific tactics for verifying each and every step contained in the routings. Using the hammer example once more, we will develop a quality plan.

It is amazing how many companies try to carry out manufacturing operations without a quality plan integrated into the process. Many managers and engineers seem to be oblivious of the large risk to their company of not having a quality plan. It is tantamount to a football team playing in a bowl game without regard for the opponent's strengths and weaknesses. This blind faith that everything will be all right as long as the process is executed properly is putting too much in the hands of the gods. A quality plan lets us anticipate potential trouble areas by evaluating our progress as we proceed. This way we can quickly mitigate problems as they occur, not when it is too late or too costly to do so. Recall the rule of 7 and the impact on costs if we do not discover deficient product quality early in the process.

Another myth about not needing a quality plan revolves about the use of inspectors. Lots of companies, when they realize that the *perception* of perfect quality is necessary to sell their product, think they can achieve it by putting an inspector in place as a sort of watchman who will prevent defective products from ever leaving the plant. There is no need to develop a comprehensive quality plan, they surmise, because the inspector will catch all defects before they ship. This is a very unlikely scenario, a throwback to the *old* concept of quality. It just doesn't work.

Eventually, companies come to realize that they need to factor quality steps into their work paradigm. But even then, unfortunately, too many think it needs to be a complex matrix overlaid on the process they employ to make their product. They often mistake process control systems for a quality plan, and hence get involved in trying to implement apples when oranges would do. I will restate:

A process control system is a methodology for measuring the organization's effectiveness in producing perfect products, with a schema for generic corrective actions.

On the other hand,

A quality plan is a specific set of actions to ensure that each step in the process of making a specific product, or subcomponent of the product, is manufactured in accordance with the design and manufacturing instructions.

Only a specific set of quality-oriented action steps linked to the process plan can have a real effect on product quality. Thus, the quality plan must be directly and irrefutably linked to a process plan. They go hand in hand. This means that a quality plan cannot exist without a process plan—ever. A process plan can exist without a quality plan, but not vice versa.

The rule for writing a quality plan is quite simple. For every step on the routing sheet, there needs to be an action that certifies that the process step was done correctly. This may sound intimidating, but it isn't. Most of the time the certifying step is nothing more than good common sense. If we are machining a shaft, would we do so without verifying that the setup on the machine is correct? Of course not. The verification is the certification action. It's as simple as that. If the shaft is simply chucked into the lathe, the certification is nothing more than the operator's making sure the chuck is secured, probably to a specified torque value. It is also the double checking to make sure that the proper tool inserts are set in the toolholder. An experienced operator would do this anyway. But by specifying that that action needs to take place, we make sure that the shaft is seated properly before machining commences and that we have selected the right cutting tools. Hence, we get a circular round shaft instead of an ellipsoidal round shaft.

Quite often the quality plan will require the operator to certify an action by recording data. This is done to make sure that critical facets of the process are being achieved, and also for statistical process control analysis. It is the process control engineer's responsibility to call for the pertinent data to be recorded, and in a way that is as unobtrusive to the flow of production as possible. Virtually all data in a properly executed quality plan are recorded by the operator who is generating them via the process under his or her control. The operator, as an integral member of the production team, is the first line of defense preventing poor quality output from moving on to the next work area. With most processes now computer-controlled or assisted, the operator is more or less a technician overseeing a complex investment in action. Therefore, he or she has to be cognizant of good or bad performance and act accordingly. The quality plan is a significant part of the guidance given to the operator regarding the range of criticality to be observed. That's why specifying what data to take and when is important for overall success.

The quality plan, being specifically linked to the process employed to make the product, looks remarkably similar to the route sheet. The similarity is intended, for the purpose of assuring complete compatibility. Figure 4-2 shows the quality plan for the hammer example. Let's see what it tells us.

The header is the same as on the route sheet, except that it says "Quality Plan." In our example, the date is a little bit later than on the corresponding route sheet (Figure 3-5). This is to signify that a quality plan cannot come into being before a method is decided upon and specified with unique details. In practice, route sheets and quality plans can be done concurrently, especially if the company employs a concurrent design philosophy.

The columns designated Operation No., Work Station, Process Description, and Unit of Measure are identical to corresponding columns on the route sheet. They are transposed from the route sheet without change because of the strong synergistic link between the quality plan and the route sheet. The only new column is the Quality Action Requirement column. This column details the quality action to be taken in parallel with the process step. Like the process description, the quality action requirement is only a brief description of the activity that is to take place. We depend on the operator and all others involved to know specifically what to do. To do otherwise would create a document that is too time-consuming to review and a waste of paper or disk space. If the document is too long, it will probably be only scanned at best. Note, however, that as for the process description, a full set of up-to-date documentation for the quality plan is maintained in strategic locations for reference as needed.

The Quality Action Requirement column specifies both the action required and who is to do it. Under operation 10 in the example, a tool and die machinist is required to certify that the forge die is properly maintained and will produce the part properly. This illustrates that not only the work station operator but many other members of the production team as well are required to perform quality-certifying actions.

In the example we also see reference to documents such as PC123E456Pt2. These are process control forms derived from the associated engineering drawing. Such a document will typically contain sketches of the pertinent sec-

QUALITY PLAN

Date: 01/29/00

Hammer
Drwg No. 123E456
Material: 316 stainless steel

Operation No.	Work Station	Process Description	Quality Action Requirement	Unit of Measure
10	Forge press*	a. Use die no. 16 b. Use std. forge practice, make 123E456Pt3	a. Certify die no. 16 has been inspected by Tool & Die for satisfactory functionality and is free of defects - T&D Machinist	100
15	CNC lathe Open headstock	a. Use 1.125 in. round stock, 12 ft length b. Feed round stock into lathe, use program 1212, make handles per drwg 123E456Pt2	a. Certify correct mat'l - Operator b. Measure & Record, PC123E456Pt2 - Operator	30
18	Purchasing	a. Purchase rubber grip, 123E456Pt1	a. Vendor Quality Certification on file - Purchasing Buyer	10,000
20	CNC drill	a. Use fixture 1 b. Use program 1213, make 123E456Pt3	a. Certify fixture 1 has been inspected by Tool Crib for satisfactory functionality and is free of defects - Tool Crib Attendant b. Measure & Record, PC123E456Pt3 - Operator	240
30	Assembly station 1	a. Assemble 123E456Pt2 to Pt3 b. Thread hammer head onto shaft c. Spot weld per process A123	a.-c. Measure & Record, PC123E456Pt2/3 - Operator	45
40	Assembly station 2	a. Assemble 123E456Pt1 to Pt2 b. Fit 123E456Pt1 on fixture 2, expand c. Fit fixture 2 onto 123E456Pt2 d. Slide 123E456Pt1 onto Pt2 e. Use process B123	a.-e. Measure & Record, PC123E456Pt 1/2 - Operator	60
50	Pack station	a. Pack 123E456 assembly per process C123	a. Audit - I.E.	180
60	Warehouse	a. Deliver 123E456 assembly to warehouse	a. Audit - Prod. Ctrl.	180

* Routing sheets normally refer to work stations by a filing number, but for illustrative purposes names are used here instead of numbers.

Figure 4-2. Quality plan (hammer example).

tions of the product where measurements will be required, a space to record the measurements, and a place for observations. It will also require a date and possibly the time of the observation and the name of the individual doing the measuring. Figure 4-3 shows a typical process control form that would be used in conjunction with the hammer manufacturing process.

Under operations 50 and 60 in Figure 4-2 we see the term "audit." This means that for these steps the quality plan does not require specific actions but that periodic checks are required to make sure no unforeseen problems occur or are about to occur. In this instance it is the process engineer who has decided that the risk of something unforeseen occurring is very low and hence no specific check is needed. But the process engineer does require the industrial engineer to check the packaging area to assure that his or her process is effective for efficient work flow and prevention of shipping damage. The process engineer is taking a similar precaution in the warehouse area, with the monitoring being done by production control personnel. If there were absolutely no quality action required (a rarity), then we would see the phrase "no action required."

Establishing the quality steps to be performed concurrently with process steps greatly affects how a work station will be managed. Quality steps are

Date _____

Work Order No. _____

Quantity _____

Checked By _____

|←D→|

L2

L1

PC 123E456 Pt 2

Hammer Handle

1. Make from 1.125 in. around stock 316 stainless steel
2. Drwg. 123E456 Pt 2. To.: ±0.003 in., Dim. D, L2; ±0.030 in., Dim. L1
3. Datum designated (0, 0, 0)

A. Material certified as per drawing (yes/no) _____
(initials)

B. Measure 20 parts from lot selected randomly. Circle out-of-tolerance dimensions.

	D	L1	L2
1	—	—	—
2	—	—	—
3	—	—	—
4	—	—	—
5	—	—	—
6	—	—	—
7	—	—	—
8	—	—	—
8	—	—	—
10	—	—	—
11	—	—	—
12	—	—	—
13	—	—	—
14	—	—	—
15	—	—	—
16	—	—	—
17	—	—	—
18	—	—	—
19	—	—	—
20	—	—	—

Figure 4-3. Process control form (hammer example).

derived from best practices, e.g., through the experience of the company itself in carrying out its manufacturing operations, and through benchmarking with best-in-class companies. Quality steps are also often dictated by customers themselves. It is not unusual for customers to direct a vendor to perform measurements and data collection and analysis to meet their specific needs. For example, if the customer is a government agency, some very specific requirements may need to be met before the vendor can even be considered for a contract. Most U.S. Department of Defense contracts require compliance with MILSPECs, which are very specific dos and don'ts on measurements and procedures. There are particularly stringent requirements on how a manufacturing process becomes qualified and remains qualified. An example would be welding on pressure vessels. The MILSPEC requires testing and certification of welders as well as certification through testing on sample production. Quite often the process to be followed needs to be agreed to by the government before production can proceed. These procedures will, indeed, dictate the choice of quality steps to be employed.

The choice of quality step will in turn be part of an iterative loop together with choice of process and how the process will be accomplished at the work station. In the hammer example, suppose a customer demanded that the spot weld be a certified weld. This means that we, the company, will have to certify that it will not fail—that we are guaranteeing that the hammer head will not fly off the handle and become a safety hazard. This could shape how we define the manufacturing process. We may elect to x-ray every weld to preclude workmanship defects. Or we may do a liquid penetrant dye test to assure that the weld is sound. The option that is precluded from consideration is the do nothing option. If we need to certify the purity of the weld, we need to do something to demonstrate good faith in assuring there aren't any weld defects. Just saying we guarantee the weld to be suitable is insufficient, because the customer needn't tolerate empty promises. The customer would just go to a competitor.

What we do, therefore, is greatly influenced by the customer. How we do the work will then impact directly on how long it will take to accomplish the task. This gets right back to the capacity and quantity issues evaluated during the process planning phase, and hence selection of the work stations to fulfill the job requirements. We can see that while the model is linear— process planning, then a quality plan to assure compliance—the reality it is not. In order to effectively plan for customer XYZ's order, we must know the customer. We need the intelligence to understand the required versus *perceived* required objectives the customer is trying to satisfy. The process of making the part may be relatively straightforward, but usually the quality steps are anything but. Here customers may be influenced by real or perceived standards that do or don't have a practical basis in relation to the specific product. Process planning is very black-and-white; quality planning deals with all shades of gray. So, in truth, process planning may need to be iteratively interweaved with quality planning. This favors a team approach, often modeled along the lines of a concurrent engineering process as described in Chapter 2.

Finally, the maneuvering through the maze presented by many customers will most likely affect the selection of the work station to do the job. Without a quality plan, it may have been practical to skip the weld quality evaluation of the hammer head to shaft assembly. After all, how many hammers fly apart with normal usage? Hardly a statistically measurable event. However, a supercautious approach may be instigated by a customer who under all scenarios must avoid lawsuits and the slightest indication of lack of care for the safety of the ultimate end user. If this is our customer profile, then doing the weld at the assembly station may not be feasible. Perhaps we need to do welding at a central weld area that is fully equipped for each and every variation of test that could be required by the customer.

TOTAL QUALITY MANAGEMENT

We have seen that the quality plan dictates the specific quality actions that need to take place associated with the work done at the work station. But is the plan enough? Is any additional training and orientation necessary for the intent of the quality plan to be accomplished? The answer is yes.

The quality plan dictates what quality actions need to be accomplished, and how they are to be accomplished, but it doesn't go into reasons for them. It simply commits the operator, engineer, inspector, foreman, and manager to specific work, work that they may perceive to be outside their normal range of duties. Being good team players, they would probably do what is requested of them but not with the vigor of one fully dedicated to the purpose. For this reason it is essential for the company to fully explain to them—in fact, to indoctrinate them in—the whys and wherefores of all of the required actions. This is accomplished through the concept of organizational continuous improvement, the striving for perfection—convincing the individual employees that they, too, will benefit from the striving for perfection, by gaining and keeping a satisfactory position in society.

Some people think that achieving ISO 9000 registration status is a synonym for continuous improvement. It is not. ISO 9000 is a statement certifying that the company has a rational process control system and associated specific quality plans, and a means of delivering on those plans with some regularity. Once ISO 9000 certification is achieved, a level of competence has been achieved. It is a bit like an engineer's achieving professional engineering registration. But it does not denote a commitment to continuous improvement. I suppose that at some point while an organization is on the path to achieving ISO 9000 certification there is continuous improvement and at that time the two are synonymous. But they are certainly not after the registration has been achieved. The only way continuous improvement is achieved is through conscious effort. There are no secret formulas. Therefore, a company serious about being a world class performer has to accept and implement quality planning as a companion to process planning. And in addition, it must commit to constantly bettering itself. In my experience, this is the only way to grow and thus earn more profits. It comes about through a decision to get better and better every day.

The trick is to be constantly aware of the need and publicize the need, somewhat like creating an ongoing Hawthorne effect. Of course, this is difficult to do. One cannot expect an organization to live daily on a high dose of adrenaline. It can't be kept up. Therefore, a way needs to be found to institutionalize continuous improvement. It has to become part of the company's culture and the way it goes about its daily affairs.

One way I have found to do this is through a pragmatic version of *total quality management (TQM)*. TQM is a fancy way of saying striving for continuous improvement by measuring the effectiveness of one's actions in achieving intended results and taking additional actions based on those measurements. Figure 4-4 shows TQM in a nutshell. But before describing it, let me state one very import corollary to TQM philosophy.

The purpose of any organization that produces a product or service is to satisfy its customers and thereby make a profit. (Even so-called not-for-profit organizations want to make a profit. They simply refer to profits in other ways beyond dollars and cents—e.g., improved self-esteem, more perks, higher salaries—instead of ROI to the stockholders.) In order to satisfy the customer, it is necessary to know who the customer is, and I don't mean the name of the company buying the product, but rather the immediate recipient of a person's work effort. Everyone has a customer, everyone in the entire chain of operations. The representative external to the organization who takes receipt of the product and then hands over money to the salesperson is

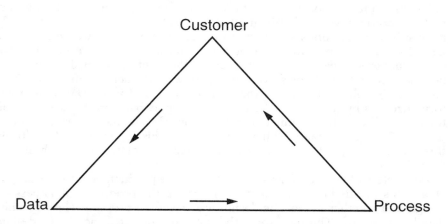

Figure 4-4. The TQM triangle: relationship of customer, process, and data in the pursuit of continuous improvement. (From Daniel T. Koenig, "Manufacturing Engineering: Principles for Optimization," 2nd ed., Taylor & Francis, Washington, 1994.)

just the last customer, paired with the last vendor, in a long chain of such pairings. The customer of the machinist making the shaft/handle for the hammer is the operator next in line, in this case, the operator who assembles the head to the shaft. The customer generically is the next operation in the supply chain, the person who receives the product in its present state of completion. That person automatically becomes the vendor to the succeeding person in the supply chain.

Now, the important part of TQM is that every vendor must strive to continuously satisfy the customer in every way possible. If this philosophy is taken to its logical conclusion, the vendor will always be querying the customer to find out if he or she is doing that—much like former Mayor Edward Koch of New York City asking his famous question, "How am I doing?" Obviously, Mr. Koch knew his TQM. He wanted feedback from his customers, the citizens of New York City, who could pay him in only one way—with their votes.

Let's look at the TQM triangle and examine its meaning. We see three titles for the three corners of the equilateral triangle—Process, Customer, Data—with arrows representative of information flow. *Process* refers to the activity carried out by the individual or teams of individuals in doing their assigned task. The process can be anything: a machining operation, preparing a billing statement, an inspection activity to assure compliance with a specification, etc. *Customer* refers to the recipient of the output of the process step. Usually it is the next person or team in the production flow of the product or service. The last customer would be the ultimate purchaser of the product, the one who exchanges money for the product and is the end user. For TQM purposes we treat all customers in the supply chain equally.

The customer receives the product and will immediately begin to pass judgment on its adequacy for the task he or she has in mind for it. This is a natural reaction; we've all done it all of our lives. In a consumer role, we all form subjective opinions about what we receive or a vendor would like us to have. In TQM parlance, we try to form only objective opinions about the part or product or service we have just received. We want to establish whether or not the received article or service complies with the set specifications. The customer is obligated to make these judgments. And in a TQM system we formalize this by requiring the customer to report back on the adequacy of the received work in a manner that is "actionable" by the performers of the process. The quality plan defines the nature of this reporting and feedback through the design of the process control steps associated with each manufacturing step.

Data refers to the customer's evaluation of the product. Within the supply chain, this means facts and figures concerning the product's robustness of design and whether or not the design was executed properly. Here specific detail is required. The data form the basis of corrective action or design improvement. The data are transmitted back to the vendor (presumably the operator) to be factored into plans for improvements in producing the next iteration of the product. Again, TQM systems institutionalize this step via the quality plan.

It is the last step, transferring data from the customer back to the vendor, where continuous improvement is launched. The vendor through his or her management of the process is sending the product to the customer and at the same time is asking Mayor Koch's famous question "How am I doing?" In this case, of course, we're asking very specific questions designed to elicit information that allows us to improve the process. This is continuous improvement.

Continuous improvement will occur only if we are successful in institutionalizing the simple but effective TQM process. If it becomes standard operating procedure to ask the recipient of your work "How am I doing?" then continuous improvement has a very good chance to become institutionalized. The remaining step is to allow operators to make changes based on the findings of their inquiries, and we need to do this without creating chaos at the work station. The best way to do this is to create an improvement opportunities log that is frequently reviewed by the operator and the support team in the area for feasibility to implement. The team would consist of the operators, foremen, engineers, quality personnel, materials specialists, and any other cognizant functions designated as support for the work station. Four sequential events precede implementation:

1. Operators log the improvement opportunities.
2. The team evaluates needs to do so versus resources on hand, time to do, and potential payback.
3. The team prioritizes implementations based on step 2 above.
4. The team keeps the customer informed of progress.

The key is to commit to improve, over a reasonable period of time, everything that feedback from the customer shows requiring corrective action. What this boils down to is that a very large portion of the work everyone does on a routine daily basis is associated with making improvements. Such a commitment institutionalizes improvement, and gets the company to adopt an ever expanding opportunist culture based on achieving perfect quality in everything it does. Is it possible? Well, the alternative to having this culture is definitely not acceptable. The trick is to make sure that progress is made and celebrated at every opportunity. This way we have success generating additional success. The interesting part is that the succeeding successes are much larger and of even more importance than the earlier ones. Who would have thought that the Wright brothers' triumph at Kitty Hawk would have led to mankind's walking on the moon less than 70 years later!

How do we motivate people to strive to live within the precepts of TQM? I believe we do so by treating them as fully functional and equal members of the production team. We treat them with respect and understand that every person on the company's payroll has specific talents that need to be exploited—somewhat like a football coach who creates esprit de corps by using players to the best of their individual abilities and forging a system of plays to exploit their talents. Of course, this sounds pontifical, and we need to latch onto a way to make these lofty ideals become reality. There is no simple way, but there is a way to "accent the positive," and that is to appeal to the innate desire every responsible person has to succeed, and not fail.

One device that I have found particularly successful is what I call the "quality credo," illustrated in Figure 4-5. These simple four statements of intent place responsibility for doing the best job possible squarely on the shoulders of those assigned the task. The credo says, I am an adult, entrusted with a responsibility, and I will do my best to fulfill that responsibility. We cannot ask any more from any one.

One more item to consider: It is essential that those we are asking to strive for continuous improvement have the skills to do so. Most idealistic approaches to quality improvement fail because they do not take into account the skills set the people need to have versus what they really possess. When this happens we have a situation akin to asking ambulance drivers to perform brain surgery. Unless the driver is a moonlighting surgeon, there's absolutely no chance it will happen. So, a very important factor in the success of any TQM system is making sure the training and skill levels are sufficient to do the job. This raises the issue of factory-specific education and time to do so, which I will cover in Chapter 10.

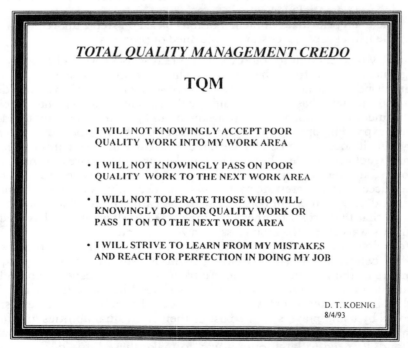

Figure 4-5. Total quality management credo.

QUALITY SYSTEM MEASUREMENT AND CONTROL TECHNIQUES

Having now laid the foundation of how a quality system should work, let's look at some of the measurements and control techniques we see impacting decisions and output at the work station.

With the modern approach to quality control, we want the operator at the work station to be the inspector as much as possible. Therefore we need to equip him or her with the tools to carry out inspection and to do it in such a way that it does not reduce the rate of production. By far this is most successful when the operator can carry out inspections within the process cycle time. Thus the process serves as a data collection function as well as providing the operators with information for doing their job properly.

The most successful tools used for controlling a process are those derived from *statistical process control (SPC)*. In the past, operators were never trained in SPC techniques because it was thought to be a quality function, not a production function. We now know the fallacy of that reasoning. We know that the operator is a full and equal member of the production team and as such is closest to the value-added activities of making the product. Therefore, it makes sense for the operator to have a significant role in measuring the results of the process. It is the operator who will have the point responsibility in fixing any problems that come along. Think of the operator as being the general practitioner or family care physician while the rest of the team consists of the specialists called in if the problem warrants their expertise. For these reasons, operators need to be trained in the basics of SPC and its derivative tools to make proper decisions.

The specific areas of SPC tailored for the work station deal with normal distribution theory and measures of central tendencies. These are all aimed at determining whether a process can deliver product within design specifications and to tell whether the process is capable of continuing to do so if operators work with reasonable and ordinary diligence. Let's look at the terminology we use in talking about SPC and then see how it is applied at the work station:

- *Specifications.* Desired attributes established by the customer and/or designer normally found on engineering drawings and data sheets. Specifications may incorporate accepted standards reached by consensus or by some governing body for the particular class of product.
- *Process.* Any combination of equipment and systems with corresponding instructions for use that, if followed, will be successful in achieving the specifications in accordance with a plan.
- *Quality.* The degree to which the output meets valid requirements as specified by the design and is fit for use as intended. Requirements are described in terms of process limits and/or specification characteristics, such as drawing dimensions or load-carrying capability.

- *Quality control.* The regulating process through which we measure actual performance and compare it with specifications. Variances are then acted upon to eliminate the out-of-specification differences.
- *Common causes.* Variations in processes that randomly affect the process output. These are the ever-present nuances about which little can be done without massive effort. Examples would be variations in ambient temperature and pressure; general condition of the equipment, such as looseness or tightness of the assemblies, ball screws, slides, etc.; and cleanliness of the atmosphere. These common causes are like the background noise of the system. When we say that a process can produce within ±0.0005 in., we mean we can't achieve ±0.000000 without some major change in how the product is made. Thus, we are saying that all the random events combined will result in a product output that falls entirely within the ±0.0005-in. range, and that since we can't further control the random events, this is the best the process can do.
- *Special causes.* Variations in processes caused by unusual, nonrandom occurrences in the process. We can assign cause-and-effect reasons to them. They are usually easily detected by SPC methods, and (unlike common causes) they *must* be corrected for process product to meet specification.
- *Statistics.* Numerical facts or data assembled, classified, and tabulated to present significant information about a subject we are interested in.
- *Statistical process control (sometimes known as statistical quality control).* Quality control accomplished via statistical methods.
- *Parts per million.* A unit used to measure quality at levels of perfection once thought unattainable. This is in contrast to the old-style quality

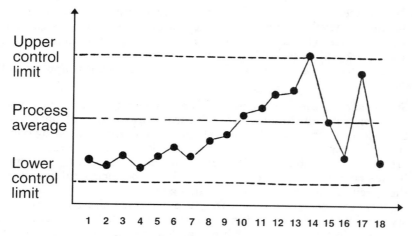

Figure 4-6. Example of a statistical control chart.

philosophy, which worked on establishing acceptable levels of defects between customer and vendor and never considered perfection as a goal worth striving for.

- *Control chart.* A tool that first determines the process limitations by detecting and recording the limits of variation and then monitors the process to determine when it is nonrandom—i.e., when some unwanted but controllable change is taking place in the process. It uses the mathematics of statistics so that characteristics of the whole can be projected by studying small samples.

Many companies are reluctant to introduce control charts at the work station because they feel that the mathematics will overwhelm the operator. This is not so. Most people working in factories today have at least a high school education. They are assumed to be conversant with simple algebra, and that is the extent of the mathematics background required for understanding statistical process control. The description of control chart theory that concludes this chapter is sufficient for the operator to successfully apply SPC in controlling his or her part of the process. Make no mistake about it: in the modern theory of quality control, the operator needs to have the responsibility and authority to manage his or her work station. This means making go, no-go decisions based on SPC data.

Control Chart Theory and Use

We will briefly review the pertinent mathematical theory necessary for understanding control charts and then describe their use.

Control charts are a practical application of normal distribution theory. We know that a naturally occurring process will have a random distribution, or variation of measurement, based on a $\pm 3\sigma$ (sigma) spread, where σ is the standard deviation. The standard deviation is a measurement of dispersion of data from an arithmetic mean μ (mu). We are very interested in controlling dimensions or process outcomes, and hence it is natural that a mathematical technique that tells us something about the likelihood of a process straying from the mean would be useful, especially if we know how wide or tight that spread is from the mean. We are interested in controlling *central tendency*—i.e., having the actual dimension be as close to the desired dimension as possible. A sample normal curve is shown in Figure 4-7; note that practically the entire area of the curve falls within a $\pm 3\sigma$ spread. It is simply a natural mathematical truth that 99.7% of all randomly occurring natural events will fall somewhere within the $\pm 3\sigma$ boundaries of the curve. We can use this fact to set dimensions and tolerance ranges and then measure to see if we are within the boundaries.

Useful formulas relating to normal distributions are:

$$\mu = \text{mean} = \frac{\sum X_i}{n}$$

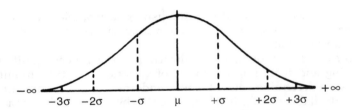

Figure 4-7. Sample normal distribution curve.

where ΣX_i = arithmetic total of all the like measurements
N = number of measurements taken

$$\sigma = \text{standard deviation} = \sqrt{\frac{\Sigma(Xi - \mu)^2}{n}}$$

For SPC purposes, by definition we try to set the process so that the value of μ is the drawing dimension or process parameter and the tolerances fall within the ±3σ spread. We then randomly measure a minimum of 20 events and calculate μ and σ. We plot these on our curve to see where they land. If they are random and fall within the limits of the curve, then the process is under control, and as long as no special causes are occurring, the process will continue to make good product.

Using statistical process control gives a manufacturer a capability of measuring fine tuned adjustments to processes. Say we wanting the process to give results within the tolerance range of the given dimension, but want to assure it is has the capability of a very tight spread about the given dimension. To be more specific, we want the actual range of dimensions produced to center at or very close to the process mean, μ, with all measurements closely or tightly packed about the mean. This in effect causes us to strive for a more robust process design. We have upped the ante and recognize that the tolerance range is no longer the only sufficient requirement to be matched to the natural spread of ±3Σ of the process. To be successful, we also need to force the process to cluster even closer to the given drawing dimension and that dimension to virtually coincide with the process mean. To tell how close we can come to achieving the tighter goal we need to have a measurement of process capability and the capability of process centering This is called measurements of central tendency. There are two of them commonly used in statistical process control: Cp (process capability ratio and Cpk (the process's capability of centering, or process capability index). Both of these are quite often required within customer's specifications to their vendors. These formulas are:

$$C_p = \frac{\text{tolerance spread}}{\text{process variation}}$$

where tolerance spread is defined as the range between the lowest and highest values of the acceptable process measurements (e.g., the drawing tolerance) and the process variation is defined as 6σ; and

$$C_{pk} = \frac{\pm(\text{specifications limit}) - \text{process mean}}{3\sigma}$$

where ±(specifications limit) is either the plus or minus value of the accept-able value for the process.

Typically a minimum value of 1.33 is considered satisfactory for C_p and C_{pk} to be acceptable. These values indicate that the central tendency of the process will generate acceptable results and the process has been set to fall within the ±3σ spread.

We can see that trying to plot on a normal curve would be quite tedious and perhaps misleading since we are taking measurements over a period of time. For this reason we use a time-dependent chart, the statistical control chart (Figure 4-6). It is important for operators to be able to take data and plot them on the control chart. They then need to interpret the data so they can take appropriate corrective actions, if necessary. The control chart is a time-dependent chart that records the measured attributes of the data. Let's describe it in detail.

First, the X-axis is the time-dependent axis. It could be delineated in any increment of time that suits the process needs. The Y-axis is the attribute axis. From top to bottom, we see the *upper control limit (UCL), process aver-age,* and *lower control limit (LCL).* If we were making a part—the hammer handle, for example—the UCL would refer to the plus diameter tolerance (drawing dimension + tolerance), the process average would coincide with the required drawing diameter, and the LCL would be the minus tolerance (drawing dimension – tolerance). If we were measuring welding process parameters—say we wanted to control voltage to assure the spot weld of the hammer head to the shaft was proper—then, instead of dimensions, we could be recording actual real-time voltages. The UCL and LCL would repre-sent the plus and minus range of acceptable voltages and the specified volt-age would be the process average.

The operator would take a series of measurements, calculate the mean and standard deviation, and plot them on the control chart at a point on the X-axis corresponding to the time period of the data collection. Quite often only the mean is recorded on the chart (if the 3σ variation is consistently less than 10% of the ± tolerance spread allowed for the process). If, how-ever, we do need to plot the ±3σ values, then we often show them as a verti-cal line at the designated time value, where the length of the line is the 6σ spread, with μ shown as a point or an "x" or some other defining symbol on the vertical line.

Figure 4-6 shows a typical set of data taken over time. Each point shown is a calculation of μ at a specific time, with the data points of μ's connected.

Interpretation is based on normal distribution theory. We know that a process can be thought of as a series of random events grouped for obser-vational purposes. Those random events will have a dispersion from a cen-tral tendency based on the controlling factors for that series of events. For machining, the controlling factors could be the speeds and feeds of the machine and how well the machine is capable of maintaining accuracy.

This takes into consideration the bearings, the machine sliding surfaces, the motors' voltage controls, and the sharpness of the tools, to name a few. There are many variables. The normal curve statistical theory says that all these many variables will create a central tendency measurement with a predetermined plus/minus range. Therefore, if everything remains the same, the process will exhibit a spread of ±3σ for 99.7% of all events. If we can match our needs for ± tolerance band within the random events that happen anyway, then we can use the theory to observe the process.

It is important to understand what the data are telling us about the process. Let's quickly review the relationship between specification limits and process limits, as illustrated in Figure 4-8. We see, first of all, that the theory is applicable only if a random event is occurring. If the events are random, then the variation is due to common causes, not special causes. An example of a special cause would be a restriction of the process, such as a severe drag on the rotational speed of the cutting tool perhaps keeping it outside the range of recommended settings. In the course of a special event the data are no longer random in the general sense but are random within the confines of the special event.

In the first graph in Figure 4-8, we see the process limits coinciding with the ±3σ boundaries of the normal curve. This relationship is what it is unless we change the process. In the next three graphs in Figure 4-8 we see the specification limits superimposed on the normal curve and the process limits. If the process limits fall within the specification limits (tolerances), then 99.7% of the output will be acceptable. If they do not, then there will be an inevitable percentage of failure depending on the degree of misalignment.

As I've said, the normal curve is not a particularly user-friendly diagram for interpreting data. We use control charts for this. There are some very reliable methods of interpretation using the trends displayed on a control chart, based on normal curve theory. Figure 4-9 demonstrate the rules of interpretation.

First, we look for randomness about the mean. Over time, there should be about as many points above the mean (the mean being, perhaps, the drawing dimension, or a nominal pressure) as there are below the mean. If this is not the case, the process and the specification are not in sync. This means that, unless there is a very small standard deviation, there will probably be failures occurring from time to time at either the upper or the lower control limit, depending on the direction in which the mean of the process and the mean of the specification deviate. The corrective action would be to correct the process so that it is centered about the mean of the specification. For a pressure or temperature setting, that is relatively easy to do. For machining operations, it may mean changes in tooling and setup, and quite often this is a trial-and-error process.

Next, we look to see if there are any unusual readings that appear to be different from the normally occurring data. This quite often indicates that a nonrandom event has occurred, an event such as a broken drill bit or something equally severe. The fix here is to look for any unusual occurrences; perhaps there is a faulty circuit breaker, or the fixture used to load

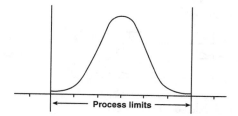

If only random variations are occurring in the process
- The distribution will be a "normal" bell-shaped curve.
- We can calculate and predict the process limits — which will include 99.7% of the output.

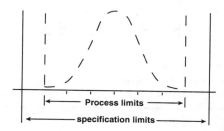

- Process llimits should fit within specification limits.
  - if not, process unit produce rejects

- But Process limits don't always match specification limits, and nonconforming material will be produced

  - The process can't meet the requirements.

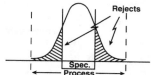

  - The process is shifted to the right (or left) of the specification.

Note: Process in control may produce product that does not meet specifications.

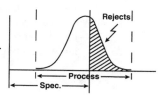

Figure 4-8. Specification limits versus process limits. (From instructor notes prepared by Daniel T. Koenig for internal General Electric Co. course, November 1985.)

■ Learn what to look for
  — Process <u>in</u> control

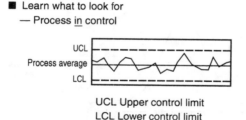

UCL Upper control limit
LCL Lower control limit

■ Process <u>not</u> in control

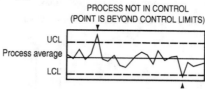

■ What action do you take?
  — Look for nonrandom variable
  — Typically readjust process

■ Process <u>not</u> in control

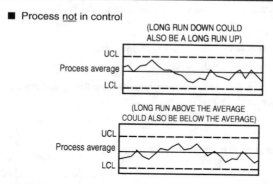

■ Watch for a run of 7* points
  — All funning up or down
  — All above or below average
■ What action do you take?
  — Look for process setting, material, or system change
  — Make necessary adjustments

*Less than 1 chance in 128 that a random variation will produce these trends

Figure 4-9. Interpreting statistical control charts. (From instructor notes prepared by Daniel T. Koenig for internal General Electric Co. course, November 1985.) *(Figure continues)*

■ Process <u>not</u> in control

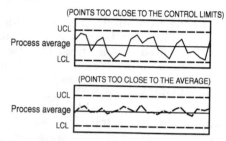

■ Watch for nonrandom patterns
  — 2/3 of data points should be in middle 1/3 of chart limits
  — Does data make sense?
■ What action do you take?
  — Look for process system change
  — Recalculate control limits if pattern continues

If process is in control
  — No trends
  — No out of control points
  — No obvious nonrandom patterns
■ Action: Don't touch it; you are likely to make it worse!

When a point is out of control
■ Ask to see a record of what action was taken
  — Ideal method is to record on back of control chart

Figure 4-9. Continued

the part was used incorrectly. Quite often, this type of fault responds well to cause-and-effect analysis, and for the preponderance of instances, there is a sole direct cause for the problem which can be corrected quickly once unmasked.

The third step is to look for trends. For a process behaving in accordance with the normal distribution, there ought not be any trends. The rule for trends is that there should never be more than seven readings in a row for which we can discern either an upward or a downward slope. Statistically, there is only a 1 in 128 chance of such an event happening randomly, less than 1%. This type of fault indicates that there is an erosion of the common cause base. Quite frequently it is something as simple as a tool wear problem: as the tool becomes duller, the results change. If readings are taken several hours apart for a day or two, such a trend will become very obvious. If the readings are taken every few minutes, we will probably miss it entirely. This is a good reason to compare historical data to see if any long-term trends are developing. The fix is to find the variation in the common cause category and correct it.

The fourth step is a little more subtle. It is to look for randomness settling about a point that is not the mean but is within the tolerance band of the process and within the required specification. This means that the output is acceptable for now but the situation is out of control and could go sour very quickly. The room for error is reduced. We *are* measuring randomness about a mean, but unfortunately the mean μ in this case doesn't correspond to the drawing dimension or the process-variable set point. The result is that we have lots of room on one side of the tolerance band but the margin of error is significantly reduced at the other end. We want the process to be centered about the *specification* mean to give us the greatest chance for success. Here we come to understand the use of the measurements of central tendency C_p and C_{pk} and see why many companies now specify their use by vendors manufacturing their products. Good measures of central tendency give a better probability of higher effective yield. When this fourth type of error is detected, the fix is to look for process system changes, determine cause, and correct.

We can see that SPC can be a powerful tool for control process quality. However, we also see that it takes considerable attention to detail to make it work. Quite often companies set up SPC regimes and then promptly forget about using the data. They think that by merely measuring data their problems will diminish and perhaps disappear entirely. Well, that's asking an awful lot of the Hawthorne effect to cure. As long as the SPC system is new and everyone has a heightened awareness of it, a certain amount of improvement will occur just because it is being given so much attention. However, as with everything else, familiarity tends to build benign contempt, and we find that the tools are in place but ignored. For SPC to work, it too has to become institutionalized. The SPC regime needs to be a vigorous part of the quality plan and must be reported on quite frequently, to the point where managers want to know the process SPC results second only to the numbers of product shipped versus numbers promised. Only with this high degree of awareness will SPC be a useful tool for producing zero-defects products.

In this chapter we have seen that quality control is an important factor in realizing the intent of the Two Knows. We see that for this more than for any other aspect of work station dynamics, we depend on the operator to achieve success. We see that the operator needs to be an integral part of producing excellent quality at the work station. It is quite obvious that checking up on an operator's performance after the fact is a methodology that just doesn't work. We cannot inspect quality into a product. It has to be designed in, and the process has to be followed precisely. This is especially relevant in the current paradigm of zero defects allowed. In order to get this type of performance we need to have the full support of the operator, and the only way to get that is to make the operator part of the team. The operator cannot just be an appendage to the machine or process equipment. We see that the best way to get the operator to be part of the team is to value his or her contributions in making the process work better. In addition, we must instill the same sense of responsibility for success within the hearts and minds of the operators as we strive to with management. This is the only path to success. We must set one high standard of performance for the entire company. All employees need to be dedicated to achieving perfection in whatever their assigned responsibilities are.

Chapter 5

Scheduling the Work Station with Manufacturing Resources Planning

This chapter is about scheduling and cycle time—how scheduling is best achieved through integrated computer-driven processes, and how schedules are affected by the powerful concepts of just-in-time (JIT) and group technology (GT). We will explore, from the viewpoint of the work station, how schedules are set and how cycle times are applied to schedules in an integrated fashion. We will also see how the integrated nature of cycle times and schedules impacts on productivity improvement strategies.

Schedules are the drivers that implement work at the work station. They are the mechanism for pressing the "go" button to commence the process. Schedules are one of the most sophisticated procedures in the entire manufacturing process, aimed at getting resources to converge on the work station to achieve the value-added goals of manufacturing. I will take you on a guided tour of the making of schedules, beginning with a historical retrospective and continuing right up to today's most modern pull system, *manufacturing resources planning systems (MRP II),*[1] all seen from the vantage point of the work station. Thus, we will consider how these techniques affect our management of the work station. Keep in mind that the end purpose of factory scheduling is to optimize utilization of capacity in order to achieve optimum profit.

To understand scheduling we will, by necessity, explore the evolution of MRP II, just-in-time, dispatching systems, and the interrelationships of group technology with scheduling. Along the way, I'll demonstrate once more that the work station operator is the key to successful factory performance. And perhaps we will slay some sacred cows of misunderstanding that are proving to be profit inhibitors instead of enhancers.

THE RATIONALE OF SCHEDULING

Scheduling is the ordered sequencing of work through a work station. It is like going to a bakery and taking a number to be waited on. Your order is filled (worked on) when your number comes up in the queue. This way there

---

[1] The Roman numeral II is used because MRP originally served as the abbreviation for *materials requirements planning,* a more primitive system.

is no pushing and shoving to get the clerk's attention. The same philosophy needs to be followed at the work station; otherwise, chaos reigns. Orders have to be filled (worked on) in a systematic manner for the process to have a chance to be optimized. Before we can examine the effects of scheduling—and subsequent effects impacting cycle time—on the work station, we need to have a working knowledge of how schedules come into being. Let's take a look.

Scheduling has been a major factor in successful manufacturing throughput for as long as factories have existed. There have been many different styles of scheduling, from complete randomness of what is to be worked on (an out-of-control process), to rigid, by-the-rules, no-exceptions techniques. The typical scheduling technique involves a work order sequence, usually based on a customer delivery commitment date; and a set of guidelines for allowing exceptions. The purpose of the schedule is to control the flow of work to the work station in an orderly manner. Effective scheduling schemes contain the following principles.

1. The sequence of work is based on the time when delivery is needed at the next work station or on a date promised to the ultimate customer.
2. The sequence of work can be batched for efficiencies of scale for a pre-selected time period—e.g., perhaps up to two weeks for products with a manufacturing cycle of less than one week.
3. Rework of defective parts can take precedence over new work as long as the schedule disruption is minimal (usually less than two days). This gives the factory the ability to accomplish two things:
   a. Allows promise dates to be maintained or late delivery minimized.
   b. Keeps the entire schedule close to the planned-for goals.
4. Because the time cost of scrap recovery can be too much of a shock to the schedule, scrap replacement work should be considered a new order, with a new sequence and customer promise date.
5. Planned start and finish times for all support activities—such as routing sheets, methods, ordering of materials, jig and fixture development and procurement, tooling allocations, and quality control requirements—are keyed off the work station schedule.

The process of scheduling starts with a demand placed on the organization to produce a product or a service. In our daily lives, we frequently agree to do something for some reason or other; we make a dinner date; we decide to purchase groceries; we go to our place of employment and commit to do our job. All of these assumptions of responsibility to undertake an action have some performance deliverables attached to them. We normally commit to a delivery date or time of completion, and we hope we can achieve it. We then live by the results of our commitments. Fortunately, most missed commitments mean very little to either our self-esteem or our ability to earn a living. Some, however, are important. We certainly want to make sure that we don't leave our children stranded by missing a pickup commitment. Nor do we want to miss a business appointment and thereby jeopardize our ability to obtain new business. Schedules for the factory fall into the "important" category. All those who depend on our output need to be able to count on us to get delivery to them so that they in turn can meet their commitments.

A business's ability to produce to schedule is the hallmark of its reputation. It does no good to have a superior product if it can't be delivered on schedule with some degree of consistency. Vendors have to be reliable if buyers are to want to do business with them. How many times have we made decisions to pay a little more for a product because we thought we would get better service from the higher-cost supplier? Many times. Reliability means we can depend on the results. It is like the surgeon extending a hand for the scalpel and knowing the nurse will hand over the correct one. Good scheduling should allow a business to be a reliable supplier to its customers.

THE PROCESS OF SCHEDULING

Good scheduling, whether a manual or a highly automated process, follows a very consistent pattern. The detailed scheduling of work at the work station is only the last of several major factors in the scheduling algorithm. Scheduling is a cascading process starting from a very broad-based, macro approach and progressing to a micro, attention-to-details level. It consists of four important steps:

- A master schedule
- Analysis of capacity and capability
- A release of an order to make a product or subcomponent
- A detailed release of a work order at the lowest detail level to the work station

Master Schedule

The master schedule is the compilation of all orders taken by the sales force for products that the company needs to manufacture over a preselected period of time (typically, one fiscal quarter to a full year). It is listed by company due date and tends to be a political as well as a tactical plan for the business over a finite period of time.

A key factor is the time between receipt of order and the promised delivery date. It is not uncommon for sales people to stretch the company's capabilities by accepting an order with a shorter delivery time than the engineered standard planning calls for. They often do this to assure competitors don't receive the order. This is a valid strategy only if the company has the know-how to shorten the normal cycle time and can count on having relatively few lapses in doing so. This is what is meant by the *political* aspects of scheduling.

The master schedule is the start of the scheduling cycle. It is initiated by the sales force and approved at the highest levels of the company. It is the only part of the scheduling process outside the domain of manufacturing. Thus it is not surprising that manufacturing observes the process very closely, and quite often has close to a veto power over what is proposed. Most general managers, while "owning" the master schedule, will feel obligated to get manufacturing to buy in before they authorize an order requiring shorter than normal cycle time.

The process of creating a master schedule consists of the following:

- *Review of the market and the competition.* In order to determine the appropriate risk to take in balancing promises to the customer with normal cycle time, it is necessary to understand the current and short-term future dynamics of the marketplace. Here the senior management of the company try to define their necessary risk profile. For example, if the company's hammers were in great demand because they were better than the competition's and hence customers were willing to wait a little longer to get them, then the master schedule could probably coincide 100% with the realities of cycle time. But since hammers are typically a commodity product and the company's hammer has no technological edge, then the choice is either to comply with the customer's delivery needs or forgo the order. If the customer's date matches the cycle time, then there is no problem. If the cycle time variance is great, then the company can either take the order, knowing the delivery will be late, or refuse the order.

- *Set goals.* Concurrently with understanding the marketplace, the company needs to establish its goals. Is the company driving for increased market share? The same market share? Should the company exit this product? Whatever the goal, it will influence senior management's reaction to any variance between desired delivery dates and capacity realities. It may also drive the need for capital expansion—e.g., procurement of additional capacity.

- *Produce the master schedule.* The master schedule is a compilation of all orders to be filled in the factory over the set period of time. While the content is supposedly "frozen" for the time period, the schedule is a dynamic document that needs to be changed as situations dictate. Therefore, master schedules need to be confined to allow for the organization's shortest feasible reaction time in response to shifting requirements. Even though the master schedule has jobs on it as far out in time as customers are willing to commit to, in practice it is governed by business cycle economics. As a rule of thumb, the length of the master schedule usually turns out to be 1.5 to 2 times the longest lead time for any stage of producing the product in the factory. It is also reviewed and updated at least quarterly.

Analysis of Capacity and Capability

With a master schedule in hand, it is necessary to analyze how the product will be made and where. The analysis of how and where is the domain of the manufacturing engineering department, which designs the method and routing, as described in Chapter 3. This step provides the requirements for materials, the production process, and the sequence of events. It also assures that there will be an adequate set of resources to allow production in accord with design requirements. All of these concerns make up the capability analysis step. Its effect on scheduling is to set the number of hours to be put in at each work station, and to determine the order in which materials arrive at the initial, start-of-process work station.

We now look at capacity, knowing that capability exists. (If it didn't, significant engineering and procurement issues would have to be resolved first.) This is like the hotel room reservation problem: the reservations clerk must know how many rooms are available on a given night and must make sure that no two customers are slated for the same room against their choice. Capacity analysis consists of looking at hours booked against a work station compared with the hours available to work. There are many solution variants of this problem, but they all boil down to same issue: the work order requires a set amount of assets (time on the machine) in a particular window of time. Either the time is available or it is not. If available, it is booked; we usually say it is *mortgaged*. The product moves through the factory in accordance with its "bookings" on the various work stations in sequential order. It is like a subway train traveling from one station to the next. If no train is ahead of it, it can pull into the station. If that's not the case, then it has to wait. The production managers evaluate how many blockages there will be along the way (none or very few, it is hoped) and prepare a sequential time flow of the work order going through the cycle. This is done on a macro level, on the basis of the time necessary for the product to go through the production cycle.

Capacity analysis has two components. The first is an assessment of work station load. By examining a series of orders going through a work station, we can estimate how far out the work station is reserved for currently scheduled work. The second component is a scheduling sequence for the specific work order that shows when the customer's order will start the cycle and when it will finish, with as much internal sequence step information as desired. Analysis of schedule for capacity reasons usually extends out for no more than six months, usually less.

A Release of an Order to Make a Product or Subcomponent

At the beginning of the next stage we know when and how an order will be filled. Now we have to initiate the process of obtaining materials and tooling, and we have to let the work station know the order is coming.

The analysis of capacity and capability has set the stage for this next step. We now know that the work station can be mortgaged for processing the product at a particular time and for a predetermined duration. This step, issuing an order, is the actual setting in motion of the activities that make the concept a reality. Release of the order is the official go-ahead to commit company resources. Here is where we actually place the order for materials, labor, and tooling, all to come together at the work station at the predetermined time. On the basis of the master schedule and the capacity and capability analysis checking on the validity of the master schedule, materials are ordered, with the proviso that they be available to work with according to schedule. The build or purchase of special tooling and fixtures is also ordered, with the same proviso.

Materials orders are very specific, being based on the information from the bill of materials (BOM). A materials order will be made up of a purchase order (PO), a contractual due date, and specification of what is being purchased. The specification will have all the form, fit, and function information the vendor needs to comply with. It will also list the quality certification requirements.

We also look at availability of the workforce at this stage. Capacity and capability analysis usually concerns itself with the capital equipment necessary to perform the intended work and assumes that the necessary personnel are available. This may or may not be the case. When an order is larger than or slightly different from previous orders, or in the case where the company is flush with current factory load, we need to look carefully at the labor content of the job. We must have the personnel available to do the job as planned and when planned for. Quite often a company will have machinery in place that is not currently being used because of a lack of orders to justify working it. This is typically the second level of output machines, quite capable of doing the job, albeit slower. Therefore, if the load placed on the factory grows to a point where the first-line machines can't keep up (for whatever reason), the second-line machines will be placed back in service. But they can't really be put back in service without the people to run them. Hence, at this stage of the scheduling process we make sure that qualified people are available to utilize them. Since moving up and down the staffing level ladder is a relatively slow and expensive process, other alternatives will be considered, too. The alternatives are threefold:

- Use overtime to make up for lack of qualified personnel.
- Double up on machines; e.g., have one operator supervise two or more machines or processes.
- Place orders with outside vendors to make up the difference between capacity with current staff and workload requirements.

The decision point will be based on the expected stability, or lack thereof, of the upturn in order levels. If it is a short-term blip, then no new hires will be added. If it looks relatively certain that this increased rate of activity will continue, then requisitions for more personnel go out. In the case of new hires, it is important to make the decision early on because of the need to get these new people thoroughly trained and indoctrinated.

The order release process creates a schedule, usually for about 13 weeks, or one production quarter. Sometimes companies use materials having a very long lead time; in that case, the extra-long-lead-time items are ordered in the capacity and capability analysis stage. But this is the exception rather than the rule.

A Detailed Release of a Work Order at the Lowest Detail Level to the Work Station

We are now at the point where the schedule impacts the work station. Up to this point the schedule has been a strategic document evolving into a tactical document. Now it becomes very much a here-and-now action plan. The hallmark of this level is the daily dispatch list (an example is shown in Figure 5-1). A dispatch list is created for each work station telling the operator what work will be done during the particular shift. It will list the jobs in sequential order of accomplishment and give pertinent information on how to do them. The information will probably, of space necessity, be in a coded format that the operator learns to decode through a briefing. It will contain information on the quantity required, the cycle time allocated for completion, the process instructions including the relevant drawings, and the quality control requirements.

With the dispatch list, the operator knows what to expect to be delivered to the work station during his or her shift. When the work arrives, it will have all the information described above, in detail sufficient to do the job. The work package will consist of the material to be processed; any specific, non-work-station-assigned tooling or fixtures; the drawing and any specification instructions; the quality requirements instructions and check sheets (including SPC if required); and a control document on which the operator enters time and duration of work. The latter is called the *traveler* and is the history of the work done at each work station in the manufacturing process. It is the way that the production control (dispatcher) function has of reporting progress against the current 13-week schedule. It is also used to update finance on labor costs.

WHY MANUAL SCHEDULES GAVE WAY TO COMPUTER DATABASE–DRIVEN SCHEDULES

All scheduling activities follow the process outlined above. As you can see, it is a very detailed and meticulous process, with very high levels of data. Obviously, it had to be done even before the advent of computers in the factory. Without the help of a computer to manipulate huge amounts of data, it was a very difficult task to do accurately, especially at the shop level, and so performance suffered from frequent glitches in scheduling the right work at the right time at each work station.

The difficulty of the task also meant that once a schedule was set, there was great reluctance to change it, so that factories were stuck trying to make do with static schedules in a dynamic, changing environment. And manufacturing is one of the most dynamic, changing environments we humans have ever contrived. Imagine how many variables and conditions have to be kept firm for the factory to operate in accordance with schedule. Now picture all the things that can vary: late material deliveries, tooling made in error, operator absenteeism, machine malfunctions. Each one of these occurrences can

Date: 01/16/00
Time: 16:56

Consolidated Dispatch Report

Id: VWP022
Page: 3

a. w/o	b. Part	1. Cap Run Total	2. StdHrs	3. Balance	4. Sales	5. Comp	6. OpNo	Tool Description	7. Queue	8. Pri	9. Next	10. P/L
LA894664	023145	935.98	8.00	—	.00	02/11/00	0010		3	50	Last	BLP
LA894666	023142	943.98	8.00	—	.00	02/13/00	0010		3	50	Last	BLP
LA895405	011798	946.53	2.55	31	91.76	02/13/00	0030	PW 2761	10	50		EXT
LA895909	025702	950.68	4.15	310	919.15	02/18/00	0030		6	50		EXT
Sub Totals:			950.68	30370	216033.02						Avg. # of days:	6

A. Work Center: 7202-00 MATSURA   Capacity: 45.5   Cutoff Date: 03/01/97

a. w/o	b. Part	1. Cap Run Total	2. StdHrs	3. Balance	4. Sales	5. Comp	6. OpNo	Tool Description	7. Queue	8. Pri	9. Next	10. P/L
LA889520	023147	8.00	8.00	1	.00	12/13/99	0010		50	50		BLP
LA895465	023743	11.10	3.10	6	.00	12/15/99	0040	MAT 1439	4	50		EXT
LA301536	023743	14.33	3.23	14	.00	12/15/99	0040	MAT 1439	7	50		EXT
LA300506	013730	16.47	2.13	16	.00	12/21/99	0050		2	50		HIP
LA894220	025928	17.60	1.13	8	.00	12/31/99	0010		4	50		HIP
LA892436	025928	19.47	1.87	52	.00	01/07/00	0010		6	50		HIP
LA300158	011271	23.16	3.70	84	717.36	01/09/00	0030	MAT 1372	5	50	LAST	EXT
LA943319	008918	27.36	4.20	60	914.41	01/12/00	0050	MAT 1494	5	50		EXT
LA894870	011269	29.85	2.48	48	386.88	01/13/00	0030	MAT 1371	5	50		EXT
LA895552	011269	32.37	2.52	42	338.52	01/13/00	0030	MAT 1371	0	50		EXT
LA894830	008742	39.08	6.71	135	1036.80	01/14/00	0030	MAT 1293	3	50		EXT
LA895794	011271	42.26	3.18	66	563.64	01/21/00	0030	MAT 1372	7	50		EXT
LA894637	023146	50.26	8.00	—	.00	01/31/00	0010			50	LAST	BLP
LA894668	023147	58.26	8.00	—	.00	02/14/00	0010			50	LAST	BLP
LA894204	023743	70.06	11.81	615	.00	02/19/00	0040	MAT 1439	7	50		EXT
Sub Totals:			70.06	1149	3957.61						Avg. # of days:	7

Description of columns

a. Work order number.
b. Part number.
1. Cumulative total to be produced.
2. Standard hours allowed to do the work based on time standards applied to the job.
3. Balance remaining for this schedule period (commonly a day or a shift).
4. Sales value of the shop order. If no value shown, either a subcomponent to roll up into a component or a rework/scrap replacement.
5. Required complete date.
6. Operation number in the process sequence and the CNC program number if applicable.
7. Number of days in queue.
8. Priority/urgency code: 50 = standard; 10 = urgent/rush.
9. Next work order to be processed. If blank, in sequence shown. "Last" indicates, don't work on unless no other work is available at the work station.
10. Code describing product line that work order belongs to.
A. Work center description line. Example is Work Center 7202-00. The machines are Matsura type CNC vertical boring machines. Capacity is 45.5 hours per day, which indicates there are two machines, each available 22.75 hours/day (24 h/day less maintenance downtime of 1.25 h/day). This schedule is based on an MRP II run Master Schedule effective through 03/1/00.

Figure 5-1. Daily dispatch list.

cause the schedule to be at serious variance with reality. With a static schedule, this spells trouble with a capital T.

In fact, manual schedules are impossible to maintain for more than a week or so before they start to break down. So the modus operandi in such a situation is to practice damage control: try to figure out what the critical variances are and make corrections for small subsets of the schedule without being too far off from where the company needs to be. This required a large workforce of production checkers to try to decipher where everything was in the factory and compare it to where it should be. Then these people, working with the operators and foremen, had to decide what could be done to move the supposedly "hot" jobs throughout the system—hot jobs referring to those on which customers were screaming the loudest for delivery, or those perceived to be essential to move expeditiously to avert disaster.

Rescheduling an entire factory is not a viable option in a manual mode, because it takes weeks to do so for even modest-sized factories; but it definitely is an option with a computer. Enter *manufacturing resources planning* systems.

THE DEVELOPMENT OF MANUFACTURING RESOURCES PLANNING SYSTEMS

Manufacturing resources planning systems, known popularly as MRP II (because MRP originally stood for material requirements planning, a precursor), are the backbone of modern scheduling systems. They do everything described previously for generating schedules—not only for the work station, but for all aspects of the enterprise that need to be scheduled and coordinated. In fact, MRP II systems are a major component of what we know as *computer-integrated manufacturing (CIM)*.

We will focus our discussion on MRP II as it affects the work station. We are interested in understanding how the system dispatches work and how it coordinates the sequence of work operations with the open availability of the work station, the delivery of material, and the queuing of essential special tools, jigs, and fixtures. This wondrous, almost magical appearance of all things necessary to do the job is a feat of engineering utilization of computers to create a dynamic scheduling tool. Until the early 1970s no one could conceive that such an amazing tool would ever be anything but a dream of science fiction writers.

The genesis of MRP II was in the materials function. With the need to purchase so many varieties and quantities of products and raw materials to make a product, the leaders of the purchasing profession saw a need to use computers to control their activities. Dealing with large dollar amounts and having payments time-phased is very much akin to the accounting calculations done by banks and other financial institutions. So it wasn't much of a stretch to apply the same, or at least similar, computing approaches to control purchasing activities. the idea of credits to and debits against an account is analogous to receiving materials and using them (issuing them to shop operations) on an everyday basis. Purchasers can then do a daily tally and see what materials they have on hand as compared with what they need. The computer supports a very dynamic schedule for the control of materials purchases because the computer can do the tallying practically instantaneously. So, in the late 1960s, purchasing departments began to far outstrip their parent organizations in dynamism.

The same logic can also be used for inventory control and warehousing activities, since they are nothing more than internal manifestations of purchasing. We can debit and credit stock to locations, and so we can have an instantaneous readout of how much material is available at any location.

This entire purchasing- and storing-driven process became known as *material requirements planning (MRP)*, now sometimes affectionately called "little MRP." It became the first computer-based scheduling algorithm used in the factory for loading work stations.

MRP was expanded to cover shop operations work stations in the early 1970s as a natural extension of the debit and credit system applied to purchase of materials and warehouse locations. In fact, it was quite a remarkable breakthrough. Why not designate each work station as a warehousing location and have material moved to it in sequence according to a schedule, and then constantly compare the schedule with what actually happens. This is exactly what we want to do to load the shop. Remember, the problem with manual schedules is that there was no way to accurately determine where a job was in the system at any one time, so there was no way of knowing precisely how the company was responding to its plan. With this computer assist, we can tell instantaneously, if desired, where everything is and react and plan accordingly. And so, using a materials algorithm based on credit and debit accounting principles, we can schedule a factory. And we have done it by accurately monitoring materials flows. This is very good, and a significant improvement over the old manual system. But it has flaws.

The MRP system does not assure that the necessary workforce hours to run the machines are available when the materials arrive. Nor does it take into consideration the need to have the proper tooling available at the proper time. It also looks at the work station as an infinite sink: it dispatches work from one work station to the next based on a predetermined cycle time, probably one derived from a computer-aided process planning (CAPP) system. It has no way of knowing what the work station's capacity or capability is. So what it does is load work into the work station in accordance with an order sequence schedule, which shows the associated hours to do the job. When the job is finished, and is reported as such, it automatically loads the work onto the next sequential work station, and so forth, until the job becomes a finished product. The problem is that it has no idea whether or not the work station can really handle all the load issued to it. It is quite conceivable that the schedule will call for many jobs to be at the work station at the same time because the computer doesn't know of any limit to what can be handled at any one instant in time. It assumes infinite capacity. Now, this isn't a problem for same-sequence, highly repetitive, and simple operations. But when a factory is in a job shop mode (and 70% of factories are) and there are many varieties of sequences, this poses a serious problem. Diversity means uneven flow, and thus variations in instantaneous capacity of the work station.

In reality, the MRP system shows how much work is currently scheduled for the work station, and how much is late—i.e., not processed through yet because it is in a waiting queue. Real capacity is ignored. Compounding this deficiency is the inability to easily determine why the bottleneck has occurred, because the system is oblivious to everything but materials movement. There is no way to know that the problem may have been caused by lack of people to run the work station, or that the tooling arrived late, or the machine was shut down for preventive maintenance. None of these factors even exist in the program at all.

The deficiencies of MRP are corrected with modern manufacturing resources planning (MRP II) systems. Notice the nomenclature change. "Manufacturing" has been substituted for "materials" and "resources" replaces "requirements." We are no longer focusing on materials as a way to schedule the shop, but instead are looking at all factors that go into making a realistic schedule.

MRP II starts off immediately by looking at capacity of a work station as the highest level of the program. It determines capacity primarily by recognizing the hours the work station has available to work in any given reporting period, usually a day. This requires direct inputs to the program from production control. Typically, the inputs include the number of shifts the work station is available and the corresponding number of hours. This is the way the people factor is entered into the equation. For example, let's say that there is only one operator qualified to run the machine and he typically works 10 hours per day. That means there are 10 hours available per day. The schedule may show a need for 12 hours on Monday and 7 hours on Tuesday. The MRP II system will load only up to the capacity level set for the work station—in this case, 10. This means that the schedule for Monday would show 10 hours and Tuesday would show 9 hours.

There are other modifying factors for people-based capacity derivations. The most important one is work station efficiency. The shop measures everyone's efficiency with respect to the currently assigned work station. Let us suppose that the individual on this work station (he is the only one; otherwise, for scheduling purposes, we would simply average individual efficiencies to get work station efficiency) has achieved a 90% efficiency rating. Then the available hours for the work station degrade to 9. This means MRP II would schedule 9 hours each for Monday and Tuesday, and 1 hour would be booked for Wednesday. Suppose also that the material for job 1 arrived 2 hours late on Monday. That means only 7 hours of scheduled work at 100% efficiency can be done instead of the original 10. This means that the next iteration of the schedule will change the work order times on the machine. This in turn will cause all succeeding work stations to be rescheduled. This is exactly what happens on a daily basis with most MRP II systems. We are constantly rescheduling, but always measuring against the original plan. Figure 5-2 illustrates the impacts of delays and downgrades of capacity that the MRP II system contends with. It can do this virtually instantaneously.

The MRP II system also handles miscues resulting in late tooling, material, and instructions in a similarly easy fashion. It is instructed not to schedule an operation on a work station unless all of the factors necessary for the work to proceed are accounted for and are present. Therefore, no resources are committed until the factory is really ready to proceed. As a practical matter, materials are handled just as in the predecessor MRP system, so this phase is the same. For other factors, such as tools, a subset of MRP II is used to manage the procurement of materials and fabrication of tools, jigs, and fixtures. Similarly, MRP II can be used to manage the engineering function's schedule for producing planning and methods instructions.

Job	Standard hours	WS capacity, daily	M	T	W	Th	F
Ideal (100% efficiency)							
1	4		4				
2	4		4				
3	4			4			
4	6			4	2		
5	8				6	2	
Total	26	8	8	8	8	2	0
Realistic (87.5% efficiency)							
1	4		4				
2	4		3	1			
3	4			4			
4	6			2	4		
5	8				3	5	
Total	26	7	7	7	7	5	0
Practical (87.5% efficiency + 1 h/day maintenance & miscellaneous idle time)							
1	4		4				
2	4		2	2			
3	4			4			
4	6				6		
5	8					6	2
Total	26	6	6	6	6	6	2

Figure 5-2. Work station loading scheme used with MRP II.

HOW MRP II REALLY WORKS

Let's look at how MRP II works. We'll see that it is remarkably similar to the manual system except that the quality of the data is much higher and we are living in a world of *available precision* instead of *acceptable imprecision.*

It will be helpful to compare the operating components of MRP II with those of the manual scheduling system. Figure 5-3 shows the manual steps for schedule creation versus the MRP II counterpart.

First notice that MRP II features no counterpart to the master schedule of the manual mode. This is true because the MRP II system deals with coordinating *existing* schedules of materials, human resources, work station capacity, and tooling. The master schedule, although an important part of the order processing system, is not part of that coordination activity; it is the *driver* of the activity. However, since master scheduling is such a necessary event, many MRP II software vendors include a companion software suite to handle the creation of the demand schedule at the front end. This package, often called master schedule, is in effect a master spreadsheet with finite amounts of orders allowed for each calendar date. This way senior management can create a logical input to the MRP II system so that it will output realistic work station scheduling.

Capacity Requirements Planning

The highest hierarchical MRP II program is capacity planning. This program does everything that occurs in the manual analysis of capacity and capability, but much faster and more thoroughly. It is capable of cascading work through the entire production facility via simulation and determining where bottlenecks will occur, and of doing it in a dynamic mode. It is especially powerful because its simulation capabilities can be used in a "what-if" mode, to show the effects of a wide range of alternative decisions. With this type of information it is possible to create packaged responses for a host of potential problems.

Manual schedule	MRP II schedule
• A master schedule	(none)
• Analysis of capacity and capability	• Capacity planning
• A release of an order to make a product or subcomponent	• Issuing of orders
• A detailed release of a work order at the lowest detail level to the work station	• Sequencing of operations (dispatch)

Figure 5-3. Comparison of the manual scheduling sequence with the MRP II program hierarchy.

Order Release

The next program down the hierarchy is orders release. Here the needs for material are placed in sequence and purchase orders are issued, along with supporting tooling design cycles and procurements. Sometimes, however, some items have such a long lead time that purchase orders are actually issued as soon as capacity and capability are verified during the capacity requirements planning phase. The orders release MRP II module is derived from the original MRP concept for materials management but also includes long-lead-time items of a nonmaterial nature, such as engineering design of the product and the design of tooling and procurement by manufacturing engineering.

Operations Sequencing

The lowest level of the hierarchy is the one that the work station sees. It is the operations sequencing module. Here, the daily dispatch sheets are created on the basis of the planned release of material and engineering tooling. The dispatch sheets become the dynamic script which shop operations will act out. The interesting thing is that the dynamic nature of MRP II allows the dispatch sheet to change as situations change. The first cut is made up in accordance with plan. All succeeding iterations are based on combinations of plan and result. This means that the system is constantly updating the schedule on the basis of the company's success with it. Every nuance of change from schedule could theoretically change the order of work.

Example. Work order 1 is temporarily stopped because of discovery of an out-of-spec surface finish. That means that work order 2 ascends to the top priority. The MRP II program can arrange this very quickly. The interruption of work and consequent modification of the dispatch list are simply inputted to the database by the operator. Typically this is done by key stroking or bar-code swiping a prearranged code into the computer terminal servicing the work station. In the MRP II world of available precision, the change in the dispatch list manifests itself as reconfiguration of manufacturing sequences.

PRAGMATIC RULES FOR WORKING WITHIN THE MRP II SYSTEM

The dynamism of the entire system is sometimes too fast for the factory, and we have to resort to freezing the sequence for a period ranging from a shift to a full production day. This cooling off prevents frustration and creates a perception that management really does have a firm grip on the situation. A more thorough way of instilling such confidence is by creating a set of rules and expectations for living in the MRP II world. Working with MRP II is definitely different from toiling in a manual system. Events tend to come much faster; thus a disciplined approach to doing business is essential. Freewheeling decision making is totally wrong, and this takes some getting used to. Consider that the driving force of MRP II is to abide by the Two Knows: know how to make the product, and know how long it should take to do so. Therefore, varying from plan and procedure will definitely reduce the knowledge base throughout the system. Since everything is integrated in an MRP II environment, a change in any aspect not adequately communicated can cause some degree of chaos throughout. For this reason it is immensely important to maintain communications excellence; hence, changes (while they can be rapid) need to be strictly controlled through agreed-upon procedures.

Most managers, supervisors, and operators are not used to this type of disciplined approach. Most have to learn the hard way that freelancing is no longer a permissible or even desirable modus operandi. To assist in getting organizations past this culture shock, I've successfully employed a reminder card (shown in Figure 5-4) for each employee of a company implementing MRP II on the shop floor. I call it the Shop Operations Ten MRP II Commandments.

The most important thing to gather from the Shop Operations Ten MRP II Commandments is that discipline is absolutely essential. If a database-

SHOP OPERATIONS TEN MRP II COMMANDMENTS

1. I will forget about the days before MRP II.
2. I will follow the MRP II dispatch explicitly and make parts in accordance with the company's quality standards.
3. I will be held responsible for missing schedule.
4. I will not sit down and wait for anyone to bring my work to me. I will actively and aggressively, with my supervisor, pursue backlog deliveries to my work station.
5. My individual work station performance will not take precedence over the overall efficiency of the company.
6. I will assist my supervisor and be responsible for maintaining the system inventories in line with physical inventories of my work station and the department.
7. I will be responsible for reporting any inventory inaccuracies so they may be corrected.
8. I will promptly report any flaws in the bill of materials or routings so they may be corrected.
9. I am really responsible for reporting accurately and closing out work orders as they are completed.
10. I understand that my contributions to the success of the company depends on my ability to comply with the application principles of MRP II, and to strive to always maintain the schedule.

Figure 5-4. Shop Operations Ten MRP II Commandments.

type philosophy is to be successful, it must be fed and cared for at very frequent intervals. And a database system is exactly what an MRP II system is. The system determines the sequence of events; therefore, it is very necessary that the data it receives be accurate and timely. In the manufacturing environment before MRP II, the rules were not as strict because they didn't have to be. The human mind is very adaptable to figuring out nuances of meaning, while a computer is not. This is a deficiency that exists even in the most sophisticated versions of MRP II employing state-of-the-art artificial intelligence. This being the case, we need to understand that procedures need to be followed explicitly to keep from confusing the computer, which takes everything literally. What a human would correctly interpret as a trivial deviation could cause the computer to have convulsions. Let us look at a simple example.

Example: Suppose we had to deviate from the lot size in assembling the hammer handles to heads because there was a temporary material shortage of bar stock to machine handles from. Further suppose that a quantity of 2000 assembled handle-to-head work-in-process (WIP) inventory existed at the assembly work station whereas the shop order requires 10,000 to be processed as one lot. Now, according to common MRP II procedure, an item or work order cannot be transferred to the next work station (in this case, applying the rubber grip on to the handle) until it is complete at the current work station. We can see why this makes sense. It is the only way to control the situation for the long term. The system knows the exact status of the work order—knows where it is, and thus knows what operations are complete and how many more are to go. It allows the MRP II program to continuously coordinate activities, and adjusts the schedule so that different activities mesh at proper times to accomplish the task. The activities it must coordinate include such things as delivery of tooling to the work station to accommodate the prescribed processes at the prescribed time. Since we know that schedules are dynamic and many outside factors can cause changes, it is not in our best interest to instigate spurious changes.

To recap, we have a work order partially completed but stalled because we ran out of materials to complete it. What do we do now? There are three choices:

- Stop and wait, thus backing everything up.
- Move the 2000 pieces to the next work station, where rubber grips are put on the handles.
- Move another work order ahead of the stalled one.

The most obvious choice is the middle one: take the assembled WIP and move it to the next work station. This keeps the production process moving. But this is terrible from an MRP II point of view. The system no longer has control, because it really doesn't know where the order is. Some of it is at one work station, and some at the next. This will foul up the system, and it will no longer be able to coordinate activities for this job because it can't locate things. Thus, the rule is, move only completed work orders from work station to work station. Most of the time this is simple to comply with and no problem evolves.

Let's go back to the choices again. The first is obviously not satisfactory. No one could possibly advocate doing nothing and simply waiting for the late material to arrive. The economic consequences are just not tolerable.

That leaves the third choice as the correct one: move that one work order aside, and move up the next one—like putting a freight train on a siding to let a faster commuter passenger train pass. This is easy for the MRP II system to comprehend. It is simply a situation where one work order will show complete before planned time, and eventually the partially completed work order will be logged as complete, as soon as the errant handle material arrives and work is completed. This will require a change in schedule, but that's what MRP II systems do well—react to the dynamics of the situation.

Now back to the central issue. With a manual system, the human controller could just as easily have moved the 2000 hammer assembly units to the next work station. She would have known it was a partial batch and acted accordingly, still in control of the schedule. Since the human controller can cope with a work order that is divided between two different work stations at the same time, knowing the remainder will catch up, she has no problem reacting to this nuance in the rules. She simply evaluates the situation and makes a decision based on presumed risk probability, most likely with little hesitation. Computers can't do that. Even computers employing artificial intelligence software can't do that, because the time for recovery is completely unknown, and thus no inference engine can interrelate with the knowledge base and solve the problem. Thus, we see the system making a more complex decision and taking more resources to puzzle it out, but the complexity is within the bounds of what the computer can understand.

Some people may think this is a setback and the MRP II system is less capable of managing the shop than the old manual system. This isn't so. In the vast majority of instances where a partial order situation creates a problem, the MRP II system is allowing the company to handle more complex issues more easily than ever before. There are no hard-and-fast benefit versus detractor ratios in this instance, but I would estimate at least a 10:1 ratio in favor of MRP II.

Again looking at the partial completion problem, we must be careful that the system's way of solving it does not just alleviate a symptom while the root cause remains. We must ask ourselves, How did the partial completion problem come about in the first place, and what do we do to keep it from reoccurring—thereby eliminating the problem and not just putting a

Band-Aid on it? Perhaps in this instance the root cause is an unrealistic lot size that manufacturing engineers have failed to recognize—that vendors, say, cannot make 10,000 sets of raw material in a time cycle to meet production needs, but they can do 2000 in the same time period. So instead of waiting with a partial order, process 5000, or 2000, orders in the same time period. Perhaps this would eliminate the hurry-up-and-wait syndrome. And perhaps one of the outcomes of this exercise would be a realistic understanding of proper lot size, based on the literal weakest link in the supply chain.

Another salient issue is the need to cooperate and work as a team for MRP II to be successful. The need for the entire manufacturing process and the support activities to be in synchrony with each other is paramount. We are trying to cope with a dynamic system using a powerful tool, the interactive database, to control the entire operation with minimal waste. We need to do this because we know that the manual mode can work only in a static situation with few variables that change slowly. However, this does not model the real world. The MRP II system does. But we have to be pragmatic about it. We need to know the limits of the software and not exceed them. In this case we need to be cognizant that if the rules under which the system was installed are violated, its dynamic, up-to-date status ability will become confused and chaos could take over. The way we prevent this from happening is to impress upon everyone within the supply chain that the rules must be followed. This is true even if we know that for any one specific instance it is quite conceivable that following the rules is the longest way to get from point A to point B. Keep in mind, however, that we depend on the MRP II system to keep track of where we are with respect to schedule. If we break the rules because it appears to be more efficient to do so in the near term, we may never know if we've reached point B. Let's look at what happens when cooperation does not take place.

Example. The ninth MRP II commandment requires that all persons running a work station report accurately what they have accomplished during the course of their work shift. In this example we have hammer heads being welded to the handles, and let us suppose it will take at least three days to complete a total work order of 650 pieces. An operator is supposed to do 65 pieces per shift and report his output at the end of the shift. Let's suppose that the operator doesn't bother to count the output of the work order completed and in fact 10 pieces of a 65-piece work order were scrapped. The operator knows some pieces were scrapped but doesn't know how many; he guesses at three. The MRP II system now knows, wrongly, that it is 3 pieces short, so an order for 3 more is booked to be added on to a work order. It should have been 10. Therefore the company will be 7 hammers short on its delivery to the customer. This in itself is not a serious flaw because of the relatively low value of each individual hammer. But what happens if this trend continues, as it likely will, given the operator's slovenly attention to detail? The cost to the company in short shipments and inventory confusion can be high. The company starts to lose control of the situation and does not know where it is with respect to the production schedule. Actual versus scheduled data are compromised. Now, if this scenario is multiplied across the factory by many operators and supervisors, then there is indeed an invitation to chaos. These types of scenarios need to be avoided in all instances, and the only way to do that is to instill a sense of ownership in the running of MRP II and to understand that cooperation is vital for success.

COMPATIBILITY OF JUST-IN-TIME (JIT) PRINCIPLES WITH MRP II

We cannot consider a discussion of automated scheduling systems without introducing just-in-time (JIT). Just-in-time is often confused with MRP and MRP II. JIT is equally as often thought to be at odds with the automated scheduling systems MRP and MRP II represent. Nothing could be further from the truth. JIT is the layman's version of industrial engineering optimization theory, while MRP and MRP II are automated scheduling systems. To put it more succinctly, JIT is all about eliminating waste in the manufacturing process. It touches on scheduling systems only in that capacity. Is the production scheduling system wasteful? If so, fix it. That is what good IE philosophy requires, and that factor is equally present in JIT.

JIT has as its core the philosophy that all activities done in a production process ought to be value-adding; if not they are ripe for minimizing and outright elimination. This philosophy applies equally across the board to all actions needed to make products. This means we need to be vigilant in process planning as well as scheduling, and as well as the process we use to design the product and the tools we use to make it with. Everything is included.

The point where JIT appeared in the past to be in conflict with MRP and MRP II is in the dispatch systems. Early proponents of JIT thought it to consist of only two things, both closely related:

- The kanban system (explained later in this section)
- The close proximity of vendors' delivery materials and thus their availability to supply the production line "just in time."

Unfortunately, those early proponents of JIT failed to realize its true core philosophy and thought it attacked the validity of the American-based MRP and MRP II (which they thought to be inferior) as compared with the Japanese-championed JIT (which, in truth, is American-based, dating back to the pioneers of industrial engineering, who were American). Kanban and close proximity of suppliers to factories do indeed reduce waste. But they do not attack the validity of a well-designed MRP or MRP II system. Let's take a look.

If the early proselytizers of JIT had looked deeper into the Toyota-invented kanban system, they would have discovered that it is a very clever *manual* production control system. If ever there was a corroboration that necessity is the mother of invention, then kanban is a certified match. At the time of its introduction, Toyota did not have MRP technology, but it did want to streamline its inventories and keep product flowing (something that we've seen MRP II does very well).

Kanban is a pull production dispatch system. It says that orders to make component parts and subassemblies ought to be in sync with the needs of the final assembly line. This means the controller of the final assembly area has to order up parts based on cycle time offsets, so she can be assured that all the parts are physically present when needed. In a true kanban system this is done with a ticket system. The ticket is the authority to proceed with production. The various part and assembly manufacturing areas can only work to fill tickets (orders) they have. Once they have filled all of their tickets they must stop. Knowing the cycle time allowed for her direct suppliers to get parts to final assembly, she gives the suppliers "tickets" to make the parts and deliver to her needs, keeping in mind that she must never ask for parts to be delivered prior to the "official" cycle time.

Notice that the dispatcher goes down only one level to pull material. This is on purpose, because it is thought that with a manual system it would be too difficult for a human to mastermind a double or triple level. It is up to the supplier to use his own kanban to get down to the next level. So, in practice, each level pulls from the next lower level. The theory is that the agreed-to cycle time covers the needs for each level to pull the next level down plus all the hidden levels below it. Figure 5-5 shows how it works for a single-series and a multiseries BOM. The obvious drawback, of course, is that large vertical BOMs become unmanageable because of the multilayers and the resulting explosion of data to be controlled. Of course, this can be handled successfully with an MRP II system in a very pragmatic way. But keep in mind that we should always strive to make BOMs as flat as possible to minimize levels, and thus minimize complexities to be accounted for.

Notice that the system is optimized for only the longest cycle time at each level. This is the critical path strategy, whereby time is allowed for the longest-lead-time items on the assumption that all other items will get done within that time and hence need little managerial attention. This greatly simplifies the management task if indeed the true critical path is identified and remains constant. Unfortunately, in manufacturing it is axiomatic that there are many unknowns that need to be coped with as they occur, and so critical paths will not remain constant. Hence, the dynamic control offered by MRP is enticing to embrace.

Kanban does tend to minimize waste by depressing overproduction. In a more traditional system, work stations make product independent of immediate current need further on down the line. This is called the just-in-case technique, and it simply builds inventory regardless of when the output will be used. Kanban tickets only allow the specified number of parts or subassemblies to be made per the ticket and only when the ticket arrives; hence,

(a)

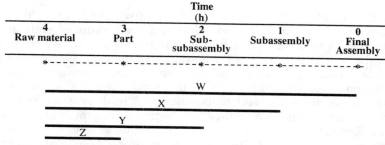

Total cycle time without queue to make product

		Time (h)		
4	3	2	1	0
Raw material	Part	Sub-subassembly	Subassembly	Final Assembly

W
X
Y
Z

Kanban ticket cycle plan-ahead time
If all cycle time between operations = 1 h, then:

- at final assembly level = W = 4 h
- at subassembly level = X = 3 h
- at sub-subassembly level = Y = 2 h
- at part level = Z = 1 h

(b)

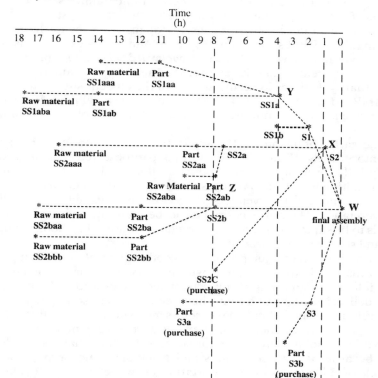

Kanban ticket at each level leads to longest (critical path) cycle time

- at final assembly level = W = 18 hrs
- at subassembly level = X = 17 hrs
- at sub-subassembly level = Y = 14 hrs
- at part level = Z = 10 hrs

Figure 5-5. Kanban work station pull relationship. *(a)* Single series. *(b)* Multiple series.

the designation "pull" system. This differs from the traditional way of dis-patching, where we start production at a predetermined start date for all components necessary for a future final assembly date. We commonly call this the "push" system. The push system, of course, assumes that all plans will be executed precisely and successfully and therefore everything will arrive on time. Naturally, we know this rarely happens, so we end up with many starts and stops and parts outages. A push production system in a manual mode, unable to self-adjust, begins to resemble highways at rush hour. Kanban manages to mitigate a bit of this as long as the critical path remains fairly constant. By not allowing production to start until a pull ticket arrives, we can minimize the traffic jam and eliminate the waste of making something too soon and hence the increased carrying costs of more work-in-process (WIP) inventory than required.

The kanban system tends to make the best of a manual system by opti-mizing "only" the critical path. It does not and cannot solve the dynamic issues. That can be done only via a computer-based system such as MRP II. But kanban does something else. It opens our eyes to the potential of making the MRP II system a pull system. And that is exactly what has hap-pened. We now have what we call *backward scheduling*, pulling all parts from final assembly and in essence issuing dynamic kanban tickets based on actual cycle times in accordance with the current situation. This means that MRP II can go far beyond optimizing the critical path. It can optimize the entire process in minute detail and modify the plan as incoming data indicate.

The early confusion on JIT applications has to do with the concept of inventory levels. Visitors to Toyota in Japan observed that there was rela-tively little inventory on the production floor and that the kanban system was resulting in tickets to vendors for frequent but small-quantity deliveries. They also noticed that vendors were close by. This led to two fallacies in interpretation: (1) that vendors had to be close by, and (2) that inventory needs to be suppressed and kept at vendor locations. Let's look at both fallac-ies and set the record straight.

First of all, the major premise of good industrial engineering practice, and thus JIT, is to eliminate waste in every way, shape, or methodology possible. It says nothing about vendor factory locations. It simply implies that deliveries ought to occur when needed. It just so happens that Japan has relatively small land mass, so it's not surprising to find vendors in close proximity to their customers. But requiring many small-quantity deliveries is not a prerequisite for success. Perhaps that occurred 30 years ago because of road conditions and truck size, and perhaps because of a lack of adequate rail transportation. The fact is that Toyota ordered materials and parts from vendors to meet its anticipated need and could not be in a relationship whereby its vendors could not optimize their production line. If Toyota had had such a policy it would have cost it more for the materials because it would have forced the vendors to utilize con-siderably more setups than normal. The kanban system really stopped at the factory door. Beyond that, the Toyota production planners needed to forecast for more extended time periods to assure that they had a smooth flow of materials entering their plants. To do otherwise is foolhardy and irresponsible.

Forcing vendors to maintain inventory at no expense to the recipient company just doesn't happen. A vendor will gladly build to stock for a customer's intended need, but only on a contractual basis. It is quite common for a company to place blanket orders for annual usages with vendors, so they can be assured of delivery when they need it. This is what Toyota did, and so do most other reputable manufacturers. A contract is negotiated, usually for a year, that states how much the buyer will pay and commit to purchase. The supplier commits to having the items the customer wants in stock. This allows the supplier to base-load facilities and achieve economies of scale. The price is set to offset the need for the supplier to hold finished goods inventory (the most expensive type, since all operations have been performed and thus all costs accrued). The vendor then delivers product to the customer on a set periodic basis or as called for by the customer. We can readily see that a base loaded product makes the vendor's scheduling algorithm much easier to manage, and so cost savings accrue. This is definitely a preferred way of doing business for all concerned. Guaranteed predictability is an asset to any business at any time. And, while it certainly follows the precept of eliminating waste, it certainly is not a revelation in business practice brought about by JIT.

REAL BENEFITS OF JIT AT THE WORK STATION

Now let's look at the real benefits of JIT at the work station. Many people have tried to codify JIT, e.g., through the seven principles of waste, or the efficiency steps. All these classifications are nice, and they help us focus our efforts, and I have also been guilty of getting into the axiom pronouncement game. The truth is, there is only one principle to keep in mind, the tried and true industrial engineering principle, and all the rest are corollaries. This principle is that we must always strive to optimize any system we employ to achieve our production aims. To put it in JIT terms, we need to *eliminate waste* in all of our systems. Let's look at a few things that happen at work stations and see how we can apply this principle. Keep in mind that no one has codified all things that can be made better, so there are still many opportunities for creativity.

Robert W. Hall, in his book "Zero Inventory" (Dow Jones-Irwin, Homewood, IL, 1983), listed six "eliminate waste" axioms:

1. Produce the product the customer wants.
2. Produce products only at the rate the customer wants them.
3. Produce with perfect quality.
4. Produce instantly—zero unnecessary lead times.
5. Produce with no waste of labor, material, or equipment.
6. Produce by methods that allow for development of people.

Putting a finite total on axioms for eliminating waste may or may not be correct. But, as engineers, we can certainly understand Mr. Hall's desire to encompass the entirety of the production universe within his axioms. Whatever the numerical count, his list does help us focus on pragmatic improvement opportunities. From my viewpoint, this is significant. The spotlight is on the opportunities, and we need to act on them.

All six axioms do apply to management of the work station. However, all but items 3 and 5 are indirect. By this I mean that the responsibility for them lies primarily with the support functions. Only items 3 and 5 are the direct responsibility of the work station; they depend on using the work station and all of its resources effectively.

Let's look at some examples of how to optimize items 3 and 5. Keep in mind that this is by no means an all-inclusive list. It is simply a thought provoker.

No. 3: Produce with Perfect Quality

This can be cynically thought of as a "motherhood" statement. If it is, that's a tragedy. We really must approach this pronouncement as a goal to strive for and creatively think about how we can get to perfect quality. If not, we never will. The simplistic beauty of this pronouncement is that it implies that producing with perfect quality is well within our reach The cynics would say we are seeking the impossible. They would say the statement is simply a ploy to mislead the uninitiated who don't know any better and don't know it can't be done, that it is a cruel hoax to separate a company from its financial reserves through projects impossible to achieve. But is it impossible? Of course not. Is it difficult to achieve? Yes, and many orders of magnitude beyond what the lay public would consider feasible in their wildest imagination. But it is possible.

What has to happen to achieve perfect quality? Let's brainstorm and list some parameters. The three major factors to always consider for optimizing a work center are materials appropriate for the task, process equipment capable of doing the job, and guaranteed operator proficiency. This would lead to perhaps the following list of requirements:

Materials appropriate for the task

- The material has to be within the tolerance band designated for it.
- The material acceptability criteria need to be easily discerned in a foolproof manner.
- The material has to be compatible with the design requirements.

Process equipment capable of doing the job

- The process has to be in control, and the six sigma spread has to incorporate the minimum to maximum tolerances. Which also means that the design for the product has to be robust enough to encompass the entire domain of process variations.
- The process equipment has to be performing perfectly.
- The equipment has to be capable of doing the designated job in an optimum manner.

Guaranteed operator proficiency

- The operator has to perform all steps of the process in accordance with the approved method.
- The method itself has to be capable of producing perfect quality, all the time.
- The operator has to be satisfactorily trained to do the specific job called for.

There could conceivably be many more considerations to ponder to achieve perfect quality, but these are the basics that are generally applicable. Now, how do we go about achieving perfect quality? First we need to define what perfect quality is, and we touched on that within Chapter 4. Simply stated, it is the achievement of the customer's expectation for the product as modified by what has been contractually accepted by both the customer and the supplier. In practice this means a specification that the vendor has designed to and is willing to support. It may involve elaborate MILSPEC definitions and measurements, or it may be based on a simple clause such as "that it will work in accordance with the customer's true needs," which may or may not be codified.

To accomplish this task, we first have to appraise where we are. This helps define the problem to be solved. In the hammer example, for instance, let's say that we have a yield of 95% good product at the end of the line that is shippable to customers. So the task is to determine what makes up the 5% reject universe (bounding the problem). We would take the materials, processes, and operator factors (the list above) and for every defect show a probable or exact cause matched to one of the items above. Figure 5-6 shows a hypothetical matrix of causes on a Pareto-style data sheet. Note that the heading topics are identical to the items we listed during the hypothetical brainstorming session. This is done on purpose, to minimize confusion. If we hadn't determined the true factors that affect achievement of perfect quality, we would have been observing defects with causes beyond the nine shown. This happens quite often, but for simplicity of illustration, I've chosen to assume that all causes were identified beforehand. In the case where they haven't been, during the data collection phase we would add new identified causes to the Pareto analysis.

In Figure 5-6, roughly one-half of the defects observed fall within 20% to 35% of the defect categories. Simply stated, it is unusual to see defect causes uniformly distributed, and they're not in this case. There are 58 defects plotted against 9 causes. The highest cause accounts for 14 defects (24%) and the lowest for only 1 (a nominal 2%). The two highest defect cause categories account for 45%, and if we extend down to the third-highest cause, we see 64% of all the defects accounted for. The remaining 36% are covered by the other six categories. This means that for problem resolution, we can achieve a very large percentage of our goal by concentrating on eliminating the three most common defects. And this is what we will plan to do. We will use good industrial engineering techniques to understand the root causes of the highest defect and solve them. As we resolve these defects, we will pro-

Hammer Defect Cause Pareto Analysis
January 2001 - December 2001

Data As Collected

Items							Observed defects								
	1	2	3	4	5	6	7	8	9	10	11	12	13	14	15
Materials appropriate for the task:															
A. The material has to be within the tolerance band designated for it.	x	x	x	x	x	x	x	x	x	x	x				
B. The material acceptability criteria need to be easily discerned in a foolproof manner.	x														
C. The material has to be compatible with the design requirements.	x		x	x	x										
Process equipment capable of doing the job:															
D. The process has to be in control and the six sigma spread has to incorporate the minimum to maximum tolerances.	x			x											
E. The process equipment has to be performing perfectly.	x	x	x	x		x	x	x	x	x	x	x	x	x	
F. The equipment has to be capable of doing the designated job in an optimum manner.	x	x													
Guaranteed operator proficiency:															
G. The operator has to perform all steps of the process in accordance with the approved method.	x	x	x	x	x	x	x	x	x	x	x	x			
H. The method itself has to be capable of producing perfect quality, all the time.	x		x												
I. The operator has to be satisfactorily trained to do the specific job called for.	x		x	x	x	x									

Data in Pareto Format

Items							Observed defects								
	1	2	3	4	5	6	7	8	9	10	11	12	13	14	15
E. The process equipment has to be performing perfectly.	x	x	x	x	x	x	x	x	x	x	x	x	x	x	
G. The operator has to perform all steps of the process in accordance with the approved method.	x	x	x	x	x	x	x	x	x	x	x	x			
A. The material has to be within the tolerance band designated for it.	x	x	x	x	x	x	x	x	x	x	x				
I. The operator has to be satisfactorily trained to do the specific job called for.	x	x	x	x	x	x									
C. The material has to be compatible with the design requirements.	x	x	x	x	x										
D. The process has to be in control and the six sigma spread has to incorporate the minimum to maximum tolerances.	x	x	x	x											
H. The method itself has to be capable of producing perfect quality, all the time.	x	x	x												
F. The equipment has to be capable of doing the designated job in an optimum manner.	x	x													
B. The material acceptability criteria need to be easily discerned in a foolproof manner.	x														

Figure 5-6. Perfect quality probable cause Pareto analysis.

ceed to the next level of highest cause, and so forth, until all defects on the Pareto chart have been eliminated.

This is the way perfect quality is achieved—through hard work and attention to detail. It is an iterative process whereby success breeds further success.

One last item. As we can see, a large component of less than perfect quality is the operator error segment. In our example, item G, "the operator has to perform all steps of the process in accordance with the approved method," is the second-highest cause of poor quality. This is not unusual, and it requires very intensive supervision and guidance to overcome. But it is the easiest, least costly corrective action to achieve. It requires truly becoming a partner with the operator to experience why he or she cannot do the job without generating defects. The ultimate mark of a good coach is being able to bring out the best in every player. And the sports analogy can end there, because teaching good performance to a work station operator is easier than teaching a person to be a good athlete. Properly constituted modern methods are planned and designed for the average person to succeed as proficiently as a sports super-superstar. What is needed is attention to detail, motivation to do the job right, and a team situation in which the operator is an equal among equals in making good, perfect-quality products.

To achieve perfect quality, we must always start with the human factors. The entire team has to be convinced that perfect quality is indeed possible and plan accordingly. The order of improvement programs is always dictated by the Pareto analysis of causes that are preventing perfect quality, and the mantra of continuous improvement has to be imprinted in the minds of the entire team.

No. 5: Produce with No Waste of Labor, Material, or Equipment

This is the classical industrial engineering step associated with names like Taylor, Gilbreath, and Gantt. First, the methodology and tools have to be provided. This we know how to do without any doubt. Second, the schedule has to be realistic in that it can be achieved as stated. This means it needs to be compatible with the methods and tooling available. To put it more succinctly, we can't ask for an automobile to be assembled in 30 minutes if the method and provided tooling require 12 hours. The third item is the direct labor component. We have to utilize the personnel available in the most effective manner.

In addition to needing to produce with perfect quality via the best application of human effort, we need to do it as efficiently and effectively as possible. We need to minimize non-value-added work and concurrently maximize value-added work.

Some people confuse efficiency and effectiveness as they apply to business activities. For our purposes, *efficiency* refers to how well we do any task as measured against a predetermined standard, while *effectiveness* means how much of our effort is consumed in value-added tasks as opposed to non-value-added tasks. Furthermore, value-added work is defined as work that directly and measurably transforms raw material or data into the finished product. Non-value-added work is the necessary support activity that enables value-added work to occur.

Example. Setting the jigs and fixtures on a vertical boring mill table so parts to be machined are calibrated and positioned properly is indirect work with reference to transforming material into finished product and hence is called non-value-added. The work of actually machining the part is the only value added work in this scenario.

Obviously for this JIT axiom, eliminating waste means eliminating all unnecessary non-value-added steps.

One common technique for minimizing waste is the "single minute exchange of dies" (SMED) process put forth by Shiego Shingo in his book "Non-Stock Production: The Shingo System for Continuous Improvement" (Productivity Press, Cambridge, MA, 1988). This process was initially developed for progressive metal stamping presses on which changeover of dies could take upwards of three days. This should give an indication of the complexity that can be involved in retooling such equipment, and the need for long production runs. This, of course, severely minimizes a factory's flexibility and capability of serving customers. Mr. Shingo said die change could be done much faster—in fact, in well under an hour. He targeted this process for single-digit numbers of minutes, and devised methods for reaching that goal; hence, the acronym SMED. While this work has extremely significant benefits for punch press applications, it is also applicable in virtually any process for any set of equipment for which shorter production runs are contemplated. It is a milestone in manufacturing progress.

Basically, the process has three components:

- Evaluate all tasks necessary to make setup changes and categorize them according to whether they can be done while the process is running or can be done only when the machine is stopped.
- Find ways to get more work to be done internal to the cycle.
- Minimize the time necessary to perform those tasks for which the process needs to be stopped.

A simple example would be if a die has to be a certain distance below the lowest extended point of the press stroke. Then a jig would be made to represent the press stroke and the die would be set in its carriage off-line to the proper height. Thus, this work does not have to be done when the new die is put in the press. An even more obvious example is to have all the tooling at the work station before the job changeover is to take place. This is simply pre-kitting. With preplanning it is possible to significantly transfer work to within the cycle and thereby minimize non-value-added time. In many respects this is nothing more than a variant of the critical path method, but in this case applied to minimizing time to perform tasks so that more Activities fit within the critical path steps.

The purpose of shop supervision at the work station is to get the entire team behind the effort to find ways to minimize non-value-added time. This is done by constantly prodding people to understand the difference between value-added and non-value-added work, and to look at the latter as an enemy to be vanquished. Make it a fun game by offering single and group awards for every minute of reduction in non-value-added activity. And at the same time make it very clear that the company's success depends on quick response to customer needs. By spotlighting this axiom of business (therefore job) success, we can create an atmosphere that goes after waste vigilante-style, for the benefit of all.

By now it is apparent that JIT is an entirely different "animal" from MRP and MRP II. Both JIT and MRP II are dedicated to making businesses run more efficiently and effectively, but from entirely different viewpoints. MRP II operates using algorithms for expeditiously scheduling operations for a dynamic situation, while JIT employs all the industrial engineering theory for operations optimization. JIT works on the *process*, while MRP II works on the *schedule* that dictates when the process is to be employed. The two are definitely compatible, but certainly neither is a viable alternative for the other. JIT principles, when applied correctly, will allow for shorter cycle times. This in turn can be picked up by MRP II in shorter schedule times, with the results being obtaining more product produced in a given period of time.

From the viewpoint of the work station, the combination of MRP II and JIT principles leads us to much more productivity because we gain well-focused information about scheduling and about how the operators can perform their job. We are orchestrating better because the MRP II and JIT systems are aimed at such optimization. The combination enhances both the desire to excel and the ability to do so. We know that we are living in a continuously improving environment with a premium for achieving beneficial change. These are the combined abstract gains we can achieve by implementing MRP II along with JIT principles.

IMPACT OF GROUP TECHNOLOGY ON SCHEDULING

A discussion of scheduling and cycle time as it impacts the work station is not complete without an analysis of group technology (GT) and how it affects performance. Unlike MRP II or JIT, GT does not have any adherents who claim it to be a way to schedule a shop better. In fact, for flow manufacturing, GT has very little to add and can be skipped entirely. GT is a way of organizing data that leads to better layout of factories and improved throughput. This may seem to be a contradiction in terms. How can GT be a way to improve throughput without being a way to schedule a shop? It can be, and is, because it is a way of finding work and organizing the shop to work with any scheduling technique a business employs. It is a secondary, not a primary, scheduling influencer. By this I mean that with GT in use, the schedule will still be created in any way a company chooses. However, what is in the schedule will be strongly influenced by GT. What GT does do, very effectively for job shops, is to beneficially impact cycle time by reducing non-value-added time. Using GT properly will reduce overall portal-to-portal cycle time by increasing the value-added to non-value-added ratio—in some cases virtually reaching the ratio enjoyed by flow manufacturing. Let's examine this and see how and why.

The Principle of Sameness

First, what is GT? GT employs the *principle of sameness*. It is a methodology of finding similarities in diverse sets of things so they may be grouped for operations purposes. For example, if we have pipes of various sizes, sleeves of various sizes, washers of various sizes, and fastener nuts of various sizes, we can find something they all possess. They all have diameters, inner and outer. They all have longitudinal lengths, albeit that washers have very small lengths compared with their diameters. They can all be made on turning equipment such as lathes. So we can see that dissimilar things can have similarities. This is the principle of sameness: looking for similarities in apparently dissimilar objects. We can even go further afield. We can say that the only thing that's similar, in our search for a similarity, is a manufacturing process. It certainly is possible for us to conceive of a ship rudder assembly and a nuclear reactor valve body as requiring similar welding and heat treatment, and therefore as an economical measure being placed in the same group for heat treatment.

The principle of sameness is employed in job shops to find items that may be manufactured together to achieve economies of scale. Group technology is a process for exploiting the principle of sameness, by devising ways to find similarities in apparently dissimilar parts. We are very interested in doing this because we know that job shops are not as efficient as flow manufacturing operations.

Flow Manufacturing

Flow manufacturing is characterized by long production runs, usually greater than 10,000 pieces, with special-purpose (usually automated) equipment and less need for skilled work station operators. As mentioned previously, we also see a more favorable ratio of value-added to non-value-added time in the chain from product conceptualization to shipping to the customer. Flow manufacturing typically has a 30:70 ratio—that is, 30% of the time, value-added work is being done—whereas a job shop rarely does better than a 5:95 ratio, or value-added work 5% of the time. Thus we can see why choosing flow manufacturing as the preferred way to produce goods has real tangible economic benefits. Unfortunately, most products made in this world have production runs of fewer than 10,000 pieces.

Hence, it is uneconomical to set up flow manufacturing operations to produce them.

Job Shop Manufacturing

Job shops are characterized by small and typically sporadic production runs, with general-purpose machines and equipment and the need for higher skilled work station operators. This all leads to increased costs to produce and to purchase. But the world is a very diverse place, and there are relatively few items that are universally appealing or even acceptable to all of us. This is why there is so much choice of products and there are so many available and successful brand names. The diversity is made possible in part because over 70% of all factories are job shops.

We all want unique things; however, we do not and in most cases cannot willingly pay for uniqueness. Therefore, the competitive advantage is definitely to those who can offer uniqueness at a price customers are willing to pay. Herein lies the application of group technology: find the sameness of dissimilar products so the factory can approach flow manufacturing efficiencies in job shop environments.

METHODS FOR ESTABLISHING GT GROUPINGS

GT principles tell us that we must find the similarities of dissimilar items in order to group them for flowlike production. There are three methodologies for doing this, ranging from estimates to precise evaluations. These are, from simplest to most complex:

- Empirical decision
- Parts flow analysis
- Classification code

Each method will place diverse parts into *families of parts* whereby all members of a family will have similarities that can be exploited for manufacturing purposes. As would be expected, the simplest method to apply will give the least precise grouping; and the most complex, the most exact grouping. Let's look at each methodology.

Empirical Decision

The empirical decision method is based on the premise that every business—even a job shop—specializes in a set or family of products. Therefore, it is possible to conceive of the variety of products that will pass through its facilities and to pregroup them into families of parts. In practice, this is done by a group of experts (people who have experience in the business over a sufficient period of time) who have seen the variety of parts the company handles. They review drawings and specifications for the array of parts that are going or have gone through the factory and group them by similarities. They usually group them for manufacturing similarities, but can also group them for design similarities to cut down on design cycle time.

Parts Flow Analysis

Parts flow analysis is very similar to empirical decision, in that it presupposes that the mix of parts going through the factory will remain fairly constant over a period of time. In fact, it is a truism that, since most companies for competitive reasons do not stray too far from their area of expertise (their safety zone), the full selection of parts will usually cycle through a factory over a period equal to about 3 to 4 production cycles. This means that an average factory will experience virtually the full variety of parts it will ever see in about 6 months. On the basis of this hypothesis, parts flow analysis will gather the routing for all orders that have gone through the factory for the previous 6 months and construct a matrix of parts versus the work station they are cycled through. By this technique, patterns begin to emerge showing the grouping of parts in parts families, and it is possible to create families of parts that are grouped for similarities in production processes.

The part flow analysis (PFA) matrix in Figure 5-7 shows a series of part numbers completed by our hypothetical factory involving turned parts of various varieties: pipes, sleeves, washers, disks, and fastener nuts.

The first thing to observe is that there isn't any pattern to the numbering system and the terminology of names is not very specific. For example, examining the matrix shows that the method for making a washer is the same as that for making a disk. Does this mean that "disk" and "washer" are two names for the same thing? It is entirely possible that this is the case. Which means that for determining family of parts, it is not sufficient to use name only.

For convenience' sake, the matrix shows work stations by process description. The results of the matrix by process category are:

Incoming material inspection	24	(all)
Cut to length	24	
Flat suface grind	16	
Weld butt ends	7	(pipes and sleeves)
Heat treat	7	(pipes and sleeves)
Turn to dia, outside	24	
Turn to dia, inside	17	
Tap holes, radial	3	
Tap holes, longitudinal	6	
Thread dia, inside	7	
Thread dia, outside	1	
Paint	3	
Galvanize	10	

Products		Processes												
Part no.	Description	Incoming material inspection	Cut to length	Flat surface grind	Weld butt end	Heat treat	Turn to dia outside	Turn to dia inside	Tap holes radial	Tap holes longitudinal	Thread dia inside	Thread dia outside	Paint	Galvanize
143A67	washer	1	4	5			2	3						
153B23	pipe	1	2		4	5	3							9
341B12	fastener nut	1	8	7			3	4	6	6	5			9
560A29	fastener nut	1	8	7			3	4			5			9
121C33	washer	1	4	5			2	3					6	
621A17	washer	1	4	5			2	3					6	
786B54	disk	1	4	5			2	3						
601B44	pipe	1	2		4	5	3		6					6
280B43	pipe	1	2		4	5	3							9
785A12	fastener nut	1	8	7			3	4		6	5			6
887C23	disk	1	4	5			2	3						
971C41	disk	1	4	5			2	3						6
101B32	sleeve	1	2		4	5	3	3						
531A23	washer	1	4	5			2	3						
771B28	fastener nut	1	8	7			3	4		6	5			9
653C29	sleeve	1	6				2	3	5			4		
221A26	washer	1	4	5			2	3						6
681C69	pipe	1	2		4	5	3							
449B67	fastener nut	1	8	7			3	4		6	5			9
532A22	fastener nut	1	8	7			3	4		6	5		9	
223C21	fastener nut	1	8				3	4		6	5			9
485B12	sleeve	1	2		4	5	3							
338C34	pipe	1	2		4	5	3							
991A44	washer	1	4	5			2	3						

Figure 5-7. Parts flow analysis matrix.

So far we can see that pipes and sleeves appear to be a specific family because they are the only components that require welding and heat treatment. But again, we have to be careful about jumping to conclusions based on descriptive names only. In Figure 5-7 we see that sleeve part number 653C29 has most of the processing characteristics of a disk or washer rather than those of the other sleeves. In fact, other than its name it has little if any commonality with the other sleeves. The moral being that, until we look at process steps carefully, we cannot form family of parts groups.

So what do we know? We see that there will probably be three family of parts groups, the first made up of washer-type products, a second consisting of pipes and of sleeves that are manufactured like pipes and probably require welding, and a third group consisting of fastener nuts. And that's all. We have learned just about as much as we can from the data presented, and now it is time to look deeper.

The second, more in-depth analysis comes about by rearranging the data but still using the same work station sequences. Now we can see why numbers in process order were used on the matrix instead of simply check marks. By regrouping, we will be able to see if there are any exact matches of different part numbers with identical processing sequences. These would be exact family of parts members, something like the nuclear family. We will also see that there are parts that go through the same basic work stations but in a different sequence order. These are near relatives and may be considered to be members of the family of parts grouping. This is particularly so if the deviations are caused by specific extra operations for specialized purposes.

Figure 5-8 shows the grouping by common name and we can see that there are four very distinct family of parts groupings. The first is a washer family, made up of washers, disks, and a sleeve. They all have the same manufacturing sequences except for special requirements. For example, the one sleeve in this grouping, part no. 653C29, has an additional manufacturing step, in this case, the threading of the outside diameter. This would imply that the part is longitudinally longer than the rest of the parts in the grouping, and so special tooling may still be required for this sibling.

The second group is the pipes and sleeves. Again, all require the same manufacturing processes except for additional special features.

Finally, we see that the third family of parts is the fastener nut family. Here all processes are the same, and again there are additional processes for additional features. We also see that finish requirements are a big variable.

This is about as close as we can get with this technique. For example, we don't know if it's really practical to group all the pipes into one family of parts group, because we do not know the size ratio. We could be talking about 5-in. outside diameter pipe mixed with 5-ft outside diameter pipe. Obviously, that would be a mismatch. The processes may be the same, but the equipment used would be vastly different. We also see a little of the limitations of PFA with the special sleeve of the first parts family. We simply cannot tell from the data presented whether the part fits

| Products | | Processes | | | | | | | | | | | | |
Part no.	Description	Incoming material inspection	Cut to length	Flat surface grind	Weld butt end	Heat treat	Turn to dia outside	Turn to dia inside	Tap holes radial	Tap holes longitudinal	Thread dia inside	Thread dia outside	Paint	Galvanize
143A67	washer	1	4	5			2	3						
121C33	washer	1	4	5			2	3					6	
621A17	washer	1	4	5			2	3						
531A23	washer	1	4	5			2	3						
221A26	washer	1	4	5			2	3						6
991A44	washer	1	4	5			2	3						
786B54	disk	1	4	5			2	3					6	
887C23	disk	1	4	5			2	3						6
971C41	disk	1	4	5			2	3						
101B32	sleeve	1	2		4	5	3	3						
653C29	sleeve	1	6				2	3	5					
485B12	sleeve	1	2		4	5	3					4		
153B23	pipe	1	2		4	5	3							
601B44	pipe	1	2		4	5	3		6					
280B43	pipe	1	2		4	5	3							6
681C69	pipe	1	2		4	5	3							
338C34	pipe	1	2		4	5	3							
341B12	fastener nut	1	8	7			3	4	6		5			9
560A29	fastener nut	1	8	7			3	4		6	5			9
785A12	fastener nut	1	8	7			3	4		6	5			9
771B28	fastener nut	1	8	7			3	4		6	5			9
449B67	fastener nut	1	8	7			3	4		6	5			9
532A22	fastener nut	1	8	7			3	4		6	5		9	
223C21	fastener nut	1	8	7			3	4		6	5			9

Figure 5-8. Parts flow analysis matrix grouped by part name.

the equipment necessary to manufacture all the siblings. However, in defense of the PFA technique, the personnel involved with manufacturing surely will know the common sizes of their products, and so there shouldn't really be too much of a surprise factor once families of parts are structured.

Classification Code

The final and most comprehensive way of creating family of parts groupings is through the classification code method. This procedure utilizes a code in which the digits and their placement in the code sequence reflect geometric, process, and performance characteristics. For example, in the PFA discussion, the sleeve that turned out to have a process sequence very similar to the washers and disks would be further clarified by geometric characteristics to see if it truly did belong in the washer family of parts. The situation with the pipe would be clarified likewise: we would know if all the pipes were of similar size so that essentially the same equipment would be used to produce them, or whether they were totally different ranging from miniature to gargantuan.

Coding can be and is also used to keep from "reinventing the wheel" over and over again. It is possible to describe a new product's characteristics and then code them and search the database for exact or near matches. This significantly minimizes the time necessary for design and process planning and is an enormous productivity improvement that allows time to market to be truncated appreciably.

Let's look now how codes are developed. Codes are either chain-type or hierarchical, and both can be computer-generated. In fact, there are many commercially available codes, many of which are associated with MRP II software.

Chain-Type Code

The chain-type code is the oldest and dates back to the precomputer era—in fact, back to the early 1900s, and some say it is traceable to the time of Taylor, Gantt, and Gilbreath. The chief characteristic of chain codes is that each digit in the chain represents a specific attribute. For example, let's say we have a code for our earlier hammer example and it goes something like this:

A238B661

This is an eight-digit code in which each digit can have 10 numerical plus 26 alphabetical values for a total of 36 values for each characteristic. As we can see, there are many different ways to set up the code, and any user can structure it to suit his or her needs. For the hammer example, one way of structuring could be:

1st digit = product identification = hammer	A
2nd digit = material = stainless steel	2
3rd digit = length/dia ratio of handle	3
4th digit = hammer head width, cm, head to tail	8
5th digit = handle material = rubber	B
6th digit = process, handle = saw and lathe	6
7th digit = process, hammer head = forge	6
8th digit = process joining head to handle = weld	1

We see that each digit in each location has only one meaning. Depending on how often we use the code, we can become proficient in knowing what each digit placement means. For example, we would probably always know that a value of A for the first digit means the product line hammer. The way this code is structured, we envision the various combinations we intend to put together in the course of running our factory. We do this by using a PFA or an empirical decision exercise to see what the likely mix of products will be and then structure a code.

The interesting thing is that it's not necessary to conceive of every possible mix right away. All that's necessary is to have the category designated. Take, for instance, digit 3, length to diameter ratio. If our company is a toolmaking concern, it's fairly definite that handles will have to be made for a variety of tools. Some will be one piece, some will go together with a joining process, and so forth. But knowing *L/D* will place us on the right type and size of machines and/or processes for manufacturing. So we set up a digit in the code to be used for *L/D*, and perhaps create ranges—e.g., a value of 0 could indicate length 0 to 5 in. and diameter 0 to 0.5 in., and so forth. It is then a simple matter to look up or measure the ratio of the part to be coded and see which code designation fits.

We can do this with virtually every characteristic of interest and build a code. But we don't have to complete the code. For example, the first digit for hammer is A. We might also have a code B in the first digit for screwdriver, and perhaps C for chisel, which might make up the current other offerings of the company. Perhaps in the future the company may want to make wrenches. Then we could use D to represent that product. But the fact is there is no need to fill in that designation in the code until it is going to be used. The same is true for most other digit locations, particularly, those for such items as materials and process designations.

Hierarchical-Type Code

The second type of code configuration is the hierarchical type. This the newer code structure designed to be used with computer databases. Here the meaning of the digit in any position depends on the value of the digit to its left, because the digit values are derived from a sort of logic tree. With this coding method it's easy to store lots of information in a relatively short code. While it's quite common for a chain-type code to have 16 and even up to 32 digits, the hierarchical code rarely gets above 8 digits. For the chain-type code, every time a new feature was added, another digit position had to be added to the code. This is not the case for a hierarchical code structure.

Hierarchical structures, as implied before, are akin to tree diagrams. While Figure 5-9 may not look like a tree, it symbolizes a tree trunk

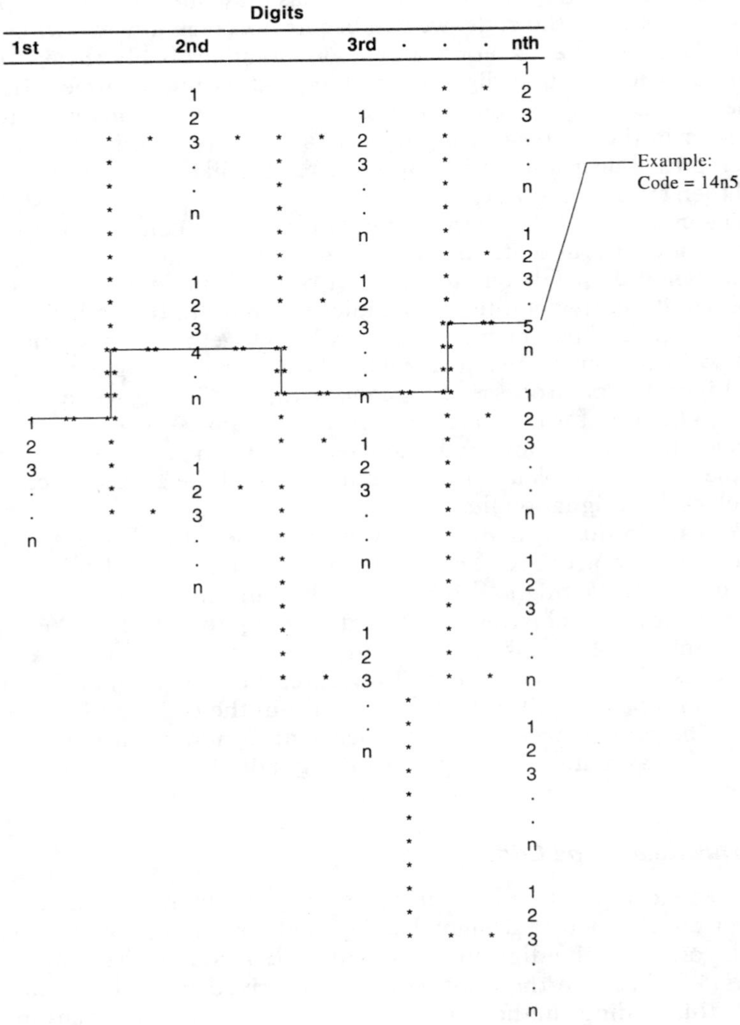

Figure 5-9. Classification code, hierarchical structure.

expanding into several branches and they themselves further spreading into smaller branches. As the branches become smaller the information contained in them are more specific. If I had used the term computer memory register, we could have been discussing the storage of memory in a computer whereby each register has sub registers under it (think of the structure for editing storage and files in a Personal Computer with a Windows/DOS operating system) each being more specific to the generic topic of its predecessor register.

A simple example is shown in Figure 5-9. We can see that the first digit determines the *nature* of the digit in the second position, and so forth throughout the entire code. This allows for a large *variety* of inputs with a short string of digits. Of course, this method is ideal for computer usage: lots of data organized in a branching network. Depending on the preceding digit, the program instructs the computer to go to a specific memory register. This way tremendous amounts of data can be stored and we need only a short code string to access it. Instead of having 32 digits, as in a chain-type code, we need perhaps only five or six digits. The one obvious drawback (if it can be considered one) is that since the nature of the data contained in a digit position varies, it is virtually impossible for the human user to recognize what a string of code means. In the chain-type code example, the second digit indicated the material the hammer was made of. In a hierarchical code, all we know about the second digit, for sure, is that it provides further information about its predecessor, the first digit.

Observing Figure 5-9, we see that the code is 14n5. Let us suppose that the first digit represents the type of tool the company manufactures. In this case, let's say it is a screwdriver. That eliminates all other tools and the characteristics associated with all other tools. Thus, when we go to the second digit, we know it is a further describer of the screwdriver. Note in the diagram that other registers for the second digit (corresponding to the values 2 through n of the first digit) are ignored, because they have no information of interest vis-à-vis the screwdriver. They are branches of the tree that at this time have no interest to us. The second digit would be expected to describe some very basic refining characteristic of the screwdriver, possibly the tip. We know that screwdriver tips can have flat shanks, or Phillips configurations, or square ends, or subvarieties of all of these. Let us say that the value 4 represents Phillips style. Now, the third digit is a further refinement down the path of a Phillips head screwdriver, perhaps representing a specific type of Phillips head. All the other registers for the third digit in this tree are abandoned because they do not represent Phillips configurations. From here we go to the fourth digit, which represents another refinement in the Phillips head family. Thus, the value 5 represents a specific characteristic common only to this type of Phillips head configuration. Perhaps it is a specific shape for the forged shaft with the exact Phillips head configuration. As we can see, this method is a very concise way of making very specifically focused code information available.

To clarify, diagrams like that depicted in Figure 5-9 are not used by persons utilizing the code. The diagram simply illustrates the logic of how the code is structured, hence the software developed. It is a simple matter of "if/then" statements instructing the application to go to the proper register (branch). Most hierarchical codes step the user through the development of a code for a product by this branching algorithm technique. The person assigning a code number to the part need not know anything about how it is structured.

Classification codes have one significant advantage over the empirical decision and PFA methods: we can use them in preparing to meet future demands, and this way have a head start in making our current work stations suitable for future work. If the company is engaged in making continually evolving products, as is the case in most power and digital electronics manufacturing, it cannot count on all its past activities to be replicated in the future. Further, it cannot count on its past methods for making *the same* products to still be sufficient in the future. Thus, whatever a company designs or manufactures, it will want to place it in an existing family of parts or to recognize when a new family really needs to be established. An optimal way of doing this is to code all characteristics of a newly received request for quote (RFQ) or newly conceived product offering at the time of inception.

The engineer reviewing the RFQ or responsible for the new product offering will use the code software program to step through the process of assigning a code number. The program will ask questions starting from the most broad to the most specific. In this manner stepping the engineer from a broad to the next more specific branch. If at any branch level in the program there is no description that applies, the software is designed to query the engineer and allow insertion of additional describers with a newly assigned digit. In this manner it is possible to use the existing hierarchical GT code to create a code number for a new item. This will concisely reveal what's new for the new product and what's the same as for an older product. This way the new product's components can be slotted into already available families of parts. This is an excellent head start in processing a quote or new product development, giving an increase in speed by a factor ranging from about 2 to 10.

Since the other two methods of forming families of parts are applicable only to past or existing products, it is impossible to derive this type of advantage with them. It would be like trying to navigate a winding road using only your automobile's rearview mirror for guidance.

RELATIONSHIPS OF GT FAMILY OF PARTS GROUPINGS TO CYCLE TIME EVALUATIONS

Now that we have family of parts techniques, how do we make use of them? We use them for two categories of productivity improvement, both involving cycle time reductions. The first is ease of preproduction planning, and the second is more effective processing of parts through the factory through emulating flow manufacturing.

Using GT with Preproduction Planning

Preproduction planning cycle time is reduced by using family of parts designations as a pointer for exactly what design and process planning must address. Family of parts technique makes it possible to use existing planning when the task is identical to one already conceived for a part made earlier. Likewise, if a previously created design is virtually the same as the current need, then there is no need to repeat the design activity. The greater the match between family of parts members, the lesser the work needed to modify an existing entity for use with the current need. It's very easy to visualize the time and effort savings that can be gained if we can find that an already existing part is within a family of parts roster. All that's needed is to find the siblings, and we do that via the three methods described previously.

Using GT to Emulate Flow Manufacturing for More Efficient Operations

Processing parts through the factory more effectively by emulating flow manufacturing becomes possible if we're making components that require similar processes with similar tooling. When this happens we can batch-load dissimilar parts to be made on the same equipment with only minimal disruptions for minor jig and fixture modifications.

The area where job shops are inefficient compared with flow manufacturing is in the transfer of materials from work station to work station. The inefficiency occurs because we very frequently have to change the devices on the machines that hold the material to be processed because of the varying nature of their geometries. Naturally, in flow manufacturing this occurs much less frequently, because we are making large quantities of identical parts. To emulate this flow manufacturing efficiency in a job shop, we would want to find parts from virtually all end use products that have matching or similar geometries. If we can use the same fixtures over and over again for making the parts, then the inefficiency is relegated to only the assembly and test operations. This would make it possible to reduce cycle time, thus increasing the productive output of the factory over a given period of time. This is where competitive advantages can occur.

Establishing families of parts and using the principle of sameness make it possible to group parts for manufacturing in such a way that setups on the various machines require only small adjustments, rather than major, as the various orders are processed through the factory. For example, we saw in the chain code discussion that we ended up with a washer-type family, with all members requiring the same manufacturing process. The difference was that siblings were denoted by different part numbers and hence were probably of different sizes. The variation can be accommodated on the lathes, grinders, and other tools by using easily expanded and contracted holding fixtures, much like multispan plumber's wrenches or a pair of vise grips. With such ingenuity, the setup change from one work order to the next is minimal and for the work station in question we are approaching flow manufacturing. This is the reason for working to find similarities. The payoffs in cost reduction and productivity improvement are large.

If we take this concept of batching a bit further, we ask ourselves, Why only set up a lathe or a grinder to handle a family of parts? Why not set up the entire production flow to handle the family of parts? Why not, indeed? We should, and we do, to really emulate flow manufacturing.

Most job shops are set up with lathe departments, drill departments, grinder departments, weld departments, etc. For a company that isn't using GT principles and has no plans for doing so, this is a good way of organizing work. People who habitually work in the lathe department can become very proficient at running lathes, and similar benefits result when people stay put in other departments. Workers become very good at running their own sets of equipment and making setups as required. But no one would surmise that such a company is approaching flow manufacturing efficiencies. If it wants to do that, and it should, then it needs to emulate flow manufacturing layout as well as procedures.

Recall that in the chain-code example there were three distinct families of parts. Each of these families had a very regular pattern of manufacturing, with some minor variations for special requirements. We know that if each one of the siblings within the families were large enough, we would set up a flow line to manufacture it. However, that not being the case, the different siblings were treated as individual orders to be processed through a job shop in a department-by-department process plan. But why not say that when grouped together, then the entire family of parts can be treated as sufficient volume for flow manufacturing? This is exactly what we do. We use the techniques described above for making single machines work as if they were within a flow manufacturing scenario, with "universally" adjustable fixtures; we make them apply for the entire process line. We go so far as to physically move equipment around the factory to place all the equipment necessary to make the product in a sequential, flow-type layout; and we create a flow manufacturing cell for manufacture of the specific family of parts. This breaks up the traditional job shop departmental layout in favor of cells dedicated to customer needs. This is a clever idea that has proven to shorten cycle times by up to 5 times over that experienced in the old job shop way. One of the major ways this happens is that transfer times from operation to operation are drastically shortened because all of the processes needed to make the product are grouped togeher, so the travel distances and times are physically reduced. Handling time in many cases approaches zero. This is indeed cycle time and productivity improvement.

There are some other very visible benefits gained by this approach. First, we create a sense of ownership within the people who are assigned to the cell. This happens because the operators get to see the manufacture of an entire product through all of its processes. We also see much more self-initiated cross training, because people understand that to advance their careers, they need to be more valuable to their companies and hence need to gain more skills. What better way than by practicing on the products within the geometric bounds of their work area.

Another visible benefit is the simplification of scheduling. Now, all that the MRP II system has to do is schedule the product to the work cell, needing to know only the portal-to-portal cycle time necessary to do the job. Everything becomes simpler. Material goes to the work cell and remains there until it is finished. This also makes it simpler to check progress and take corrective action if required. No longer do managers and schedulers have to wrestle with the complexities of many departments needing to be coordinated. Now they deal only with one, thus simplifying the control task substantially. All of the above advantages are true and proven in practice. However, there is a school of thought that says that by rearranging the factory to create work cells we end up with underutilized equipment. After all, that's why job shops always grouped their equipment together, so that they could work on many different types of products and hence keep the machines busy.

There are two fallacies to this argument. The first fallacy is that long setup times in traditional job shops (because invariably the next work order scheduled will not be similar to its predecessor) significantly detract from run time. Thus, the machines aren't running all the time. In fact, years of observation show that machines in family of parts–constructed cells run about the same amount of time as machines in traditional layouts. Thus, there is no disadvantage for machine utilization with cellular layouts.

The second fallacy is that keeping the machines running more of the time equates with greater profitability. This is actually not true. Total portal-to-portal cycle time reduction equates with greater profitability, not longer machine run times. The ability to shorten the cycle between order placement and shipping to the customer is the only factor for improving profits. Everything else that happens in the area of run time is simply suboptimization and needs to be avoided.

To suboptimize costs time and money and doesn't really shrink the overall cycle time. It is like the critical path scheduling strategy. Those things that happen internal to the critical path lead times have no bearing on getting the job done to schedule, and therefore little effort needs to be applied to making them perform better. To do so only creates more waiting time. Think of an avenue in a city with virtually every intersection controlled by a traffic light. What is the purpose of accelerating at a rapid rate only to have to stop at the next corner for another red light? It is much better to get in synchronous flow with the traffic signal time sequence and thereby create a steady velocity. Using this analogy, running a machine tool all-out to make product only to have it piled up in front of a down-the-line work station is waste. It is simpler and cheaper to let the machine remain idle and reapply the personnel to other tasks. There is no benefit to suboptimizing by striving to have the machine always running.

We can see that from a strategy viewpoint GT cells make sense for improving profitability via shorter cycle times and a simplified scheduling algorithm. If that were the only reason to employ the GT cellular layout concept, it would still be an excellent strategy. However, I believe there is an even more compelling reason to use GT cellular layouts. It is the development of people's capacity to be better, more proficient employees.

Look at what happens when we set up GT cells. We are in effect creating small enterprises dedicated to making and selling a specific family of parts. We end up with a very manageable group of people and facilities dedicated to the specific product line. People can see the entire process from start to finish. They become aware of all the peculiarities of making the family of parts, and in effect become expert in all things about it. They can also appreciate the external customer's needs more readily, because they are no longer many layers removed from the ultimate user. They can see results of decisions faster. They become more adept at participative team performance. They truly become owners, stakeholders, in the entire process.

Nothing breeds creativity and resultant improvements better than considering oneself to be attached to the enterprise for one's personal success. By being part of a team operating a family of parts cell, one that is practically bounded, the members have a sense of ownership and thus a stake in its success. We see considerable improvements in the rate of suggestions and interest in the entire process. People try harder if they feel they have a personal stake in the success of what they're doing. It's human nature to do so. It's hard to put a value on this, but it's certainly greater than zero and must be considered as a significant competitive benefit for applying GT cellular concepts. This is team building for free. The money for GT cellular layouts is already cost-justified; it is icing on the cake, and what makes companies world class.

In this chapter we've seen how scheduling and cycle times affect productivity. We have explored how schedules are set and how cycle times are applied to schedules in an integrated fashion. We also observed how cycle times and schedules are integrated into productivity improvement strategies.

We defined and explored the drivers that implement work at the work station—specifically, the MRP II family of computer-controlled scheduling algorithms. As it turns out, this is one of the most sophisticated procedures in the entire manufacturing process, aimed at getting resources to converge on the work station to achieve the value-added goals of manufacturing.

To understand scheduling, we explored the evolution of MRP, just-in-time (JIT), dispatching systems, the relationship of the perfect-quality ethic to JIT and scheduling, and the interrelationships of group technology (GT) with cycle time reduction and scheduling. We found that JIT is not a competitor with MRP II but rather an interesting subset of industrial engineering theory applied to factory effectiveness. We discovered that GT is a way of reducing cycle time and is also very compatible with the goals of MRP II and JIT.

Along the way, and integrated throughout, we found once more that the work station operator is the key to factory performance success, because what the operator is capable of doing is directly responsible for the output of the factory. If all the systems put into play do not make it easier for the operator to accomplish his or her mission—i.e., to make products—then all is for nothing.

Chapter 6

Techniques for Developing Tools, Jigs, and Fixtures

We have discussed aspects of design, quality, scheduling, and the methodologies of instructing work stations on how to do work. Now it is necessary to delve deeper into the development of those devices that are vital for performing work at the work stations and ways of facilitating that development.

So far we have seen how to describe the work that will be done at various work stations and the sequence of doing it. But we haven't precisely described how the work is done. We have stated that the work station gets instructions on how to perform work and have made the assumption that the operator knows how to set up the work to do the value-added job. This may or may not be a correct assumption. It is entirely possible that the operator can set the workpiece on the work station without any additional information or technical and supervisory support. It is also entirely probable that different operators will set the same job up differently if not instructed how to do the job the way the company prefers. These scenarios do unfold in many factories where it is left to the skill of the operator to decide how best to present the work to the machine. I doubt that many managers subscribe to this strategy if optimizing the work flow is a priority. Skilled machinists do pride themselves in making do with general-purpose securing devices for clamping a part to a machine table and then machining it to drawing requirements. However, an increasing percentage of manufacturing operations are requiring development of more specific methodologies of securing the workpiece to the process equipment and transforming it physically to a finished product. The effort of developing those methodologies makes up *tool, jig, and fixture design*, and that's what we will explore now.

WHAT ARE TOOL, JIGS, AND FIXTURES?

Recall that the basic tenets of manufacturing are twofold: (1) know how to make the product, and (2) know how long it should take to do so. This implies that we have detailed knowledge of the process including how to hold the part during manufacture and what devices will be used in the transformation process. It further implies that considerable thought has been applied in determining what we will do. In fact, this is the third part of the design process described in Chapter 2 on design, the *manufacturing facilities design*.

Manufacturing facilities design comprises the specific designs for tools, jigs, and fixtures and many times also processes that are necessary to perform the work at the work station. This design work is as complex as the design of the product itself. It is a commonplace that for any product there are more designs for jigs, tools, and fixtures than there are for the product being produced—how many more depending on the product. We can safely say that there will be at least twice as many associated tool, jig, and fixture designs as there are product designs, and in some instances as many as 10 times more. We can see that tool, jig, and fixture design is an enormous task and not one to be treated lightly. In fact, the bulk of productivity improvements in businesses today emanate from clever approaches to tool, jig, and fixture designs.

Definitions

Unfortunately, the terms tools, jigs, and fixtures are erroneously used interchangeably. They are mistakenly thought to be identical in meaning. Of course they're not, and to treat them so unnecessarily clouds discussions of the topic. Let's establish the definitions of these terms:

jig: A small device, rather simple, of a semipermanent nature used for supporting a workpiece on the work station, so that value added tasks can be performed.

fixture: A device that is precisely designed to support a workpiece on a work station so that value-added tasks can be performed in an optimal manner. A fixture is more specialized than a jig and is also designed to be used over and over again in connection with the designated tasks. It is typically associated with complex setups and correspondingly longer production runs. Sometimes fixtures are so complex that they constitute specialized additions to generic machine tools or processing stations used to make the product.

tool: A device, either simple or complex, that is used to actually perform the value-added work in conjunction with a machine or process line. Creating a tool to produce the desired results usually requires complex design analysis.

Jigs

Jigs can be an on-the-spot creation of the operator to fasten the workpiece to the work station. Setting up a jig is creativity in its most direct form and tends to be reactive to a need rather than proactive. The operator observes the task to be performed, visualizes how the workpiece ought to be presented to the tool, and then conceives of a way of doing it and sets out to assemble the jig as expeditiously as possible. Many times only a core of an idea exists and the operator ad-libs her way to the final solution as the availability of suitable materials and resources manifests itself. We'll use the hammer example once more to illustrate this ad hoc creative principle.

Example. Let's assume that we need to position the hammer shaft to repair a cracked weld where the head and the shaft are joined. Since we don't expect to have to do too much of this type of work, elaborate fixture design is not a viable solution. Instead, we would opt for a simple solution using existing materials and devices. First we need to conceive of how we would fix the hammer, and then develop a simple methodology for doing so. You might think that there needs to be a discipline to codify the selected resolution of the problem, and, yes, there should be. But it oughtn't be a process requiring lots of documentation and certification. Remember, we are trying to fix an existing situation, and not incur costs to the point where it is more economical to scrap the cracked hammer and start all over again.

The Problem: The tack weld securing the hammer head to the shaft exhibits a crack as revealed by a routine dye penetrant test. Two things have to be done. First, we have to discern the root cause of the crack and take corrective action to prevent reoccurrence. We will not go into that process here; rather, we will assume that the root cause issue is being addressed elsewhere. Second, we have to determine how the defective hammers will be repaired. Whatever repair procedure is decided upon, it will be documented via the process control procedures already established for the company. This way the data do not remain ad hoc, and procedures will not have to be relearned every time the same situation or a similar one occurs.

The Fix: We have a cracked weld. A probable solution decided upon by the process engineer would very likely call for the crack to be ground out, retested with penetrant, re-tack-welded (probably by hand, rather than by automated process), ground smooth to a cosmetically acceptable finish, and finally subjected to yet another dye penetrant test to prove that the repair was sound. We'll see how this entire procedure requires nothing more specialized than a jig to hold the hammer.

The Jig: Remember, a jig is a simple device. In this case the operator need not invent anything special. Probably all that's needed is a V-block sufficiently high above the work space, with a pair of C-clamps to hold the V-block onto the table, and another pair of C-clamps to hold the hammer in the V-block. Since this equipment is readily available at the work station, there is no need to instruct the operator to use these general-purpose jigs. Ninety-nine times out of a hundred the operator will proceed to do what we just described and get on with the task of repairing the hammer(s). Of course, management has to be prepared to assist the operator's thought process, as required, to assure success.

Sometimes the process is not as clear-cut as the one described in the example. Perhaps the right V-block is not present in inventory; then the operator will have to go further afield to achieve a solution. When this happens, we need to be sure that the operator has received enough training and has had enough similar experiences to jury-rig an acceptable solution. We would hope that the operator has received some value engineering training (we will explore value engineering later in this chapter) and is thus able to discern the problem and formulate a solution. For the hammer difficulty, the solution may be as simple as clamping the defective assembly off the edge of the workbench, thus making the cracked head accessible for the necessary grinding and welding. Here the jig is even further simplified, to just one pair of C-clamps.

Jigs are always simple, expedient devices that solve the here-and-now problem with very little prethought. They also are used primarily for one-time fixes and are usually not meant to become specialty devices for repeat or permanent use; that's the domain of fixtures.

Fixtures

Fixtures perform the same function as jigs, but with two important differences: they are permanent in nature, and they are optimal solutions for a process. A jig, on the other hand, is often thought of in connection with a repair process, something that wasn't planned for in the first place. A fixture is most often predesigned to make the manufacturing process more efficient and hence less costly. Fixtures are truly phase 3 design items that need to be designed before the project is launched in the factory. Let's follow the development of a fixture, from concept through actualization.

For the hammer example again, let us refer to the route sheet in Figure 3-5. In operation 30, at assembly station 1, we see that we need to assemble the head to the handle and that the necessary tasks are thread fitting and tack welding. If we were making only a few pieces, say, fewer than 100, it probably wouldn't be cost-effective to design and build a fixture for this operation. But because that is not the case—we are, in fact, required to produce 10,000 pieces—there is a definite advantage in fixturizing the operation. We are trying to remove as much non-value-added time from the operation as possible and at the same time trying to shorten the value-added time through efficient utilization of materials and processes. Thus, the design goal is to eliminate non-value-added time and to minimize actual work performance time. For the hammer example, we need to examine the process to be performed and try to fixturize it to make it easy and fast.

First, what are the goals we need to achieve? They are probably the following:

1. Easily thread the shaft to the head.
2. Tack-weld the head to the shaft so that the threaded handle doesn't back out during use.
3. Minimize the times for both.

With these goals in mind, we can start to visualize how we can approach a solution. Obviously, with 10,000 pieces we are going to need some sort of automated approach, but it has to be something fairly common since 10,000 really isn't enough volume to justify a fully automated transfer station type of device. Most likely, our solution would have to be a combined operator-machine approach. We can envision some kind of device whereby there are two simple progressive feeds—one for the handle and one for the hammer head—loaded by one or two operators and coming together at an assembly station. Here the hammer or the handle can be rotated onto the other part, which is held stationary. Then the tack welding is done. Finally, an operator off-loads the finished hammer assembly. The fixture would have to be designed to align both the head and handle correctly during the loading process.

Obviously, there are many approaches that would achieve a satisfactory solution. The key points to keep in mind are that the solution has to be doable in the specific factory and that it needs to meet the economic constraints of the factory in order to make a profit. For this reason, fixture design, like product design, goes through several iterations and design reviews to continually optimize the results until a consensus is arrived at. Very rarely is a fixture designed and approved without some iteration. The iteration might be as simple as the methods engineer's discussing concepts with the work station operators, or as involved as establishing a concurrent design team as described in Chapter 2.

Let's look at one possible solution, of which Figure 6-1 is a schematic diagram. It shows hammer heads loaded onto a carousel mating with shafts on an intersecting carousel. When the mate is made, the handle is power-threaded into the head. Then, before both carousels are indexed again, the head and the top of the shaft are tack-welded with a commercial tack welder. Then the finished assembly is lifted out of the merged fixture by an operator.

This is an example of a semiautomated process that should be sufficient for a medium-volume production run. With this schematic in mind, the methods engineer can consult with shop operations people to see if they can live with this sort of process, and also look for improvements. The methods engineer would also discuss the concept with industrial engineering to get a feel for the time cycle involved. There would be no sense proceeding further if this operation as conceived appeared to require more time than the totally manual method of the operator's threading the shaft into the head and then placing the assembly into a holding fixture and tack-welding it. In fact, the time savings would have to be sufficient to also justify the cost of purchasing and/or building the semiautomated line.

There are many points of debate in the schematic that we would try to iron out in the iterative process. First, of course, we would have to agree that the concept would work. For example, the handle needs to be threaded into the head. We might envision this being done by the operator stepping on a foot pedal to engage the handle and at the same time lift it into position to be spin-threaded into the head. In this scenario, the lifting and engaging is straightforward: the foot pedal can create enough force to push the handle to the threaded hole of the head. But we need to make sure that the handle and the head line up properly; otherwise, there is no way to successfully thread. We also have to assure ourselves that the spinning rubber wheels will create

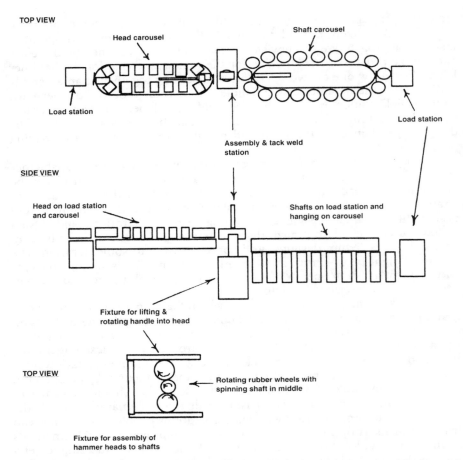

TOP VIEW

Head carousel

Shaft carousel

Load station

Load station

Assembly & tack weld
station

SIDE VIEW

Head on load station
and carousel

Shafts on load station and
hanging on carousel

Fixture for lifting &
rotating handle into head

TOP VIEW

Rotating rubber wheels with
spinning shaft in middle

Fixture for assembly of
hammer heads to shafts

Figure 6-1. Schematic diagram of hammer semiautomatic assembly fixture.

enough torque to successfully spin the handle into the head. The torque
would have to be great enough the even if there were slippage due to insufficient friction at the engagement end, the handle could still be driven home.
The torque values can be calculated and would be. The results of the calculations might lead to further iterations.

Some further iterations may involve the design of the product (the hammer) itself. For example, suppose it was determined that the motor necessary to rotate the rubber wheels would be too big and unmanageable to do
the job of spinning the shaft into the head, so that unless the design of the
shaft was changed, the concept would have to be abandoned. In this case, we
could see that asking the design engineer to add a knurl onto the hammer

might solve the problem. The knurl would give the handle more friction during the spin insertion process, possibly eliminating the unacceptable choice of a bigger motor. Of course, this could require another manufacturing step of putting on the knurl, or the material would have to be purchased with knurling already in place. In both cases, the cost of implementing the idea—adding the knurl—would have to be less than the savings associated with this form of spin assembly. As we can see, choices are usually plentiful. It is up to the formal or informal team to select the best way feasible considering the constraints placed upon it.

Also notice how iterative fixture design is. The methods engineer is engaged with the operators, design engineers, and cost accountants, to name a few, in the quest to solve the manufacturing optimization problem at the lowest cost possible. At the same time, the methods engineer is under a time constraint to produce the design and then the finished fixture as soon as possible. In fact, in many short–cycle time industries, such as semiconductors, time to produce the fixture becomes a more important constraint than cost. This is simply because the product life cycles are so short that there is a definite possibility of missing the market entirely if the product doesn't ship from the factory quickly after its introduction.

Tools

Tools have to be precisely designed for the function of creating the desired added value to the workpiece. Fixtures can be many and varied to carry out the function of holding, transferring, and positioning material to be transformed into a product. As we saw in the preceding discussion of fixtures, fixtures have to optimize these three functions, but there are no clear-cut right and wrong choices. Tools, on the other hand, need to be a precise fit with the intended outcome, and there can be only one intended outcome. Tools need to be specifically oriented to carrying out a specific function.

Tool design calls for an understanding of what the required outcome needs to be vis-à-vis the engineering drawing or instructions. For this reason tool design must be an exact follow-up to the design of the part itself. For example, suppose the hammer handle needed to have an undercut between the last thread and the shank portion. The drawing would so indicate, and operation 15 on the route sheet would refer to the drawing, which in turn would call for a special lathe tool that would machine the required undercut. For all practical purposes, the design engineer would select a common radii tool, and it would be called for by the BOM as an expendable item. If, however, the undercut had to be of a nonstandard configuration, then the tooling engineer would have to design a forming tool to cut the shank to the proper configuration. In any event, the tool would be *precise*, in that its proper utilization would result in the required undercut and, for all practical purposes, it would be suitable to perform only the one function.

Tool design starts with an understanding of the task to be performed. Knowing that, and the process to be used, the designer creates a tool that fits within the process equipment and has the necessary geometry and strengths to perform the designated task. Most often, the tool designer will download the CAD configuration of the part to be made with the tool and will use the same exact geometry for the interface surface between the tool and the raw material. With the proper in-feed and motions, the end result will be the inverse of the tool itself. A simple example would be a form tool used to polish a concave telescope mirror. The mirror itself will be concave, but the polishing tool will be convex. The important factors the mirror and the polishing tool have in common are shared radii and angle of curvature.

This points out another frequent issue in tool design. The designer quite often has to think of the inverse of the final form in designing the tool. For this reason, effective tool design is not intuitively obvious and takes considerable concentration. While fixture design presents an opportunity for brainstorming and group thinking, tool design tends to be practiced in solitude. Also, while fixture design often benefits from interaction with work station operators—e.g., in finding ways to minimize the fixtures' setup time and hence reduce waste—this is seldom the case with tool design. Good tool design is very closely tied in with the design of the product and is part of the requirements package dispatched to the work stations. Very seldom do operators partake in this phase of product realization. To ask them to do so would be tantamount to asking them to serve as design engineers. Good manufacturing practice, on the contrary, requires the operator to *use* the designated tool and to report back whether or not it produces the desired outcome. If not, then the tool designer has to analyze the process to understand why the tool has failed. This tends to be a lonely process involving complex geometry and static and dynamic forces, usually all beyond the knowledge and familiarity level of the operator.

THE PHASE 3 DESIGN PROCESS

We saw in Chapter 2 that design consists of three phases, all based on complying with the dictate of good design attributes. The interesting concept of *authorship* of design has changed design for the better in the last 10 to 15 years. With the realization of concurrent engineering as the preferred way of organizing preproduction work, we find that the three phases of design tend to merge so that design is less compartmentalized than before. This means that inputs from all functions are integrated, making it easier to achieve overall portal-to-portal optimization. The existence of a concurrent approach means that there is more iteration between the phases instead of simply a series effect whereby no manufacturing facilities (fixture or tooling) design takes place before the concept and producibility design phases are completed. The result of this concurrent engineering process is a work station design, a fixture design, and a tool design that are more compatible with the product design and are usually less expensive than when created under the series approach. It stands to reason that with a concurrent approach, designs at both ends of the spectrum are fine-tuned to get the best overall cost and performance synergism possible. This means that a product design can and should be modified to suit fixture and tool design as long as the modification doesn't compromise or degrade the original purpose of the design specification.

All phases of design are carried out as concurrently as possible. This saves a considerable amount of time and money. The concurrent approach also makes it easier to assure that decisions are not suboptimized, because it calls for members of all functions to be present on the team. In fact, the only real difference we should see in applying the concurrent approach would be who assumes the lead function, and that depends on what phase of design is being worked on. The first phase of design is the concept design, which is typically co-led by marketing and design engineering. The second phase of design is the producibility design, and that is usually led by design engineering. And the third phase, manufacturing facilities design, is normally headed up by manufacturing engineering. Each phase has its peculiarities, but for our purpose of understanding work station dynamics, the most critical to us is the third phase. Let's take a look now at how manufacturing facilities design, primarily concerned with designing fixtures and jigs, factors in the attributes of good design.

ATTRIBUTES OF GOOD DESIGN FACTORED INTO FIXTURE AND JIG DESIGN

The five attributes of good design apply to all three phases of design. All five attributes are important for fixture and jig design, some more than others. Figure 6-2 shows the relative importance of the attributes to fixture and jig design.

| | Applicable To | | Importance Compared to | |
Attributes of Good Design	Fixture Design	Jig Design	Concept Design	Producibility Design
1. Producibility	Major	Major	same	same
2. Simplicity	Major	Major	same	same
3. Lowest Feasible Cost	Major	Major	more	same
4. Esthetics	Minor	Micro-Minor	less	less
5. Ability to Meet Quality Requirements	Major	Major	less	less

Figure 6-2. Relative importance of the attributes of good design to fixture and jig design.

We see in Figure 6-2 that while all attributes must be complied with, some are significantly more important than others. This does not mean that less important attributes vis-à-vis fixtures and jigs can receive lesser attention, just that they may not have the go, no-go, kill-or-keep-the-project aspects of the other design attributes. They still need to be attended to as part of the process of creating the overall work plan for the customer's job order.

Example. A furniture cabinet top is glued to the cabinet and needs to be secured in place by a simple series of C-clamps while the glue dries. The clamps constitute a jig that would usually be designed by the operator; the jig does not have to be esthetically pleasing to do its work. But form usually does follows function. The simplest forms *are* for the most part more pleasing to the eye, but as it happens they tend to work better, too. So it is in this case. If a jig consists of a battery of different-sized C-clamps instead of clamps of a uniform size, it doesn't look nice, and it usually won't work as well. Why? Simply because the large C-clamps in the array can apply more pressure than the smaller ones, and hence the operator may mistakenly apply uneven pressure and the finished glue joint may not be uniformly strong across the entire length. In fact, the uneven pressure may cause wavelike distortions so that the top is not as flat as it should be. The possibility of a failed glue joint would be minimized by using esthetically pleasing, uniform-sized C-clamps, because the pressure applied would less likely be different from clamp to clamp.

There are indeed differences in importance of the various design attributes among the three phases of design. Of the five attributes, we see that producibility and simplicity are equal for all three phases. Lowest feasible cost is a major factor for fixture and jig design, as it is for producibility design. However, in concept design lowest feasible cost is not considered as important. We can explain this by recognizing that concept design must first satisfy the design functionality requirement before cost can be considered. It makes no sense having a lowest-cost product if it can't perform the intended function. To take it to the absurd level, it would be like having the lowest-cost jetliner by doing without the wings.

Now let's look at ability to meet quality requirements. This attribute is a major applicable factor for fixture and jig design but nonetheless is not as important as it is in concept design and producibility design. Why? Mainly, because both concept and producibility design will have major interfaces with the customer, while jig and fixture designs normally do not. But not in every case. Suppose a customer is interested in six sigma performance, which means zero defects. In order to achieve this level of performance, virtually everything the company needs to do would have to be approved by the customer, because the customer is ultimately paying for the service. And in realistic, pragmatic terms, this results in extra effort usually above the normal level expended by the company. So, in this scenario, ability to meet quality requirements would have the same level of importance to fixture and jig design as to producibility and concept design.

THE PRODUCTION OF FIXTURES, JIGS, AND TOOLS

The production of a company's products is controlled by the seven steps of the manufacturing system and governed by the Two Knows. What about the devices that the company needs to make its products—fixtures, jigs, and tools? In the past, this has been handled on an ad hoc, as needed basis, and so the record of success has been spotty. Now, with the advent of applications of manufacturing systems cornerstoned by MRP II, fixture, jig, and tool production and procurement are coordinated in the same manner as creation of designs and work station instructions. All three are handled in a similar manner but with some variations. Let's take a look.

Procurement of Tools

Tools are very seldom made in-house, especially cutting tools. High-speed steel, diamond-tipped, carbide, ceramic, and other tools are commercially designed and marketed through numerous firms specializing as tooling suppliers. Most tool suppliers carry extensive inventory of various geometries meant to fit virtually all toolholders used in numerous machine tools. With the wide variety of commercial enterprises selling tooling, there is no need for a company to manufacture its own tools. To obtain the proper tools, the engineer simply selects tools from a catalog and makes sure that the tools are part of the bill of materials for the work order. In this way the MRP II system handles the purchase of tooling as it does all other materials necessary to build the product.

Occasionally a firm needs to design a tool from scratch for a very particular reason. Perhaps a specific radius is needed to assure that a stress riser is not established in a very highly loaded structure. Most often, in these types of cases, the concurrent engineering team will call in the tool supplier and use its expertise to create a special tool for the purpose. Once again the tool requirement would be placed in the BOM and ordered with proper lead time via the MRP II system.

The Creation of Jigs

Jigs, as we know, are temporary fixtures of a relatively simple nature. The C-clamps of the glued furniture top example are jigs. The hallmark of jigs is that they are holding and positioning devices that normally allow no movement. This means that, once set, neither the part nor the process device it is attached to will move independently. Of course, it is possible for the jig to move during an operation. For example, V-blocks used to set a piece on the table of a vertical boring mill will rotate along with the part and table during the machining operation.

Since jigs are simple holding devices, they tend to be universal and can thus be purchased ready-made. It is a common practice to outfit a machining work station with a set of V-blocks and C-clamps and a host of other hold-down devices that the operator will use as required. Although the jigs may easily be stored in a cabinet at the work station, their distribution is not a matter of happenstance; to optimize productivity we want all uses of jigs to be preplanned and grouped for use with their mated job orders. The purpose of preplanning is to design the jig utilization beforehand and not on the spur of the moment when it is discovered that a jig is necessary. This way non-value-added time is avoided and the optimum application of jigs is better established.

Because of their relative simplicity, the design of hold-downs using jigs is very straightforward and accomplished as part of the development of the production method. The method sheet will specify how a part is to be held or positioned for the value-added work to be performed. It will specify what jigs to use and tell the operator where they are to be placed. Just as an automobile manufacturer will design a jack pad for lifting the chassis to change tires, design engineers should designate where hold-downs and other positioning devices are to be placed to assure proper manufacturing. This is becoming more and more prevalent now that concurrent engineering is becoming commonplace. This way we are assuring that the forces exerted during machining, cutting, welding, etc., are not being translated in such a manner that we end up with parts and products twisted and bent in ways that make them unusable.

The proper use of jigs is also an opportunity to instill feelings among the operators of belonging to a team. By making them part of the decision-making process of how jigs will be set to optimize a job, we are making use of their pragmatic experience for the benefit of the customer. We are minimizing the trial-and-error approach appreciably, as we have to do if we want short cycle times and six sigma quality results. When we encourage operators to be contributing members of the creative team of making the product better but with less cost, it's not surprising that most jig utilization improvements originate with the operators and not the engineers.

Fixture Development

Fixture development is very much akin to prototype development. A lot of work goes into the design of a device that will never be mass-produced. Fixtures are more complex than jigs by many orders of magnitude. In many instances they take as much design creativity and analysis as the company's products itself. Think of a fixture as a machine to position material in order for a value-added activity to occur. Sometimes the fixturing device dwarfs the value-added device and it is even difficult to tell where the line between the process and the fixture is. Automated assembly lines are good examples. The fixtures carry the parts to the assembly station, present them in proper aspect, release them into the assembly work center for value-added work, and then regain possession of them for transfer to the next station, at the same time perhaps changing their orientation.

Fixtures in themselves do not add value to the product. But without fixtures, particularly those used for complex assembly line and flow manufacturing, value added would be less effective and perhaps be unable to achieve design objectives. This is true because fixtures are the paramount items for assuring that the tools can be used to their design intentions in creating the product. If we look at drawings and other instruction that define shape, form, and function, we see that the typical dimension is referenced to a particular datum point in space. It is the fixture's job to assure that the tool can be presented to the material so that the corresponding points match in spatial location according to the design specifications. This means that the design of a fixture requires an exacting understanding of the product it will support. It means that dimensions, obviously, have to be known and it has to be possible to comply with them.

A lesser known but equally important product design feature that has to be well understood is the elasticity factor. When raw material for a part is held in a fixture, it needs to be firmly supported so the process forces don't skew it out of alignment while the work is being performed. Beyond that, the fixture needs to hold the part with forces below the yield point of the material to assure no permanent set takes place after release of the part. To illustrate these last two points, let's look at a relevant example of constraints to be considered during fixture design.

Example. Suppose we are faced with the task of holding a stainless steel 36-in. outside diameter 2-in.-thick ring in place to machine concentrically to within ±0.0015 in. and putting in six equally spaced 0.25-in.-dia ±0.0005-in. holes perpendicular to the plane of the ring at a 35-in.-dia bolt circle. The production run is 2100 per day, and it is anticipated that the part will remain in production for a minimum of six months. We can see that this is a rather large ring and will have to be machined quickly at a rate of 700 per shift. The volume precludes manual placement of the part on the machine (most likely a CNC verticle boring mill (VBM) and requires a fixture design to both place the material on the machine and hold it during machining.

Judging from the tolerances presented, the part will have to be gripped in four places, 90 degrees apart, and the gripping pressure will have to be identical to keep the part in equilibrium. This is to assure that there is no uneven distortion, which would give the ring an ellipsoid shape after machining when the forces holding the ring in place are released. We will also have to obtain exact centering of the ring on the machine table with respect to the cutting tool so that both the inner and outer diameters are cut concentric to each other and are concentric to the imaginary center of the ring circle. These are the two major fixture design considerations to contend with.

Possibly, the solution would be to have a four-position gripper actuated by a four-position sensor switch on a transfer table. Here, when all four switches are contacted by the part (see Figure 6-3), it activates a hydraulic cylinder that extends the gripper assembly over the ring and then down over it. When the gripper assembly, in turn, contacts the sensor switches, another relay is closed, which then extends the gripper horizontally to grip the ring. The four grippers have load cells built into them to assure that only the programmed force is used to hold the rings. The gripper then lifts the ring and swings it through a 45-degree arc and places it on the machine tool table. The gripper then goes vertically down once more and, utilizing another set of load cells, this time placed vertically, holds the ring on the table with equal force on all four supports for machining. Concentricity on the machine is assured by design of the pivot arm of the gripper assembly in that it can only come to a stop over the machine table in the position where it is programmed to do so. This is done in the manner used to fine-position machine tool beds, such as with precision ball screws. Finally, after machining is completed, the gripper lifts the ring and rotates another 45 degrees and drops the ring into a specially designed collector bin. Then the gripper retracts and rotates in the same direction another 270 degrees and resets for the next ring transfer and position.

The completed fixture design comprises all the components necessary for the gripper with its load cells; the transfer table, including the platform with the sensor switches; the finished ring off-load bin; and the rotating table that moves the gripper assembly through its three active positions.

We now have a scheme for accomplishing the fixture design task, and we've seen that the tasks encumbers many facets of design and is just as complex as the product design itself. In fact, in the example portrayed the task for designing and building the device envisioned for the solution to the ring problem may be even more complex a design task than the product it supports. And by no means is this an unusual occurrence.

Operators have little direct input into fixture design. Since this design is typically as complex as the product design, the operators' inputs would be the same; e.g., an advisory or sounding-board role. In the case of the ring machining, as part of the concurrent engineering team being led by a manufacturing engineer, the operator would be responsible for pragmatic evaluations for feasibility of the proposed fixture on the shop floor. However, it is important to include and not exclude any member of the production team from the fixture design exercise. Good fixture design requires a feel for the process to be performed, and while engineers may be able to define forces and deflections as well as moments of inertia and other pertinent technical realities of the situation, it isn't unheard of to have a winning idea come from the operator who lives with this type of situation day in and day out.

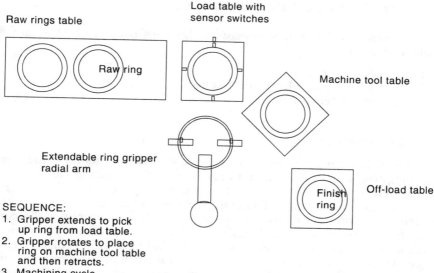

Raw rings table

Load table with sensor switches

Machine tool table

Extendable ring gripper radial arm

Off-load table

SEQUENCE:
1. Gripper extends to pick up ring from load table.
2. Gripper rotates to place ring on machine tool table and then retracts.
3. Machining cycle.
4. Gripper extends to pick up ring from machine tool table.
5. Gripper rotates to off-load table and releases ring.
6. Gripper continues cloackwise rotation and retracts to start position.

Figure 6-3. Fixture for positioning rings on a machine tool table.

HOW VALUE ENGINEERING IMPROVES COST OPTIMIZATION OF FIXTURE DESIGN

As we can see, good fixture design, like good product design, requires a creative and yet a team approach to achieve the best and most cost-effective solution. One of the best ways of achieving a cost-effective grouping of solution alternatives is through the *value engineering* technique. Let's look at this process and see how it can be applied in a concurrent engineering scenario.

What is value engineering? A useful definition is provided by the Society of American Value Engineers:

Value engineering is the systematic application of recognized techniques to identify the functions of a product or service and to provide those functions at the lowest total costs.

Value engineering deals with the utility of the offering as well as its cost and strives to optimize both for the benefit of the company and its customers. However, value engineering is not another name for cost improvement or cost reduction, because it focuses on making the product better, not simply cheaper.

THE VALUE ENGINEERING PROCESS

The value engineering process consists of three distinct phases. These are, in sequential order:

1. Identification of goals
2. Brainstorming to select a methodology
3. Plan recommendations

Identification of Goals

The concurrent engineering team is likely to conclude that a value engineering project is needed when it appears that a formalized methodology is required to solve a particularly perplexing design problem for either a fixture or the end product. The concurrent engineering team defines the functions the product or fixture needs to fulfill. It also defines the constraints the design is under. And finally, some sort of value measurement scheme is assigned that defines success or failure of the project. These three items (functionality, constraints, and value measurements) are defined so that the goals of the value engineering exercise can be properly focused.

Brainstorming to Select a Methodology

With the goals defined, we can focus on looking for ways to improve the product or process. We do this typically by *brainstorming*, which is a formalized way of putting forth ideas for improvement.

Brainstorming yields lists of ideas, some better than others, for the particular problem we are trying to solve. Brainstorming techniques are described in many project management books and articles. Briefly, the techniques is to allow each member of the team a turn to put forth a suggestion on how to solve the problem. This is then recorded for all participants to see. Quite often, the previous suggestions act as a catalyst to stimulate additional suggestions. Many rounds are accomplished, giving each team member virtually unlimited opportunities to make suggestions. The last round occurs when no team member has any additional suggestions. There is one very important caveat to keep in mind during the listing phase: do not criticize any idea; nor should an idea be praised. At this stage the goal is to list as many ideas related to the subject at hand as possible. We do not want to inhibit free flow of ideas by passing judgment as soon as one is put forth. It is not unusual for an idea that at first appears trivial or irrelevant to really have a virtue that leads to the ultimate solution of the problem.

The next step is to rank the listed ideas. One way of doing this is through a voting method whereby each team member ranks each idea and then the scores are tabulated to give total ranking. The total ranking is put on a Pareto plot for ease of visualization. The ideas are then evaluated with the highest score first, then the second highest score, and so forth, until the team feels that there are enough valid ideas to solve the problem. In practice, usually fewer than half of all ideas put forth need to be evaluated to solve the problem.

Plan Recommendations

In order to recommend a series of steps toward solving the problem at hand, the first thing is to make sure that all ideas presented are prioritized. The question we ask when prioritizing is what ideas are most likely to result in the improvements sought. Every idea is measured against a fictional stand of 100% certainty to yield the desired results. Therefore, we grade each idea much like a judge rating a diver's performance—not against one another, but against a perfect score. This way each idea is evaluated objectively and independent of all others.

With the evaluations done, it is a simple matter to list the ideas in priority order form the most likely to yield desired results to the least likely. Now, the task turns to the company's ability to implement the ideas. The simplest way to do this is to list the steps necessary to implement each idea and the resources required. You might wonder why this is necessary. If the number 1 idea has the greatest chance of success, why not just adopt it? In a perfect world with unlimited resources, the answer would be yes, go and do it. However, suppose idea number 1 requires a sum of money beyond the company's ability to spend. This means that number 1 may be the sure-fire way to go but the company can't use it because of a lack of financial resources, so we are forced to look at the number 2 suggestion. Idea number 2 may not have the same probability of success as number 1, but it may be affordable to try. In that case, trying idea number 2 makes sense. It is within the company's achievable range and the probability of success is probably worth the risk.

A professional sports analogy can illustrate using an idea with a lesser probability of success. The best way to win a professional baseball game is to have your pitcher toss a no-hitter. Then the probability of success is very high. However, the chosen idea requires a superior pitcher who demands an enormous salary, which may be beyond the team's resources. The next choice is to have a less capable pitcher who can minimize the number of runs scored by the opposition. The strategy is to score runs and hope the other team's offense is just a little bit less effective than yours. It makes no difference in the league standing how you win and by what margin. So if the number 2 strategy allows the team to pay the salary of the pitcher who is relatively good but not superior, then there is a reasonable probability that the team can win. Lacking the resources to afford the no-hitter pitcher, this is the best the team can do and what it should do.

With the prioritization of ideas set down alongside their costs in time, funding, process capabilities, and skills defined, the team then makes recommendations to senior management on how to proceed and why the choices were made. The immediate task is to sell the recommendation to the decision makers using the logic of pragmatic realism described above.

There rarely are absolutely right or wrong choices. Normally the choices need to be based on this pragmatic philosophy. Value engineering forces the company to make these realistic choices, and by doing so it often prevents the company from tackling tasks it ought not. Another way of explaining this pragmatic choice system is to say we can quantify value. We can say value is defined as the sum of positive aspects divided by negative aspects of the product or service. It is up to the organization producing the product or service to determine what constitutes positive and negative value. The following equation applies:

$$\text{Value} = \frac{x_{a1} + x_{a2} + \ldots + x_{an}}{x_{b1} + x_{b2} + \ldots + x_{bn}}$$

where x = magnitude of the value
  a = positive perceived value
  b = negative perceived value

An outcome greater than 1 defines an acceptable product or service. Conversely, an outcome less than 1 indicates an unacceptable product or service. Through quantitative analysis used to evaluate ideas for achieving the desired goals, we can more often than not have a higher success rate than by operating by chance alone. Therefore, the purpose of value engineering is to identify the project choices that create the highest number greater than unity possible for the value equation. We will see in the succeeding sections how the values of the unknowns in each term are determined through value engineering techniques, and how these techniques give us a better chance of achieving the highest value greater than unity.

VALUE ENGINEERING TECHNIQUES

Value engineering techniques are focused on finding the proper aspects of a product or service to improve. The techniques are primarily aimed at defining what actions should be taken to achieve the desired end results. We need to do this because properly aiming company activities toward efforts having significant payback is the most difficult thing for management to do. We are trying to "aim, aim, aim, then shoot," as opposed to the often tried but rarely successful philosophy of "shoot, shoot, shoot, then aim" that companies all too often fall prey to. These same techniques used for the planning steps can and should be used later on to verify that the improvements made were indeed true improvements.

The functional analysis and quantitative analysis techniques are long-standing methodologies used by teams employing value engineering to solve process and product improvement problems. As such they are considered the core of the value engineering process. We used brainstorming to get to solutions for the process or product that needs to be upgraded. Now, for each of the brainstorming ideas we want to evaluate, we need to go down one more level of specificity to really fine-tune the process. We do that with functional analysis and quantitative analysis.

The techniques of functional analysis and quantitative analysis, and the associated measurements processes, appear in many textbooks. The explanation that follows is based loosely on that put forth in the article authored by David J. DeMarle and M. Larry Shillito in "The Handbook of Industrial Engineering," 2nd ed. (Gavriel Salvendy, ed., published by the Institute of Industrial Engineers and John Wiley & Sons, New York, 1992).

Function Analysis

The purpose of function analysis is to determine whether a function of the offered service or product is primary or secondary. Think of it as a must or a want: a primary function is a must, in that the entity cannot exist without it; whereas a secondary function is a "nice to have," a want of varying degrees of desirability. Then determine whether the function can be eliminated or improved to the advantage of the customer and the company. (Note: The actual improvement investigation and planning occurs in later phases of value engineering.)

Generally, the primary function cannot be eliminated, only improved. Keep in mind that the goals identification and brain storming processes have identified the function to be improved or eliminated. Now, we want to see what subsets of the function can be improved or eliminated, and in what order of priority to give us the best bang for our buck.

A primary is a component or subcomponent that has to exist for the product or service to exist.

Example. For a hammer to be able to drive nails it has to have a head.
1. Function: Hammer—drive nails (component—primary).
2. Function: Hammer head—impact nail in driving action (subcomponent—primary)

A secondary is a subcomponent that may or may not exist for the product or service to exist, but in some way enhances the item's ability to do what it is supposed to.

Example. The color of the hammer head is black except for the strike disk.
1. Function: Hammer head—impact nail in driving action (subcomponent—primary).
2. Function: Hammer head color—give esthetically pleasing appearance to the tool (subcomponent—secondary)

All primary functions must remain in place but are candidates for improvement. All secondary functions can be eliminated and should be unless their removal lowers the tangible or intangible worth of the product or service.

The function analysis process begins by breaking down all products and/or services into their basic components and subcomponents. A common technique, described in the DeMarle and Shillito article, is the "verb/noun process." The process works as follows:

1. Use only one verb and one noun to describe the function.
2. Verb answers the question "What does it do?"
3. Noun answers the question "What does it do it to or with?"
4. Avoid passive or indirect verbs such as provides, supplies, gives, is, etc.
5. Avoid goal-like verbs such as improve, maximize, optimize, etc.
6. For each component or subcomponent make lists of two-word (verb/noun) combinations that describe the function(s).
   a. Example: For an electric stove burner element—create heat, emit light, cook food, color room, etc.
7. List the word combinations in priority order that best describes the most important function of the component or subcomponent.
   a. Note: It is entirely possible for a component or subcomponent to perform more than one function, either independently (*example:* range burner—create heat and color room) or dependently (*example:* create heat, cook food—can't do the latter without the former).
8. Use the word combinations to evaluate the functions of the components and subcomponents for their relative importance to the product's or service's reason for existing. Then determine if it is a primary or secondary subcomponent function. And finally, rank in importance for improvement priorities.

Let's use the DeMarle and Shillito verb/noun process to describe the process improvement selection procedure for an ordinary light bulb. Remember, we are trying to determine what is most important and what is least important in the functionality of the light bulb in order to set task projects in place to improve it. The last thing we want to do is end up working on a facet of the light bulb's functionality that has a low relative importance.

We make up a chart with the headings shown in Figure 6-4. First, we list the subcomponents. Then, for each component we create a verb/noun pair and list the pairs in the function column. As you can see, it is quite probable that each component will have more than one function attached to it. However, not all of the functions will be primary functions.

Now, with the Subcomponent and Function columns completed, we skip over to the Primary/Secondary column and determine whether each function is primary or secondary. We do this on the basis of our familiarity with the product and some old-fashioned common sense.

Next, we rate the relative importance, and from that we obtain the improvement order. Relative importance is just that, a scaling of how important each function is to the effective performance of the light bulb's mission.

This is not a forced ranking. In fact, it is permissible to have as many ties as the group doing the ranking think is appropriate. With the relative importance set, it is a simple matter to prioritize the order of project work to make improvements. It is simply in the order of highest score first. Note that we have made no attempt to determine the firm's capability to carry out one project as opposed to another, so the improvement rankings are assumed to be equally achievable. We do not appear to have a case where the company is forced to reject a higher-ranked item for lack of resources.

Note that no attempt was made to use a quantifying process to determine primary or secondary functions, or relative importance, or priority for improvement. It was all done subjectively by simply having the concurrent engineering team express their opinions and come to a consensus. This is not an oversight. In order to use quantifying techniques, it is necessary to understand the relationships of the subcomponents to each other. Which means we would have to understand all of the variables of design, manufacture, and use. Then we would have to evaluate a host of other environmental and situation factors. All of which are beyond the pale of reasonable expectations of handling unknowns for creating pragmatic solution matrices.

My experience has shown that a subjective group evaluation made by knowledgeable people (in the example, that would be lighting engineers, manufacturers of light bulbs, and marketers of light bulbs) will come up with very representative and practical ratings that can then be used to pursue improvements. Any more effort to achieve more precise ratings is a waste.

Once a priority listing is made, the final part of functional analysis can be done. The finale is deciding whether a change can be made to improve the product or service from the viewpoint of both the customer and the company. For primary subcomponents, the decision is whether a modification is feasible and desirable. By definition, a primary subcomponent function can-

Component: Incandescent Electric Light Bulb

Subcomponent to improve	Function	Relative importance (10 = high, 1 = low)	Primary/secondary	Order
Globe	Contain vacuum	8	P	3
	Decorative shape	1	S	8
Filament	Flow path	6	S	6
	Resistance element	9	P	2
	Emit light	10	P	1
Socket	Hold parts	7	S	5
	Transmit electricity	8	P	3
	Secure globe	5	S	7

Figure 6-4. Function analysis process value selection.

not be eliminated. The decision for secondary subcomponents is whether the functions can be eliminated. If the answer is no, then the next question is whether a modification is feasible.

Constraint Analysis

Functional analysis gave us a breakdown of the part or process we are trying to improve by creating primary and secondary categories and rankings. We now delve deeper. Constraint analysis looks at the results of the functional analysis to see if there are any impediments that would affect adopting its recommendations.

For primary subcomponents and their functions, we need to check whether there are regulations, laws, codes, or standards that prohibit change or require extensive analysis before change is allowed. We also need to check whether the technology is available to make the desired change. Here we are once more looking to see whether the company can realistically do what it wishes with its current resources. The choice of how the product is made and will be made in the future needs to be considered. The same is true for services. Are they still relevant, and do they warrant further improvement efforts? The essence of the question the constraint analysis has to answer is, do the design and manufacturing procedures employed in the development of the product still apply? Or have new developments occurred that make them no longer relevant? For example a functional analysis may point out that a toaster can meet a new external influence requirement such as environmental compatibility by lowering the resistance of the heating elements; e.g., use less electricity (this assumes there is a need to conserve electricity to minimize fossil fuel burning). The constraint could be that to lower the resistance we can no longer toast bread in a reasonable time. Hence the constraint would probably preclude going forward with an otherwise acceptable solution.

For secondary subcomponents and their functions, quite often the functional analysis would recommend elimination. So, for this situation, the constraint analysis evaluates whether elimination is a net plus for the product or service. If it is not, then project work should be scheduled to improve the function.

Not all secondary characteristics can be readily quantified: some are *intangible* benefits, and we know instinctively that to say they have no value or lesser value is incorrect. For example, the globe of the electric light bulb could be candle flame–shaped instead of spheroid; does one shape have greater value than the other? There is no yes or no answer to that question. For this reason there is also room for subjective judgment to determine whether a change is worth the bother. It is easy to see that if we were in the decorator electric light bulb business, then optimizing how to produce candle flame–shaped bulbs would be important. Conversely, if we were making bulbs primarily for industrial purposes, say, oil refineries, the answer would be, no it's not important.

For the hammer example, the head as originally designed is black. A decision whether to devote finite resources to investigating a change in color would be handled by the concurrent engineering team with a marketing lead. Marketing would look for indications that color influences sales. If some sort of correlation were found, then there might be a reason to put forth an improvement project to have different color hammer heads. Perhaps the industrial engineering team member would be assigned to study the cost of manufacturing multicolor hammer heads to see if it is economically feasible. If it is, then it still comes down to playing a hunch as to whether there is a justification for making this change and initiating an improvement project. To reiterate, there is no right or wrong answer; the outcome of constraint analysis often depends more on hunches than on objective facts.

Constraint analysis follows no firm procedure except to simply list all the known changes that functional analysis has identified and then to ask the question, Are there any accompanying technological limitations or other factors that would preclude going forward with the recommended project? If there are none, the process goes forward. If the answer is yes, there are, then the concurrent engineering team needs to reach a consensus as to how to proceed based on the customer's and the company's needs.

Value Measurement

We've now gone from brainstorming to functional analysis to constraint analysis. We have rankings and modifiers of those rankings to the point where we are in danger of getting lost in trivialities. We need to have some sort of measurement to use as a value reference. In value engineering, we call this the value measurement technique. This technique is an attempt to evaluate the worth of any subcomponent with respect to all or to other specific components. It is used to validate the results of the function analysis and constraint analysis. It can be considered a sort of last check to make sure the subcomponents that are targeted for improvements are indeed the ones that have the higher intrinsic value for the customer and the company.

Again, attempts have been made to use numerical quantification techniques. These techniques help but do not have a true basis in the objective methods of science, and they have to be used with this in mind. They are attempts to make a subjective decision process as objective and impartial as possible. There are many regression analysis–type techniques that can be used. Most, in my opinion, are gross overkill. The goal is to be able to discern the value of one subcomponent's worth versus another's. Most of the time this relative worth is known to the people involved in the study because of their familiarity with the product or service. Otherwise, they wouldn't be members of the concurrent engineering team.

Probably the only two useful numerical techniques are also the simplest:

- Relative worth analysis
- Value ratio

Relative Worth Analysis

Relative worth analysis can be performed in two ways. The *total comparison method* consists of the following:

1. Select a subcomponent that can be given a worth value. Quite often, this would be a dollar value, for the sake of universal applicability. This is needed because we really *are* trying to compare apples and oranges.
2. Set a value for the selected subcomponent. Then construct a table showing whether or not all other subcomponents are of either greater or lesser value.
3. On a comparison basis, then assign a value to all other subcomponents.
4. The subcomponent with the highest value would then be the one that should be targeted for the first intensive look at improvement.

An alternative is the *one-on-one method*, in which the selected standard component is compared against only one other component:

1. If the standard is judged higher than the first comparison component, it is kept as the standard.
2. If the first comparison component is judged higher than the original standard, then it becomes the new standard.
3. The process is continued until the full gamut of comparisons are made, and whatever choice is left having the highest value at the end is given the highest priority for further investigation.
4. This process is continued after the first winner is retired and is iterated until there are no more choices to be made. The result is a relative ranking of all the subcomponents.

Figure 6-5 is an example of the total comparison method of relative worth analysis, using the light bulb functional analysis results. We will choose

Subcomponent	Function	Greater Than or Less Than	Dollar value
Globe	Contain vacuum	L	$0.85
	Decorative shape	L	$0.10
Filament	Flow path	L	$0.60
	Resistance element	L	$0.90
	Emit light	N/A	$1.00
Socket	Hold parts	L	$0.65
	Transmit electricity	L	$0.75
	Secure globe	L	$0.50

Figure 6-5. Total comparison method.

"emit light" as the standard subcomponent of the highest perceived value, and let it equal $1.00 for the cost of operating for a month. We will do the total comparison method first.

As expected, the rankings follow the relative importances of the function analysis (Figure 6-4). But note that we have interpolated between subcomponents that had equal relative importances in the function analysis. Again this is a subjective rating system. It is quite possible that the concurrent engineering team could have set some ground rules before doing the evaluation. For example, they could have said that delivering light was more important than the cost of doing so, i.e., the cost of electricity. Then the ratings would be as shown. However, if the ground rules were that the operating costs were most important, then items such as resistance element and transmitting electricity would become more important than the quantity of light emitted.

Let's now look at the one-on-one method, as illustrated in Figure 6-6. Using the same relative importance shown in Figure 6-4. The results fall in the same order as in the total comparison method: emit light, resistance element, contain vacuum, transmit electricity, hold parts, flow path, secure globe, and decorative shape—which would indicate the dictate that functionality of the product is more important than cost.

Value Ratio

The value ratio technique uses a variant of the classic worth formula we saw earlier in this chapter:

$$\text{Value} = \frac{x_{a1} + x_{a2} + \ldots + x_{an}}{x_{b1} + x_{b2} + \ldots + x_{bn}}$$

where x = magnitude of the value
a = positive perceived value
b = negative perceived value

An outcome greater than 1 defines an acceptable product or service. Conversely, an outcome less than 1 indicates an unacceptable product or service. We use the formula to rank the subcomponents in worth order and therefore to help us determine the order of investigating them to gain improvements for customers and the company.

Whether a subcomponent ranks greater than or less than unity is also significant. Less than unity would indicate that the subcomponent is not viable and should be changed (if primary) or eliminated (if secondary).

Let's look at an example. Using the variant of the formula

$$V = \frac{x_a}{x_b}$$

we first find a value for the subcomponent "contain vacuum":

$$x = \text{magnitude} = 8$$

COMPARISON GROUP I
Contain vacuum/decorative shape
Contain vaccum/flow path
Contain vacuum/resistance element
Resistance element/emit light
Emit light/hold parts
Emit light/transmit electricity
Emit light/secure globe

RESULTS I
Contain vacuum
Contain vacuum
Resistance element
Emit light
Emit light
Emit light
Emit light (highest)

COMPARISON GROUP II
Contain vacuum/decorative shape
Contain vaccum/flow path
Contain vacuum/resistance element
Resistance element/hold parts
Resistance element/transmit electricity
Resistance element/secure globe

RESULTS II
Contain vacuum
Contain vacuum
Resistance element
Resistance element
Resistance element
Resistance element

COMPARISON GROUP III
Contain vacuum/decorative shape
Contain vaccum/flow path
Contain vacuum/hold parts
Contain vacuum/transmit electricity
Contain vacuum/secure globe

RESULTS III
Contain vacuum
Contain vacuum
Contain vacuum
Contain vacuum
Contain vacuum

COMPARISON GROUP IV
Decorative shape/flow path
Flow path/hold parts
Hold parts/transmit electricity
Transmit electricity/secure globe

RESULTS IV
Flow path
Hold parts
Transmit electricity
Transmit electricity

COMPARISON GROUP V
Decorative shape/flow path
Flow path/hold parts
Hold parts/secure globe

RESULTS V
Flow path
Hold parts
Hold parts

COMPARISON GROUP VI
Decorative shape/flow path
Flow path/secure globe

RESULTS VI
Flow Path
Flow Path

COMPARISON GROUP VII
Decorative shape/secure globe

RESULTS VII
Secure globe

Bold = highest value for each comparison group.

Figure 6-6. One-on-one method. The parameter having the highest value in each comparison group is shown in boldface.

(the relative importance found in the function analysis);

$$a = \text{benefit value of the subcomponent} = \$0.85$$

(from the relative worth analysis);

$$b = \text{cost value of the subcomponent} = \$0.10$$

(an estimate of how much it costs to create the vacuum after the bulb is assembled; it should be noted that the decorative shape would have the same cost for this analysis); and

$$V = \frac{8 \times \$0.85}{8 \times \$0.10} = \$8.50$$

Following this procedure for each subcomponent, we construct a table for the value measurement created by the value ratio method, as shown in Figure 6-7.

Once again we have created a priority ranking for investigating the subcomponents of the selected product or service for potential improvements. In this case the order of investigation would be contain vacuum, emit light, resistance element, flow path, transmit electricity, hold parts, secure globe, and decorative shape. We see that the order of ranking between the methods is not the same (Figure 6-8). They are relatively close—the top three are still the top three, and the bottom two are identical—but otherwise we get different results. The two methods are equally valid but the rating systems involved are subjective. The important point is that they are not totally dissimilar, and we could expect equally satisfactory outcomes from implementing either plan.

We can see that value engineering is a complex methodology for determining what opportunities for improvement to pursue. It is effective and

Subcomponent	Function	Relative importance (magnitude)	Relative worth a	Cost value b	Value measurement V
Globe	Contain vacuum	8	$0.85	$0.10	$8.50
	Decorative shape	1	$0.10	$0.10	$0.10
Filament	Flow path	6	$0.60	$0.15	$4.00
	Resistance element	9	$0.90	$0.15	$6.00
	Emit light	10	$1.00	$0.15	$6.67
Socket	Hold parts	7	$0.65	$0.33	$1.97
	Transmit electricity	8	$0.75	$0.33	$2.27
	Secure globe	5	$0.50	$0.33	$1.52

Figure 6-7. Value ratio method.

Relative worth analysis	Value ratio
Emit light	Contain vacuum
Resistance element	Emit light
Contain vacuum	Resistance element
Transmit electricity	Flow path
Hold parts	Transmitt electricity
Flow path	Hold parts
Secure globe	Secure globe
Decorative shape	Decorative shape

Figure 6-8. Comparative outcomes of the relative worth analysis and value ratio methods.

useful for complex activities. Fixture design many times falls into this category, as does product design, probably to a lesser degree. Not always, however, in either case. I have presented value engineering as a legitimate technique of investigating options for improvements when the stakes are very high and the company is engaged in a very competitive situation. When that happens, fixture designs that save pennies per piece can eliminate millions of dollars in production costs and add significant increases to bottom line profitability. That's reason enough to carry out value engineering and to tolerate the complexity of the process. However, once tried we see it turns out to be nothing more than an exercise in good engineering logic.

Designing and developing tools, jigs, and fixtures requires good engineering judgment. It is just as complex as designing the product itself, and usually involves significantly more parts than the product itself. Imagine something as simple as a hammer, made up of a head, handle, the handle rubber grip, and a fasten method to hold the handle into the head. Only three parts. Now imagine all the tools, jigs, and fixtures needed to manufacture those parts economically. We've touched on quite a few already in this text. It is easy to see that for a simple three-part assembly we will probably have well over two dozen internal designs that have to be executed to create the devices necessary to manufacture the part. I hope this serves to explain and illuminate that a considerable amount of engineering has to take place behind the scenes and it is as necessary to do right as is the product design itself.

When we engage in tool, jig, and fixture designs, we need the entire creative ability of the company involved. Because if we can't optimize the cost of manufacture, the best product designs will never be competitive and will never reach the marketplace. For this reason we use the concurrent engineering team to manage this task and assign it a value equal to the product design itself.

Chapter 7

Work Station Configuration to Perform the Intended Manufacturing Operations

The way work stations are configured depends on the type of work to be performed, the equipment the company provides for it, and the skills of the operators who will be staffing the work stations. In previous chapters, we explored how product designs are developed, and how processes are designed to execute them. In Chapter 6 we saw how jigs and fixtures are developed for the work station. But so far we haven't designed a work station that will support the jigs and fixtures and will serve as the venue for transforming raw materials into finished product. Nor, once the work stations have been configured, do we yet know how many of them to call for. To know this, we have to be able to predict capacity. In the ensuing discussion, we will explore all of these issues within the context of the Two Knows.

We will delve into the generics of good work station configuration, and see what a significant influence it has on the ultimate cost to produce and the resultant quality. But instead of viewing this task as simply an engineering exercise to optimize motions and to store and then use materials, we will emphasize how good work station configuration can optimize operators' potential. We will also look at ways to match work station configuration with the quantity of work that is expected to journey through the area. It would be folly to design a totally satisfactory work station only to find out that its capacity is insufficient for the volume requirements. So, as part of work station configuration, usually the last phase, we need to analyze capacity to do the entire job. It is often said that a mechanic is only as good as his or her tools. It is also a truism that operators should come to the workplace with a prescribed minimum level of competency, because no degree of work station design trickery can overcome lack of skills to do the job. These opposite ends of the spectrum are both very true and form the basis of good work station design. But good tools and adequate operator skills are not things we can define simply to cover all cases. There's a good deal of give-and-take in choosing the right tools for the operator and the right operator for the work station, so work station configuration actually requires a compromise between operator skills and tool selection. From this paradoxical viewpoint, let's now explore work station configuration.

THE GENERICS OF A WORK STATION

Good work station design takes into account the skills and experience levels of the intended workforce. Although we would prefer to ignore the competency level of the workforce and design for optimum equipment placement at the work station, we cannot. We must tailor the work station to the average factory employee's level of competency and skills. By skills I mean mental abilities as well as physical strengths and dexterity. A good example is ability to lift objects from pallets to work benches. If a factory employs mostly female operators, then the materials to be lifted to the workbench will have to be lighter than for a predominantly male workforce. This is not discriminatory; it's just a fact of physiology. The average man has greater upper body strength than the average woman. Therefore, it would be prudent to size the workpieces so that they're no greater than what an average woman could comfortably lift. Thus, small jib cranes might be necessary, whereas that might not be the case if demographics showed the workforce to be mostly men. On the other hand, women exhibit greater dexterity, so a work station in an area staffed primarily with female employees would make less use of adjusting devices for positioning small, lightweight workpieces that require precise positioning. For these same workpieces, small, tweezer-like devices might be called for to assist male operators. Both of these examples demonstrate the human factors that need to be considered in work station design, particularly, the type of workforce available to do the intended work.

What this means, besides having the work station populated with the correct machines and processes to do the job, is that there are other important factors to consider; the important ones are ergonomics, methods, material handling, good operator-machine harmony, and automation thresholds selection. They tend to be interrelated and are all somewhat dependent on the makeup of the workforce. Let's delve deeper, starting with ergonomics.

Ergonomic Factors in Work Station Design

Ergonomics is the study of optimization of effort through proper placement of people and their tools to do the job. Basically, ergonomic considerations depend on the work to be performed and the placement of that work on the work station. It's obvious that the workpiece itself has to be presented in a manner to aid the value-added operations. But what of the operator? Does it make any difference if the operator is a man or a woman? Perhaps. Ergonomics strives to find the least fatiguing way to work. It will tell us that sitting is more productive than standing. That moving an object with fingers is less fatiguing than using an arm. Which in turn is less tiresome than using an arm and a shoulder. We also know that men have greater upper body strength than women as well as a longer reach. So it is conceivable that a work station design for a man could employ longer reaches and heavier lifts than one for a woman. But also keep in mind that the differences between male and female physical capabilities are not significant. Hence, the likelihood that male versus female work stations would be employed is not very high.

What ergonomics does teach us is that we need to take into account energy levels needed to do work and strive to reduce them through proper work station design. Energy level minimization by operators has been codified to the extent that we can compare human motions required to do any job with these standards and know virtually immediately if there is an ergonomic problem. Good work station design should always strive to minimize the operator's fatigue levels.

There are some important ergonomic factors to evaluate for the consideration of the work station design; Figure 7-1 lists them. While any of these considerations may be nothing more than common sense, it is surprising how many are simply ignored, and the ignorance factor dominates.

- Strive to have humans do analytical and control work at the work station instead of physical work whenever possible.
- Comply with principles of motion economy:
  - Find the lowest human energy utilization method of doing work. Set up work stations to favor:
    - Using hands before hands and arms
    - Using hands and arms before hands, arms, and shoulders
    - Using hands, arms, and shoulders before hands, arms, shoulders, and back
    - Minimizing use of back in any work operation
  - Keep work within arm's reach as much as possible.
  - Minimize distance operators travel doing work.
  - Keep work at waist level as much as possible.
  - Prefer operator sits rather than stands.
- Prefer parts or materials move rather than operators.
- Lay out tools and work in an arc, radius equal to average length of human arm, rather than in a straight line.
- Keep work in sight of operators at all times, never behind them.
- Analyze tool needs before work is initiated, and provide the tools.
- Designate location and set pallets for transferring materials as close to work area as possible.
- Provide devices for lifting materials in accordance with all regulations and laws, but above all using common sense.
  - Train all operators to lift correctly.
- Provide proper task lighting adequate for doing the specific task.
- Provide proper clothing and protective devices compatible with the job-specific requirements. Comply with all OSHA and EPA regulations.

Figure 7-1. Pragmatic ergonomics considerations for designing work stations.

The first bullet is often overlooked. The reason we have work stations with machines in the first place is to expand the capability of a human, be it strengthwise, or speedwise, or agilitywise. We want machines to do work, not humans, because of their inherent advantages over people in these areas. We want humans to do the thinking and analyzing because of their inherent superiority over machines in this domain. Which means we want to go with human strengths. Once more, the sports analogy: Field the best team possible.

This leads to *principles of motion economy*, the study of energy levels necessary to carry out universal tasks—e.g., using arms, legs, backs, etc., to do physical labor. While it should be our goal to utilize the power of the machines to do all physical labor, economically that is probably not feasible. We still largely depend on operators to present the work in proper aspect to the process tools to perform the actual value added tasks. We all know how complex a robotic positioning device can be and how easy it is to disrupt or confuse it. Therefore, some manual work is inevitable even in the most automated factories. However, when we do that work we want it to be done with the least amount of human energy possible. This allows the person to stay on the job longer and tends to keep the attention sharper because there is a lesser fatigue factor. Figure 7-1 lists the major motions we use in factory-type work and shows which are the least energy-consuming. When designing work stations, if we are cognizant of these factors, we should do a better job of making the work station compatible with lesser human energy expenditure. Obviously, this is good for business and for the operators.

The list also states that we should move materials, not people. This, too, goes along with the proposition that we must spend human energy miserly if at all. Also, by moving materials we will force the issue of planning how that should be done. If we tell people to move, most likely we won't specify the most expeditious path, but simply let the individual figure it out. By planning how to move the material (it can't on its own volition move itself), we will find a way that will be the best for the situation and nominally the best path. This probably means less time, less cost, and more moves over the course of the work shift. This all leads to more throughput and hence more profit.

Considering making the work station something other than rectilinear and straight-flow is often overlooked. But it shouldn't be. If we state we want the operator to be stationary and preferably seated in order to conserve energy, we must factor in how the person will work. The best method is seated and working on parts in front of her, usually in an area within one foot outboard of each shoulder to a depth in front of the operator of up to two-thirds of an arm's reach. Also, all tools should be in an arc of radius equal to the average arm's length, left and right. We also need to keep all tools within reasonable sight of the operator. To do this, the arc of the work area should be about 120 degrees and never more than 150. Figure 7-2 diagrams all these preferred dimensions.

It is also imperative that no work or tools be behind the operator. This is for safety reasons and for efficiency and quality reasons. Safety reasons are self-evident. We do not want movement of materials—which may possess considerable inertia and hence could cause harm if striking a person—to be

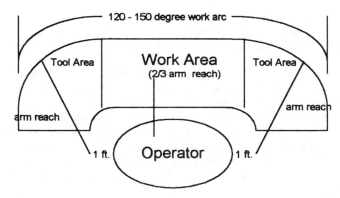

Figure 7-2. Work station optimum work area for the operator.

out of sight of the person. She could conceivably back into a moving piece of material or a tool, jig, or fixture and be injured. Second, we want the operator to be focusing on the work. By turning her back to it, she loses concentration and is more apt to make mistakes when returning. Therefore, we want all tools, jigs, and fixtures along with the workpiece to be in simultaneous view of the operator. This maximizes concentration, thus making it less likely that an error will occur.

We see the principles of good ergonomic layout dramatically played out every time we view a medical operating suite drama. The instruments are all within easy reach of the doctor, who never removes her eye from focus on the task at hand, no matter what. If it is physically impossible to have all the tools of the doctor's trade laid out in normal sight lines, she asks for them and has them put in her hand by an assistant without once lifting her gaze away from the patient. This, of course, is done dramatically in television and movies, but nevertheless the principles are sound. They are ergonomic principles, invented and exploited by engineers, and the best way to accomplish work. We need to have the same thing happen in factories. We want operators concentrating on value-added work, not searching for tools and losing concentration in the process.

Effect of Methods of Manufacturing on Work Station Configuration

Chapter 3 covered the process of developing methods for producing a product. We observed how the product design will focus the engineer on what processes need to be employed to actually make and assemble the product. We also saw that the volume or quantity of parts to be made, either in a one-time work order with a high probability of never being produced again, or in an order repeatable over time, will dictate the choice of methods to be used. This means that capacity considerations are always lurking in the background when methods are selected for a particular job. The method we choose needs to be compatible with both production needs and our capabilities. The techniques for calculating capacity will be covered later in this chapter.

In most cases, the factory already has established work stations and the design of the work station is not an issue. Perhaps some tweaking is necessary to suit a peculiarity of the design. In the hammer example, perhaps a material of certain strength and corrosion resistance is required for the spot weld of head to shank. And perhaps the weld wire is not available for spot welding but only for TIG welding. In that case, the work station needs to be modified to accept TIG welding. Then ergonomic considerations would be factored into any changes employed. But this is the exception rather than the rule.

Choice of methods does strongly affect work station configuration when a company embarks on a new process or initiates a new manufacturing line. The method will dictate what the operator needs to do and what the physical process has to accomplish. The idea is to make the work station compatible with the method of production and to optimize production of the product. Let's look briefly at the hammer example again.

Example: Suppose the method of producing the hammer required drilling and pinning the head to the shaft. With the volume of 10,000, we would want a semiautomatic process, and the work station would have to be designed accordingly. Starting with the work station shown in Figure 7-2, we could envision a suitable system (as shown in Figure 7-3) whereby totes of heads and shafts could be placed on separate nonpowered roller conveyors, both working inward. The operator takes a head and a shaft and places them in a fixture containing a drill and a pin insertion piston. She then steps on a pedal to begin the drill sequence, followed by an automatic pin insertion sequence. At the conclusion of the second sequence the operator places the assembled hammer on a powered continuously moving conveyor that transports the hammer to a gravity-fed tote box. The tote box is periodically retrieved by move personnel and taken to the next operation.

In this example we see how the method influenced the way the work station was configured. The work station needed to be entirely compatible with the method in a manner that allowed for optimum productivity to be derived. But we also see that good ergonometric principles were not compromised. Note in Figure 7-3 that all the guidelines for ergonometric success per Figures 7-1 and 7-2 were complied with. For example, we see that the totes with the parts to be assembled are delivered at table height level, thus eliminating a bend motion the operator would otherwise have to make to place the parts in the fixture. The telling point is that methods influenced work station configurations, but ergonometric design still needs to be complied with.

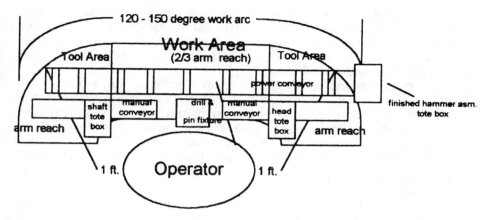

Figure 7-3. Work station optimum work area for the operator, hammer assembly.

Material Handling, the Works Station's Transportation System

We always need to keep in mind that value-added work occurs only when we're transforming materials into something essential to a finished product. The cold reality is that all other efforts are waste and do not get us directly to the goal of presenting a finished product to the customer. This is such a misunderstood fact that most people are shocked to learn that the best factories in the world are creating value added only 30% of the time. (This is for flow manufacturing. Job shops are fortunate if they approach 5% value-added time.) The rest of the time is planning for work, or moving materials about from work station to work station, or simply waiting for a turn on a facility to do value-added work. We can see, then, that being able to move materials to and from work stations quickly and in such a manner that they can be worked on when they arrive is a critical factor. Therefore, proper work station configuration needs to take into account the methodology of transportation to and from the active value-added entities. I say "entities" because they can be machines or people.

In Figure 7-3 we see provisions for moving materials to and from the workbench in a manner that allows the operator to be almost oblivious to the arrival of parts and the departure of completed assemblies. We see a solution that always makes same part deliveries to same destination locations. Obviously, this is not by accident. The material handling scheme has been thought out integrally with the design of the work station, and all has been planned to be compatible with what is to happen at that work station. In the Figure 7-3 example, handles and hammer heads arrive at the proper location for a drop into a fixture where a pinning operation is to occur. An additional detail, not shown in Figure 7-3, is that in a configuration of this nature, the same aspects of identical parts will be placed in the pinning fixture every time. This allows the operator to employ the same motion pattern for every cycle and assures that we can optimize the cycle time. By doing so we can improve output productivity.

Thus, repetition and sameness are desired qualities, and our material handling schema needs to support that. For this reason we must create a plan for materials support for the work station. And the critical factor is how we will deliver materials to the work station that actually arrive when needed, and in the proper aspect for the intended uses.

There are only a few material handling techniques to chose from, mainly:

- Conveyors of all types
- Cranes of all types
- Vehicles of all types
- Human carriers of all types

Conveyors can be overhead, on the floor, at waist level, or at any level and angular plan desired. They can be powered or nonpowered, roller belt or chain. They can be shelflike in that material rests on them, or they can be hook-type, whereby materials are supported from them. Conveyors are typically for large-volume, relatively small parts or assemblies and are very prevalent in assembly operations.

Cranes are usually used to move large items, which tend to be bulky and/or heavy. The parts are usually more complex than conveyor-transported parts and tend to stay at the work station longer. They usually require the crane to support the setting of the piece into the work station, and sometimes even to hold the piece during value-added operations. When this happens the material handling device essentially becomes a fixture in support of the value added tools.

Vehicles range from common forklift trucks to wagons, to special-purpose independently controlled devices for carrying materials. The most recent addition to this last class is the automated guided vehicles (AGVs) programmed to go to certain work stations and dispatched by certain triggering devices. Some vehicles even become the work station itself when merged with the value added performing tool. This allows for the workpiece to set up correctly with respect to datum points and then to be transported to different process-performing locations throughout the factory.

Human transportation of materials, perhaps with pushcarts, is the simplest and also the least efficient method of carrying out the transportation task. This is so because people have the smallest capacity to carry and/or push goods about the factory. This system works only when the volume of material movement is small and the weight is well within the range a person can carry in a sustained period of time—usually up to 10 pounds at a time frequency for the work shift, with adequate rest breaks.

Most factories start out depending on vehicles to deliver materials to the work station and then find that there is too much ad hoc placement—hence wasted time—in performing the value-added activities. They then set about to actually design material handling systems compatible with the principles of motion economy that are being applied at the work station. Drop-off and pickup in such systems need to minimize operator expenditure of energy and to be unobstructive to the value-added work occurring. The way this is done is for the manufacturing engineer to think in total system concepts rather than just how to do the value-added work. Instead of simply puzzling through how to do the job, the engineer has to extend the boundaries of the problem to consider how the material will arrive, how it will be placed in a position to be worked on, how the work will occur, how finished work will be removed, and how the removed work will get to the dispatch station to be sent to the next work station. With all these sequences to contend with, the designer has still another factor to consider: how to make the process work smoothly so there are no long periods of idle time while a particular sequence is concluding. This is called *internal work station line balance*. The goal is to make the flow of operations like laminar flow of fluid in a pipe.

Internal line balancing means that the operator is not delayed waiting for material to arrive or for the machine to finish a task. It also applies to the machine as well. We can readily see that the productive output of the work station will drop if either the machine or the operator is idle while waiting for the other to complete a task. This means we must strive to assure that the balance of time with respect to tasks is proper for the job to be done. We will look further into the balance between operator and machine later in this chapter in the section on man-machine harmony. But first let's look at line balance with respect to material handling.

Without material to work on, there is no reason for the work station to exist. Therefore we must assure that materials are always available for as long as we want to operate the specific work station. We want material to arrive on time and then to be removed before it clogs the work station so work cannot effectively occur. To do this we need to set up some protocols to adhere to. These protocols are basically common sense, but like so many right things to do they tend to be ignored if not pointed out beforehand. The protocols are:

- *Understand the usage rate of materials at the work station.* This means knowing the cycle time necessary to complete the entire manufacturing cycle at the work station, portal to portal.
- *Understand the cycle time from requesting material to actual delivery of material.* This means establishing a classic max/min inventory control process for the individual work station as opposed to the entire factory (see Figure 7-4). The theory is the same, except now we focus on the individual work station. We want to determine an optimal pacing of material deliveries, as well as an optimal delivery size. With a finite amount of material on hand, and knowing the rate of usage, we can calculate the time until materials are exhausted. Then, knowing the time it takes to load a tote and transport it to the work station, we can match the delivery cycle time with the depletion rate by requesting replenishment at just the right time to make sure that the remaining on-hand material will run out just as the new material arrives. The delivery size for the new material should be at least equal to the amount consumed in the time it takes for the material handling system to generate another

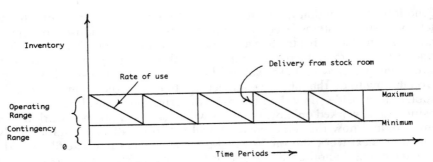

Figure 7-4. Work station material max/min chart.

replenishment trip. The amount of material present at the work station after delivery should be the maximum the work station will ever see. But given that stipulation, there is yet another factor in determining the delivery size, as Figure 7-4 illustrates. Because there could be unforeseen circumstances where deliveries are delayed or the rate of production increases, or other unplanned-for events, it is also wise to have an additional safety or contingency reserve of material on hand. So the work station needs to be designed to hold that much material. Of course the physical constraints of the work station will also have to be considered in setting any contingency levels.

The basic equations for maximum/minimum inventory are as follows:

Maximum material at work station = calculated minimum
+ calculated return trip regeneration usage rate amount
+ contingency reserve
Calculated minimum = (rate of depletion)(time to replenish)

Let's look at an example of their use.

Example: For the hammer assembly work station shown in Figure 7-3, we wish to complete 120 assemblies an hour. We know through time studies that it takes 10 minutes to load two totes (one with handles and one with heads) in the stockroom and that the trip from the stockroom to the work station also takes ten minutes. Unloading of the totes at the work station, retrieval of the totes with the assembled hammer heads, and replacement with an empty tote for the assembled units all takes an additional five minutes. We need to calculate the maximum and minimum inventory levels to be maintained at the work station so the line balance is maintained. Let's assume that the contingency level is set at 20% of the minimum level.

First we calculate the minimum inventory level:

Calculated minimum = (rate of depletion)(time to replenish)
= (2/min)(10 min load + 10 min transport to WS
+ 5 min unload)
= 50 heads and 50 handles

Next calculate the maximum inventory level:

Maximum material at work station = calculated minimum
+ calculated return trip
regeneration usage rate amount
+ contingency reserve
= 50 + (2/min)(10 min return to stockroom) + (0.20)(50)
= 80 heads and 80 handles

If the material handling system were supplying multiple work stations, then the transport time to the work station and back to the stockroom would not be equal. Suppose, for example, that the particular work station is second of six in the delivery cycle and the distance between work stations is five minute. Then the calculation for maximum and minimum inventory needs to be adjusted for the additional time to support the other five work stations. In our example, that would be:

Calculated minimum = (rate of depletion)(time to replenish)
= (2/min)
× (10 min load + 10 min transport to
WS + 5 min unload + 5 min trans.
between WS1 and WS2 + 5 min
unload WS1)
= 70 heads and 70 handles
Maximum material at work station = calculated minimum
+ calculated return trip regeneration
usage rate amount
+ contingency reserve
= 50 + (2/min)(10 min return to stockroom after last stop)
+ (2/min)[(5 min unload + 5 min
travel)/WS](5 additional WS)
+ (0.20)(50)
= 180 heads and 180 handles

As we can see, the maximum and minimum inventory levels are very much dependent on the amount of time it takes to replenish. This has to be very carefully considered when designing the work stations. It means that the final design must be compatible with how the production system is going to operate.

For the system to operate correctly, we need to designate spaces at the work station for delivery and take-away. These spaces have to be configured to support quick removal of materials in both loading and unloading. We also saw in the example that time is critical in having the proper levels of inventory and it is very dependent on the rate of usage. This means the operators and the material movers need to be sufficiently trained so the optimal methods of loading and unloading are always followed. If this is not the case, the calculations will be in error far beyond any contingency factors and we will be constantly either starving or bloating the work stations with materials. In both cases line balance will have been lost and productivity downgraded.

This points out once more the importance of the human element in manufacturing. Operators and all other support people need to be trained in adequate utilization of resources for the endeavor to succeed. The next segment of work station configuration continues this theme of integration of man-machine resources and the need for compatibility.

Man-Machine Harmony

Putting together an efficient work station design requires considering one more significant factor: what separate roles are assigned to the operator and the machine. Obviously, the machine is going to do the real physical work, while the operator is assigned the controlling activity. The trick is to have the person and the machine work in harmony as a team so that total portal-to-portal cycle time is the least amount possible. This is true productivity; anything else is nothing more than a trivial pursuit of suboptimization, which leads to little gain, if any, for the company.

The concept of man-machine harmony is very simple and is as old as the profession of engineering. We use machines to transform raw materials into useful goods, and we want these machines to never stop operating. Therefore, any controlling-type work the operator needs to do must be done within the cycle time of the machine. If we accomplish this goal, we are maximizing value-added time at the expense of non-value-added time. Thinking of it in another way, anytime the machine has to stop to allow the operator to perform his or her function is waste and needs to be minimized to the greatest extent possible. There is a premium to be earned if we correctly analyze the division of tasks to make sure there is minimal non-value-added time within the total portal-to-portal time.

There might be some confusion in defining portal-to-portal time with respect to actual machine cycle time to make the product. Total portal-to-portal time encompasses material handling, inspection, and engineering adjustments to processes as well as the cycle time of the machine tool or process. Portal-to-portal time with reference to man-machine harmony is only concerned with machine tool or process cycle time. Total portal-to-portal time usually exhibits no more than 30% value-added time for flow manufacturing and only 5% for job shop or intermittent flow manufacturing. However, when we examine that portion of the total time dedicated to machine tool or process cycle time, the percentages are much more favorable toward value-added. Usually greater than 65%. This is true because we are analyzing the producing cycle, not the total cycle. Don't become complacent and think that 65% is OK. It isn't. Our goal for man-machine harmony should be 100%: the necessary work done by the operator should be totally doable internal to the machine cycle time. Therefore the operator's work is not on the critical path but simply an adjunct to the main process. Figure 7-5 visually portrays the time advantage gained by operators who have been trained to work within the cycle time of the machine processes. It is really just another way of expressing the philosophy of concurrent engineering, whereby as many tasks as possible are done at the same time or within the critical path cycle time.

Suppose we need to maximize the parallel-profile portal-to-portal time as shown in Figure 7-5. How is that done? A very pragmatic approach is through the use of man-machine charts. One column of such a chart is a time line that shows when the machine is working and is idle, and another

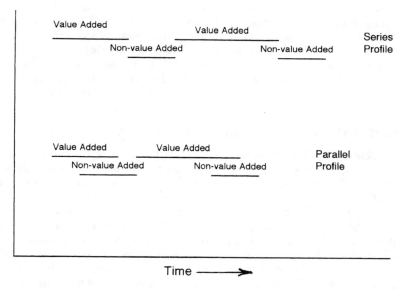

Figure 7-5. Portal-to-portal time: man-machine harmony.

column of the same chart (usually parallel to the machine time line) is a time line showing when the operator is working or idle. We then look at each work step the person is performing while the machine is idle and ask a simple, straightforward question: Can the person's work be done concurrently with the machine's work, so the production output will not be slowed waiting for the operator to finish his or her task? If the answer is yes for some steps, then we accept that step without modification and assign it to be done while the machine is operating and go to the next step. If the answer is no, we look at the content of the work step to see if there is a more time-efficient way of doing it or an alternative to doing it that has shorter cycle time. Often there is no choice but to stop the machine and allow the operator to do his part. A typical scenario where this would be the case is with checking the setup on a single table VBM. The machine is stopped for the operator to verify that the physical settings of the jigs and fixtures are correct. There can be no value-added work until this task is completed.

We go through all operations this way. Then, after making the corrections (or improvements) to the original human operation profile, we once again look for areas to improve so the machine stop time is minimized. We iterate this process as many times as we feel necessary to get the most productive sequence of operations. Figure 7-6 shows a typical man-machine chart.

Keep in mind that none of this work is being done in a vacuum or in isolation. At the same time we are reviewing the man-machine chart, others may be reviewing and possibly changing jigs and fixtures. When these changes come about, the man-machine chart will change once again. So there is no preset limit to the number of iterations that may ensue. Also, to make things even more interesting, we are concurrently analyzing man and machine movements vis-à-vis time standards to evaluate calculated movement times. We do all this to ensure that the work station we design is as good as we can make it. Obviously, the iterative process has to eventually come to an end, and that occurs when the investment in engineering and shop operations time reaches a point of diminishing returns in profit.

Automation Considerations in Work Station Configuration

Another factor to look at in work station design is the degree of automation contemplated. A work station that is fully automated will look different from one that isn't, for an obvious reason: the human factor considerations are significantly minimized. This means that for doing the same work as would be done on a manual machine the man-machine chart will be considerably altered. In addition to the traditional tasks assigned to machines, automated machines do a high proportion of the things that humans traditionally do at the work station. They take over many of the factors of control that used to be the domain of the operator. This means that the training the operator undergoes is quite different. For the most part, operators working at automated work stations tend to be technicians rather than skilled machinists or

CNC Lathe Open Headstock
Hammer Handle Machining

Operation	Cycle time	Man activitites	Machine activities
1. Receive 1.125 in. round stock, 12ft lengths	5 min	Verify, then certify receipt of material	Idle
2. Set up machine for 123E456 Pt2	2 h	Do setup for program 1212	Idle
3. Make 10,000	333.33 h	Idle, monitor performance of machine	Machine cycle rate at 30/h
4. Audit quality	Internal to operation 3	SPC check 3 hammer shafts per hour; record on PC123E456 Pt2	Machine cycle rate at 30/h

Figure 7-6. Man-machine chart.

process operators. The task to be performed is more akin to overall systems maintenance rather than direct hands-on control of the process. This has a profound effect on work station configuration.

With automated work stations, the traditional ergonomics focus on the principle of motion economy is largely replaced with a concern for optimizing system dwell times between value-added activities. We no longer have to be concerned with fatigue factors but become more involved in transportation times and reasons for the extent of dwell times between operations.

In fact, the only true human interface ergonomic situation we still need to contend with for automated machines is the safety and comfort issue for the operator. And even here it is not critical for performance. For manual machines, it is possible to conceive of a situation where, to make an operation safe to perform, we must sacrifice process speed and thus output per time period. Many cases can be documented where the safe way of doing things is the longer way. Guarding of punch presses and stamping presses is an example. It is common for a punch press to have a safety activation switch that the operator has to activate with both hands. This is undoubtedly safer but slower. Contrast this with the automated-feed punch press. In this case, the operator is an observer, ready to shut down the machine if anything is outside the desired parameters. Here, ergonomics comes to play only to assure that the operator is in a safe position to observe and can do so effectively. Since the operator is not part of the process activity, we can do what needs to be done for his safety and comfort without having to be concerned with productivity losses.

Material handling is also quite different with automated work stations. In nonautomated work stations we tend to tolerate a more casual attitude toward the way materials are brought to and from the work station. While all well-designed work stations need to have designated materials receiving and departing areas, for the automated work station these areas have to be precisely laid out. Therefore, the design of the work station has to really extend into the material transfer aspects of factory design, and we need to have a more systems-synergistic approach toward design.

Automation implies computer control, which is actually the case in over 90% of all automated work stations. With computer control, we need to minimize the number of choices involved; otherwise, the control algorithms become too cumbersome for the factory to cope with. Thus, the movement of material to and from the workplace needs to be very precise, with virtually no variation from load to load. To accomplish this, many designers require that a common datum point for the delivery of materials and the positioning of the value-added tooling be set at the start of every cycle. This, of course, is not true for manually operated work stations. As an illustration, a manual lathe operator is not going to care where the next part to be machined is waiting in queue as long as it is easy to get at it and to place it in the head- and tailstock chucks. Contrast this with an automated lathe, feeder-type. Here, the next piece has to be positioned on the transfer tray ready to be parallel-pushed into the lathe bed in such a way that it can be secured to the head- and tailstock chucks. If the material is simply at the work station but not on the transfer tray, the machine cannot function. It's as if the material is on Mars, as far as the work station is concerned.

Automation requires very precise understanding of all the value- and non-value-added activities so they can be accounted for in the design of the work station. The reason is that the automated machine has a computer instead of an operator in control. And quite frankly, computers are neither as smart nor as creative as humans. Thus, more activities have to be orchestrated before hand, rather than ad-libbed on the spot. For design of work stations, this means more difficulties to overcome, because to be successful all likely scenarios have to be considered. It takes longer to cover every contingency, and it is more costly and error-prone. It is not unusual for automated work stations to take years to be fully developed, while manual work stations tend to be fully developed in months.

CONCEPTUALIZING THE WORK STATION TO FIT THE FLOW OF MANUFACTURING

We've looked at the points that have to be considered in creating a work station configuration. Now let's back off a bit and see how the type of work to be accomplished will affect choices for configuring the work stations and where those work stations will be with respect to one another. The big picture will be dependent on the products the factory has to make, the volumes, the processes involved, and the compatibility of the processes. All this is tempered with the economic reality of the current business situation.

It's obvious that work stations need to be compatible with the product the company produces. What's perhaps not so obvious is what the product will require of the work stations and how they need to be arranged. Perhaps the easiest way to explain this is to equate the bill of materials (BOM) and the routing directly with the product. The BOM is essentially a goes-into type of document reversed. We start with the completed product and then break it down to its fundamental raw materials through several layers. At each level an operation is performed, either a transformation of raw to semifinished or finished status, or an assembly operation. The interesting thing is that each operation is dependent on a preceding activity. It is this order that dictates the shape of the factory, how the factory's work stations are designed, and how many of each type of work station are required.

To do the job of laying out the workplace, we invert the BOM and create the prototype route. This is the path the various materials will take through transformations and subassemblies to reach the final assembled state. This conceptualization will establish a work station to perform one or more operations dictated by the route. Depending on the complexity of the work to be done, it will set the requirements of the work station, including its physical size, the processes employed, and the number of people required to operate it. So we can see that the flow of work is dictated by the BOM, and the work stations are segments of the flow. The task is to have enough work stations to do all the transformations and assemblies as required and at the same time minimize handling as much as possible.

The exact nature of the individual work station is totally dependent on what it is supposed to do. The operations assigned to it will dictate its configuration. Also, we have to take into account whether the product will run for a long period of time (flow manufacturing) or is a relatively short run that, once finished, would probably not come back again for a long time, if at all (job shop manufacturing). The former will yield work stations totally dedicated to the particular product and will tend to favor automation. The job shop based scenario will gravitate to general purpose machines that can do the intended work and many similar kinds of work, but not as efficiently as work stations can work in mass flow work. We also see more space dedicated to semiuniversal type jigs and fixtures at job shop work stations than at their flow manufacturing counterparts. We can see that the flow manufacturing work stations are going to be more precisely laid out to dictate the needs of the product and as a result will be more efficient and productive.

Unfortunately, the vast majority of manufacturing is job shop in nature, and thus not at the efficiency levels we would like to see. But by understanding the requirements for the product, it is possible to combine those with other products the company makes utilizing the group technology principles discussed earlier. So, as a general rule, it is always preferable to create manufacturing cells for job shop manufacturing rather than by process-oriented layouts. This allows some of the advantages of mass flow to be enjoyed in a job shop environment. This is the reason we see so many more semiuniversal fixtures in job shops now instead of the specialized fixtures of the past.

PEOPLE SELECTION BASED ON WORK STATION CONFIGURATION

It is superficially apparent that the more automated a work station is, the fewer skills the operator needs to possess. At the first, conscious level, this is certainly true. An automated lathe having a sophisticated CNC controller will direct the activity of the machine for even the most complex machining operations. We also know that producing the same complex part on a manually controlled lathe will take an operator of substantial skills. That operator probably has more machinist's knowledge than the operator of the CNC lathe. However, the manual machine operator needs no knowledge of CNC to do the job, while the opposite is true for the operator running the CNC lathe. So we see on a second level that the knowledge to run automated equipment is not less than that required for manual equipment; it is simply different.

When it comes to staffing a factory, it is essential to understand the types of skills needed. Looking at the first level only, we find that job shops require more process skills knowledge than does flow manufacturing, because job shops usually employ more general-purpose machines capable of a wider variety of operations than flow manufacturing businesses. Flow manufacturing companies, with their larger and longer production runs, can afford to pursue special-purpose equipment to squeeze out the last ounce of productivity advantage. Usually, this equipment consists of automated devices that require little human intervention. Therefore, by conventional wisdom, we say that the skills levels required are less than for job shops. Of course, this is true only for manufacturing processes directly involved in the transformation process. The typically overlooked factor is that the skills now required are computer operator or programming skills.

We see that the knowledge levels are not higher or lower within job shops or flow manufacturing. They would be essentially the same if we could measure them on a scale of basic intelligence for operators. They are simply different. This means that an important factor of work station configuration is to determine the types of skills necessary to do the job and configure accordingly. For example, in a job shop there is less need for real-time communications, because of the relatively slower pace and smaller volume of products being worked on. In a flow manufacturing activity, on the other hand, the pace is faster and problem resolution needs to be faster; otherwise, a lot of "bad" product can be made in a shorter period of time. Therefore, in flow manufacturing, communications aspects built into the work station have to be more proactive rather than reactive. The people involved need to be adaptable to this type of environment, usually more team-oriented, than the job shop operator. The job shop operator tends to operate more independently with less contact with others while doing the job. These differences will affect choices of personnel. Just as processes have to be compatible with each other, it is essential that operators be compatible with the philosophy of operation the company employs.

A CAPACITY CALCULATION PRIMER

Before work station design is considered complete, it is necessary to either verify that sufficient capacity exists or to design the required capacity into the process. There are two types of capacity to consider. The first, already alluded to in discussions, is the calculated capacity based on the methods and time standards developed to produce the product and is called the *theoretical capacity*. The second type of capacity is the true capacity that we need to understand to set the production output budgets in place for the factory. This is called the *practical capacity*. Practical capacity is a derivative of theoretical capacity downgraded by pragmatic considerations of things that interfere with the ability to do work at the work station. Since these pragmatic considerations are different for every factory—and, indeed, different for every work station—the values that we end up with are estimates and need to be on the conservative side. Also compounding the ability to calculate practical capacity is the fact that situations surrounding the factory change every day.

Now let's look at the techniques for calculating both types of capacity. In both cases we will be using a part manufacturing situation. But we will see that these methods are equally competent for assembly operations and for providing of services in non-product (physical) producing companies.

How to Calculate Theoretical Capacity

Theoretical capacity is derived from mathematical calculations based on the prescribed method of making a product. It is based very specifically on the basic tenets of manufacturing, the Two Knows:

1. Know how to make the product.
2. Know how long it should take to make the product.

We have explored a good deal of the thought processes and techniques used to apply these tenets to the manufacturing process, so they won't be repeated here. Suffice it to say that those techniques are used throughout the process. My purpose here is to describe a concise, perhaps a summarized, process for finding theoretical capacity sufficient for sizing the factory and ultimately designing work stations. There are five steps in defining theoretical capacity; we will briefly explore each of them:

1. Isolate the part to be studied from all other operations.
2. Make a detailed list of all the steps necessary to make the part.
3. Determine the time to perform each step.
4. Add the times for the various steps to get a base time for doing the work.
5. Divide the time to do the work by eight hours to get theoretical capacity per shift per work station.

1. Isolate the Part to Be Studied from All Other Operations

Carefully define the part for which the capacity study is to be done. This means we make sure the only value-added activities we are looking at are specifically for the subject part and not shared by any other parts or assemblies. If this is not possible, then we must prorate the portion of an operation that can be dedicated to the subject part. For example, if a part is customarily machined in the same work center as another part, it would be necessary to determine how much time the subject part will be allowed to consume on the work center. For quick capacity analyses, this can be done by estimating volumes and machine times each competing part needs to have and then using the appropriate fraction for the capacity analysis for the subject part. When this scenario is encountered, it is quite proper to do an entire analysis and then back off by an estimated percentage to take into account the effects of other products going throughout the work station. We do the necessary segregations at the very end of the analysis of practical capacity.

2. Make a Detailed List of All the Steps Necessary to Make the Part

A list of steps can be obtained from the methods sheet developed for the product. Developing the methods sheet for the product usually occurs during the design and process development phases, as discussed in Chapters 2 and 3. If it doesn't occur then, a rough-cut visualization of the method would need to be prepared. This rough method is similar to preparing a quote, and it is often used by job shops, which have no responsibility for design, only for manufacturing. When this method must be used, the engineers evaluating how to make the part must pay special attention to the true requirements of the job, and must make sure that what they are proposing to build is indeed what the customer has in mind. The best way to do that is to discuss the product and its documentation with the customer until there is a thorough understanding of the requirements.

3. Determine the Time to Perform Each Step

There are three ways to determine the time for each step, ranging from the fastest but least accurate to the slowest and most accurate:

    a. Estimates based on previous experience
    b. Stopwatch time study
    c. Predetermined scientific time standards

The use of these techniques was introduced in Chapter 3 in the discussions of creating process instructions. In many ways, we are actually doing a rough-cut methods analysis in order to determine the capacity of the factory for making specific products. Instead of the end results being a methods sheet for doing the work, we are using the output to understand how much work can be done in a specified period of time. As we can see, this is very closely allied with doing methods studies, and can have more than one useful end product. So, with that in mind, be aware that our discussion of determining the time to perform each step is as valid for setting up process instructions as it is for establishing a capacity factor.

a. Estimate Based on Previous Experience

Here the time to perform each step is based on what those involved think it should be. Obviously, it will only be accurate only insofar the person(s) making the estimate understand the nature of the work and are familiar with similar work. The method is usually sufficient for work that is the same as or similar to previous work. In the hammer example, spot-welding the head to the shaft is a very typical spot weld activity, and a supervisor or operator experienced with spot welding could give a decently accurate time estimate to make a wide-range capacity evaluation. But as we saw in Chapter 3, this is not a preferred way for setting times for doing the work.

The accuracy of estimated times is reasonably sufficient for all jobs that are low volume and for specific operations that are not critical path activities. In other words, if the operation being studied for capacity is not the prime concern of the company because other activities are already known to be limiting, then estimated times will always be sufficient for the purpose of documenting the capacity level. If this is the case—i.e., if the capacity study is for a secondary operation and is not crucial to a go, no go decision process—an estimate is satisfactory.

b. Stopwatch Time Study

The middle-level way of determining step cycle time is through stopwatch studies. This method is sometimes called the compromise level, because it portends to be scientific but in fact can be swayed by many nonstandard factors. However, since it is used to set process times in many industries, with considerable history of success, it is also sufficient for many capacity studies.

Stopwatch time study involves observing the operator or a person doing the task and measuring the portal-to-portal time it takes to do it. The important caveat in obtaining an accurate evaluation of the cycle time is twofold. First, we have to be sure that the person being timed is really doing the work in a manner that represents how it will be done during actual production in the real world. Second, we have to be certain that the pace the operator is working at reflects reality, including all the typical obstacles the operator will encounter.

The first caution is eliminated by the evaluator's thoroughly understanding how the work should be performed. In other words, she should be familiar with the methods sheet sequence and what the proper layout of the work station is to achieve the intended outcome. The evaluator also has to make sure that the sequence is followed during the timed evaluation. And further, the evaluator must make sure that the observed performance is being carried out in a manner in line with the methods instructions. No ad-libbing allowed. Many times the stopwatch study is first done observing a fellow engineer doing the work in an off-line situation so the observer becomes familiar with the work sequence beforehand.

The second caution is addressed if the person being observed is aware that the observer understands what a normal work pace is. The problem is usually a speedup of the cycle time to do the job, not a slowdown. Most people want to look good when being observed, and inevitably they put forth an effort that isn't sustainable over the course of a work shift. Obviously, this leads to erroneous evaluations which show capacity values higher than they actually are. The ways to mitigate this are simple. First, explain the situation to those being observed. Make sure they understand that the normal pace must be maintained. This may take considerable persuasion, particularly if the observation is occurring in a situation that has had labor/management confrontations in the past. Second, make sure that multiple observations are made, and preferably with as many different operators as possible. This averaging effect will mitigate many aberrations from normalcy. The observer also has to be careful to validate each measured cycle to assure that is a normal cycle without any unusual factors that could bias the portal-to-portal times.

With these points in mind, it is possible to get valid cycle times from stopwatch time studies. But doing anything less would make the results invalid and an unacceptable compromise. It should be pointed out that a good stopwatch time standard takes longer to establish than the uninformed would think. It's not unusual for a good study of something as simple as spot-welding the hammer head to the shaft to take several days of observations to be sufficiently accurate.

c. Predetermined Scientific Time Standards

Using scientific time standards is the most accurate and slowest method of measuring cycle time. When completed, there is no doubt that it is accurate and dependable. The drawback is that it has to be done by an engineer trained in the technique and will take upwards of a week to do it right. The greatest time spent is in preparing to do the work. The cycle is very precise and is based on the principles of motion economy (see Chapter 3 for definition). Scientific time standards will give precise cycle times for process instruction. Therefore, it is equally effective when used for capacity analysis. In fact, where a study has large ramifications for a company's future, there is no choice but to use scientific time standards.

4. Add the Time for the Various Steps to Get a Base Time to Do the Work

This is the summation step. We simply add all the method time steps together to get the total time to do the job. But keep in mind that all we need to do is sum the critical path operations, because all other operations can be done internally to those and will not affect the capacity evaluation. And here we deviate from the process instruction model. When developing process instructions, we need to know the time for each operation to set the resources needed to do the job. For capacity analysis, we need only add up the critical path factors to get the portal-to-portal times and understand the total envelope of product quantity over a finite period of time. We can do this because we know that the company has the necessary capability to do any non-critical path item within the cycle time of the critical path activity.

Remember, for capacity studies we're looking for bottleneck activities that limit output. We're not concerned about the staffing and equipment instructions and needs for doing all operations. This can be confusing at times. But think of it as a baseball game. We keep statistics about hits and errors, and earned run averages, but the only thing that matters in the end is which team scored the most runs. Developing process instructions is like optimizing the production of hits and batting averages, and assumes that if we do this to the best of our ability we will score runs and win the game. On the other hand, capacity analysis goes to the core issue—how many runs scored—and nothing else counts. We want to optimize scoring runs, not optimize batting averages. In manufacturing evaluations, process instructions assure that we keep costs down while making product. Capacity analysis tells us how much product can be made, and that is limited to the critical path activities—i.e., the bottleneck operations.

5. Divide the Time to Do the Work by Eight Hours to Get Theoretical Capacity per Shift per Work Station

Since we traditionally measure output on a per shift basis, it is common to express capacity as units per shift. This, of course, can be further refined to production per hour or any other increment of time. This is the last step, or the culmination of the process, in developing theoretical capacity. We use this information as a benchmark for comparison against other factories or other combinations of facilities within the same factory.

Theoretical capacity is a good way of measuring progress in productivity improvement programs. If we say our current capacity is X, we then can use it as a comparison over different time periods against other capacity evaluations. The caution here is to make sure that the methodology of defining process cycle times is done the same way every time. Otherwise, we are in danger of compromising the accuracy of the comparison.

Note, however, I haven't said we can use the calculation of theoretical capacity to set factory performance goals. We can't do that because we need to fully consider all of the variables that can affect the factory's ability to do value-added work. The only way to approach real capacity is to calculate practical capacity, something we'll do next. But before we go through that exercise, let's make sure we understand what theoretical capacity is used for: it is used for comparison purposes, specifically, to see whether the firm is making progress in improving productivity. Practical capacity, on the other hand, is used for setting actual production schedules.

To do comparisons, it is necessary to have stable measurement. Theoretical capacity is just that. There are no extenuating or transient circumstances to contend with. We simply blot them out of existence so a simple and effective comparison between dates in time can be made. This way we can assure that the comparison is true and unaffected by outside influences.

Comparisons, however, are not very useful in setting a production schedule. Here we have to know what we can really deliver to customers today. What we can do today is what the company can stake its reputation on today. Tomorrow may be a different matter altogether and has no pragmatic relationship to the here and now of today. So we need to find the current practical capacity to satisfy our scheduling needs. Let's look now at how we find practical capacity and how that differs from theoretical capacity.

How to Calculate Practical Capacity

Practical capacity differs from theoretical capacity the way an actual factory differs from a photograph of one. Practical capacity is the "down and dirty" look at reality with no holds barred. Here we are stating a value that can be used to make real promises against, and we're willing to bet the company's future survival against it. These strong statements tell us that this value has to be real and must be viewed through very clear lenses. To determine practical capacity, we need to understand the workings of the factory right now. We cannot be concerned with what it could be in some future time when the factory has absorbed the many lessons of optimal performance. Practical capacity deals with understanding the deductions from theoretical capacity that reflect the realism of the situation.

To illustrate how practical capacity is derived, let's look at a simple product with basically only one operation. This will allow us to clearly define the deductions without any other collateral issues to consider, and yet all factors of the technique will be fully demonstrated. The example we will use is an injection-molded lid for a picnic cooler. The process is straightforward. We place a die in an injection molding machine, we heat the die, and then under pressure we force plastic into the mold to form the part. The mold is cooled below the freezing point of the plastic and the piece extracted. We repeat this process as rapidly as we can, the major constraint being how fast the mold can be heated and cooled.

The formula for practical capacity is:

$$\text{Practical capacity} = \text{theoretical capacity} - \text{capacity deductions}$$

The capacity deductions are:
1. Setup time
2. Personal time
3. Absenteeism
4. Interference time
5. Manufacturing losses
6. Efficiency

Using the example of making cooler lids, the following demonstrates the process for calculating practical capacity. We will state that theoretical capacity is 60 injection molded lids per shift off the one injection mold press.

The process will be one of calculating the effect of all six of these deductions and subtracting from theoretical capacity to get the answer we need.

1. Setup time

Setup deductions have to be prorated over the entire order of identical parts ordered for the same production run. We should also recall that the methodology is identical for assemblies as well. So this example is universally applicable. Again, for simplicity purposes let's state that the production run is for 600 lids. With this in mind, the process for calculating the setup deduction is:

a. List the steps necessary to set up the workpiece on the work station to do the work.

Example: Set die in machine, adjust, bring up to temperature.

b. Estimate the time to do each step, and sum the times to get a total setup time.

Example: Set die in machine = 0.50 h, adjust = 0.25 h, time to bring to temperature = 1.00 h. Total = 1.75 h.

c. Prorate the setup time over the entire production run. The ratio of setup time for a shift is the setup hours divided by the hours in a shift, and in the normal case, a shift is eight hours. This has to be multiplied by the number of shifts required to make the order quantity of parts. Then to determine the number of parts to deduct from theoretical capacity we need to multiply the results by the theoretical capacity. This gives us the setup time deduction in parts per shift.

Example: X = setup time ratio; Y = number of shifts; Z = theoretical capacity setup time. Deduction = XYZ.

$$\text{Setup time deduction} = \left(\frac{1.75 \text{ h}}{8 \text{ h/shift}}\right)\left(\frac{60 \text{ parts/shift}}{600}\right)(60 \text{ parts/shift})$$
$$= 1.3125 \text{ parts/shift}$$

2. Personal time

Personal time tallies the amount of time an operator uses for breaks of all types. Management tries to codify and schedule those breaks so as to minimize the impact of these work stoppages on production output. These breaks are classified as production deflators and capacity deductions even though they are very necessary to sustain high-quality output and to maintain an effective and alert workforce. Typical of these breaks are rest breaks, lunch, and cleanup at the end of the shift.

If breaks are planned for, they have the least effect on production. For example, if it is known that there will be a 10-minute coffee break at 10:00 a.m., production control can schedule work activity up to that time and know that it is most likely to occur. Also, materials personnel know that between 10:00 a.m. and 10:10 a.m. there will be no movement of materials to work stations. Knowing these facts makes planning more definitive and hence more optimum.

The problems occur when an unplanned break happens. Perhaps an operator has to take an emergency telephone call—in itself, a minor incident. But if that operator holds a key position in an assembly line operation it could literally shut down the entire line. For this reason most companies try to prevent unplanned breaks or at least their effects. Companies running assembly lines often go to the extent of having relief operators on the payroll just to cover such incidents. They feel that the cost of additional personnel more than offsets the cost of lost production when a line goes down. This is particularly true when a flow operation consists of many dissimilar operations and balancing the output of one work center with the input of another work center it feeds is difficult to maintain. This is a phenomenon of trying to balance work centers with different inherent flow rates—a matter of bottleneck prevention and control.

Let's look at the calculation for the personal time deduction.

a. List the time allocated for each break, and sum the break times to get a total personal time.

Example: 2 rests @ 0.167 h = 0.333 h, lunch = 0.50 h, cleanup = 0.167 h. Total = 1.007 h.

---

b. Divide by 8 hours to get the fraction of the entire shift used up by personal time.

Example: 1.00 h/8 h per shift = 0.125 shift.

---

c. Multiply the personal time fraction of a shift by the theoretical capacity, to calculate the personal time deduction in parts per shift.

Example: (0.125 shift)(60 parts per shift) = 7.5 parts/shift.

---

3. Absenteeism

Absenteeism is the nemesis of all management and creates the most anxiety in trying to calculate practical capacity. Absenteeism is a highly personal thing and therefore hard to predict. In addition, not all absenteeism is equal. It is much more serious for a key operator to be off the job than for a peripheral occupation to go untended. As an example, a CNC machine operator holds a key position, and a maintenance oiler a peripheral one. The machine doesn't run without the operator, but it can run for a period of time without the oiler's presence, depending on the current state of machine maintenance. With this in mind we can see that percentages of absenteeism we use to calculate this deduction can be misleading. However, think of an analogy with quantum mechanics: while a particle may not be in a specific place at a specific time, on average we say it will be there as predicted. The same is true for absenteeism deductions. On a specific day, the effect of an absent worker can be minimal or maximum. But on average it will reflect the degree (percentage) of absenteeism experienced in the factory.

For the above reasons, to calculate the loss of capacity caused by absenteeism, we use the average attendance factor as its basis. If the company is experiencing an average 2% of its workforce absent on any given day, we would use 2% as the factor for the calculation. The method is to multiply the average percent absenteeism by the theoretical capacity. This is the absenteeism deduction in parts per shift.

Example: (0.02)(60 parts/shift) = 1.2 parts per shift.

Remember, this an average deduction and may not reflect the actual situation occurring on a particular day. To be more accurate, it would be necessary to determine who's absent and what capability the company has to cover the particular absenteeism. This is a tedious process, and for practical considerations its not done unless the production rate is tied to a very critical order.

4. Interference time

Interference time occurs when everything is in place for shop operations to do productive work but it doesn't occur because of some type of distraction or outside disruption. Some common issues that fall into this category are lack of material at the work station to work on, a maintenance problem slowing or stopping the machine, or a lack of engineering instructions on how to proceed.

The calculations for this deduction are again based on averages of past experience and may or may not be accurate for a specific instance for reasons similar to those mentioned in the discussion of absenteeism deductions from capacity.

To obtain a value to deduct from capacity for interference time, it is necessary to have a good understanding of idle labor categories. Idle labor is nonproductive labor. A timekeeping system ought to have various categories to log time against. If we expect to pay operators for being on the job for eight hours, we want to optimize productive versus nonproductive labor. One way to do this is to keep score of what percentage of time is nonproductive and why. Knowing why gives us opportunities to eliminate occurrences of nonproductive time. For this reason we set up categories of idle time to collect, analyze, and develop programs to minimize lost time. Figure 7-7 is an example of time records used to collect idle time information on a daily basis.

With time breakdown records as a basis, we can calculate the percent of interference time. I have to emphasize that we must be careful to make sure that we do not double-count idle time from other categories as interference time. Not all idle time is interference time. Therefore, the time categories we use in keeping track of nonproductive time have to be as specific as practicality permits. It is important to keep in mind that keeping score of how time is used during a workday cannot become all-engrossing and time-consuming in itself. Figure 7-7 gives an indication of what is

Labor Time Categories

Name_____

Date_____ Shift _____

Department_____

Instructions:
  * Show all hours worked.
  * Total recorded hours must equal total hours worked.
  * Break down into categories as shown.
  * Round to nearest tenth of an hour.

	Time (h)
Direct labor on direct work (value-added time)	_____
Direct labor on indirect work (non-value-added time)	
Administrative time:	
Training time	_____
Attending meetings	_____
Personal time	_____
Absent	_____
Setup time	_____
Manufacturing losses corrective labor time	_____
Interference time	
Waiting for materials	_____
Waiting for instructions	_____
Waiting for maintenance	_____
Inspection time	_____
Total non-value added time	_____
Total time recorded	_____
Total time worked	_____

Figure 7-7. Time breakdown record.

practical in timekeeping, and shows how interference time is itself broken down.

With the historical data available, we divide by eight hours to get the fraction of an entire shift used up by interference time. Let's say that the time log average shows 0.50 hours as interference time. Then we divide by 8 hours to get the portion of shift lost to interference time.

Example: 0.50 h/8 h = 0.0625 shift.

The lost shift time due to interference time is multiplied by the theoretical capacity, to obtain the interference time capacity deduction.

Example: (0.0625)(60 parts/shift) = 3.75 parts per shift.

3.75 parts per shift is the average number of parts lost every shift due to interference time. Once more, the same admonition raised in the absenteeism capacity deduction holds. It is good for average use, but not necessarily correct for a specific shift.

5. Manufacturing losses

Manufacturing losses are divided into the following categories:

a. Operator error
b. Process failure
c. Design error
d. Defective materials

Manufacturing engineers keep close tabs on manufacturing losses to monitor the overall effectiveness of the product-producing activity. They catalog reasons for manufacturing losses in order to try to minimize them and, in some instances, eliminate them entirely. Manufacturing losses are good labor expended for parts that cannot be used because of a deficiency as measured against the intent of the design. For example, if a lid is to be airtight and the mold has allowed porosity paths to open between the inner and outer surfaces, so that the lid is not airtight, then the resulting product will not do its intended job. The labor and material have been wasted. This is a manufacturing loss. The engineers need to know why it happened and what steps can be taken to prevent it from happening again.

Operator errors are losses that occur when operators have not followed the prescribed method: the operator made a mistake. The corrective action is to understand why the operator varied from the prescribed method and take steps to assure he knows how to do it right in the future. A good deal of operator discipline results from operators' not caring enough to always do the job correctly. Next to chronic absenteeism, this is the largest cause of operator dismissals and punitive time off. The secret to minimizing operator error is to make operators part of the process development team and to assure that the methods to be followed are sufficiently explained and sufficient training is provided.

Process failure is a loss that occurs when the process itself is not robust enough to always give satisfactory results. This means that the yield factors are significantly less than 100%. In Chapter 4, on quality control, we saw how statistical methods can be used to measure a process's ability to perform within specification and how we measure to determine if a process is under control. These are the main tools for eliminating process error. Manufacturing engineers need to measure, adjust processes, remeasure, adjust again, and iterate as often as necessary to get the tolerance band of acceptability to fall within the six sigma spread of normal distribution. There is no particular right or wrong way to do this. Every process will have its range and limitations as established by the physics and chemistry of the procedure. The engineers have to understand the science behind the process and react accordingly, first, to predict what it should be, and second, to adjust as data either validate or refute the predictions. Getting processes under control is the one primary task that manufacturing engineers have to perform successfully for a company to prosper.

Design errors are pure and simple mistakes made by the design function for the product. If operators are performing to methods, process tolerance ranges meet the maximum and minimum range of the design tolerance, and still the part fails, then the error is a design error. The all too familiar recalls of manufactured products are manifestations of design errors. Everything was done in accordance with plan, yet the part still doesn't function correctly as intended. This means the original solution to the design need was faulty. These types of failures cannot be fixed in the factory but have to go back to the design development itself. These losses, when they occur, tend to be large and can, in severe cases, literally cause a company to go bankrupt. Fortunately design errors are the least frequent cause of manufacturing losses.

Defective materials are vendor items, raw materials or component parts that were allowed into the factory but did not meet the design specifications. When this happens, the best intentions go awry and products come out defective. The cause of such occurrences is twofold: first, not properly documenting the specifications to the vendor; and second, not properly assuring that the vendor has the capability of meeting the specifications. Both kinds of failure are shortcuts too many companies take; they then wonder why their quality levels are not what they should be. Allowing defective materials into its products is a classic example of a company's being penny-wise and dollar-foolish. No matter what the situation, vendors need to be evaluated for their ability to produce in accordance with specification. But often the ability to do this is retarded by the company's own lackadaisical attitude toward defining measurable and accurate materials specification. Most vendor-related manufacturing losses are not vendor-caused. They come from sloppiness in enforcing adherence to design specificity outside the factory's fences and imposing it on vendors. Most vendors will do as required, but no more. It is up to design and manufacturing engineering, working through purchasing, to assure that vendors are valid members of the supply chain and as such understand fully what has to be produced and the ramifications of not producing it. Nothing less is acceptable.

These are the four causes of manufacturing losses. Now, for the impact on capacity, all we can do is surmise that the level of losses will remain as is, unless a specific, pinpointed effort is under way to change some aspect of it. If the level remains constant, the manufacturing loss capacity deduction is an estimate of extra parts made per shift to overcome scrap and/or rework. This is usually done by averaging the number of scrapped or reworked parts per shift over a reasonable period of time, anywhere from one week to three months, on average.

One thing to point out regarding estimating the effect of manufacturing losses on the deduction from capacity: Since reducing manufacturing losses is usually a high-focus activity of any respectably functioning company, there tends to be an optimistic impression that things are going to get better and soon. Do not fall for this. Capacity evaluations have to be realistic and conform to the pragmatism of the situation. No one wants to be involved in failure, and manufacturing losses are failures in procedures; therefore, the tendency to paint rosy pictures is strong. Failures occur because we don't know how to do certain things. And the things that fail the most are typically the hardest things to do. So it is prudent not to give the benefit of the doubt when it comes to manufacturing losses. Use the historical data to determine the capacity deduction related to manufacturing losses.

Example. Let's assume that the data show manufacturing losses of three parts per shift.

---

6. Efficiency

For capacity deduction purposes, efficiency refers to the planned time to do a job divided by the actual time it takes. To estimate efficiency, we use a variant of this formula in which the time is held constant and instead we divide the Actual number of parts to be made per shift by the number of parts planned to be made per shift. We use the theoretical capacity in parts as the stand-in for planned time. In the lid example this is 60 injection-molded lids per shift. We then look at recent production (back two or three days for a quick-cycle product like injection-molded lids). Let's say this was 54 parts per shift. We then divide the recent average yield by the expected yield under the theoretical capacity to obtain an efficiency value for the practical capacity calculation.

Example: 54 parts per shift actual/60 parts per shift theoretical capacity = 0.90, or 90% efficiency.

The reason we use the recent performance values instead of a historical average is that when setting practical capacity, we want to do just that. If our best operators are no longer working on this particular product, then we must reflect on current circumstances. There are other ways of computing efficiencies, and, by all means, use them if your company has the proper data on hand and can focus its measurements directly and only on the products related to the capacity study. Many companies calculate efficiency but only for the overall work of a department. In other words, they group all products together to come up with a composite efficiency value. Quite often this evolves about standard hours earned versus standard hours planned in a certain department and is not focused finely enough for a particular part or assembly, or at least cannot be without significant effort to filter out unneeded information. Whatever the case, use the best specific value of efficiency available for calculating the efficiency capacity deduction.

Now, to calculate the efficiency deduction, the efficiency value is multiplied by the theoretical capacity. Then the result is subtracted from the theoretical capacity to arrive at the efficiency deduction in parts per shift.

Example: (60 parts per shift) – (0.90 efficiency)(60 parts per shift) = 6 parts per shift.

We've now obtained values for all the deduction factors. The last step is to tabulate and sum them and deduct the total from theoretical capacity to obtain practical capacity:

Theoretical capacity:	60 molded lids per shift
Deductions:	
Setup time	–1.3125 molded lids per shift
Personal time	–7.5 molded lids per shift
Absenteeism	–1.2 molded lids per shift
Interference time	–3.75 molded lids per shift
Manufacturing losses	–3.0 molded lids per shift
Efficiency	–6.0 molded lids per shift
Practical capacity:	37.2375 molded lids per shift
Practical capacity: rounds down to	37 molded lids per shift

37 is the output number we would use to size the factory—to determine the number of work stations required—and to make delivery commitments against. It is reasonable to expect that on any given day the factory might be able to make more, but the numerical results indicate that it cannot be expected to do so for a sustained period, and no delivery promise should be based on a higher number.

This concludes the discussion of work station configuration. We see that there are many factors to consider, ranging from ergonomics, to material flow, to what method of manufacturing is being pursued, all the way to pragmatic aspects of capacity analysis. Pragmatism and interrelationships of manufacturing engineering techniques are the key words here. If I've accomplished but one thing in the discussion of workplace configuration, I hope it is a sense of the practical bonding of many techniques and different ways of looking at the same problem—a sort of checks-and-balances approach toward achieving a workable work station configuration. With this checking and double checking, engineers can set up a factory that is competitive and that responds to customer needs in virtually all circumstances and in virtually any geographic location.

Chapter 8

Raw Materials and Work-in-Process Inventory Control in the Factory

Keeping the factory stocked with raw materials and purchased subassemblies is essential for optimum shop operations performance. While this may be a trite statement, it is not necessarily a simple task to accomplish. This is so because we do not have the option of overstocking the factory with materials. First, there likely wouldn't be enough space to store excess material, and it would cause internal logistic problems. Second, we could hardly afford such an extravagance. Keeping the factory properly stocked with materials means making sure the factory never runs out of critical materials and at the same time minimizing the cost of doing so. In this chapter we will review the strategies employed to buy materials and to achieve proper inventory controls, both for the input of raw materials and for movement of materials within the factory.

In Chapter 5, I described how MRP II is the dominant factor in scheduling the shop. In that chapter the emphasis was on work station scheduling. In this chapter, I will demonstrate that MRP II is also the dominant factor in purchasing and inventory control. I will not repeat the descriptions of how MRP II works. Suffice it to say that purchasing schedules are derived from the master schedule and are coordinated with production schedules in a way that allows buyers to place orders compatible with need. The same scheduling algorithms used to create operations schedules also drive the purchasing schedules. I will demonstrate the technique for satisfying need throughout the discussion. But since the thrust of this book is on *work station* optimization, we need to understand the contributing roles and responsibilities of shop operations personnel in controlling materials inputs into and within the factory and how they ally themselves with materials personnel.

THE PROCESS OF SCHEDULING IN MATERIALS MANAGEMENT

In discussing scheduling, we saw that there were four cascading factors, going from a strategic viewpoint to the very pragmatic, here and now actions. These four factors, first introduced in Chapter 5 are:

- A master schedule
- Analysis of capacity and capability
- A release of an order to make a product or subcomponent

- A detailed release of a work order at the lowest detail level to the work station

These are equally true for the materials phase of scheduling. Let's briefly see how these four factors apply to materials management.

A Master Schedule

The master schedule sets the overall game plan the company will follow. As a result of management's setting a master schedule, the materials buyer understands the magnitude and timing of the company's plan and can plan purchases accordingly. This assures that materials are on hand as needed.

The buyer also has an opportunity to review new products and to compare them with products the company has made before. For repeat products, the buyer can review her performance in obtaining materials in accordance with schedule. This performance review allows her to correct delivery parameters as required. For new products, the buyer can look for similarities between current and past products from the viewpoint of purchases and plan accordingly. Having a master schedule allows the purchasing team to *act* rather than just react to current situations.

Analysis of Capacity and Capability

The rule of thumb is to have materials on hand as needed and to minimize the just-in-case philosophy. Just-in-case encourages hoarding of materials, creating storage problems, and inflates expenses. All companies want to avoid that, and to do so we need to know the usage rates.

By having a capacity and capability analysis available, we can calculate usage rates and calibrate materials order and delivery rates to meet "real" needs. Also, understanding capability allows purchasing to help engineering. This is especially true in tolerance zone activities. By assuring that raw materials and component parts are compatible with capability, the buyer can enhance a company's process yield. By making sure materials are within the range of machinability or at proper net tolerances, a buyer can reduce the times necessary to process the parts and also increase the yield. Without a coordinated scheduling activity, which in turn supports a concurrent engineering philosophy, it is unlikely that such activities would occur, or even be considered.

A Release of an Order to Make a Product or Subcomponent

An order release schedule allows purchasing to create schedules compatible with dates that have been offset to assure on-time delivery. There are two "active" scheduling scenarios MRP II driven companies use: orders release, and dispatching. Orders release is the primary schedule for purchasing, because it is offset to allow the company to establish a short-range schedule of perhaps up to 60 days. Purchasing, knowing the orders release schedule, negotiates with vendors to release materials and deliver them to the factory.

When orders are issued to vendors, the goal is to have the supplies arrive on time and at a sufficient rate to support production. This is often misconstrued to be the classical just-in-time (JIT) concept we think of when describing the Japanese production system (although we saw in Chapter 5 that this is a secondary benefit of JIT). Many people erroneously believe that this means that materials arrive off a truck right at the work station just when needed to supply the process. What we really mean by having materials arrive on time is that they are available for the company to process prior to use.

There are many factors that militate against having materials arrive directly at the work station. The critical one that comes to mind is the need for perfect coordination, which rarely occurs, because it presupposes perfect communication. We want to keep manufacturing operations as simple as possible to minimize possibilities for error, and depending on perfect communication is a stretch, at best. But consider what *wouldn't* happen if materials were delivered directly to the work station as soon as they arrived. Ordinarily, material first has to be received into the inventory and financial systems. It has to be counted, and someone has to verify that it is as ordered. Then it has to be inspected to assure that it is at the quality level required for production. These are nontrivial procedures. There is always a possibility that the vendor made an error, so that what is expected is not what arrives, either in quantity or quality or both. Therefore, it is unrealistic to expect that materials can be received and dispatched immediately to the work station. A buffer is needed, and that's the receiving inventory warehouse.

This buffer situation, along with a calculated amount of additional material to maintain the buffer, is coordinated with the MRP II orders release process with feeds from the master schedule. Orders release in all practicality manages this buffer.

A Detailed Release of a Work Order at the Lowest Detail Level to the Work Station

This is the work station dispatch system. Production control releases daily schedules to each work station. Materials management, through its inventory control subfunction, dispatches materials to the work stations in accordance with the daily schedules.

The materials release schedule tends to be ahead of the daily dispatch schedule by at least a work shift and possible up to two days (using a shift of eight hours as the typical duration of the work day) in order for materials to be available at the start of the shift. Since production schedules are often made for two to five days at a time, the coordination is not hard to accomplish.

The desire is to dispatch inventory already on hand. For reasons already mentioned, by working with on-hand inventory we know we are sending validated inventory to the work station. With the inventory we have, there is a high probability of knowing it will be usable. The last thing we want is for poor-quality materials to be sent to work stations. At best, this material will take extra work to be made usable, and at worst it will result in scrap. This is a sure productivity deflator and needs to be guarded against.

Let's now expand on these four factors of scheduling via discussions of the materials function, its relationship with shop operations, and the responsibilities of both of them for controlling the uses of materials for production.

THE MATERIALS MANAGEMENT FUNCTION

In its strictest interpretation, the definition of materials management is the procurement, storage, and distribution of raw materials and purchased parts used to manufacture a company's products. However, most organization charts also add in scheduling, transportation, and distribution of finished goods to customers to the list of materials management responsibilities. Many companies also add purchasing of nonproduction materials to the set of responsibilities. For our purposes, we're interested only in a strict, narrowly confined interpretation of responsibilities.

Materials are managed externally by purchasing, and internally, before release to shop operations, by inventory control. Let's take a look at those functions to better understand the roles they play in the integrated manufacturing scenario.

The Role of Purchasing

The purchasing department is the sole procurement agency of the production function. Its job is to obtain raw materials and outside purchased components at the lowest prices possible and at the required quality level. It must do this in a manner that fully supports the real-time phased needs of manufacturing. The department is populated by professionals who are knowledgeable of commodity prices and component part prices. They also need to have a realistic understanding of the cycle times required to make the parts or deliver the materials that will be used to manufacture their company's products.

The purchasing agent (often called a *buyer*) has the same role—even more pronounced—as the leadoff batter of a baseball team. Like the leadoff batter, he has to get on base to be advanced and batted in by power slots in the batting order. He has to make sure that the products needed to start production are on hand as needed (akin to reaching base), and he cannot fail. Lost time due to late materials is like all other time-based losses: it is irretrievable. So all is lost if the company does not have the material on time; there is no second hitter to make up for the leadoff batter's failure. This may seem harsh, but unfortunately it's true. With lead times between product conception and sales at the local store ever shrinking, time lost because of a late start is extremely difficult if not impossible to rectify. This means that the onus is on the buyer to make sure critical path materials are available as needed. To do this, the buyer has to know what to buy and when. Let's take a look at what's involved in doing so.

The MRP II Based Materials Schedule

The buyer bases his purchasing decisions on the MRP II scheduling algorithm, the inventory on hand, and the anticipated cycle time from order placement. The knowledge for making correct choices depends on understanding the way MRP II creates schedules, the rate of materials usage in the factory, and the production methods of suppliers, which determine the "real" lead times the company will encounter.

The MRP II schedule is the same as discussed in Chapter 5. The only difference is that the buyer is interested in the *offset* of when materials need to be ordered versus the start production date. Order release planning is the module of most interest. It determines the sequence in which purchase orders should be released.

The professionalism that's involved in this function is understanding when to buy to get the right price and to have the supplies available as needed. Knowing when to buy is part knowing the market and part knowing the factory's inventory levels. The laws of supply and demand prevail, with the buyer striving to always be buying when there is more material available than currently needed. The buyer needs to be constantly cognizant of pricing trends and to always be in a negotiating mode with his vendors. A penny saved in procurement of supplies goes directly to the bottom line, with no further value-added activities required.

MRP II systems generate material usage needs schedules for all identified parts and subassemblies the company chooses to track. This gives the buyer a road map to follow for when the items will be needed and in what quantity. The decision on what items to track is based on a method called the ABC method. According to this method, class A items are either very expensive items or those that are difficult to obtain. Difficult to obtain frequently means that the lead time is long and therefore orders have to be placed considerably before they are required. Forgings for steam turbine spindles would be an example of a class A item. They are very expensive, and take upwards of two to four months to produce. Class B items are of medium relative expense, but are critical to the internal manufacturing process. They can have long lead times also. But generally speaking, they're shorter than class A procurement times. Class C items are commonly called *floor stock*. These are the nuts, bolts, and washers, etc., used for assembly purposes— vital for success, but individually relatively inexpensive. MRP II normally does not manage or predict needs for class C items. For ease of control they are kept in bins, barrels, and tubs, and when the level of items in the container falls to a certain prescribed level, purchasing then reorders. This is a visual inventory management system and works quite well as long as shop operations personnel monitor the floor stock levels and request resupply when the trigger level is reached. In summary, MRP II tracks usage of class A and B components, while class C items are generally managed by shop operations personnel.

Figure 8-1 shows how MRP II presents information to the buyer to manage purchases of class A and B parts or raw materials. The header identifies the part with a number and description. It also describes such things as unit of measure, order lead times, the shrinkage factor to guard against a too rapid utilization of the part (e.g., scrap, or wasting of materials), a standard purchase cost (usually the lowest price paid in recent measurement periods), and various stocking codes. It also shows the quantity on hand at the start of the measurement period.

The body of the report is a usage schedule for the products being manufactured consisting of a balance on hand after procurements are received and again after stock is depleted. This is identical to carrying a running total in a checkbook as funds are spent and deposits made. In the MRP II case, inventory gains are being posted electronically upon receipt of materials at the shipping dock and upon depletion of materials—i.e., both when goods reach the warehouse and when they are shipped to the customer. Note that the report contains history, the present period activity, and the future schedule. By analyzing the requirements and comparing with on-hand quantities and scheduled needs, the report suggests to the buyer when to replenish stock.

Prior to MRP II, this calculation of stock needs was done manually and laboriously by purchasing clerks for the many different items necessary for production. As one would imagine, this took the energies of many people. Now, with MRP II, the computer does it all. It can handle many more items, and do it faster with unerring accuracy.

The inventory levels also fluctuate due to changing rates of consumption in the factory. But these are more predictable than, say, commodity prices, because there are fewer variables. The variables are usually just the rates of

Part Number: 123E456Pt.1   Description: hammer rubber grip
U/M: each   Lead Time: 4.2 weeks   Safety Stock: 600
EOQ: 1000   Multiples: 1   Shrinkage %: 0%
Order Strategy: max/min routine (600 min)
On Hand: 575   Standard Cost: $0.29 ea.

	History		Present		Future Schedule	
	7/15/98	8/15/98	9/15/98	11/15/98	12/15/98	1/15/99
start	575	575	1575	-8425	575	1575
receipts	0	1000	0	9000	1000	0
requirements	0	0	10000	8425	0	0
available	575	1575	1575	9000	1575	1575
suggested buy	1000	0	9000	1000	0	0
end	575	1575	-8425	575	1575	1575

Figure 8-1. Example of MRP II part usage schedule.

usage and spoilage. In Chapter 7 we discussed usage rates calculation with respect to resupplying the work stations. The exact same concept is used to resupply the factory. This means that understanding true inventory levels is extremely critical. We will discuss more of this with the study of inventory control management.

Lead Time Evaluations

Why is lead time important? Because hoarding materials actually increases costs. And it does so two ways. First, having lots of just-in-case inventory on hand requires storage space to house it. Space costs money, and storing material in it gives precious little return on investment. Second, cash has to be spent to buy materials. Having more inventory than actually necessary becomes waste—again, virtually no return on investment. Compounding both of these negative incentives for having more rather than less material on hand is the fact that most companies have to "rent" money to operate. They borrow it against a line of credit which costs whatever the prevailing interest rates are. So we see that more inventory simply costs more to have, and with no reasonable additional return on investment. The strategy, then, is to minimize inventory purchase lead times and use materials as quickly as the company can. This minimizes the cost of manufacturing and indicates why we want the shortest lead times possible. Generally speaking the more inventory *turns* per year a factory has, the better its profit margin will be.

Determining lead time parameters is purchasing's responsibility; the parameters are used for assuring that materials are in stock when needed. The buyer also uses this information in leveraging to get the best deals for his company from the suppliers. Lead time is set as a function of raw material vendors' manufacturing time and transportation time to the manufacturing site. An estimate of cycle time starting with order placement is requested from vendors, who may or may not be willing to supply this type of information. If the vendor feels that it is his competitive advantage not to divulge cycle time, an estimate has to be done internally by manufacturing engineering for purchasing. They do it in a manner similar to calculating factory capacity: they extract from the method, interpolate within it, and apply it to vendors for getting the best schedule delivery dates possible. Penalty clauses are also occasionally used when the items being purchased are expensive and/or critical to success. Let's look at an example of lead time calculation and the specific methodology many purchasing functions use.

In the hammer example, we saw that the rubber grip of the hammer, part no. 123E456Pt1 (see Figure 3.5) is a purchased part and must be present to accomplish operation number 40. Therefore, purchasing must order it with enough lead time to have it arrive on time. To do so, the buyer must place the order on time for the vendor to extract the product from inventory, load the order on a truck, and have it arrive at the factory in time to be received financially, inspected, and dispatched to the work station. Figure 8-2 illustrates the process the buyer goes through to assure on time delivery. Let's use the process to determine lead time for the hammer rubber grip.

1. Understand vendor's manufacturing cycle time by doing the following:
   a. Ask vendor, and/or
   b. Verify by internal manufacturing engineering evaluation
      (1) Estimate by comparing with similar parts made in the factory
      (2) Perform rough-cut methods study for parts not compatible with internal capabilities
2. Determine whether vendor has the part in stock and it is for sale.
   a. Not reserved for other customers
   b. Evaluate seasonal relationships of the product to demand
   c. Evaluate price fluctuations and whether they are factor in the vendor's decision to release for sale
3. Determine transportation time from vendor's warehouse/factory to the manufacturing facility.
4. Determine receive/inspection cycle time required at the manufacturing facility.
5. Calculate maximum and minimum time ranges for items 1–4.
6. Evaluate risk factors* for using minimum times
   1 = no risks,   0 = guaranteed poor choice
   (Item 1 risk factor)(item 2 risk factor)...(item n risk factor) = total risk factor
   Interpretation: 0.5 = split time between maximum and minimum
                   0.25 = use 75% of maximum time
                   0.75 = use 25% of maximum time
7. Use the sum of the selected times for each of steps 1 through 4 to determine the lead time. Convert to expected work times, not calendar times.
   <u>Example:</u> 24 hours will be 3 work days if the work time is only one 8-hour shift per day.

* Risk factors are internal specifics related to steps 1 through 4, individually. They vary in accordance with the nature of the steps for the particular transaction.

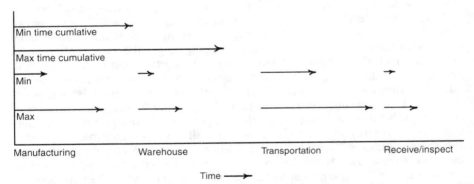

Figure 8-2. On-time delivery process for purchased parts: how to forecast lead times.

Step 1

The first step is to understand the vendor's process for making the grip. Since this is significantly different from anything done by the factory making the hammer, the best bet is to persuade the vendor to tell what the cycle time is. This can be done by simply asking, and the answer can then be verified with a plant tour. A tour can easily be arranged if the vendor needs to comply with specification-imposed quality standards. Since most specifications require demonstration of ability to hold certain tolerances and physical/chemical characteristics, it is quite common for customers' technical people to make process evaluation visits. If this is the case, they will be able to discern what the approximate cycle time is. Of course, the company can also undertake a technology search via the Internet or other reliable reference sources to learn the typical processes used to make rubber grips and then do a rough-cut time estimate.

Let's assume that it takes a maximum of 125 hours to make 10,000 hammer grips (the order quantity required) as stated by the vendor. Let's also assume that an Internet search resulted in a rough-cut cycle time of 75 hours. Note: It is not uncommon for a vendor to pad the actual time in order to create some buffer for potential problems during production. This margin of safety would minimize the vendor's risk of ever paying a penalty for late delivery. So we see we have a 0.60 probability risk factor built into the estimate.

Step 1. Manufacturing Cycle Time

$$a = \text{probability of occurrence} = 0.6$$
$$b = \text{manufacturing optimum cycle time} = 75 \text{ h}$$

$$\text{Manufacturing cycle time} = \frac{b}{a} = \frac{75}{0.6} = 125 \text{ h}$$

Step 2

With cycle time established, the next step is to determine warehouse cycle time, and at the same time evaluate whether it's necessary to contend with a warehouse cycle at all. If the hammer grip is a common item used for many applications—perhaps rake handles or competitors' hammer offerings—it is conceivable that the vendor makes this product for many different customers and tends to keep it in stock. If so, the vendor's marketing department may also be surveying the potential for sales and deciding how many to make for stock with the confidence that there will be customers for them. Therefore, the number of grips the vendor wants to keep in stock may be a variable. If this is the case, and if product is normally available, then the lead time is impacted primarily by how fast the vendor can literally process the order, pack the shipping cartons, and load on transportation (in this case, usually trucks). Therefore there is no significant warehouse time to contend with.

But it is not as easy as this. We have to be assured that the vendor will sell the grips on a first come, first served basis and this may not be the case. Suppose a rake manufacturer has entered into a long-term agreement with the vendor guaranteeing a certain amount of business on an annual basis for a set price. In return, the vendor guarantees always having adequate stock on hand to deliver to the rake manufacturer. Then, when our hammer manufacture's buyer approaches the vendor to buy grips, she may be in competition with another buyer who has guaranteed access to the in-stock product. If that's the case, the hammer manufacturer may be forced to deal with manufacturing cycle times even though in-stock inventory exists. The moral of the tale is that the buyer has to understand how dependable the in-stock source is, and this has to be factored into determining lead time.

The source reliability factor is evaluated on the probability of gaining access to existing stock when needed. Factors to consider are:

1. Is the product seasonal? If it is, then buying from stock in season is a lot less reliable than buying out of season.
2. Does the vendor have tight or excess capacity? Tight would mean difficult to get; excess, the opposite. This is so because a tight-capacity factory wouldn't be likely to have the option to build for stock. It would be hard-pressed to build for received orders.
3. Is it a commodity whose prices fluctuate with demand? If so, the company may not be willing to pay inflated prices, because of their potential erosion of profit margin. Here the material may be available, but for an unacceptable price.
4. Does the company have a long-term JIT type of contract with the vendor? If the answer is yes, then the likelihood of being denied a purchase for in-stock materials is minimal.

Let's say that the hammer manufacturer has entered into a JIT contract with the vendor, and therefore the probability that the vendor can supply stock out of current inventory is high. We will say 90%. (Never use 100%; that disallows any unforeseen situation, such as, for example, a wildcat labor strike suffered by the vendor's rubber supplier.) The next judgment to make is how long it should take to process an order. With a JIT contract, not too long. The hammer company would not have to undergo a credit check before release of supplies to the warehouse. Most companies try to turn over in-stock inventory in less than a day. Therefore we would use 1 day as the cycle time.

Step 2. Warehouse Cycle Time

$$a = \text{probability of availability} = 0.9$$
$$b = \text{turnaround time} = 1 \text{ day}$$
$$\text{Warehouse cycle time} = \frac{b}{a} = \frac{1}{0.9} = 1.11 \text{ days} = 26.66 \text{ h}$$

Step 3

The next step in the process is to determine the likely elapsed time it will take to ship the goods from the vendor's facility to the location where they will be used. Delivering the hammer grips to the production line will depend considerably on the mode of transportation selected, and this is entirely in the hands of purchasing. Since most purchase transactions in the manufacturing domain are FOB point of purchase, the hammer manufacturer will select the way the product will be transported to the factory. The choices are many. Some of the common ones are company-owned trucks, common carrier freight forwarders, express shipments such as provided by UPS and FedEx, the U.S. Postal Service, and, for intercontinental transportation, ship or air. Sometimes the need for the parts is so acute that drastic measures are undertaken, such as calling upon courier services or dispatching employees to go get the material. The goal is to use the lowest-cost transportation that guarantees delivery by the forecasted need date.

Keeping in mind that having inventory on hand longer than needed increases cost just as not having it does. The purchasing agent has to balance these opposing potentials for waste and do the right thing. This is not easy to accomplish in its entirety without some risk. The purchasing agent has to factor the accuracy of manufacturing and warehousing cycle time estimates against the internal manufacturing need date. If the agent feels the previous two factors are relatively well known and they do not eat up too much of the time before production needs kick in, then the solution would be to book a transportation scheme of the lowest cost that will still have material arrive on time. Any deterioration of the assessment will require a speedier transportation selection, but at additional cost. Typically, if the buy is for an extended period of time with several releases, the choice would be the least expensive transportation, with the vendor partnering to let the agent know if there were any foreseeable delays pending. This working with the vendor simplifies the process for the agent. Also, many contracts call for the vendor to arrange shipment and simply put it on the bill.

Transportation costs are normally not a factor. We simply use the lowest-cost method's cycle time for the lead time evaluation. We can safely reason that if the vendor is late, or our order is placed late, we will simply absorb the additional cost for faster transportation. Purchasing will always make the strongest effort to assure material arrives before the need date. So we will use the best-cost method for obtaining transportation lead time.

Assuming that the grip maker is located within 500 miles of the factory, we would assign 24 hours for this factor. Five hundred miles is considered the norm for rail or truck transportation in one day. But we should also know what the shortest cycle time would be. In this case, we would also use one day, because to do otherwise would imply accuracy greater than the process presupposes to have. As a point of information, the fastest time would be courier service, and that would be within 48 hours from anywhere in the world, and in most cases within a day. Purchasing agents, as a matter of course, keep tabs on specific cycle times for all sorts of transportation options, and many keep it as an insurance policy backup to use if required.

Step 3. Transportation Cycle Time

$$a = \text{probability of accuracy} = 0.9$$
$$b = \text{transportation (truck) time} = 1 \text{ day}$$
$$\text{Transportation cycle time} = \frac{b}{a} = \frac{1}{0.9} = 1.11 \text{ days} = 26.66 \text{ h}$$

Step 4

The last step is to calculate the total receiving time at the hammer maker's factory. This is entirely within the domain of the user company, but it must be calculated, and it, too, will have some potential variability.

Receiving cycle time has two components, which should overlap as much as possible: financial receipt, and quality receipt. Financial receipt is the logging in of shipments as received inventory. The inventory has monetary value and is logged as a "payable." In other words, it is a financial liability that the company has to honor. In most cases, this means getting the receipt in the queue for payment. However, finance should not pay for anything until there is a definitive check to assure that what was ordered was received—or, at least, until it is known what has been received and what needs to be paid for. Second, finance should not pay the invoice until the quality function verifies that the received goods do indeed meet the specifications set out in the purchase order.

So we see that financial receipt is simply the receiver's logging in of the shipment. No attempt has been made yet to add it into the inventory count for the particular item. That happens only after quality releases it for production. Until that time the material is like a passenger arriving after an international flight. She has arrived in the country, but is not yet legally permitted to be there until she clears customs and immigration.

The incoming quality inspection needs to be thorough but should not be bureaucratic or take a long time to accomplish. An incoming receiving quality plan should be in place prior to purchasing the material. It would usually consist of a review of the specification imposed on the vendor and a verification that it has been complied with. Many times companies prequalify vendors, certifying that the vendor has the system and controls in effect to assure that the product will be made in accordance with the specification. This is done through a site visit by quality, purchasing, and design engineering. They present their needs to the vendor, who in turn demonstrates an ability to comply. If the site visitation team is satisfied, the vendor is certified, and thereafter the vendor's goods are considered as if they were made within the buying company's factory. Then the vendor's own internal inspection documents and quality assurance procedures are verified at receiving inspection (not a full inspection) reducing the cycle time considerably.

If there is no such certification, then quality will have to carry out a statistical quality sampling procedure to assure that the goods are acceptable. Since this can take considerable time, it is to all parties' advantage to have vendor site qualification visits and certification beforehand. This assures materials of excellent quality getting into the factory, and quicker payment for the vendor.

In the case of the grip supplier, let's assume that the site visit was successful and the receiving cycle time is four hours—one-half of a shift. If the site visit wasn't accomplished, it is conceivable that the receiving cycle time could be as long as five working days. Once the material passes the receiving hurdle it is officially entered into the inventory count and is available for use.

Step 4. Receive Cycle Time

$$a = \text{probability of accuracy} = 0.9$$
$$b = \text{receive cycle time} = 4\text{ h}$$

$$\text{Receive cycle time} = \frac{b}{a} = \frac{4}{0.9} = 4.44\text{ h}$$

To arrive at a lead time we sum all four steps to get a value that is conservative but realistic for our needs. We can be assured that the lead time will be a pragmatic value that allows the hammer manufacturer to minimize exposure to excessive materials carrying costs, and at the same time protect the factory from unnecessary stock outs. The value would be the following sum and would be used in the part usage schedule (Figure 8-1) after appropriate interpretations:

Manufacturing cycle time = b/a = 75/0.6 =	125.00 h
Warehouse cycle time = b/a = 1/0.9 = 1.11 days =	26.66 h
Transportation cycle time = b/a = 1/0.9 = 1.11 days =	26.66 h
Receive cycle time = b/a = 4/0.9 =	4.44 h
Total lead time =	182.76 h
	7.61 days

Round to 8.00 days.

We see that the lead time is the equivalent of eight working days if the entire process—all four steps—is carried out in 24-hour (three-shift) workdays. But since this is highly unlikely, we need to modify our lead time to take into account the realism of true work time. A manufacturing firm will not choose to work a three-shift workday unless it is in extreme need and can afford to do so (triple its supervisory staff, etc.). Therefore we must assume that the manufacturing cycle time will be done in increments of one eight-hour shift per day. In fact, the only step that we can assume will occur in a continuous 24 hour a day cycle would be the transportation. This being the case, the lead time would look like the following:

		Work hours per day	Work days
Manufacturing cycle time =	125.00 h	8	15.625
Warehouse cycle time =	26.66 h	8	3.33
Transportation cycle time =	26.66 h	24	1.11
Receive cycle time =	4.44 h	8	0.555
Total lead time =	182.76 h		
	7.61 days		20.62 days

Round to 21 days.

We now have to realize that factories also try to work only five days a week to avoid overtime pay at the traditional time and a half for Saturdays and double time for Sundays. So we do one final calculation. We divide 21 days by 5 to obtain a lead time of 4.2 weeks. This would be the lead time for purchasing the hammer grips. We can be assured that there would be no stock outs by using this value for lead time for this particular part. This may sound like a significant period of time, and it is, but it is realistic. Consider that hammer grips must compete with hosts of other items at the vendor's factory, and the factories of the vendor's vendors. I think this also tends to show why we say that, in a manufacturing plan to make a complex product, average value-added time is only 5% of the entire cycle time for a job shop strategy and improves to only 30% for a flow manufacturing strategy.

Relationships with Vendors—Supply Chain Management

In today's world of compressed cycle times between product conceptualization and delivery to the customer, we cannot afford to let a cat-and-mouse game be played between buyer and seller. In fact, business success is more than ever based on consortiums of companies acting together as if they were one virtual company. The way these relationships are structured is commonly called *supply chain management*.

In its most basic format, supply chain management is an attempt to equalize attention to the details of planning among all sources of production. It means that the ultimate seller of the end product to the consumer is the lead strategist in bringing the product to market. All the companies in the supply chain, from raw materials to component parts, subassemblies, and, eventually, final assembly receive build instructions that have been coordinated by the lead company. All the various manufacturing work stations are scheduled as if they were owned and operated by the lead company. This means the consortium strives to have common design, manufacturing, purchasing, quality, and, in some cases, even personnel policies. It can be thought of as an industrial version of NATO. In fact, the first arena where we saw workable consortiums adhering to a common supply chain management philosophy was in the defense industries. Most modern aerospace and weapons systems are developed this way. And perhaps the most successful and recognizable commercial pursuit of this philosophy has been Airbus, in its competition with Boeing for jet airliner supremacy.

Of course, saying that supply chain philosophy will work doesn't necessarily mean it will. There are problems making it do so. But before we try to understand them, let's first understand what commonality is essential. The list, of necessity, needs to be tailored to the specific product; however, the following are the common trends:

- Design standards have to be common, and feedable into a common database.
- Lead times for production have to be understood and must be reliable.
- Measurements of productivity have to be common among all partners. There cannot be any suboptimization of one partner at the expense of another.
- Quality standards for all phases of purchasing and production have to be designed to a common denominator capable of being achieved by all.
- Profit levels among the members of the supply chain have to be equitable and should depend on the effort put forth by the individual partners.
- Scheduling has to be accomplished in accordance with a master schedule that is compatible with each partner's MRP II algorithm or manual equivalent.

- Technology needs to be shared openly if it is related to the supply chain–controlled product.

The clear implication is that communications have to be free, with no parochialism allowed. Coupled with that is free access to each partner's facilities, as if they belonged to all of the other partners. Thus, methods of production need to be shared, with good ideas transported from one member company to another. The concept that the strength of the organization is only as strong as its weakest link needs to be realized, and all players need to help that weakest link become stronger.

In the purchasing domain, the concept of a supply chain means that prices will be negotiated among members on the basis of their higher-level agreement on allowed profits and shared expenses. This is very similar to what occurs between divisions of large companies that buy and sell to each other. Since corporate profit is a sum of all the individual profits, there is no "corporate" incentive for sister divisions to try to get more profit from one another (even though this happens from time to time, when a manager, motivated by internal corporate politics, wants to look good regardless of the cost to other divisions). In real terms, purchasing negotiations between supply chain partners are more a matter of gaining commitment to manufacture on time than of setting specific prices. The only variables in prices will be raw commodities prices in the open market. Whatever these prices, they are usually absorbed in an equitable manner, thus preserving the individual partner's profit margin.

This type of negotiation can get very complicated. For example, does all of the commodity being purchased go against the supply chain's product, or is some of it outside the scope of the agreement? So we see that purchasing negotiations are not about "Will we buy from you?" but rather "What is a fair price for what we are contracted to buy from you?" The need for lead time analysis also simplifies: there is no need to check the accuracy of the manufacturing lead times, or to be concerned that product will be held back to get a better price.

All in all, supply chain manufacturing is a positive innovation. It takes considerable effort to reach that "communications excellence" level and to be in sync vis-à-vis methods of operation. But once that is achieved, we have a large virtual company that can react like a smaller company and at the same time retain the advantage of a multiresourced corporation.

The Role of Inventory Control

Just as purchasing is the external arm of materials management, inventory control is the internal agent. Once a product is received into inventory, it is no longer under the control of purchasing. From here on it is the responsibility of inventory control. The job of inventory control is very straightforward:

- Manage the storage of materials.
- Dispatch the materials to the start-of-production work stations when needed.

- Keep track of on-hand inventories so as not to run out at inopportune times.
- Place requests to purchasing for restocking per shop operations needs.

Let's look at these assignments and understand how they're accomplished.

Manage the Storage of Materials

Materials arrive on a daily basis for virtually every manufacturing company worldwide. Just count the trucks on any stretch of highway in any populated area, and you will see the vast complexity of deliveries under way. Now, deliveries don't happen in some kind of haphazard manner. All of these shipments have been arranged between a buyer and a seller in accordance with a schedule of some type. Inventory control, privy to that buyer/seller schedule, is expecting the goods and takes control of them as soon as they arrive. When materials arrive at the receiving dock, a set activity takes place. It may seem very ritualized, but it is very important that it be done properly; otherwise, the records will be inadequate, and then shop operations may not get the materials on time to maintain production and finance may not allocate funds from cash flow to pay the vendor, in turn causing a future credit problem. The accuracy of inventory may become so bad as to adversely impact the company's financial statement. This could affect its ability to raise funds in the financial markets, putting it at a competitive disadvantage. All these detrimental things can happen and all too often do, because of lack of proper receiving control.

The very rigid (and they have to be) receiving controls are:

1. When the material is ready to be unloaded:
   a. Verify that the load is destined for the receiving factory.
   b. Review the bill of lading and/or packing slips for quantity of materials listed.
   c. Count the items as they're being unloaded, and write the number and type on the corresponding bill of lading and/or packing slip.
   d. List discrepancies, if any, on the bill of lading and/or packing slips.
   e. Review the content of the shipment for obvious shipping damage. Record shipping damage on the bill of lading and/or packing slips.
2. Record keeping associated with receipt of materials:
   a. Enter receipt of shipment into the receiving log, containing the following:
      (1) Date received
      (2) Purchase order number.
      (3) Supplier name, and transportation company name if different
      (4) The company's part number
      (5) The warehouse location the material will be dispatched to (this should be on the company's purchase order)
   b. Fill out a material move ticket and send the shipment to its first location within the company's facility. Note: Quite often there will be an intermediate step indicated on the purchase order for the mater-

ial to be sent to incoming inspection prior to release to its inventory storage location.

c. Enter receipts into the MRP II system prior to dispatching materials from the receiving dock. The receiving warehouse location also enters receipt into the MRP II system after it has counted and identified the material. *Note:* This double entry system of sending and receiving materials is followed every time material is moved: from warehouse to warehouse, warehouse to work station, work station to work station, and work station to warehouse or shipping station.

Dispatch the Materials to the Start-of-Production Work Stations When Needed

In accordance with the daily dispatch system maintained by production control, inventory control will dispatch materials to the start operations. Most companies maintain a weekly dispatch system so inventory control can kit materials the day before to be dispatched before the beginning of the shift.

As part of its daily routine, inventory control will search the database to determine what materials are needed at each start operation and gather all the necessary materials, count them, and prepare the necessary move tickets. It should be pointed out that in factories under very good controls, nothing is moved without a move ticket and an input into the database (typically by bar code). Except for the initial move of materials from the warehouse to the start operation, all move record keeping is done by shop operations. This means operators are trained to scan bar codes of materials moved off their work stations and also to scan all incoming materials. Just as materials personnel have to account for the exact whereabouts of materials, so too do shop operations personnel. But by far the most critical dispatch of materials occurs when inventory control releases them to the shop. This is a passing of the baton. Up to this point inventory control has maintained security for the material. It has verified that it is as required (usually with QC incoming inspection assistance) and at the proper quantity levels. It has counted out each component designated for the start operation, and when the kit is complete inventory control releases it.

What happens when the number of parts in inventory is insufficient for the release? At that point, production control needs to decide whether or not to break up the work order into smaller quantities that can be supported by on-hand inventory levels. If it makes sense to dispatch a smaller quantity, then it is authorized and released. If not, the order is held until sufficient material is available.

Keep Track of on-Hand Inventories So As Not to Run Out at Inopportune Times

Obviously, when there are shortages, purchasing reenters the fray and has to correct the situation. It should also be pointed out that shortages will not take people by surprise in a well-run inventory control activity. With proper exercise of the MRP II system, there is little chance of a shortage. However, it does happen from time to time, especially as a consequence of quality defects that require emergency resupply. Even in these circumstances, shortages should not come as surprises that don't give inventory control enough time to react with purchasing. Usually, quality defects require quick response. But if the need for a complete resupply of the work station comes up, leaving the company out of inventory the next day, then inventory control has probably cut it too close in setting the minimum level to keep on hand.

If a shortage occurs that causes the next day's lack of inventory to be a surprise, then there is a data entry problem in maintaining inventory. This typically happens when inventory deletions for materials sent out for use are not happening correctly. Let's look at how this can happen.

First, inventory needs are set by the bill of materials. This document, as discussed in Chapter 3, determines how much raw material and how many parts and/or subassemblies go into a finished product. These individual "pieces" are summed in their respective categories via the MRP II system and form the basis for purchasing buy requirements. This is typically handled via the running total of inventory on hand (see Figure 8-1). However, the running total has to account for when these parts are used so that the part count is always correct. If it is not correct, then inventory control doesn't really know how much material is in the various warehouses, and hence the factory can get surprise outages.

Thus, it is critically important that usage be recorded as it occurs and the inventory ledger be debited. We call this *relieving inventory*, and the simplest way to relieve inventory is to deduct one of everything when a finished product is sent to shipping or finished goods storage. We do this by deleting one of everything listed in the bill of materials. This is why it is critical to have an accurate bill of materials when an MRP II system is instituted.

Inventory control maintains records of each item of the A and B categories. Simply put, it uses a ledger balance system. It updates entries into and withdrawals from the account to give a running balance. In manual inventory systems, companies use what are called bin tub files. (A bin tub file is a deep rigid file box filled with ledger sheets, each separately framed, containing lines for manual debit and credit entries. It is usually kept along side the desk of the clerk specifically responsible for a series of assigned BOM parts). In the manual system, the inventory control clerks all have certain segments of materials and/or parts to monitor and update daily. They have typical bank-type double-entry ledger books where they meticulously enter withdrawals every day and inputs when new purchase orders are received. They get information from the shop floor when items are used, usually via a manual material usage slip, and they use the receiving logs to enter inventory additions. As you can imagine, this is a fatiguing, mind-numbing exercise, but absolutely necessary.

Fortunately, MRP II can do this work with unerring accuracy (provided that the data are inputted correctly) and extremely fast. In fact, most of it is done behind the scenes and never needs to be reviewed by anyone. MRP II is in actuality an exception system: the adds and deletes are done against a setting for max/min inventory levels that alarms if there is a discrepancy with needed levels. Figure 8-1 is the closest thing modern MRP II systems traditionally show that can be construed as a ledger card. Note that it gives suggestions on what to buy, with enough lead time to get materials in-house as needed (the example in Figure 8-1 shows a negative amount, but it becomes positive before the scheduled manufacture date). However, the ledger for inventory by part can be shown, typically as a special report, if required.

Figure 8-3 is the normal inquiry report that MRP II has in its database for viewing by interested personnel. It is called the *item inquiry file*, and there is one in the database for every part and subassembly in the system. But notice that it does a lot more. It gives information on quantity on hand, but also information on location where stored, product type, whether there is a substitute item that can be used, whether it is a purchase or make item, number in inventory allocated for future use, purchase price, how many bought year to date, and how many of the parts have been sold, with selling prices (if applicable). This is a host of data. And now, with the advent of relational databases, inquiries can be tailored for very specific information needs on an ad hoc basis.

Place Requests to Purchasing for Restocking per Shop Operations Needs

The next procedure goes hand in hand with the item inquiry file, which in turn is driven by the continuous update of the inventory levels per the inven-

Item File Inquiry

1	Item	Hammer Rubber Grip	12	Location where stored	warehouse 1
2	Part Number	123E456Pt.1	13	Standard cost	$0.29 ea.
3	U/M	each	14	Purchase price, last buy	$0.285 ea.
4	EOQ	1,000	15	Quantity buy, last	1000
5	Shelf Life	5 years	16	Quantity buy, YTD	3000
6	Product Type	accessory	17	Sell separate? (Y/N)	No
7	Min. Inv. Required	600	18	Quantity sold, last	0
8	Quantity on hand	575	19	Quantity sold, YTD	0
9	Quantity future use	10,000	20	Selling price, last	0
10	Make or Buy	buy	21	Standard selling price	0
11	Substitution	none			

Figure 8-3. Item inquiry file.

Daily Purchasing Suggestion Report

Date: Sept. 28, 1998

	Item	Part Number	Standard Cost	Inv. On Hand	Inventory Allocated	Minimum Required	Suggested Buy
1	Hammer Rub. Grip	123E456Pt.1	$0.29ea.	575	-9425	600	10025
2	316 St. Steel bar stock	123E456Pt.2	$38.56/12ft.-0.125dia	40	-800	40	880
3	316 St. Steel forge stock	123E456Pt.3	$2.75-4in.dia.rnd.1/3lb.ea.	1000	-2500	500	3000
4							
5							
6							
7							
8							
9							
10							

Figure 8-4. Daily purchasing suggestion report.

tory relieving system. When the MRP II system detects an item that has fallen to the minimum inventory level, it enters the item into the *daily purchasing suggestion report* (see Figure 8-4). Purchasing has access to this report on its MRP II terminals and is constantly viewing for action needs.

The database excerpt shown in Figure 8-4 lists all items that are at or near the reorder point. Purchasing then decides what actions are necessary at this particular time. For example, if there is no further contemplated production for several months and there is a lead time of only one week, then purchasing ignores the suggestion and does nothing. The fact that MRP II only makes suggestions is significant: no system would have enough intelligence to make decisions on launching orders without human intervention. We are all aware of the very dynamic nature of business. We know that orders are orders only after a contractual commitment is received and there is no such thing as a sure thing. For that reason MRP II systems simply output information based on an arithmetic algorithm. It is up to the human operator to put the proper spin or nuances on the need presented by MRP II.

THE INTERACTION BETWEEN SHOP OPERATIONS AND MATERIALS

The interaction between shop operations and materials management needs to be close and in many cases transparent. Materials is the life blood of manufacturing, and just as engineering information is critical to success, so are materials. Work station operators are entirely nonproductive without materials to work on. Obviously, it's critical for these functions to work together as a well-disciplined team. Operator and supervisor have very distinct and necessary roles to play in successful materials management. Let's look at these important assignments for success.

Reporting Usage

We've seen that the inventory control and subsequent purchasing system depends on accurate information about stock on hand and usage rates. Theoretical usage rates are set by engineering in determining the rates of production. In the discussions on methods, time standards, and capacity analysis, we observed how the theoretical rates of production are determined. These are absolutely necessary factors that have to be known to inventory control and purchasing for sizing warehouse space and making initial preproduction buys. However, after the initial pilot production phase is completed, it is the actual usage that dominates the decisions made for materials purchases and storage locations. Shop operations has to report its usage rates in a timely manner so that materials management can judge the flow of materials required to keep the work stations gainfully employed.

Reporting is done by logging completion of jobs at each work station dynamically—i.e., as it occurs. This information, as we previously discussed, is used to update schedules and as the basis for the next work period's schedule. But it is also used to update materials status: every job completion is a trigger to delete the particular specifics of materials from the account ledger, or inventory balance. We saw previously how this information is presented in various reports (Figures 8-1, 8-3 and 8-4) to be used as tools for instigating further actions. But we must be very cognizant of the fact that this information needs to come from the shop floor, and it is the operator's responsibility to input it.

Countless control schemes in manufacturing today are paralyzed and made useless by poor shop floor reporting. In the past, I thought that proper reporting of actions occurring on the factory floor was second only to the actual carrying out of instructions. But I was wrong. It is equally important. In order for management to make correct decisions leading to optimized costs of production, the key ingredient is proper information. What would the competitive results be if the operator assembling the hammer grips to shafts thought he was too busy to bother to bar-code in completions? Possibly late delivery of replenishment hammer grips and perhaps a temporary layoff of the operator himself for lack of work due to unavailability of materials. This is not a far-fetched example. As ridiculous as it seems, it happens all too often. Operators fail to report status. Therefore, inventory control is blind to a need. Material orders are not placed on time. Inventory arrives late. And consequently the company has no product to sell, or at best it disappoints its customers and cannot deliver on time. This is not a happy scenario.

All of this can be avoided if management is cognizant of the absolute need to report progress (or lack of it) at every work station and function area on a timely basis and to be a stickler for enforcement of this dictate. Reporting back actions taken at all levels of a company is critical to success. It is surprising how many intelligent, well-meaning people do not seem to grasp this. The key to being a successful and low-cost manufacturer is communications excellence, and nothing more. You may say execution of work at the work station is more important. But it's not. The truth is that execution at the work station is a given. The ability of process systems to perform is an engineering function and is preordained before the company entertains the thought of entering a specific market. Communicating properly is a soft technology issue, perhaps more psychological in nature than we care to admit, and it takes a lot of hard work to do it right.

When I was a lowly "swab" (a first-year cadet, a freshman) at the United States Coast Guard Academy, one of the most intensely ingrained habits of a good officer was instilled in me during summer indoctrination. It was simply reporting back on the status of any assignment in a timely manner. Of course, the fourth class system did it through stress, some humiliations, and lots of tension. But every successful cadet learned this lesson, or he and the academy soon parted ways. If I look back on my experiences some three and a half decades after graduation, that habit of reporting back, completing the feedback loop of the communications system, was one of the most universally applied rules for organizational success. Whatever assignments I've had or management positions I've held, the one truism for success has been to get the entire team to understand how important reporting status is. When we were successful, the reporting of status was superb. When I was considerably less successful, it was because I didn't do a good enough job to assure timely reporting of status.

The key to manufacturing success is to get people in all positions to constantly report status. And the most important reporting of status revolves about how we are doing in manufacturing the product we are going to sell to our customers. The most important communicator in this chain is the "point man," the work station operator. If he does his communications job well, we know what's happening and can react quickly to virtually any situation. Manufacturing, being the dynamic entity it is, requires quick response to problems. We do not have the luxury of time to contemplate responses. Therefore, failure to report status in a timely manner is doubly destructive and cannot be tolerated. I've often said that given the choice of state-of-the-art equipment and lack of a good reporting system versus an excellent reporting system and a mediocre set of equipment, the latter is far and away the best choice. Excellence in communications always beats good equipment, because it's the ability to execute decisively and quickly that counts, not excellent equipment idle due to indecision.

Nowhere in the manufacturing endeavor is excellence in communications more important than the interface between materials management and shop operations. This is so because materials deals with both internal and external resources. External resources are not as easy to control as internal ones. Externally, we are at the mercy of many competing needs for the same capabilities and cannot dictate who goes first, as we can internally. For this reason it is crucial that shop operations dutifully and accurately report back progress including usage rates of materials. We know that purchasing will have a difficult time in short-cycle expediting of materials into the company. Therefore, as much advance warning as possible is required to assure an uninterrupted flow of materials.

You may ask, Why isn't the planned rate of usage sufficient for scheduling resupply deliveries? It probably would be if all that were required was for the engineers to have done their work properly and accurately calculated what each work station could really do. But even if they did this successfully, there are still, as we have seen, so many indeterminate variables involved that we need to constantly compare plan with reality and make adjustments. This is the main reason MRP II systems have three levels of planning: strategic, within the master schedule domain; tactical, at work release time; and dynamic, at the daily dispatch time. Unfortunately, the major portion of success lies on the shoulders of those who manage the dynamic portion of scheduling, and to be successful they need to be vigilant of the vagaries of the dynamic variables, the things that happen on a daily basis. These can range from absenteeism of key operators to crashes of computers driving the processes. And it all hinges on accurate, timely reporting.

With regard to reporting rates of material usage, suppose we had an inexperienced operator pressed into service because our key operator was injured in an automobile accident and could not work the machine. In this case it is likely two things would happen: the output of the work station would be less than planned for, and the rate of material use per quantity of good parts would increase because of more errors. So, on the one hand, the usage rate would decrease, and on the other it would go up. The one certainty is that it wouldn't be the same as planned. We would also expect the ratio to change as the new operator became more competent with practice on the job. All these factors would play themselves out and be observable if we had timely measurements. If we didn't, we would be blind, and perhaps terribly surprised one morning to find out that we had run out of material a few days before replenishment was due. Knowing in advance is no guarantee of being able to avoid bad results. But assuredly we have a chance to do so if the reporting system is adequate.

The lesson learned is simple: make sure shop operations understands the absolute necessity of timely reporting of status, that it does, indeed, follow the communications scheme set up to report results. And that it understands that reporting results is equally important to actually doing the job. One is not complete without the other.

THE DIFFERENT STRATEGIES IN MANAGING INVENTORY FOR CLASS A AND B ITEMS, AS COMPARED WITH CLASS C ITEMS

Class C items, as previously noted, are floor stock. These are the large categories of fittings, fasteners, nuts, bolts, and screws that are relatively inexpensive and easy to obtain. But they are also vital to success. If we lack a mounting screw for a bracket and that bracket has to hold a unique control device for a complex machine, the unit will be incomplete. The unit is no less incomplete than if the unavailable part were a highly critical and expensive computer chip. The conclusion is that we can no more afford to run out of class C items than we can of class A and B items. The only difference is how we manage them.

Class C items are managed by shop floor personnel, who monitor quantities on hand and report to purchasing when replenishment is required. Class C items are managed this way because it's straightforward and because these items—being commonplace and readily available—don't require the more complex, slower, and more expensive method of inventory control used for the more expensive and harder to obtain items. Portal to portal speed decreases and complexity increase as the abstract nature of the control system increases. Complexity requires more actions usually involving more people, hence portal to portal time increases (Note; the computer data generating portion of the system is very fast, but people have to inter-react with it). For clase A and B items we use the full capabilities of the complex MRPII software and all the supporting human controllers as decision makers. For class C items we need not use the computer system. We use a very simple visual system, conducted by one or at most two people.

Recall that the basis of inventory control is the bill of materials and the reporting of completions. Once a product is completed, the items and their quantities used to make it are deleted from the specific item part count. This is similar to keeping a checkbook register current; to do it requires good reporting and constant vigilance in tracking actual versus reported usage. I will explain how this is done shortly.

The more complex system is maintained for class A and B items because of their high value and/or the long lead times in obtaining them. Class C items are easy to buy and are, comparatively speaking, cheap. Therefore, each individual item by itself has very little monetary value. Whether we have 5000 or 5052 on hand is meaningless. These items are simply a commodity; approximate values are sufficient. The key dictate is, *Don't run out of stock under any circumstances.*

As I said, class C items are maintained by shop operations personnel. We call it bin supply stock management. The process is as follows:

Bin Supply Stock Management
1. Calculate a period usage rate (usually one month).
2. Buy a quantity of parts equal to two periods' usage.
3. Set up bins at the point of use capable of holding one period's supply.
4. Place a mark on the bin to indicate when the stock has been drawn down to the 90% consumed level.
5. Fill the bin with one period's floor stock.
6. Use stock as required to support production.
7. When the 90% consumed marker line is visible in the bin, the operator informs the stockroom.
8. The stockroom delivers another period's floor stock and asks purchasing to order another period's stock.

Since we are managing by sight levels, there is no attempt to precisely pin down the exact quantities of screws or nuts are in each bin. They are not purchased that way (they're commonly bought as so many dollars per pound or kilogram), and there is no real reason to know. The key to the success of the whole process is to never let the floor stock go below the 90% consumed marker.

This is a system wholly managed by the operators who consume the stock. It is as ritualistic a process as the daily checking of the dipstick on a machine's oil sump. Part of the operator's training therefore needs to be focused on this need, and policy plans need to be set in place for the training.

In order to appreciate how simple the control of class C items is, let's look at how class A and B items are controlled. First, let's describe how we assure ourselves that we really know how much class A and B inventory is on hand.

Class A and B inventory items are all items listed on the various bills of materials used throughout the company. Class C items are not listed on a bill of materials as specific parts for inventory control purposes. For example, if we had a motor-driven pump assembly, the bill of materials would list a motor, a pump, a flange, perhaps a special gasket, a control circuit board, a power cord, a UL label, and a packaging kit. Notice that there is no direct mention of the nuts and bolts and epoxy glue used for assembly. These are floor stock items and are excluded. How does the operator know what floor stock items are necessary to complete the assembly? It is included in the methods sheet, which is the engineering document instructing the operator how to do the job and how long it should take to accomplish it. Recall that the methods sheet also contains information as to what jigs and fixtures are required. These, too, are not on the bill of materials.

The exact number of each class A and B item is contained on the bill of materials. The job needs exactly that many for completion—not one less, not one more. All part numbers and quantities represented on the company's total bill of materials for all released and planned-to-be-released jobs for production, plus a safety margin (the max/min system), should be in inventory at any one time. This means that the company has an inventory value (both numerical quantity and monetary value) of every class A and B item it owns. This is like the balance in the checkbook. Every time we use or consume a class A or class B item, we need to delete it from the inventory balance. This is like writing a check and subtracting the amount from the previous balance in the register. This is where the fun begins. How do we do this and do it accurately?

We could assign an accountant to each work station and meticulously record each item as it's used, then enter the database and delete it from inventory. This would work for inventory control purposes, but it would be terribly expensive, to say nothing of the slowdown in production. Therefore we choose not to do it that way.

Another way would be to periodically take full physical inventories of all stock in the factory warehouses and work-in-process inventory. This actual "nose count" is tedious and takes time. Sometimes it takes as much as two to three days, depending on inventory quantities and individual part quantities. It requires the factory to stop work, to "freeze in place" because it is necessary to get an accurate picture, not of something that is constantly changing, in order to know what's on hand and can be used as the new baseline. Having a new baseline, we would then deduct planned usage amounts—probably weekly—to estimate inventory levels until the next physical inventory. But this projection *is* an estimate at best and it requires considerable effort to prepare. Most companies find they need to make such an estimate annually to satisfy financial reporting dictates and only secondarily use it for inventory control purposes. However, many companies find they need to make such inventory projections quarterly, because they do not have any trustworthy way of maintaining inventory accuracy based on a sophisticated materials management system. Again, this is not the preferred way of managing class A and B inventory.

The preferred way of managing class A and B inventory is by first establishing an accurate inventory count and then maintaining a secured stock area where materials are kitted for release in accordance with a schedule, the kit being defined by the bill of materials. Then, once the kitted items are actually used, they are deducted from the specific part account ledger. In practice, this happens when the assembly is completed and the product is put into the finished goods warehouse (or, if we are fortunate, shipped to a paying customer). We also take periodic physical part counts of significant items and compare them with the current tally levels, making adjustment as required.

This system is practical and sufficiently accurate for reorder purposes. But it does require accurate bills of materials, along with secured stockrooms and the discipline to make it work. The discipline includes making sure that no unrecorded usage of materials occurs, e.g., that the shop doesn't use more than specified quantities without proper requisition documentation. This situation occurs if materials are wasted through processing errors, or perhaps are no good. Usually, what goes wrong is that the erring supervisor extracts more materials without documentation and hence the reorder system is blind to the fact and has a wrong count. The other discipline error is non–entry of receipt of materials into finished goods or shipment. This means the system doesn't recognize that the job was indeed completed and hasn't deleted the materials from the inventory count. Again, the result is a missing deduction and a false sense of security vis-à-vis the level of inventory on hand. We can mitigate a lot of these failures through periodic part counts of critical items. But the real solution always comes down to improving communications excellence. The need to report in an accurate and timely manner is mandatory for the system to succeed.

I alluded to the fact that many companies suffer from this malady of highly imperfect inventory control systems. And this is a needless waste. The erroneous argument I commonly encounter here is, We can't afford to put in an MRP II system, and therefore we can't do anything about it. My answer is, *You cannot afford not to put in an MRP II system if you intend to stay in the manufacturing game.* This is an absolute truism of management today. But even in the unlikely event it's true in your specific case and you can't adopt MRP II, you can still institute an inventory control system that will tremendously improve your inventory costs. Might I add, this will also penetrate right to the bottom line (and then you'll be capable of affording an MRP II system).

The process of implementing an inventory control system is outlined in Figure 8-5. Notice that it is a combination of materials, shop operations, and engineering management activities. Since engineering and the shop operations management activities are covered elsewhere, let's look at the inventory control aspect, which may need some elaboration.

The first necessary accomplishment is to assure that the bill of materials (BOM) is complete and represents all the products the company makes. "All" is all-inclusive. Theoretically, that does mean everything. But in practice, if we can achieve 85% coverage, the company will gain significant benefit. The only way I know of to check to see if a BOM is accurate is to audit an assem-

Implement a max/min inventory control system as a subset of the MRP II system development, in the following order:

- Complete an inventory count by doing a physical inventory.
- Concurrently implement BOMs for all currently offered products.
- Determine max/min inventory levels for all BOM line items based on usage volume and reorder delivery cycle time.
- Input data to the Item Master log (inventory log by item description and quantity on hand).
- Modify the materials usage system (either manual or MRP II based) to flag BOM line items when reorder points are reached.
- Establish a reorder policy for (automated or manual) reorder and audit requirements.
- Set up secure stock locations and develop policies for restocking and authorizations to withdraw materials.
- Set up a policy for floor stock on a visual bin resupply system for class C items.
- Set up a policy for receiving raw materials and component parts into inventory (Item Master log), incoming from vendors or from internal off-line manufacturing.
- Set up a materials dispatch system integrated with the daily scheduling algorithm.
- Set up a policy for inventory relieving system to keep the WIP and raw materials inventory levels accurate. Probably automated by bar coding at the time a completed product exits final assembly.
- Set up a policy for creating a finished goods inventory count and relieving system when finished goods are shipped to customers.
- Establish a report system based on the needs of the company but as a bare minimum containing
  - Daily inventory counts by commodities and serialized part nos. for all stock locations.
  - A daily schedule for parts to be dispatched to support the daily scheduling algorithm.
  - A max/min report showing parts/assemblies requiring reorder actions daily
  - A finished good inventory count
- Develop a training program for all individuals who will be involved in any phase of the system.
- Develop an implementation schedule and implement.

Figure 8-5.   Inventory system implementation plan guideline.

bly of a product and meticulously check off each item as it is used. This takes time, but for new-product introduction particularly, it is a worthwhile exercise. Considerable future problems are avoided by assuring that the BOM is adequate for the product. This will minimize idle time by making engineering seat-of-the-pants adjustments a rarity.

I believe the work station operator is the ideal choice for auditing a BOM. Since he will be coexisting with the product as long as it is produced in the particular factory and he will want his job to run smoothly, the operator has a vested interest in understanding the nature of the parts and/or the assembly. The way an audit is conducted is simple. We give the operator a clipboard with the BOM attached. As he completes each phase of the work, he checks off the parts he used. At the end of the day, any items that aren't checked are reported to engineering for investigation. You might think this is a waste of time, but it's not. There are many instances where the operator simply miscounts or ignores items that are listed on the BOM. These are human types of mistakes; therefore we must be willing to assist and be part of any corrective action. On the other hand, at times it appears that the BOM has neglected to call for something that's needed. When that happens, the operator reports it to engineering, but in this instance he is asked to suggest what should be done to correct the BOM—what he thinks is missing. Perhaps the operator has tried something to make up for the missing piece of the puzzle, and it might have been a very pragmatic solution the engineer wouldn't have thought of. It's quite common for engineering to receive excellent ideas from operators, and this cooperation must always be encouraged. It's a truism that nobody knows better than an experienced operator who has to live with the product all day long.

While BOMs are engineering's responsibility, materials management has a strong interest in their successful development and implementation. A set of correct BOMs makes inventory control theory feasible. This leads to the next step in implementing a successful inventory control system: creating a baseline inventory database.

Inventory databases are lists of materials and parts the company maintains to build its products along with the quantity of each item on hand. For this reason it is most often referred to as the *item master database*. This database should correspond to the sum of all the parts listed in all of the BOMs the company has on record. In practice, it usually comes close but also contains other parts. Primarily, these others are leftovers from obsolete BOMs, perhaps not scrapped but kept for potential spare parts business. As stated previously, accurate inventory is necessary to prevent surprise outages during manufacture. Therefore, in order to apply the debit-and-credit method of inventory balance, it is necessary to start with an accurate quantification of each part or raw material and to periodically validate this number. Using a familiar analogy once more, this is like balancing a personal checking account monthly: we have to count everything we have on hand throughout all the factory and company spaces where inventory may be kept. This is the taking of physical inventory.

Taking a physical inventory is an all-hands exercise. All people involved in manufacturing are usually given the opportunity to participate. The nature of the job is to count everything, tag all items as they are counted, and then enter the tally for each individual part, assembly, and raw material in stock onto a copy of the item master. We then compare the copy with the current item master database to see how accurate it is (like balancing the checkbook). The task, then, is to try to reconcile any differences and finally to update the item master to this most current physical inventory.

As you can imagine, a physical inventory in any company needs to be planned and executed well. Figure 8-6 is a list of common tasks that have to be planned for to accomplish a physical inventory.

With a physical inventory baseline, and a reliable and complete set of BOMs, it is possible to set up an inventory control system. We employ the max/min strategy to know how much inventory we want to carry and to determine how far to deplete stock before generating a replacement order. The max/min process was described previously. The point here is that a baseline has been set and now it must be maintained by debiting and crediting inventory as it is received and used. To help in that, we do one other strategic thing: we create secure stockrooms. A secure stockroom is one where inventory of all types and description is accounted for as it is received and as it is dispatched to the various work stations. In practice, it means a caged or locked area with limited access, to prevent unauthorized release of materials for whatever reason.

The last item concerning establishing an inventory control system is to periodically verify that the debit and credit balance is accurate without having to do a complete physical inventory. We do this via statistical checks. We call these *cycle counts*. On a monthly basis, stockroom clerks count specific line items off the item master to assure that the debit/credit system is working properly. A routine is set up for stockroom personnel to count items according to schedule. Usually, the most critical items are included, and in total perhaps 15% of all line items are counted this way. We then use statisti-

Steps to take:

- Set target date to take inventory.
- Define items to count.
- Set inventory count procedures.
- Establish ground rules for validating inventory values.
- Set up schedule for validating inventory values.
- Define format of results needed to satisfy financial and inventory control needs.
- Define methods of inputting data.
- Define and set up computer resources.
- Create schedule for doing count and inputting data.
- Establish teams of counters.
- Establish data input teams.
- Train counters, data entry checkers, and validators.
- On selected day, shut down production and take inventory.

Figure 8-6. Physical inventory check list.

cal inference to determine if the inventory balances are accurate enough to continue. A company doing all the measures and techniques described above would probably have an accuracy rate of 98%. This, coupled with a reasonable buffer stock as part of the max/min settings, would more than likely be the basis for an effective inventory control system. In fact, maintaining such a high level in most cases would preclude the need to do even annual physical inventories for financial reconciliations.

We've now had a detailed look at how the materials function supports shop operations. The interesting aspect of materials control is how closely it works with shop operations. Unlike engineering, which can become isolated from the day-to-day happenings on the shop floor, materials doesn't have such leeway. The shop floor depends on a constant stream of parts and materials to work on. Their exact needs have to be satisfied all the time for the factory to keep working. This is in contrast to the engineering support that shop operations requires. Engineering efforts peak and wane with the introduction of new designs and or technologies. When they are new, engineering has an intensive presence on the shop floor. As the technologies become more commonplace, there is less need for engineering support. This, of course, cannot happen with the materials function's role. We have just as critical a need of materials for the 52nd or 3034th lot production run as for the first. This being the case, shop operations often has closer ties with materials management than with any other function.

When we look at MRP II, we see that the differentiation between purchasing and production control is slight. The latter deals with internal schedule, primarily people resources; while purchasing is externally focused, using the same system and programs but to manage materials movement into the factory. With so much in common in management tool usage, it is no wonder that there at times seems to be a merging of the functions all under the banner of an entity simply called operations. And this is as it should be. We only divide the tasks because it is more convenient and efficient to do so. I have never met a good materials manager who wasn't also a good shop manager. And I believe you can't be successful at either unless you fully understand the other and can perform both roles. Using my baseball analogy once more, you need to be a complete player to successfully compete in the major leagues. The same is true for manufacturers.

Chapter 9

Work Station Maintenance for Optimum Productivity

Up to this point I have implied that work stations will by themselves perform to their predetermined capacity levels except when operators behave inappropriately by not following the prescribed method, or where there is a shortage of required materials. But there is a third, equally important reason why work stations might perform at a subpar level: sometimes the equipment is simply not working properly, or, in the extreme, not working at all. It is these two threats that maintenance contends with. The maintenance organization is required to minimize and sometimes eliminate under performance situations due to breakdowns, either complete or partial, of production equipment.

In this chapter, I will explain how maintenance goes about accomplishing this task both on its own and in alliance with shop operations. This alliance is critical for living by the excellence-in-performance credo necessary for sustained optimum productivity. Let's explore how an effective maintenance program can be a significant factor in sustaining and improving a factory's productivity level.

THE ROLE OF EFFECTIVE MAINTENANCE IN THE ABILITY TO ACHIEVE PLANNED CYCLE TIME

We all recognize that a "broken" facility will not achieve planned-for productivity levels. All equipment will eventually spiral down to unacceptable performance levels. The only question is how long it will take to reach that level. The job of maintenance is to stretch that decay spiral to as long a time as possible—virtually infinite would be the ideal—by scheduling periodic rejuvenation programs. The role of maintenance in the manufacturing strategy is based on understanding what to do and when. Just as we adhere to deliberately orchestrated methods and sequences to make a product, we similarly follow well-planned maintenance strategies to keep the machines and processes running. Let's look at what that strategy consists of; the main points are listed in Figure 9-1.

First, the goal is to field as many usable machines and/or processes as possible for every working day, assuring that they can perform properly when called upon. We do this by carefully monitoring key features of every machine and process. The tactic is to measure these key features

1. Measuring the ability of machines and processes to operate ("down and limping" report)
2. Preventive examinations against set standards of performance
3. Ongoing preventive maintenance during operations (daily, weekly, monthly, etc.)
4. Taking equipment out of service for periodic rebuilds when tolerance range is exceeded
5. Responding immediately and effectively to unplanned outages

Figure 9-1. The preventive maintenance strategy.

against defined standards of acceptable performance. Each machine and process is evaluated for its ability to yield results deemed acceptable, e.g., in number of units made per shift. We issue what is called a *down and limping report,* a report that makes straightforward distinctions. If the facility is producing product within the expected range, with all external influences accounted for (for example, uptime required to run to meet production schedule), then it is an *up* machine. If it cannot perform within the range, then it is a *limping* machine. If the work station cannot operate at all, then it is a *down* facility. The down and limping report, the very basic and primary measurement technique of all maintenance strategies, is the key to all further activities and the link to current production capacity for production control's scheduling algorithms. I will describe the process of setting up a down and limping report in a later section of this chapter.

Second, we set in place preventive examinations of the equipment to assure that the natural deterioration rates are minimized as much as possible. We do this with varying degrees of aggressiveness, depending on the specific manufacturing situation, by developing specific tests and examinations for each machine and process equipment. These tests are designed to measure performance against a set standard. Usually this standard is very compatible with if not identical to the specifications the machine or process had to meet when first purchased and put into use. We say "compatible if not identical" because, after putting the equipment to use, we may have found that original purchase specifications were not quite correct or optimal for the real need. This happens frequently in implementing new products, particularly those employing new technologies. These tests should be of short cycle and designed to test the process capability of the specific work station. Commonly for machine tools, we do sample cuts at various feeds and speeds for specific shapes and contours and then measure the results against a capability standard, e.g., a standard set of tolerances. For example, we would test the ability of a CNC machine to cut a true circle at a set radius tolerance, which is one of the most difficult things for it to do. With CNC machines we also commonly test for ability to hold concentricity for a series of circles about a common center. Usually this type of test is done weekly, at the beginning of the shift. It means loading a special program into the machine and letting it run, and then evaluating the results against a set standard. In many ways, the simple tests computers put themselves through when we turn them on are a form of this second step in the maintenance strategy.

Third, we design a series of preventive maintenance activities to be carried out by operators and maintenance personnel to assure that what can be done to prevent deterioration is done. Again, the degree of aggressiveness depends on the specific manufacturing situation. The caveat here is that the preventive maintenance (commonly called PM) activities should not take too much time out of productive manufacturing. Preventive maintenance consists of simple activities such as checking sump oil levels and cleanliness, replacing filters, recording bearing temperatures, and noting other items that measure symptoms of impending failures. The core commonality is these activities tend to be done while the work station is in operation or shut down for only a short period of time. For machine tools, we would also include removing chips and other excessive materials that could get into the workings of the machine and potentially cause damage. These short-cycle PM activities are traditionally done by the work station operators, and specialized maintenance personnel are involved only if the operator discovers an out-of-specification situation.

Fourth, we periodically take work stations out of service to rebuild them back to "as new" condition. The time between rebuilds is established by anticipated mean times between failures for key components of the work station. These may be operating hours recommended by the various vendors for the work station equipment, or times established by down and limping report data. Whatever the method for establishing when to take the facility out of service, it must coordinate the company's short-term production needs with the need to keep the equipment operational for the company's long-term good. The best way to schedule work station out-of-service time is through the MRP II scheduling system. This way we can anticipate the separate needs for major PM and production and reconcile the differences. The main thing is not to create surprises. We cannot at the last minute tell production control that the facility is not available because it didn't get back on-line on time, nor can we tell maintenance after extensive planning for the overhaul that their effort was for naught and they can't work on the machine. In every way the noncommunicating situation is a lose-lose situation. The customer loses because commitments cannot be maintained. The company also loses when extensive PMs are canceled. Perhaps key vendors had been scheduled to do work; now they won't. This may entail cancellation fees and also may make it difficult to reschedule in the future. It also means that a facility will deteriorate more and probably cost more to fix whenever the PM is rescheduled. And further, the yield of good products will decrease, therefore costing more per unit to produce and adversely affecting profits. The point is, creating a PM downtime schedule needs to be a joint effort of all affected parties. We must respect the data that tell us the PM needs to be done and at the same time comply with the needs of the customer. The fact that these types of PMs are readily predicted means that they can be scheduled to occur at the most convenient time. This is what's done in practice. And when the scheduling precautions fail, it is usually because one faction or another has ignored the needs of others. Unfortunately, the most frequent offenders tend to be the sales staff, who may be oblivious to other than sales needs. Progressive management needs to work hard to correct these situations.

The final part of the strategy is not scheduled at all, but it is planned for. This is the quick and effective reaction to unplanned downtimes. Every well-run maintenance department needs to be able to respond quickly to unplanned downtimes and get the situation stabilized. In fact, most organizations require this task to be the highest priority when it occurs, even at the expense of ongoing PMs. But the objective is to make the response and recovery time as short as possible so the entire manufacturing organization can quickly return to normal operations. To do this, many maintenance managers have developed response scenarios to preplan how they would react to certain situations. Then when these or similar situations occur, the company can quickly respond by being "prefocused" on the task at hand. Obviously, not all scenarios can be preplanned. But the fact that potential crisis plans exist makes it easier for the maintenance organization to create a mind-set that will allow creative problem resolution to get going faster. This is much like the volunteer fire department: the members do not know what the next emergency will be; however, they are trained to take action responses. So, too, should maintenance repair men and women be trained.

A PRIMER ON MAINTENANCE METHODS

The main focus of maintenance is to prevent loss of capacity through unplanned-for underperforming or down work stations. Therefore, as shown with the strategy employed, we normally emphasize preventive methods as the normal course of conducting the maintenance business. For this reason, generally speaking, the maintenance philosophy will always favor preventing downtime instead of being very proficient in reacting to unplanned outages. However, having capability to react to unplanned outages is still a necessary factor in planning maintenance's capabilities. The basic structure of the maintenance organization is one aimed at maintaining a vigorous PM program while at the same time maintaining a reserve capability to react to unplanned downtime. But the thrust is always an offensive one of prevention rather than a defense against potential breakdowns. However, to present a full picture, we must recognize that PM-type strategies aren't always selected. It is conceivable that a reactive approach is suitable especially in situations where the equipment is relatively straightforward and little PM is feasible—for example, where most work is done via nonmoving jigs and fixtures to assist highly skilled manual operation, as in jewelry manufacturing.

The interactive strategies are as follows:

- Reactive
- Predictive
- Preventive

Let's take a look at these three strategies.

Reactive Strategy

Both the preventive and predictive strategies strive to eliminate or at least minimize downtime with proactive actions on working machines and processes before there is any indication of problems. The reactive strategy, by contrast, is one of minimizing the effects of downtime by fixing the problem as soon as it's discovered. Reactive is the oldest strategy. Some people call it the "if it isn't broke, don't fix it" strategy, which at first glance would appear to be just good common sense. But it isn't. When a machine breaks is not predictable. Therefore, the ability to plan for an outage is very limited. In the reactive mode we are in essence nothing more than superb volunteer firefighters. We may be able to put down the blaze, but not without unplanned for cost. And as we know, unplanned outages will cost more because we need to respond quickly. When we respond quickly it is usually a priority to do so and any ability to control costs becomes secondary to getting the job done. Pure reactive strategies just are not optimum from the viewpoint of profitability and therefore are seldom a prime maintenance strategy. We use a reactive strategy as a secondary approach to respond to spontaneous outages that weren't precluded by proactive techniques.

A reactive strategy for a company having simple machines, jigs, and fixtures is really a hybrid. It will include simple PMs done at the beginning of shifts or internal to the manufacturing process (as long as it doesn't lengthen the time to accomplish the prescribed manufacturing work). These PMs will be accomplished almost exclusively by the work station operators. This is so because most reactive strategies occur in smaller manufacturing activities where the maintenance staff is very small and in many cases also handles janitorial and facilities upkeep roles.

Predictive Strategy

The proactive preventive and predictive strategies try to intervene before work stations have deteriorated to the failure level. The difference between the two strategies is essentially where in the life cycle of the work station the intervention will take place. The predictive strategy is based on calculations of mean times to failure. To say it in simpler terms, we calculate the number of cycles the equipment can go through until its weakest link fails—for example, how many on and offs a light bulb can undergo before burning out, or, more generally, how many times the equipment can be revved up from a total stop to full throttle and still reach steady-state running. Using the host of fatigue equations employed in machine design offices, we can with some accuracy predict the number of cycles the machine will undergo before failing. The predictive strategy says, on the basis of such information, replace parts just before they actually fail. Of course, this means replacing components that are still performing satisfactorily, and this is the main drawback for this strategy—but also its main strength. We rarely, if ever, have unplanned outages, so we never suffer the high-cost consequences of the reactive methodology.

The process is simple in concept:

- Calculate the number of cycles to failure for the major components.
- Set up a procedure to record operation cycles (like a baseball pitcher's pitch count, up to a maximum before being taken out of the game).
- Estimate when the cycle count limit will be reached, and schedule a deliberate outage for shortly before the limit occurs.
- Remove the components that have reached their prescribed cycle counts, and replace with new parts.
- Dispose of the removed parts even though they appear usable.

By following this process we tend to sufficiently shorten maintenance down periods but the costs are significantly higher than those of the older preventive strategy. The other drawback is in the ability to actually calculate with a high degree of certainty the number of cycles to failure. This assumes we know what the weak link in the system is and we can actually do the fatigue cycle calculation. Since no competent engineer would stake a reputation on such accuracy, in practice significant safety factors are added in to assure no unplanned outage occurs. What this does is raise the cost of maintenance by disposing of perfectly usable components significantly prematurely.

Preventive Strategy

The preventive strategy is the compromise between the predictive and the reactive strategies and the most widely used. It differs from the predictive method in that we undertake prescribed upgrades at specific times only if we discover the first signs of deterioration, Otherwise we leave things alone. The preventive strategy depends on doing investigative period audits of the condition of the equipment. We determine how often we ought to look for deterioration and we couple this with prescriptions of known "good things to do" to further stretch out the time before deterioration could cause unplanned failures. This is the common strategy of prescribed downtime for examination and prescribed preventive tasks in between downtimes.

Figure 9-2 illustrates a typical plan based on a preventive strategy.

Let's look at some of the key factors this strategy relies on as shown in the figure. I developed this plan for a woodworking factory, but it is applicable for virtually any factory using machines and processes for producing its products.

The first thing to note is I divided the factory into its major producing categories and the facility itself. Often companies buy subcomponents and have significant assembly operations. Also, quite often the assembly operations

GENERIC PREVENTIVE MAINTENANCE

GENERAL REQUIREMENTS item	MACHINES frequency	(As Applicable) est. time to do	done by	est. annual hrs. per machine
Clean (remove debris)	daily	10 min.	operator	39
Check guages & controls for problem	daily/on-going	—	operator	—
Check oil levels, grease, misc. lub.	daily	—	operator	—
Change oil, grease, lub. & filters	monthly	1 hour	oiler	12
Inspect brgs, gears, hydraulics, air	annual	16 hours	tech/maint	16
Inspect motors & controls	annual	8 hours	tech/maint	8
Inspect PC controller/logic circuits	annual	4 hours	tech/maint	4
Inspect lead screws/structure/align	annual	16 hours	tech/maint	16
Tumpane testing for accuracy	5 yr. intervals	24 hours	tech/maint	5
Major overhaul/clean/paint	5 yr. intervals	40 hours	tech/maint	6
			painter/h-man	2
		Total Annual	S.O.	39
		Time/Machine	Maintenance	67

GENERAL REQUIREMENTS item	PROCESSES frequency	(As Applicable) est. time to do	done by	est. annual hrs. per machine
Clean (remove debris)	daily	10 min.	operator	39
Check guages & controls for problem	daily/on-going	—	operator	—
Check moving parts for proper ops.	daily	—	operator	—
Lubricate	weekly	10 min.	operator	39
Inspect steam/air/hydraulics/etc.	monthly	1 hour	tech/maint	12
Inspect motors and controls	annual	8 hours	tech/maint	8
Major overhaul/clean/paint	annual	16 hours	tech/maint	10
			painter/h-man	6
		Total Annual	S.O.	78
		Time/Process	Maintenance	36

GENERAL REQUIREMENTS item	BLDG SYSTEMS frequency	(As Applicable) ets. tiem to do	done by	est. annual hrs. per machine
Inspect steam system; traps, pipes valves, etc	annual	320 hours	tech/maint	320
Inspect dust collection system	annual	320 hours	tech/maint	320
Inspect oil fired boilers	annual	80 hours	tech/maint	80
Inspect wood fired boiler, silos, feed system	annual	80 hours	tech/maint	80
inspect air condition system	annual	40 hours	tech/maint	40
Inspect and repair stretchers	annual	500 hours	tech/maint	500
Pain bldg, Internal	5 yr. cycle	continues	painter	1856
		Total Annual	Painter	1856
		Time	Maintenance	1340

SUMMARY	Number		Shop Operations	Tech/Maint	Painter
Machines	100		3900	6700	
Processes	75		58500	2700	
Building Systems				1340	1856
TOTAL HOURS			9750	10740	1856
TOTAL MANPOWER/YEAR			5.23	5.79	1.00

Figure 9-2. The generic PM system.

consist of multiple sets of automated work stations. If that is the case, these companies would have a different grouping emphasis. Perhaps instead of a machine group they would have an automated assembly group. The important point is that the structure of the preventive maintenance (PM) plan should match the factory.

Under each category, we list the activities for investigating the state of deterioration, or a simple preventive activity designed to minimize and stretch out deterioration. Again, I should point out that deterioration is inevitable for any device that has moving parts. Our purpose is to slow down the rate of deterioration as much as possible to assure that the equipment can perform in accordance with its specification as long as possible. Note that I have divided the tasks into categories sorted by time intervals between actions. In the figure, the tasks go from daily to five years. Each company needs to decide what the intervals should be to suit its particular needs. This depends on the rate of natural deterioration you would expect for the machine or process, the only rule of thumb being that the shortest inspection period for the intended investigation should be less than the theoretical time it takes the machine or system to reach an unacceptable level of deterioration for proper performance. For example, we would inspect a machine's bearings annually, because a set of roller or ball bearings would probably be satisfactory for at least one year, possibly 18 months, in normal usage.

Notice that these are general requirements for all the machines, processes, and buildings. A full plan would use the model to detail specific requirements tailored to the particular machine, process, or building system.

Continuing horizontally across the form, the third column lists the estimated time it should take to complete the task. Of course, for this generic figure the times are averages. When making up a specific PM plan for the factory's equipment, these times can become more accurate for the specific tasks. In fact, industrial engineers will often do a time standard analysis on the PM times to get a more precise time to carry out the PM. This is then inputted to the MRP II scheduling system to allocate time for that purpose in the overall schedule.

The fourth column identifies the position assigned to do the task. In the example, we see operators, technicians or maintenance specialists, oilers, handymen, and painters. Usually, the shorter-time and most frequently done items are assigned to the work station operator, the only caveat being that the task should be within the expected capability of the position assigned to it. This means that the operator has to be trained to do the PM tasks assigned to his or her work station. Also, performing the PM segment has to be part of the operator's official job description, and so does the time allocated to do it.

The fifth column sums the annual time consumed in doing each PM—how much productive time must be subtracted to maintain the equipment and how many people will be needed. We use this information to determine the staffing requirements. Note that we show the staffing requirements by category of labor. In the example, we have shop operations, the maintenance staff, and a painter. For convenience' sake I grouped the handyman and oiler into the technician/maintenance category, knowing that the latter is the next higher career step for the two junior positions as the incumbents gain experience. Knowing total hours and dividing by 2000 h/year we arrive at a staffing level.

The figure shows that shop operations will lose the equivalent of 5.25 people a year dedicated to PM. This is very necessary work, but it does reduce capacity and has to be accounted for in the MRP II scheduling system. It's accounted for by scheduling PM as a job going through the work station. The work station load sheet will show all the jobs assigned to the particular work station for the particular shift, including the planned-for PM. By this method we know that maintenance is being done and accounted for. To further emphasize the importance of PM, shop supervision is measured on its ability to do all jobs assigned efficiently, not just value-added jobs.

Similarly, the calculations for personnel needs are done for the technician/maintenance specialists, only here, this becomes an overhead expense rather than a deduction from time to do value-added work. On the contrary, it is additional work that has to be done so value-added work can be done.

The PM program as outlined in Figure 9-2 and its specific development for the particular factory are only the ultimate summation of the planning process for PM. We plan PM just as we do production jobs. We determine the method to be employed. We then estimate the time to do the job, using whatever technique is appropriate, making choices as we do for production work. Knowing the sum total of all PMs necessary and the time to perform them, we can create a time phased plan (this is the Two Knows specialized for maintenance work) to achieve the desired outcome. When the plan is integrated with the company's planning and scheduling system, vis-à-vis the MRP II system, we have created a synergistic system that functions virtually automatically. And this is what we strive for: in the case of maintenance, we aim for the longest uptime at the lowest possible cost. We can see that maintenance's contribution is to keep as much capacity available to make the company's products as it possibly can at the lowest possible cost.

MEASUREMENTS OF MAINTENANCE EFFECTIVENESS

Before we look at how we measure the effectiveness of a maintenance organization, let's recap the three approaches to extending the deterioration cycle; it is important to understand this to know what is vital to measure:

Reactive   Fix quickly after it breaks
Predictive   Remove and replace before it breaks
Preventive   Fix before it breaks

The major measurements we use to evaluate the effectiveness of the maintenance organization are:

1. Response time
2. Mean time between failures

3. Percent downtime
4. Budgetary control
5. Number of outages per time period

Figure 9-3 shows how each of the three major management strategies approaches these measurements.

The figure shows the relative emphasis each strategy places on each of the measurement categories. The types of measurements an organization uses to evaluate its effectiveness need to be able to judge objectively whether the selected strategy is succeeding or failing. This is true in general and particularly so for maintenance. In addition, we have the down and limping report, which is universal for all maintenance strategies. While we may think that all measurements are equally important, they are not necessarily so, and they further vary in importance depending on the strategy employed. Let's examine the importance of different measurements by comparing the measurements with the three strategies.

Reactive Maintenance Measurement Criteria

For the reactive strategy, as expected, the most important measurement criterion is response time. Since this strategy relies on "if it's not broke don't fix it," the most important measurement is how fast we can fix a down or limping machine or process to get it back to normal.

The next level of importance would be the mean time between failures, because this is an indication of how well the maintenance organization last performed when it had to fix something. It indicates how well and thoroughly the repair was accomplished. Equally important is the cost associ-

	A Response Time	B Mean Time Between Failures	C % Down Time	D Budgetary Control	E Number of Outages per Time Period
Reactive	1	2	3	2	3
Predictive	3	1	1	1	1
Preventive	2	1	2	2	1

1.= highest priority
2.= medium priority
3.= lowest priority

Figure 9-3. Maintenance strategy measurement criteria.

ated with the repair. This is the only way that reactive strategies can be compared with the other two. If we can show that reactive strategies cost significantly less than predictive or preventive, then they are a viable alternative for management to consider.

There are two measurements that are of lowest priority: percent downtime, and number of outages per period. We say percent downtime is a least important measurement because a reactive strategy doesn't try to prevent downtime, but only to minimize its extent through fast reaction. Of course, if too many short downtimes occur—e.g., if so many work stations are down at one time that they significantly affect capacity—then the reactive approach will be judged a failure for the particular company.

This leads to the fifth measurement, also rated lowest priority: the number of outages per period. Since the strategy reacts to outages, without trying to prevent them, this measure is quite irrelevant. In fact, proponents of reactive maintenance say that the only value in measuring the number of outages per period is to indicate whether the machine or process is reaching the end of its useful life. They say the measure can then be used to justify capital expenditures for replacements, but it has no meaning in evaluating the effectiveness of maintenance.

Predictive Maintenance Measurement Criteria

The predictive strategy is the most scientific maintenance strategy, in that it uses series of fatigue and probability equations to predict component parts' useful life. Proponents attribute its success to its ability to significantly shorten downtime by replacing parts before they exhibit any indication of impending failure. The key to the strategy is using massive data on like parts to understand the number of cycles to failure. If we know this number, we can productively change out the part before it fails; we simply have to count cycles and take out the part that will statistically fail at a cycle count of X before it reaches X. The trick, of course, is to have reliable data to do this.

Since predictive maintenance is such an enticing concept, a lot of research is being conducted to learn how to predict cycle times to failure with more accuracy. But even today, there is enough knowledge to accurately predict failure of most bearings and virtually all lighting fixtures. One promising technique is signature analysis. For example, machine shafts will exhibit certain acoustic *signatures* before journal bearing failures. Another signature analysis is temperature-related: thermal sensor probes show characteristic rises in temperatures as bearings enter the end phase of their useful lives. There are also strain gauge systems that allow us to predict when materials are getting close to their yield points hence are ready to crack and fail. These are just a few of the newer engineering techniques that make predictive maintenance possible. One of the drawbacks, however, is difficulty in predicting with accuracy the time delay between a precursor being observed and the actual failure. Obviously, there needs to be sufficient time to plan for an outage when the precursor is detected.

Predictive maintenance is still a risky business; it is really possible to be throwing away perfectly usable parts on the basis of a theory of failure instead of observed fact. Since a large part of the theory is based on statistical inferences, the simplest being averages of past experiences, it is reasonable to expect the important maintenance measurement criteria under this strategy to be those related to these calculations, and they are. Predictive maintenance, if done correctly, would maximize mean time between failures (these should be rarities) and minimize downtime (intentional downtimes should be planned in advance to change out parts on a schedule for replacement). So mean time between failures is a primary measurement. And so, too, would be the number of outages per time period.

In addition budgetary control is equally important. The company is being asked to spend more money for new parts rather than less money to fix worn but repairable parts. These parts will have some additional life in them after repairs, but not as much life as new parts. Any value gained for having virtually new machines and processes most of the time has to come from achieving higher usable capacity than a less expensive strategy. Coupled with the budgetary control is the number of outages per period. This is an important measurement that needs to be low to justify disposing of still functional parts.

The least important criterion, and by a wide margin, is response time. With predictive theory, there is no need to have a well-trained team to respond to outages, because outages will be so rare, according to proponents, that rapid response is moot.

Preventive Maintenance Measurement Criteria

Preventive theory is perhaps the middle ground, although, in truth, it leans more toward the scientific character of predictive theory than toward the rough-and-tumble of the fix-it-if-it-breaks-and-do-it-fast philosophy.

The preventive strategy has only two tiers of importance for measurement criteria. The two in the higher tier are the mean time between failures and the number of outages per period. The reasons are much the same as they were for predictive. By shutting down machines for planned inspections and minor replacement of parts (we do consider bearing oil, filters, and greases to be parts), we should be catching all causes of failures before they happen. The measurements internal to the inspections themselves should assure the grander measurement scheme that mean time between failures is at least being kept in check and hopefully growing. Similarly, if shutdown adjustments are being done correctly, the number of outages per period should remain low. So the outage count is a strong direct measure of the efficacy of the theory.

The secondary measurements are useful but do not really pass judgment by themselves. Budgetary is a secondary measurement for the preventive strategy. It is not as significant as in the predictive strategy because the need for entirely new parts is less. We are fixing existing parts when required, and replacing them at a less frequent rate; hence, costs are lower.

Percent downtime is also a secondary measurement. A company can have more downtime than under the predictive strategy but needs to be less than under the reactive. The cost of the strategy is less than that of the predictive strategy (from a planned-purpose viewpoint), so the balance sheet will tolerate less productive capacity over the time period than for predictive. But the downtime has to be less than experienced with reactive, because we are taking the work stations down for planned evaluations and preventive work based on those evaluations. By doing so, we are betting that there will be fewer unplanned downtimes.

The last secondary measurement is response time. The only strategy that emphasizes this criterion is reactive. But the preventive strategy, being a sort of middle-of-the-road strategy, has to perform reasonably well in this category. The predictive bases its existence on the fact that it can prevent unplanned downtime due to failures because it knows when to put in new replacement parts. The preventive strategy doesn't make that claim. It relies on periodic inspection to determine wear rate and assumes that even though a part shows wear, it can sometimes perform well enough to do the job. We figuratively keep suspect parts under careful watch, and perhaps at the next inspection period we will fix or replace them. So there is definitely a probability that we're waiting too long and there can be an unplanned outage. If that occurs, the maintenance team needs to respond. So response time is a measurement a maintenance organization operating under this strategy has to be cognizant of.

HOW TO CHOOSE A MAINTENANCE STRATEGY

The choice of maintenance strategy depends on the type of factory the company has. And this boils down to the complexity of the equipment. By complexity, I mean ease of understanding the nature of potential failures. If we understand the nature of potential failures and can predict them, then the predictive strategy would probably be employed. If we understand the nature of potential failures but cannot predict with any reasonable certainty when they will occur, then a preventive strategy is called for. And finally, if the equipment is relatively simple and thus potential repair choices are minimized, then a reactive strategy would probably be sufficient. Figure 9-4 is useful in helping to select the best strategy for a particular company's set of circumstances. Let's do a brief tutorial based on the figure.

Figure 9-4 is based on the premise that various manufacturing scenarios can be predicted and thus matched with a preferred strategy, as mentioned above. The figure lists characteristics of factories which the user employs to guide his or her selection of a probable best-matching maintenance strategy. The user checks each statement that pertains to the particular factory, while skipping those that do not. Then the various scores shown for the selected

	Criteria	Strategy Choices		
		Reactive	Preventive	Predictive
1	flow production	1	3	2
2	job shop	3	2	1
3	0 – 10 work stations	3	1	2
4	10 – 50 work stations	2	3	1
5	greater than 50 work stations	1	3	2
6	similar machines @ work stations	3	1	2
7	dissimilar machines @ work stations	2	3	1
8	mix of same/not same machines @ work stations	3	2	1
9	less than 25% computer control	3	2	1
10	more than 50% computer control	1	2	3
11	product mfg. cycle less than one week	3	2	1
12	premium for up-time critical	3	1	2
13	seasonal manufacturing	1	3	2
14	precision tolerances required	1	3	2
15	more than 2 axis movement	1	3	2
16	controlled environment	3	2	1
17	special training required	3	2	2
18	special diagnostic tools required	3	1	2

Instructions:
  [1] select criteria applicable to specific factory.
  [2] add point values of selected criteria for all three strategies
  [3] highest point value indicates probable strategy choice

Figure 9-4. Maintenance strategy selection matrix.

statements are added up in the respective columns for each of the three strategies. The strategy with the highest point score is the most probable match.

The word "probable" is the key factor. No one can possibly conceive of all the various permutations and combinations a factory can have. So at best, the user of Figure 9-4 and similar devices uses it as another data input factor among several. For example, consider availability of expert resources: sufficiently trained people who are capable of doing the diagnostic job. This is equally as important as the strategy chosen. There is no sense employing a reactive strategy, even if the numbers add up that way, if there is no ability to react quickly and with assurance that the breakdown can be repaired properly. It would be much better to use a preventive or predictive strategy where still-functioning parts are abandoned on a time schedule in order to take advantage of probability theory. Using an alternative strategy can often reduce the chance that a breakdown will occur that will require an expert to fix.

Remember, the choice of maintenance strategy needs to be compatible with all the pertinent characteristics of the factory. We can go through a maintenance selection matrix and have it indicate that a preventive strategy is the proper choice, and if all company cultures were the same this would be end of story, we would do just that—put in place a preventive strategy. But what if we had a company culture that tried to react to every sales opportunity regardless of whether it was feasible for satisfying the customer's needs? A sales-driven company that constantly changes schedule to meet the latest customer crisis regardless of expenses and disruptions is a company that has no internal discipline and wreaks havoc on all schedules. Every time an opportunity presents itself, this type of company would prefer to abandon all plans in an effort to secure the sale, even if it meant scuttling long-standing and prepaid preventive maintenance shutdown plans. Can this company support a preventive maintenance strategy? Most likely not. The choice becomes a reactive strategy and hoping for the best, even though logically a preventive strategy would be a cheaper way to go. So, compatibility with company culture is a must in selecting a strategy, and often this is the most important factor in the selection process.

An Example of Choosing a Maintenance Strategy

Let's look at an example of employing the maintenance strategy selection matrix (Figure 9-4). We will use the hammer producing factory as the subject. In this case we will assume that the company culture will be compatible with any decision the analysis recommends.

First we list the criteria from Figure 9-4 that apply to this facility. The items that apply are:

2. *Job shop.* An order for 10,000 units is relatively small for this type of product, and the company is classified as a small-lot job shop.
3. *0–10 work stations.* From Figure 3-5, the route sheet, we see that there are six active work stations in this factory.
7. *Dissimilar machines at work stations.* Again referring to Figure 3-5, each work station is different, and there are no similar machines or duplicates at any work station.
10. *More than 50% computer control.* The major work is done on computer-controlled machine tools.
11. *Product manufacturing cycle less than one week.* The magnitude of manufacturing cycle time for hammers is hours.
12. *Premium for uptime is critical.* Job shops need to perform quickly for clients to justify higher operating expenses.
14. *Precision tolerances required.* The nature of the product and its assembly requires machine tool-like tolerances.
15. *More than two axis movements.* The fact that CNC machines are employed indicates that multiaxis machining is a distinct probability.

17. Special training required. CNC machines require expertise in programming and electronics maintenance as well as normal machine tool maintenance.

18. Special diagnostic tools required. CNC machines typically require analysis equipment to check the "health" of the computer as well as the alignment and wear on critical drive train components.

We now add the point values for these selected criteria for reactive, preventive, and predictive strategies. The one with the highest point total would be the best-matching maintenance strategy for the hammer manufacturing facility. The results as shown in Figure 9-5 indicate that a reactive strategy would be best for this facility.

This is not surprising. The example is a small facility with fewer than 10 work stations. Most small shops have one of a kind pieces of equipment and are engaged in job shop activities where the premium is on uptime and delivering orders quickly. They also typically cater to the spot market, so having all equipment always running is paramount to success. In this case a reactive strategy is called for. PMs would be bare-bones and normally done on weekends, on holidays, and between orders, because the company can't afford downtime.

	Selected Criteria	Reactive	Preventive	Predictive
			Strategy Choices	
2	job shop	3	2	1
3	0 – 10 work stations	3	1	2
7	dissimilar machines @ work stations	2	3	1
10	more than 50% computer control	1	2	3
11	product mfg. cycle less than one week	3	2	1
12	premium for up-time critical	3	1	2
14	precision tolerances required	1	3	2
15	more than 2 axis movement	1	3	2
17	special training required	3	2	2
18	special diagnostic tools required	3	1	2
	Total Points	23	20	18

Best probable strategy is Reactive

Figure 9-5. Maintenance strategy selection for hammer manufacturing facility.

Note that if the hammer facility had more than 50 work stations, which would mean the premium for uptime would not be as critical, there would be a change in favor of a preventive strategy. Criterion 3 would be replaced by criterion 5, and criterion 12 would be eliminated. This, too, makes sense. When we have a great deal of equipment we not only can afford the time for PM during the production day but actually need it to prevent the probability of large numbers of outages at the same time. If this happened, the maintenance staff would be overwhelmed to the dismay of the company and its customers.

THE DOWN AND LIMPING REPORT

The down and limping report is the most important report produced by the maintenance system for both external and internal use. It is also universally used regardless of maintenance strategy employed. Every company that has a maintenance department employs some variation of this report. It is a simple report that tells management the status of all of its equipment by simply stating which are not available for use under any circumstances, and which are available for limited use. This is a casualty report for industry and enables management to adjust production capacities and to update information to customers about schedules. It also allows management to redeploy product manufacturing through different routes and sequences, to minimize disruptions.

As useful as a down and limping report is, I am too frequently disappointed by senior management's ignorance of its existence. I know, I want to know, how well my company can comply with schedule each day, first thing, when I arrive at the factory. This is my key on how we can react to customer needs. Along with material shortages and people absenteeism, the daily down and limping report gives me the most advanced warning of schedule problems looming in the near term future. And the more timely warning I have of potential problems, the more likely I can bypass or at least mitigate them.

Many senior managers seem to be caught off guard when machines go down, as if they expect these things never to happen. The down and limping report brings realism back to the planning meetings, reinforcing the knowledge that all machines and processes eventually fail. This knowledge is critical for another reason. It assures that the company is not viewing manufacturing through rose-colored glasses and underfunding capital for equipment upgrades and replacements. Many companies that ignore down and limping status seem to also ignore the need to fund replacement equipment. By logic then, senior management should insist on daily down and limping reports, because they are a simple accurate barometer of how well the manufacturing operation can perform in the near to medium term. They are also a good indicator of how much it will cost in the future to maintain a manufacturing capability.

Down and limping reports are simple in concept and execution. They tell at a glance what work stations are down, i.e., not capable of doing any productive work. They also point out what work stations are below stated capacity but still functioning to a lesser degree. In addition, they predict when the situation will be solved and show the reason for the deterioration from standard. Figure 9-6 shows a typical down and limping report.

By just glancing at the report, management has an idea whether or not the company will have manufacturing capacity problems. A small list of down and limping facilities says capacity is not too bad, and a longer list that it is. Looking at the Days on List column and the promised recovery dates (uptime) gives a magnitude estimate of the issues. Besides this intuitive analysis, production control will use the daily report to adjust capacities at various work stations. When a company possesses a modern MRP II system, this capacity adjustment will result in schedule adjustments throughout the factory on an almost real time basis. This synergy allows management to properly plan its actions in an orderly manner and from a basis of precise knowledge. This leads to reduced costs and higher profit. Once more, the axiom of the Two Knows is demonstrated. Modifications of capacity will affect the time to make a product and will lead to modified ways to make it. The down and limping report, while simplicity in itself, is a communications excellence practice that needs to be encouraged for use in every factory. Since communications excellence is the most important factor in competitive success, this tool is a natural competitive advantage. Those who neglect to use it do so at their peril.

Date 1/11/99

	Days on list	Promise Up-Time	Comments
Down Machines/Processes			
1. CNC Lathe 2W3K	1	2/15/99	ordered spindle bearings
Limping Machines/Processes			
1. Anneal Furnace	3	1/12/99	Requires replacement of 2 heater controls. Can only be used in manual mode.
2. Tig Weld Station	17	1/27/99	1 of 7 machines down. Electric motor for fan needs rewind. In repair shop.

Figure 9-6. Down and limping report.

THE MAINTENANCE ORGANIZATION'S PERSONNEL REQUIREMENTS

Maintenance organization people are special types unto themselves. We see from the nature of the work they do that they are always on the critical path of the company's track to success. But in perhaps a negative way. They do not make anything, nor do they plan for how products will be created. What they do is keep the company functioning when it suffers facilities setbacks. They are combination artisans, technicians, and preachers of conservatism in utilization of resources.

Successful maintenance people are neither engineers, technicians, nor operators but share traits with each. With the engineer, they share a kindred technical understanding of the equipment they are charged to keep operational. With the technician, they share an ability to fix complex equipment, often without the aid of drawings and schematics. With the operator they share an understanding of how to make products using the equipment. The one unique trait they possess is how to synergize all these roles to fix equipment and keep the factory running under adverse conditions. They do this at any time of the day, any day of the week. Successful maintenance personnel exhibit a can-do attitude, and very rarely, if ever, when they're called to attend to a down or limping machine, do they give the excuse that they're "waiting on someone else's work to be done" before they can do their own. They pride themselves in can-do and make-do.

How do we develop such people? Obviously, they require experience beyond the level of the work station operator. But the work station is where most good maintenance people come from. The necessary attitudes and skills are those of people with a great curiosity about why things work the way they do, coupled with a love of machinery and processes. They have to be capable of success in classroom technical sessions and have the pragmatic sense to apply their learned skills to real equipment problems. They need to be able to learn from experience and to have a sense of cause and affect that will help them bridge the unknown. And equally important, they need to work with a sense of urgency, keeping in mind that they are not puttering around in their basements but their actions can determine the success or failure of an entire company. Maintenance people are often thought of as blue-collar workers, and perhaps they are, but their superior skills set them apart from typical blue-collar workers. They, as much as managers, can set the course a company will follow. Companies can only utilize state-of-the-art equipment if they have an infrastructure to support it. The maintenance team is that infrastructure.

Maintenance personnel are most often promoted into their positions from a work station operator's job. From then on they undergo continuous on-the-job training, the first being a buddy system where new and junior people are teamed with more senior maintenance personnel. This is a sort of throwback to the old apprentice system, where journeymen practitioners learn through an internship with more knowledgeable people. The senior's skills are transferred to the junior via observation and practice on real problems. In addition, maintenance personnel attend training sessions given by vendors of the equipment the company has or will purchase. Here the vendor's experts provide guidance on troubleshooting and preventive maintenance.

Maintenance is not a haphazard attack on problems. It is disciplined and well organized. The people are well trained and undergo continuous training. They document what works and what doesn't and value benchmarking with other companies' maintenance personnel. It is a profession recognized by most manufacturing personnel and held in high regard.

Maintenance operators also frequently find themselves to be members of concurrent engineering teams. This is very prevalent when a new product will have a uniquely assigned production area with unique processes and equipment. The maintenance representative will advise the team on PM and predictive maintenance scenarios that the team should consider as it formulates its plans for the product. Many times maintenance personnel will accompany the manufacturing engineer to vendors' facilities to witness and learn firsthand about the equipment being purchased for the new product. They will also have a significant role in teaching proper usage of the equipment to shop operations people when the equipment arrives and is installed. Also, as you would surmise, a maintenance role is critical in installing the new equipment. This firsthand knowledge is extremely valuable in diagnosing down and limping problems later on. The maintenance role greatly affects the capacity of the work station. That is why maintenance people are often included on concurrent engineering teams.

THE RELATIONSHIP OF SHOP OPERATIONS TO MAINTENANCE

Maintenance is a service function to shop operations. The primary focus of the entire business organization is to support the value-added activities of the company, i.e., shop operations. Maintenance, along with manufacturing engineering, designs the maintenance strategy to be followed by the company—the most common one, of course, being a PM strategy. This middle-of-the-road strategy requires periodic duties to be performed with and for each specific facility. As stated earlier, some of the PM tasks are well within the capability of shop operations personnel to perform. Things like checking oil levels, maintaining a clean work place, and perhaps changing filters are items assigned to work station operators to perform.

Maintenance gets directly involved only in the more comprehensive PM periods when the equipment is taken out of service for an overhaul. It is good practice for the operator to be present during these overhaul periods to assist and give information on how the equipment has fared since the last overhaul. It is also a way for the maintenance technician to teach the operator more about the workings of the facility. This is invaluable experience that can be beneficial in the future if and when the operator has to report down or limping equipment for repair. With all PM activities, it is important for shop operations and the maintenance organization to develop a team relationship. Maintenance recognizes that shop operations is its only customer and treats shop operations as a valued commodity. On the other hand, shop operations people need to understand that excellent support by maintenance will allow them to achieve the production goals. They need to do everything they can to support maintenance requirements, the most important being the release of the facility to maintenance per schedule. Taking a shortsighted view that the maintenance schedule is not as important as the production schedule usually leads to less profit and perhaps less opportunity because the machines simply can't perform to their maximum capability.

Sometimes PM is not enough, and down and limping situations occur requiring rapid response by maintenance. When this occurs, the operator becomes the prime source of symptoms information to maintenance and is a critical factor in diagnosis. Here, the relationship of the maintenance operator as a partner with the work station operator can be significant in minimizing the effect of this capacity-reducing incident. We want full cooperation between the organizations to minimize the detrimental effects of the incident. The best way to do this is through good teamwork and appreciation of all parties' inputs to the solution.

This concludes our discussion of work station maintenance. We see that, just as a work station needs equipment, materials, and instructions to be productive, it also needs a good "pit crew" to keep it going. Two companies starting out at the same time with the same equipment will be hardly differentiable in the beginning. As those companies get older, the one with the better maintenance support will prosper far more than the other. And perhaps it will be at the expense of the other.

Chapter 10

Creating an Effective Shop Operations Team

Without a cohesive and effective production team, a manufacturing company will fail. There is no doubt about that. And yet, most members of senior management tend to simply assume that a shop operations organization will be effective. This overconfidence in shop operations management's ability to create effective shop operations teams can be a prescription for disaster. Assuring that shop operations management's skills are at the level necessary to achieve a cohesive and effective team is probably the lowest of all business function priorities. This means there is a danger for hosts of well-executed strategies and tactics to be nullified by poor performance on the shop floor. All this can be avoided if we focus as much effort on how to manage shop operations as we do on managing sales and engineering and the rest of the traditional support functions.

So far I have focused on the impact of all the direct and indirect inputs to the work station from the various support functions of the business organization. These are critical for success of manufacturing, but not sufficient. We have to make it jell with excellent management of shop operations itself. In this chapter I will present the case for developing progressive participative management on the shop floor and define and demonstrate the tools for doing so. I believe that having strong shop management that motivates its personnel in doing the jobs required of them is essential for manufacturing business success. It is entirely possible to manufacture products with vague and incomplete instructions if the factory can focus on the desired end results. But the reverse is not true. A vague factory operation, always in a constant fog of indecision and misunderstanding, cannot be overcome by superior engineering and support skills. In this chapter I will demonstrate how superior shop operations management skills allow a company to take advantage of superior engineering and support services.

THE FACTORS IN PROGRESSIVE MANAGEMENT

The first step of good management is assuring that all employees fully understand what they need to do and why they must do it in the way they're told. In addition, management has to see to it that the members of the organization buy into the legitimacy of its goals and support those goals. In manufacturing, the transfer of this information has two components: first, management's explanation of why the company needs to make its products at a reasonable cost; and second, all employees' (especially those in shop operations) understanding of the Two Knows. It is imperative that how to make the product and how long it should take to make it is common knowledge, dispersed to, understood by, and agreed upon by all. Knowledge achieved via good communications is essential. There is always a premium on communications excellence.

For a company to succeed, its employees (all of them) have to have:

1. An understanding of the company's goals
2. An agreement with and an assertive buy-in of the goals
3. The necessary skills to accomplish the goals
4. Sufficient resources to allow the goals to be achieved
5. An adequate reward system that spurs them on to achieve the goals

Let's amplify these statements a bit to demonstrate why they are correct.

1. An Understanding of the Company's Goals

In the past, the theory of need to know was used in a negative manner. Knowledge was thought to be power, and unless you wanted to dilute your power, you didn't share knowledge. Therefore, an astute manager would tell subordinates only what he or she thought they needed to know to do their jobs. Hence, information was handed out piecemeal, and rumor reigned supreme. What's wrong with this? A lot. Let's look at a few potential problems.

First of all, information was being censored in such a way that short-sighted and perhaps misguided managers who hadn't fully bought into the company's strategies could scuttle a project through slightly bending the intent of the information. There is no check or balance on interpretation. Obviously, equal access for everyone to vital information will make for a more cohesive drive for success.

When only one person possesses all of the information, we find creativity is stifled. People are not stupid. They know quite readily when there is more to the story than told. And when they feel they are kept in the dark they will err on the side of caution in taking initiatives. They do this for fear that their large investment of effort could turn out to be misdirected, thereby making them look like fools. True creativity occurs when people understand the real end goal and can freely think "outside of the box" to find a solution. How many people would do that if they didn't know the domain of the problem, and hence the acceptable reach out from the box? Usually, a very small minority.

If, for example, we needed to reduce the cycle time for making hammers by a factor of 5 but management was reluctant to say why, there would be few if any bold ideas. Let us suppose the need to reduce cycle time was generated by a desire to become a big-time player in hammer manufacturing, going from the nominal job shop total build of 10,000 to 10,000,000. But suppose also the company didn't relate this to the operators, instead saying only that they needed to produce 5 times faster. The operators wouldn't be impressed. They'd likely ignore the challenge. In fact, it is highly unlikely they would think outside of the box. If they did anything, they might stick to ways of improving job shop efficiency and playing it safe. It's unlikely that the creative sparks would fly and perhaps reach out as far as ideas about mass flow processes. Also, I doubt the operators would have much faith in management, because they would know the likelihood of achieving a fivefold reduction is virtually zero. The results would be not much—at most, a desultory, halfhearted effort to look as if they were complying with the request for suggestions.

Now, what would happen if the company had given all of the information? A lot of activity to generate ideas would occur. The company is specifying why it's looking for the fivefold increase. It would generate excitement. After all, it is natural to want to be part of growth and success. The operators will know the company had a good reason to ask for ideas, and that there was no hidden agenda. The company would get their full support.

Not providing full information can often have negative consequences. For example, not stating the reason why the company wants the fivefold increase could lead to all sorts of rumors. Some of them could be very disruptive. A rumor purporting the company's hidden agenda was a desire to cut the size of the workforce in order to save money could be very harmful. The rumor would be erroneously validated by stating that a five times faster operation would mean a layoff of all but one-fifth. This would not only be counter to getting good inputs on how to increase output fivefold, it would do the opposite. There would be an unconscious slowdown because operators wouldn't want to place their jobs in jeopardy by working their way out of employment. As a rumor like this gained credence through the company's failure to explain the situation fully, the ability to get cooperation from the workforce would diminish. Along with it, the ability for the company to grow and profit would be depleted. But if the information were shared, there would be no fear, and operators would fully participate in generating ideas. Indeed, they would feel wanted, and there would probably be an increase in productivity through no management action whatsoever, other than demonstrating that operators are significant members of the company's team.

2. AN AGREEMENT WITH AND AN ASSERTIVE BUY-IN OF THE GOALS

Very closely allied with understanding what the company is striving to accomplish is the workforce's positive acceptance of those goals. Not only do they have to buy into them, but they have to think of them as "our" goals, not "their" goals. If they remain "their" goals, there's no great loss if the goals are not met. It's like saying the United States bobsled team failed to win an Olympic gold medal in the last games. Many Americans may feel regrets about this, but hardly any would have great remorse. If they're relatives or friends of the team members, they may feel more sympathy for the failure, but still not great remorse. If they're team members, they suffer great remorse and probably vow to do better given the next opportunity. We want our factory operators to be like the team members. We want them to feel great remorse at failure and vow to do better next time. We want fire in the belly to strive for success.

Only true believers do great things. Therefore it is paramount for management to express goals in a manner that assures complete buy-in by the entire team. In the case of the hammer expansion, it can't happen unless the entire team feels its a good idea that needs to come to fruition. Assuring them there is a good reason for buy in is achieved through skills, resources, and rewards, as we shall see.

3. The Necessary Skills to Accomplish the Goals

If we want our shop floor teams to succeed, we need to assure they have the necessary skills to succeed. Just wanting good things to happen is not sufficient. The workforce can be as motivated as humanly possible and still fail if it does not possess the proper skills to do the job. No matter how you look at it, there is no substitute for the prerequisite skills necessary for the organization to succeed.

Shop management must understand the skill set(s) required to do the assigned job. They must make sure that the operators also understand what those skills are. But more so, management must assure that the operators themselves have correctly judged their respective abilities to do the required tasks. This is self-assessment and it is a necessary step before management and operators can agree how the operators stack up compared to the real need. If they agree with the diagnosis that certain levels of skills are lacking, the task of setting up training activities to spur skills development is worthwhile and will have positive effects on employees. What we are essentially saying to the operators is that the company values their previous commitment and desires that they augment their skills to encompass the new challenges facing the company. The company, by doing this, demonstrates a bonding with the employees, and that says the goals' success is important to all parties. In this manner, management gets buy-in and support. And in the bargain, its employees increase their value to themselves. Bluntly put, more skills, more earning potential.

4. Sufficient Resources to Allow the Goals to Be Achieved

Sufficient resources go along with proper skills. Both are necessary for a company to succeed with its plan. Proper skills alone will not suffice. In order for the most skilled practitioners to be successful, they have to be provided with the required resources to use with their talents. We would not ask a gifted surgeon to perform open heart surgery on a kitchen table; nor would we procure a sailboat when a search-and-rescue cutter is required. Why, then, do we find management quite often willing to waste skilled operators with inadequate machines? It makes no sense at all. It's like saying that getting to third base is sufficient even though the goal is to score runs.

For a company to succeed, management needs to make sure that resources suitably up to the required tasks are provided to its employees. It is also a matter of perception. If management has gone through the efforts to have employees understand the goals, then get concurrence that they are worthy to accomplish, and finally assure that operators are trained and capable of achieving those goals, why would it be willing to now say, we're sorry, we can't give you the resources to achieve the goals? Obviously, there is no reason to consciously do this, but many companies do just that by their implied decisions to skimp on proper resources. The body language is saying it's all "play acting," we want you to fail, even though the truth may be just the opposite. The fact is, if management wants its company to succeed, pre-planning necessary resources is a very important step. It has to be done when considering the entire strategy, and if there is no financial way to achieve those resources then the strategy must be abandoned for one that is affordable.

This is not to say that only money counts. There are numerous cases of business success where the winning competitor has far less money resources than the other firms. It just used its resources better. The lesson is, providing proper resources is part of an overall prescription for success, but it has to be in the context of the company's means. For example, say we have a strategy calling for utilizing a CNC lathe with lots of advanced control systems that emulate a very complex tool path required by the design. This in turn requires a moderately skilled operator and an equally skilled engineer. We can see that the machine would be the highest-cost item, the resource needed. It could cost upwards of $300,000—a sizable investment for most companies. Let's now suppose the company can't afford that amount. The result would be that the moderately trained operator and engineer would have to work on a lesser machine, with perhaps less probability of achieving the required tolerances. So, the success of the venture is in jeopardy. The company has a higher probability of failure. Every phase of managerial tactics was attended to correctly but this one—providing resources to allow the goal to be achieved. There is a disconnect. How do we fix that? We make sure that all the steps are compatible with the company's capability of achieving. In this case we would need to invest more effort in the skills attainment step. We would have to train the operator to become more proficient with a lesser machine and we would have to upgrade the skills of the engineer to be able to match designs with the lesser machine's abilities.

It is these types of managerial decisions that are so often lacking when we try to motivate personnel to achieve the company's goals. The pragmatic step of planning how to provide affordable resources is often overlooked. This review needs to be tied into understanding and agreeing to the goals, as well as matching the skills the company can provide.

5. An Adequate Reward System That Spurs the People On to Achieve the Goals

If we want people to strive to reach a goal, there has to be more of a reward than a sense of a job well done. A simple thank you may be part of the reward package, but it is not sufficient in itself. We can be cynical and say that there should be some sort of financial reward and anything else is window dressing. In many cases that may be correct. But it is never entirely correct.

Work on the factory floor is the closest modern manufacturing comes to true physical labor. While it is rare for operators to become physically exhausted, conditions are definitely not as attractive as so-called office work. Therefore, shop people tend to bond through common shared experiences more than do white-collar workers. Shop operations, more than any other function of a company, tends to instinctively form "we versus they" teams. Another trait is the workers want to be on the winning team. Thus, the reward system which is most effective is a team award. Usually, recognition for reaching a milestone or goal is also well received, and even more so if it is a team recognition situation. It could be as simple as a special memo from the company president with a cake and coffee shared during a work break. It also could be something more complex, such as a profit sharing plan that "kicks in" for achieving a planned milestone. The point is that team recognition is the key concept. This recognition is something that says management salutes the team for its accomplishment, for reaching a plateau of success, and here are the spoils to you, the victors. If the operators know there will be some type of recognition at the end of the road management wants them to travel, then there is every expectation that this fifth step has been successfully complied with.

We've set the stage with the five points of success. Now let's look at how we go about building the effective operations team.

BUILDING A TEAM WITH PEOPLE SUPPORTED BY SYSTEMS, NOT VICE VERSA

Shop operations' task is to make the product with the facilities, instructions, and materials provided. The one thing the managers and supervisors have to do is apply the workforce to the task at hand, and do it in a way that gains sufficient profit for the company. Shop operations management needs to motivate the operators to do good work in order for the company to succeed. The axiom

People make products supported by machines and information

succinctly states the philosophy successful shop managers need to follow. The emphasis is on getting and employing the best people available for each and every task that needs to be accomplished, and doing it in a manner that gets the best effort from them. This means that the daily task of managing is to stay people-focused before looking at process and equipment. The axiom is, find and employ good people, and then enlist their help in achieving the assigned goals.

There are many philosophies of management, from autocratic to participative. I believe the latter to be much more effective, particularly since the modern American workforce, through cultural affinity, tends to instinctively ask "why" for virtually every step of a work assignment. I also believe this is a good thing, because it forces management to think through every phase of an assignment to assure it is the best way to approach it. It also encourages suggestions for improvement, and, I believe, this is a paramount reason why American factories far outpace all others for sustained productivity improvement.

A typical list of people-oriented shop operations management tasks is shown in Figure 10-1. Notice how virtually none consist of telling employees directly what to do. Most are a matter of providing the necessary infrastructure so the operators can understand how to do their value-added jobs. For example, we see that the first item concerns labor reporting,

- Assure labor reporting is accurate, by instructing employees on proper reporting procedures.
- Coordinate work flow in the department (people, equipment/tooling, and materials).
- Coordinate work flow between departments.
- Coach employees in proper procedures for carrying out their assigned tasks.
- Provide guidelines and monitor procedures for assuring proper performance of method of manufacturing.
- Facilitate development of relevant measurement metrics.
- Provide resources for allowing employees to work within EPA and OSHA safe workplace guidelines.
- Work with employees to create an optimal ergonomic workplace.
- Coordinate maintenance activities.
- Be the first-line technical support resource for the employees.
- Work with engineering as part of a concurrent engineering team.
- Supervise the Engineering Change Notice activities on the shop floor.
- Coordinate quality control activities on the shop floor.
- Facilitate labor and machine utilization strategies with employees.
- Manage integration of new processes via coaching and soliciting suggestions from employees.
- Conduct evaluations of performance with respect to achieving set goals.
- Manage tool crib activities for dispensing equipment to employees.
- Maintain accurate records for attendance and payroll.

Figure 10-1. Shop operations management responsibilities.

making sure it is accurate. It's not achieving production goals for the day. In fact, that isn't even mentioned in any of the items. Why? Because telling operators what the quota for the day is, is not necessary. This is so because we have many more concise ways for conveying that message integrated with the daily work routine. The most direct is the daily dispatch sheet that tells the operator the sequence of work and the jobs to be done in the specified work period. But it is necessary for the information flow to be correct so the schedule we are using is a reflection of reality. Therefore, accurate labor reporting is a valid people-oriented management task.

Notice, also, how many of the specific duties of the manager involve the words coordinate, support, work with, and other counseling-type phrases. This implies a participative approach whereby the manager, while still in charge and ultimately responsible for results, is more of a facilitator than a director. She rarely needs to tell people what to do, but rather provides the wherewithal so they can do it. This can be as direct as assuring materials arrive on time or as abstract as participating with engineering in resolving product design issues. The point is, we need to assure that operators fully understand why they have to do things a specified way as much as how to do them. In this manner we gain commitment from operators to strive for success. We are actively encouraging buy-in for the process, creating ownership and thus a stake in being successful.

We can see that a system in which operators are to feel truly responsible for the outcome of their work requires a commitment to these people. We must recognize that people are a company's most valuable asset, which makes good business sense. After all, people can still think better and be more creative than any computer ever conceived. And if the day comes when this is no longer true, then machines will have replaced humans as the dominant intelligence in our world. It is foolish to think that machines will replace people. Sure, machines work faster, and are certainly more adept at repetition. But they cannot react to changes in stimuli very well, if at all. They cannot adapt to changing market forces without major retooling. People can. All that's necessary is for the leaders to succinctly explain what the realities are and sell the case for change. If we treat people as partners in the enterprise, this becomes remarkably simple. If we treat them as ciphers worth less than the machine, we get resistance, mistrust, and sometimes actions countervailing what is needed.

The goal of management is to merge people with machines to get a synergistic best scenario. The machines do the things they do well, and the people take care of the human things—e.g., control and coordination—creatively and innovatively to find ever more effective ways of utilizing the machines. But this happens only if we get operators' buy-in and ownership of the factory processes. If we don't get buy-in, if we impose autocratic rules, operators will simply run the machines per the directed method and rarely if ever suggest better ways of accomplishing the task. This is called operator tune-out as compared to buy-in. This is the manufacturing equivalent of societal trouble. We see discontent, lethargic performance, and continuous labor-management bickering. We also see the rise of a bloated and costly "human resources" organization charged with maintaining labor peace through arcane rules and compromises that never result in improved productivity. All of these negatives create a climate under which short-term rather than properly constituted long-term goals are the focus. And obviously these goals are never optimum. The ultimate result of all of this is underperforming companies undertaking plant moves and closings and living by the grass-is-always-greener-across-the-street philosophy. We see the chase to obtain overseas factories, the thought being that they will offer an escape from productivity problems. We see the illusion that cheaper labor costs are the solution. Obviously they are not, but are only a stay of execution. If the old domestic labor policies are employed overseas, ultimately the same end results will be achieved. Also, cheaper labor costs are a farce as a reason for abandoning domestic plants for foreign sites. The simple economic equations show this to be true, even to the first-year economics student. If modern industrial experience shows direct labor costs to be only 1% to a maximum of 10% of the entire cost of doing business, how can that be a significant factor in making a decision to move a factory? It can't. The payback in labor savings to cover for loss of skilled labor and infrastructure support is very long in coming. Most companies that have run away from labor problems experience decades-long anxieties before equilibrium is achieved—if it ever is truly achieved.

THE OPERATOR AS THE LINE MANAGER OF THE WORK STATION

The point of this discourse is to show that treating the shop operator as an extremely valuable resource is much easier and much more productive for the company than the alternative. In fact, it leads to an interesting concept of management—looking at the operator as the line manager of the work station where he or she works.

If we follow classical management theory, we do four things:

1. Assign a task to achieved.
2. Provide resources.
3. Set about doing the task
4. Measure results and make changes as required.

We do all these things all the time with every work station on the factory floor right now. Reviewing Figure 1-1 once more, we see that all four classes of activities are present. The only thing we don't do is designate the operator as the "boss" of this bounded system. Most manufacturing entities ignore the presence of the operator entirely. He is simply part of the topography and taken for granted. If we really do want to be optimum, we need to engage this person in more than a passive observational role pushing a button or moving a part in choreographed and scripted fashion. We need to assure that we know what the end result needs to be and then set out to allow the "manager" the scope to do it. And this scope should be as large as we can possibly make it for the operator (i.e., manager) to act within. If we have provided the right resources, including proper training, then the operator ought to be able to manage his way through the task in the most expeditious way possible. And, most likely, it would be at the lowest possible cost.

The philosophy of the operator as line manager of the work station is quite straightforward. It is the macro results that count—that must be agreed upon by all and thus cast in concrete—while the exact way of getting them is the operator's prerogative. This certainly gains buy-in and ownership on the part of the operator. Concurrently, if the reward system is sufficient, the probability is high that the operator will prevail and achieve the result, and it is a win-win situation for all. You might think, well this is a throwback to the old piecework system under which an operator was paid for his output and only his output. True enough, but the operator as the work station manager goes beyond that. He is truly responsible for all the factors of production affecting the output of that work station.

For the concept of operator as line manager to work, the operator needs to fully understand the "game plan" employed. He has to be fully briefed on what is expected of the work station, exactly what resources are available, and what constitutes success. If we level with the operator and give him the full picture of the business situation, we can expect him to view the work from a different, more worldly viewpoint. Instead of being an appendage to the machine, one who tends to its well-being so it can perform properly, the operator is a manager of a valuable company resource placed under his supervision. This is a subtle difference in practice, but it makes a huge difference in attitude toward achieving company goals. In his mind the operator becomes a decision-making member of the team who is important to the team's success. The operator becomes a colleague to other managers and will strive to make them feel that their trust was not misplaced. It is very important that management believe this, too. Without mutual respect this concept doesn't work, and participative management fails.

Along with this shift in attitude toward the importance of the operator as the manager of the work station, there has to be ample reward. The best way of giving this is through group incentives shared by all the operator/managers and their supervisor. They have to feel that they are all striving to meet suitable and achievable goals and when they achieve those goals they have a reasonable award to share. The incentive to be successfully creative needs to be there. We need to recognize good work publicly and make sure those who have achieved their goals are lauded for reaching the milestone.

Have you ever participated in award ceremonies? Notice that everyone feels good, because notable achievement is being celebrated. Those who are receiving the awards are given the incentive to do good work again, because peer recognition is a narcotic. Once achieved, forever strived for again. It also acts as an inducement for others to achieve awards. They, too, want peer recognition. It is a continuous improvement cycle once started that can only reach higher levels.

Notice I haven't said the rewards have to be monetary. They certainly need to have some aspect of financial gain; after all, most of us work to support our basic needs and not for pleasure. However, rewards for achievement other than money certainly can be a significant portion of the award. How many Nobel Prize winners consider the money as the most significant factor? Very few, if any, and the prize is a large sum of money. Most Nobel laureates are primarily delighted with the peer recognition and the fact that they have been certified as the best in their vocation and are only secondarily interested in the financial aspects of the prize. The key point is, plaques, certificates, medals, etc., probably have as much positive impact on morale and improved performance as straight cash. And they last much longer. Plaques and certificates continually remind recipients that they did a good thing that was recognized by the organization. In addition, all who see the awards know the recipients are worthy of respect because of their achievement.

This type of recognition is the cornerstone of continuous improvement. It is important to understand that people respond positively to praise—especially if it is nontrivial and from the heart. The participative program demands true, sincerely felt respect for achievement. Operators cannot be allowed to surmise even in the slightest that management is trying to trick them into giving more effort than they should by instilling a false sense of togetherness. Participative management has to be honest with facts and reasons and measurements. Respect for all members of the team is essential. There cannot be any false friendliness or trickery. If there is, the we versus they situation takes over and the stage is set for confrontation and discord. Recognition has to be sincere. There can be no sugarcoating of the facts of the situation. Honesty must prevail. If it does, the operator-as-line-manager philosophy will yield productivity far greater than any other management approach to shop operations.

HOW TO TRAIN THE SHOP OPERATIONS TEAM

Motivating operators to perform to the best of their abilities is a necessary condition for successful shop operations. But it is not a sufficient condition. The team needs to have the skills to complement its desire to do the required jobs. The approach management takes to effect sufficient training is very important to success. Not only will training provide the skills, but how it is approached will either add to or subtract from the team's motivation to succeed. Let's look at methods and techniques that can aid rather than detract from employee morale, and at the same time improve the productive capacity of the workforce.

1. Create Reasons for Wanting to Learn

Companies having a participative management style often tie promotions to higher qualifications achieved through successful completion of courses. For example, if an operator wants to become a lead person in CNC machining, he or she needs to complete a course of instruction in CNC theory and application as part of the prequalifications. This linkage between a better job and acquiring skills assures that only qualified persons gain the higher-paying jobs. There may be other requirements, such as time in grade, i.e., experience in prerequisite jobs, before a promotion occurs. But it soon becomes very evident to the employees that learning skills is necessary to be promoted. The more the employee learns, the more important he or she is to the company and to him- or herself. The company is *rewarding people for learning*—a very important part of participative management.

Besides pay incentives, we need to demonstrate that learning is an ongoing purpose of the company so it can continue to successfully compete. The organization must be willing to set aside time for instruction out of the production day. By doing this the company transmits the message that it values learning as part of its method of operation and as part of its development of a stronger competitive position. This means that training definitely has to impart additional skills so that the company can gain profitable benefits. These benefits, to list a few, would include better productivity through more efficient utilization of equipment, the whole range of applied SPC techniques, and improved communications skills. The manner in which we impart these skills is also important. I believe there should always be a carrot tied to the end of the stick. We want every new skill learned to make it easier for the operator to understand his or her job and to do it more proficiently, so that the operator will have a higher probability of success, and along with it awards and recognition.

We should also always link personal success with company success. We should never give the impression that the teaching is for the sole benefit of the operator. It is not, and the operators know that. By creating a situation for mutual benefit, a win-win combination, we achieve the goal of setting mutual needs that can be satisfied only if the operator improves his or her skills.

Creating the desire to learn is the first step. Let's look at the next phase of training.

2. Create a "Learning Organization" by Pursuing Excellence

We've just seen how companies create an atmosphere in which the learning of skills is a desirable as well as a rewarding pursuit. Such an atmosphere affords the opportunity to encourage curiosity about better ways of doing things. A company that thus encourages a desire to pursue excellence is what we call a "learning organization." Seen from the opposite viewpoint, a learning organization is staffed by people who have an insatiable curiosity about how things work and why and whose management encourages both their curiosity and their desire to act on it.

The goal is to appeal to the natural curiosity all people have and channel that into a desire to understand their surroundings and make them better. This is a proper goal, but to be successful at it, it is necessary to put people at ease about learning. It literally has to be easier to want to participate in learning than not. This could be a challenge to management. Many people have a fear of learning, mainly brought about by unfavorable experiences in their formal schooling situations. It is not unusual for shop operations to be staffed by individuals who were not very successful in their mandatory school years. Since shop operations has been known for hands-on, brawn rather than brain occupations (obviously, not entirely true), it has tended to attract people who feel working primarily with intellectual abilities is beyond them. They feel uncomfortable in the lecture, show, test situations of formal schooling. Since that is the case for a sizable portion of the workforce, it is necessary to create situations where the fear of the learning process is abated. There are some tried-and-true ways of doing this. Let's look at them.

The main thing is to prevent any student from feeling embarrassed about his previous education achievement shortfalls and to present a situation that is nonthreatening. The last thing we want is for an employee to feel intimidated by the schooling process and be reluctant to participate. We mitigate this by creating environments where learning becomes secondary to having fun with peers while investigating new things. We make sure we never put anybody on the spot by asking questions going to the heart of the matter in a way that would cause shame or embarrassment to the student. This means never having formal tests in any subject unless they are mandatory for safety or other overriding reasons. We judge competency by actions, not answers to written examinations. We make it easy for the employees to demonstrate they've learned the skills the lesson was designed to impact. This is done by allowing them to put the new skills into service and show by doing that they understand. Figure 10-2 shows the dos and don'ts of shop floor instruction. Following these simple guidelines will definitely allow the company to enjoy a satisfactory training program.

Another very effective way to mitigate fear of learning is through the "buddy system." The buddy system ostensibly pairs a person who understands the topic to be taught with one who doesn't, or sometimes pairs people with different rates of learning. In both cases, the one who is more knowledgeable or faster helps the one who isn't. Again, it is important to make it a stress-free situation. We certainly aren't going to announce that we're pairing Joe with Sam because Joe is a slow learner and Sam is a good student. We simply say we're pairing so we can share different lifetime experiences related to the topic, or some other such euphemism to make sure that we do not embarrass Joe.

The buddy system can be very conducive to learning because it is very nonthreatening. The pair go about the task of learning usually at a pace that is comfortable to both. The system makes it easier for the slower learner (usually the one who is embarrassed to demonstrate difficulty in learning by asking questions) to actually ask for help from the instructor because he can do so with the backing from his buddy. In effect, they're both asking questions, not each alone, and therefore the potential for embarrassment is lessened. With the buddy system the slower learner is more willing to try putting new skills into service because there is less fear of making a mistake. He will not cause his partner to laugh at him, because his partner is his close confidant. Again, the key is establishing a less threatening situation.

Do	Do not
1. Present topics at a level the participants can understand.	1. Be condescending to the participants by letting them know this is a "watered-down" version.
2. Create a relaxed situation with no visibly apparent agenda to be covered.	2. Set a goal for a certain amount of material to be covered during the session.
3. Set the number of learning points per lesson that needs to be retained to the capability of the slowest learner.	3. Set fixed goals for retained learning points for each class and dogmatically drill to assure success.
4. Allow interruptions or questions at any time and answer politely in a nonthreatening, nonadversarial manner.	4. Put off questions until the set question-and-answer period to maintain the flow of the presentation.
5. Direct hard questions to the group, not to an individual, unless you are sure the person knows the answer.	5. Direct questions to a person who probably doesn't know the answer.
6. Admit you don't know the answer to a question, if you really do not. Say you will look it up and get back to the questioner, and really follow through.	6. Try to bluff your way past tough questions you are not sure of.
7. Use visual aids and hands-on demonstrations at every opportunity.	7. Rely on descriptions instead of visual aids and hands-on demonstrations.

Figure 10-2. Guidelines for a successful shop floor training program.

The buddy system works well provided that:

1. The pair get along reasonably well.
2. One of the pair is capable of absorbing the lesson plan materials and can help the other learn.
3. Both members have a positive attitude toward learning as a team, and there is mutual respect.

If any of these conditions are not fulfilled, the buddy system will not achieve what it is supposed to. The amount of shortfall depends on the total shortfall among the three conditions.

A final thought on combating the fear of learning: The most important thing to do is make the situation nonthreatening. This means doing everything to create a relaxed, fun-seeking situation, even though the subject matter may be very serious or technical or even vital to the company's survival. Take the student's mind off proving mastery of a set of skills and instead focus on the fun of exploring new ideas and ways to do things.

3. Establish Routines for Instruction That Fit the Culture of the Organization

Every company has its specific culture. We want any company's culture to include continuous learning among all members of the production team.

However, what we do to include it cannot go directly opposite to whatever course the company is following. It can be targeted to changing the culture, but not as a frontal attack. It has to be more like a sailboat tacking upwind. Let's look at the kinds of learning situations we can create and keep in mind there are many different company cultures. Remember, a learning situation that is antithetical to the culture will not succeed.

I believe a participatory culture is the most effective one for successful manufacturing operations. So what follows will favor that philosophy. I believe we should gently nudge those companies that don't subscribe to the participatory philosophy with the tactic of tacking up wind to achieve that result. We should use training as another tool in achieving the company culture that best suits the organization. Again I will state that my preference is one heavily favored toward participatory.

On the Job

An on-the-job instruction routine is a version of the buddy system whereby we train workers who need to gain a skill by pairing them with knowledgeable workers. This is a low-key approach and is useful as a way to gain acceptance for learning, thereby upgrading skills from within. Most management teams recognize this as a necessity, realizing that all new skills inputted into the company cannot be achieved through outside hiring. It is also the employees' first indication that the company has a vested interest in retaining them, because of the time invested to impart skills. Most companies equate shop operations time with product produced, and if a direct expenditure of labor produces no product, then it had better be an investment in future growth.

Another reason an on-the-job instruction program is successful in gaining a foothold is that most people do not even recognize it as a learning situation. They simply view it as a means to tell new or junior employees how to do the job.

On-the-job learning is as informal as instruction gets. Therein lie its strengths as well as its weaknesses. It's reasonably nonthreatening because it is a peer-to-peer situation where the new employee is being indoctrinated by the longer-service employee—and that longer-service employee is at the same company social rank as the new person. If the seasoned employee knows his or her "stuff" and is capable of transmitting it to the new employee, then the training is a success. If the older employee is not properly knowledgeable of the process, then the new person either doesn't learn the necessary skill or learns techniques that are not proper. This is a dangerous way of transmitting erroneous techniques and habits that needs to be guarded against.

To ensure that on-the-job training is done successfully, the company needs to train the trainers. After making a conscious decision to use on-the-job training, the company then pretrains designated individuals in specific skills prior to using those people for training purposes. For establishing a learning organization where one never existed before, this is a technique that has a high probability for success. It's relatively easy to gain agreement that certain trusted "old hands" be given help so they can more effectively train the "rookies"—the typical logic being that the old hands wouldn't be burdened as long with the rookies if they could get the training done faster.

On-the-job training needs to be part of the learning organization's arsenal of tools. It is easy to set up and readily accepted. It also complements other techniques as an adjunct or reinforcing mechanism. It supplements classroom or group floor sessions with practice at the workplace, in much the way labs are an adjunct to physics and chemistry classes. On-the-job training should be considered the pre-requisite of a formal training program. It is easy to implement. It can be either a structured approach utilizing prepared lesson plans for the trainers to employ, or it can be an ad-hoc approach used when opportunities present themselves for improving workforce skills. No matter what level of intensity is employed, we should recognize that it is a valid managerial tool. It is important for shop operations success and should be used.

On the job training is used in companies practicing virtually all styles of cultures. However, in participatory styles the results are faster and perhaps more creative because of the more permissive atmosphere.

Classroom

Classroom training implies formal sessions with prepared agendas and lesson plans and specific goals to be achieved. It can be and often is. Since it is by nature structured, classroom training tends to be favored more by companies demonstrating cultures that are hierarchical rather than participatory as the prime source of training. However, it can also be as informal as on-the-job training. Let's look at both extremes.

Formal classroom training can be used to indoctrinate new employees in the company's rules, procedures, and culture. It is also effectively used for specific program sessions when the company needs to teach its employees specific process techniques or procedures. The classroom setting has the advantage of freedom from outside distractions that would disrupt students' attention. It is also an appropriate place for setting up all kinds of visual and audio learning aids. Formal training implies use of structured lesson plans and perhaps some sort of verification that the intent of the lesson has been successfully transferred from teacher to student—in other words, that learning has occurred.

The setting of the classroom should be advantageous for formal learning. However, when dealing with shop floor personnel, as mentioned previously, we need to be cognizant of the high percentage of people who suffer in some degree from "fear of learning." The classroom may remind some people of past failures, and therefore the experience needs to be mitigated. How do we do that? Perhaps there is no easy way, but I've always had success by making sure that we were meeting in a conference room, not a classroom, and assuring workers that the purpose was to solve mutual problems—how to implement, use, or understand the subject matter so that we could improve our performance. I always set the stage by saying that this learning situation was really a group problem-solving session. That way I disguised the fact that it was really company-sponsored school. I'm sure those with a fear of learning knew it was a euphemism, but it gave them a way to save face and tended to relax the students. I also virtually never used a test where any one individual is put on the spot to demonstrate competency. Rather, I used the facilities of the classroom to provide for group practice of techniques and to observe the groups for indications they had mastered the lesson's objectives. I like to pair people up so neither has to face public embarrassment. As you can see, I believe maintaining a person's dignity is very important for learning to occur, either in a formal classroom setting or any other venue.

Formal classroom settings are very good in focusing everybody on the subject matter at hand. People come to the class to learn. They are exposed to formal lessons with set goals (but only after they are put in a stress-free situation). And mostly, learning occurs quicker than in any other situation.

Informal classroom sessions occur when people need to get together to discuss new methods, techniques, etc., and then refine ideas using the chalkboard (or modern erasable-marker white board) to record their deliberations. Such situations may not be as fast or as efficient as formally structured learning situations, but the classroom can still be a useful setting for informal learning to occur—not structured learning, and not specifically planned, but learning nevertheless. Students (e.g., operators trying to learn new techniques) can use the facilities to practice skills learned in other venues or to generally enhance learning that could probably have taken place elsewhere but would have at a less efficient pace. By allowing workers to have these "jam sessions" in a locale favorable to learning, where we set the stage for learning, we encourage the procedure and get it done faster. I know this from experience and can attest to the fact that creating a favorable learning situation sets the stage for success. Let me relate one such incident.

In the early 1980s I was an engineering manager of a division losing lots of money. we had hosts of problems, ranging from poorly trained operators to lack of cohesive goals. The nature of the problems is not germane to this illustration, except to say that the division was in severe trouble and needed to do something. That something turned out to be to find a way to identify the root causes of the problems and create a road map for fixing them.

We tried to do just that within the factory and adjacent offices for over two months. It didn't work. We could never bring ourselves to find what the problems were, and hence we rambled all over the place. The fact of the matter was we were too close to the real-world pressures to ever release our minds to think "out of the box." Then our general manager had an inspiration: to take us all to a conference center over a weekend to debate all the issues away from the pressures of the site. And by all of us, I mean virtually the entire management structure of the division. We had the same host of problems as before that we couldn't come to grips with, only this time we were in a locale that encouraged thinking and discussion and nothing else. It was a conference center that had every known device for recording, comparing, and visualizing ideas and teaching concepts. The interesting thing was that after one intensive weekend in the right setting, one conducive to exchange of ideas, we created the strategy to save the division. The plan was put in place after we returned and was successful in a matter of months. Now, this is not to say we wouldn't have done the same thing by staying home, but I'm convinced it wouldn't have happened anywhere near as fast if we hadn't made that trip. Here we had the surroundings ready made for us to produce a successful solution if there was one. This illustrates how the informal classroom can enhance learning.

Correspondence Courses

Correspondence courses are probably the least effective way of training shop floor personnel in general, but can be effective for properly motivated individuals. While these courses can be well constructed and have excellent tutorial capabilities, they rely solely on the motivation of the individual to succeed.

Correspondence courses are successful only if the student has a strong desire and favorable circumstances to succeed. There has to be a payoff for the individual to take the course. Plus, there needs to be a situation that encourages the individual to pursue the course. In addition, if the course is difficult, there will be few if any sources for assistance to turn to, so motivation to continue needs to be stronger even than the desire to start this type of learning. With these constraints in mind, let's look at where such courses may apply.

We can see a need for correspondence courses in situations where job promotion depends on acquiring certain skills and there are no qualified schools or instructors readily accessible to the student. It is not unusual for operators to need certain skills to qualify for promotions or higher pay. A company may require many dissimilar skills, and it wouldn't be unusual to find that qualified instructors are not locally available for all the desired skills. In this case the operator either gives up his or her quest for additional knowledge or looks for alternative methods of obtaining it. One of the purportedly attractive alternates presented to the student may be a correspondence course. If the operator's desire for the knowledge is strong enough, he or she may sign on and start the course. Whether the operator completes it or not will depend more on how the course material is presented than the student's intelligence. If it is a dry, very objective approach, chances are good that after a lesson or two the student will abandon the project. If, on the other hand, the material is presented in a spirited and challenging manner, the probability of a successful conclusion is much higher. But when all is said and done, if it isn't fun to do, it won't be done.

These types of instruction work best when they are directed at very specific needs. For example, if a machine operator requires knowledge of

CNC programming in order to qualify for jobs in a new company facility, then the operator will work hard in the correspondence course to acquire the skills. Here we have a very direct path toward achieving a goal. The operator knows that the only way to qualify for a posting at the new plant is to achieve the new skill and will do that. Management can help this along too, by being available to assist in whatever way possible to help the operator complete the course. Often, managers have access to alternative sources of information that may help the student better understand the course materials. In that case, the manager should offer to provide the information if the student finds a need for it. In general managers should encourage operators to pursue this form of independent study, but they must be pragmatic about it. They should talk to the operators about their potential—whether they really have the background and maturity to start and finish a correspondence course. I have no doubt that any operator can learn via a correspondence course. The question becomes, Can the operator finish it, and will the experience be a positive one for both operator and company?

Another factor in the probability of success is the time available for working on the course. Should we be willing to give up time during operators' work shifts for correspondence course work, or should we require operators to do it on their own time? The answer is not always clear. We have a strong interest in operators' gaining skills if it can beneficially affect their ability to make products. If that is the case, we can certainly justify supporting study time during the work shift. The other viewpoint would be that the employee has been hired to do the current job and that job shouldn't suffer in the interest of potential improvements at some undefined time in the future. If we had a large percentage of employees wanting to take correspondence courses during the work shift, their unavailability could effectively shorten the production day, thus creating bottleneck situations and having serious consequences for the company's ability to maintain schedule. This scenario is unlikely, of course, but it is a factor to consider. If a company is successful beyond any expectations and has many correspondences course takers, then study time could become a factor to reckon with. In that case then probably the best compromise would be to make a quiet place available for study during lunch and break periods.

Another alternative to consider: If we have sufficiently large numbers of people who want to take correspondence courses, it might be feasible to develop a course to be taught in the factory based on the most frequently taken correspondence courses. This eliminates the correspondence course altogether along with all of its drawbacks. Instead we revert back to the more traditional kinds of courses, which have a much higher degree of success.

Most companies do not have a "quiet study hall" situation for their workers, and so it can be tough for workers to study. After hours, the student is tired and less alert. And on work breaks, there are many distractions to make it hard to concentrate. So, in order for the operator to complete the course, the company should try to provide materials to make study more entertaining and interesting. While companies can't take the time to develop every correspondence course their employees will subscribe to, they can certainly be aware of factors to look for when reviewing courses they may potentially offer. Some things to consider would be:

- Shorter lessons, with only a few lesson objectives to be covered
- Good evaluation examples
- An easy way to know if students' comprehension of the material is satisfactory
- Relatively few official exams to demonstrate competency, and an "open book" format for those that are needed
- An effective way of gaining positive feedback, such as answers to quizzes with explanations for the correct answers
- A good bibliography of support materials
- Lots of illustrations and diagrams

Correspondence courses can be useful, but one last caveat: Remember, we are striving to build participative teams, and teams work most effectively when we teach all members concurrently. This way we create no prima donnas, and the sense that each member is carrying his or her share of the burden is reinforced. Individualized courses, depending on the subject matter, could foster the opposite: the "star" performer who can do much more than the "rest of us." We certainly don't want to encourage a person or a few people to become the lead singers of our opera while the rest are simply spear carriers. With this final thought, use correspondence courses where there is a true need, and not indiscriminately.

Other Types of Effective Group Training Technique

The traditional methods of shop floor education are on-the-job training, classroom training, and correspondence courses, but there are other methods that can be just as effective—some say even more so, because they also work well as team-building exercises. These so called nontraditional methods are used as supplements to the three traditional education activities. They can teach skills that have direct application to enhancing process performance, but they are better suited for the "soft" or attitude-type subjects and hence are of value for team building.

These techniques go by many different titles and have many different variations. Let's look at some of them from the viewpoint of effective team building. We'll investigate:

a. The birthday club
b. Round tables
c. Quality circles
d. Lunchtime learning
e. Operator inspection tours

All of these ideas tend to support the building of participatory cultures. So they may have trouble being initiated in the more hierarchical and authoritative culture biased companies. However, I urge that they be given an opportunity to be used. If nothing else they will improve the perception of the human side of management to the operators and put faces with managerial dictates. Once operators see and learn that managers are people like them and that they can be approached with problems we have gone a long way towards achieving an effective production team.

a. The Birthday Club

The birthday club is a monthly event to get a cross section of all company employees together for informative meetings to discuss the state of the business and what each team member (individual employee) has to do to make the company successful. People are chosen because their birthday falls within the month and for no other reason.

The program is led by a senior manager, typically the plant manger or general manager. Whoever it is, this person has to be known by the participants to have clout to make things happen. Usually, the agenda is focused on the company's need to compete successfully, and quite often it has a total quality theme. The leader welcomes everyone and spells out the agenda. Most commonly, representatives of the various functions present the state of their function as it relates to the company's current goals. These presentations are usually less than 10 minutes each, and an attempt is made to keep them compatible with each other. There is also time for questions and answers, but usually the size of the meeting is too large for participants to be willing and comfortable to speak out (unless the individuals are comfortable with public speaking). So a dialogue is not a real part of the goals for the session.

There is also an opportunity for some formal learning to take place, usually through a TV video or satellite presentation on a topic germane to the theme of the presentations. Alternatively, it is possible for the seminar leader to prepare a short lesson plan. I have found this medium very effective for getting across the concepts of and responsibilities for quality and for such things as introducing the philosophy of zero defects by explaining how it works and what "we" have to do to make it reality. It is also a good idea to hand out mementos of the lesson for attendees to keep. For example, the quality credo discussed in Chapter 4 (see Figure 4-5) would be a good topic to build a short lesson around; at the conclusion, the group could be handed laminated wallet cards with the credo printed on them.

Following the lesson plan, the group then has a simple birthday party, with a birthday cake, candles, and the rest. Some companies even go so far as to have a luncheon and some small company gift. So it makes for a festive occasion and a great team-building exercise. This is so because employees from all functions are hearing the same talk and getting the same direction for the company's needs and their own personal success. The birthday club is management's pretext for gathering this diverse cross section to receive a demonstration on working effectively together for their own and the entire organization's success.

b. Round Tables

Round tables are similar in concept to the birthday club but contain many fewer people. They are informal in nature and designed to elicit discussions about the company's performance, problems (hopefully with directions for resolution), and future plans.

True round tables should have representatives from all company functions, so that problems and topics from different venues can be expressed. This way attendees can learn by becoming familiar with others' perspectives. By creating this learning situation, we hope to have workers gain a more tolerant attitude toward the way things are done in other areas of the company, and to have them also learn from experiences gained in other areas of the company. But round tables may also be convened consisting of members from single functions, such as manufacturing's shop operations. This is so because functions like shop operations are usually broken into several departments, typically by process, so it is still possible to get a cross section of employees with different viewpoints of the company gained from different vantage points.

The setup for round tables is simple. Eight to twelve people meet with the host manager in a conference room during work hours to discuss company problems. The people are drawn at random from "all walks of life," so we get a representative cross section. (Sometimes the selection is constrained a bit, particularly in union-represented organizations, where strange interpretation of contracts and law requires a union representative to be present when management talks to bargaining unit people. In that case a union representative is always invited to participate.) Usually the host manager is the only manager present. Quite often a representative from HR (human resources) is present to take notes, and that constitutes the extent of the formality.

As I said, the setting is a conference room, with all sitting around a table, the usual amenities being present (coffee, etc.), along with notepads and pencils. The manager opens the session by welcoming everyone there and asks the attendees to introduce themselves. After that icebreaker, she sets the stage with very brief opening remarks—probably a brief review of company performance—and then asks the attendees how they can improve performance. From there the manager's job is to facilitate discussion. Quite often employees will start slowly and be reticent about speaking out. Here the manager has to present a nonthreatening atmosphere and extract comments from the participants about things she knows they know. This will usually work to get the group talking, and before long they should be right into the discussion as if they were talking with their families at the dinner table.

The manager will receive quite a few complaints at first before suggestions for improvement start flowing. It is important for these items to be recorded and some post meeting action to take place, with report back to the attendees. Here, the HR representative has an important responsibility to understand the nature of the complaint and coordinate post meeting investigations. It is important for the host manager to get on with the purpose of the meeting—the gaining of buy-in to company programs and goals—but she must not abruptly cut off complaint discussions. This is an important part of the process of allowing employees to "vent" and to be heard in a sympathetic manner. This common courtesy helps make employees feel that they are an important part of the team and management really does care about their opinions. If we get nothing more than this out of the meeting, it has been a success. The results are positive because we are getting employees to give management the benefit of the doubt when it comes to doing things differently or for new reasons. We are eliminating some level of resistance to change.

Round tables virtually never have planned lesson formats attached to them. Instead they have as their goal creating both understanding and the will to try to work together for the benefit of all. The informal atmosphere, the willingness to listen, and the positive reaction to fixing complaint items help to create a positive, can-do team atmosphere.

c. Quality Circles

Quality circles are derived from round tables and are similar to them except that the participants come from a more focused group. A quality circle consists of people from the same department who gather periodically to review how they are doing in achieving accepted goals and what they can do to improve their performance. They are all coequals with no assigned leader. However, to provide continuity and direction as well as a link to higher management, there is usually a facilitator assigned to the circle. The facilitator may or may not be the department supervisor, depending on the number of teams in the department and other assigned duties.

Quality circle meetings are more or less structured to elicit ideas for improvement. The meetings are kept as short as possible, usually scheduled for an hour in a meeting room or classroom, and virtually always on company time. They most often start out with the facilitator going over the pertinent current statistics and reporting on actions taken based on previous circle decisions. This is followed with discussions on how the circle team can make improvements and decisions on how to put those ideas into action. The facilitator will advise as the process goes on and will act as a funnel for information and support from higher management.

Quality circles have a high rate of success as long as the managers react in a timely fashion to requests for assistance. They are also somewhat dependent on the Hawthorne or novelty effect for success. As long as the members feel that the circle is exciting and gaining results, as well as respect from management, the circle will be successful. As soon as this is not the case, a circle tends to diminish in effectiveness.

A successful way for management to keep up the interest in a quality circle is to guarantee a percentage of any savings derived from circle-initiated ideas. But for this to work, the company must first devise a method of evaluating and calculating savings and advertise that system well to all employees. This a powerful direct cause-and-effect tool that will generate savings for the company. However, I must point out that any organization planning on having more than half a dozen or so active teams will need virtually a full-time administrator.

Quality circles can also be an effective teaching tool as an offshoot of the buddy system used in traditional on-the-job training. Here, the circle decides on new ways to improve the company's performance, which often means acquiring new skills. Let's suppose the circle members decide that there has to be an extension of statistical process control (SPC) into parts of their domain and to bring it about they need to teach additional people how to operate the SPC system. This need becomes a strong candidate for on-the-job training. In this case, since the idea is circle-initiated, it is suitable for experienced circle members to teach inexperienced colleagues. Training in this way is also a powerful exercise in self motivation. The circle knows it will receive a monetary award when one of its ideas generates savings, so it is in the circle's collective best interest to make sure that the necessary skills are present within the group. This puts a strong incentive on the circle to train effectively; hence, learning takes place. It's easy to see then, that learning will be accomplished if there is a direct relationship to success when the learning is demonstrated. Therefore, quality circles can be an effective tool for skills improvement among the workforce.

d. Lunchtime Learning

Lunchtime learning, as the name implies, takes place at lunchtime. It is a technique for imparting new information and sometimes skills to members of the workforce while they're consuming their lunch. The way the process is structured, the company will put out a syllabus of topics that will be presented at each scheduled session. The employees are then allowed to pick and choose what sessions they'd like to attend and then show up for them. There is no coercion to get people to come, except perhaps to make sure that if they sign up they need to honor the commitment and indeed show up. This is done to make sure employees sign up only for what they're interested in, and for logistics purposes, to make sure there is enough room for everyone and enough light refreshments. While it is customary for the company to provide soft drinks and the like, it is expected that employees will provide their own lunches.

These sessions last as long as the lunch period and are designed to fit the time slot. This means that a topic is often carried over for several sessions in order for enough material to be presented to make the process worthwhile. Also, the instructors are asked to provide a handout at the end of each session, so the attendees have some reference notes. Some companies go so far as to provide attendees with binders and have instructors prepare notes in accordance with a specified method.

Lunchtime learning is a serious attempt to cover topics of need for the company and at the same time present material that is of interest to its employees so they can gain more competence. It is often sold as a method whereby employee makes themselves both more valuable to the company and at the same time more marketable in the current job market. So its appeal is simultaneously to group loyalty and individual self-interest.

Lunchtime learning is only as successful as the instructor's efforts make it. The company tries to line up instructors who are more than passingly knowledgeable with their subject. It does this by enticing employees already possessing the skills and the knowledge of content to be instructors. In fact, sometimes this program is known as the "bootstrap academy," so called because colleagues take turns being the instructor, thus hoisting everybody's abilities by one or two notches. Companies also recognize that for those not regularly in a teaching mode, preparing lesson plans can be difficult. When help is needed, companies can assist instructors in structuring their materials by encouraging a buddy system of experienced instructors. Sometimes there are people on the HR staff who have experience generating lesson plans, and they are assigned the task of coaching instructors on lesson planning and delivery. Many companies go even one step further by offering some sort of honorarium for instructors, as recognition for agreeing to take on added chores on behalf of company and colleagues.

Lunchtime learning is an excellent tool, provided that it is sold effectively as a nonthreatening gathering to enhance individuals' skills. It cannot be a situation in which employees feel they have to attend to show the boss they're team players. It has to be totally voluntary, with no attendance records kept and no implied threats for not attending. It has to be one of those things the company offers as a benefit to employees and nothing more. If kept in this context and the syllabus hits the nerve of enough individual desires for skill enhancement, it will be a success.

e. Operator Inspection Tours

Inspection tours are not really learning activities in a direct sense but are in a secondary way. They are an opportunity for operators to see the effect of their work well after it has left their department and so to judge whether their efforts were satisfactory. Inspection tours were conceived as a total quality technique to foster quality improvements. But they serve an equally important purpose as a training aid to point out cause and effect of process viability and skills improvement.

The process starts out similar to round tables. Individuals are selected at random to participate in an inspection of the finished product(s) with the appropriate manager (usually the plant manager or manufacturing manager) and quality control representatives. The same rules apply for union representation as with round tables. The inspection tour team meets at the appropriate place at the designated time and begins to do the inspection under the tutelage of the quality representative. The members will be performing the same task the quality control personnel normally do, using the same checkoff and reporting forms.

At the conclusion of the inspection, the team reconvenes in a conference room to go over the results and recommend corrective actions. In this manner individuals from many departments can see firsthand the results of their work and understand what constitutes success or failure. They can bring the message back to their comrades and hopefully effect productive changes. If the individual on the inspection team also happens to be on a quality circle, the report might be made to the circle for consideration for additional action. In any event, the publicizing of defects and their point of origin is a powerful cause-and-effect learning tool that does have impact on performance.

While operator inspection teams are not primarily training events, they definitely have the benefit of raising awareness. The experience helps companies improve their employees' skills and is thus justifiably regarded as part of the training regime.

PARTICIPATORY MANAGEMENT PRACTICES

How we manage people has a great bearing on how well they deliver best performance for a company's competitive needs. We all know that in today's competitive global village, performing at one's best is not a mere luxury or nice thing to have. We need to get the best out of every employee every day all the time. In this chapter we are dealing with forming an effective shop operations team. In previous chapters we looked at best practices across the entire spectrum of making work stations perform optimally. In all cases I have either stated or implied that all of these techniques work best when used with an engaged and actively participating workforce. Now I'd like to specifically address what I believe to be the important factors in participatory management, and relate them to the creation of an involved shop operations team.

Participatory management is not the abdication of leadership and decision making. It is simply a process of allowing those who would be affected by the results of decisions to express ideas and concerns and recommend cogent courses of action. I was told by a mentor a long time ago that a good leader gets his way by convincing his followers that what they are setting out to do was their idea. That is sage advice and gets to the point of what participatory management is all about.

Let's look at three simple scenarios to illustrate the transition from autocratic to participatory management styles:

- *Autocratic style.* "Make two bolts using the Bridgeport milling machine."
- *Transitional style.* "Make two bolts using the Bridgeport milling machine because it is available and perfectly capable of doing the job."
- *Participatory style.* "Make two bolts. There are several choices of machines available. I recommend using the Bridgeport milling machine because it can cut the thread to the tolerances we need. What do you think?"

What do you notice right off? Managing is obviously slower under the participatory style than under the others. With the autocratic style, management simply dictates that employees do something as directed. Transitional-style management, on the other hand, gives employees an explanation why they should do it a certain way, but not necessarily a complete one. Participatory management also gives explanations, but it tries to make them complete and offers subordinates an opportunity to express their opinions. A participatory style always implies that management can adopt subordinates' suggestions as company policy.

We also note that autocratic management doesn't bother to consider the opinions or feelings of the employees whatsoever. It is extremely paternalistic: management always knows best, regardless of the situation. Managers are delegated the authority to make decisions in specific areas, and they need consult with no one prior to making their decisions. This is the divine right of kings expressed in the modern era. Quite frankly, it doesn't work very well, because only a few brains get to run the business instead of all the cerebral capacity available if all employees are involved.

The transitional style is an attempt to soften the edges of the autocratic system. It tries to make people more accepting of dictates from management by offering explanations of the actions they are told to take. Sometimes discussion is permitted, but rarely at the instigation of management. Its almost like asking your benevolent monarch for permission to speak. The transitional style came into vogue around the time of the Second World War when women entered the workforce and felt no cultural restriction on asking the question "why?" It didn't disappear after men regained their positions in industry after the war but gradually became entrenched and has been evolving to participatory styles.

The participatory style definitely elicits the best ideas and performance from a workforce. But it is harder to practice on the part of management and requires more time to make decisions. We see from the simple scenario that there are four steps involved:

1. Define the goal to be achieved. If the reason for it is not entirely obvious, explain it.
2. Describe how the goal could be achieved, to the best of your understanding.
3. Ask for suggestions for better ways of achieving the goal.
4. Consider alternatives offered; then select the best, either the original or an alternative. Proceed with the implementation.

Figure 10-3 demonstrates how the three styles of factory management relate to instructions given to operators. There is no doubt that it takes longer and requires more patience to operate in a participatory style. Autocratic management uses only the first part of step 1 before proceeding. Transitional management adds an explanation but not necessarily a thorough one and then proceeds. Only the participatory style requires all four steps.

I am totally convinced that world class manufacturers have to use the participatory style to be successful. There is no choice. With today's well-educated workforces—especially given the prevalence of the Western educational mode of teaching people to question and ask why, not just learn by rote—it stands to reason that employees will not tolerate being dictated to. A questioning workforce may be unruly and at times sloppy, but in the end engaged people will create the best results. And that will be only through a participatory style of leadership. In setting up the shop operations team,

Steps in participatory management decision implementation	Occurs in		
	Autocratic	Transitional	Participative
1. Define the goal to be achieved. If the reason for it is not _a _b obvious intuitively, explain it.	1a	1a	1a & b
2. Define how the goal could be achieved, to the best of _a _b your understanding.	n/a	2a	2a & b
3. Ask for suggestions for better ways of achieving the goal.	n/a	n/a	3
4. Consider alternatives offered. Select the best (the original _a _b or an alternative). Proceed with implementation. _c	4c	4c	4a, b, c

Figure 10-3. Styles of management—participatory versus predecessors.

we need supervisors schooled in participatory management skills. Let's look at these basic skills and see how they apply to shop operations.

BASIC PARTICIPATORY SKILLS FOR SUCCESSFUL MANAGEMENT

Various advocates of participatory management stress many so-called soft-science or psychological skills, and they make very compelling arguments for them. The trouble with all those rules is that they tend to be intimidating to those who are not familiar with the precepts of psychology, and therefore they tend to be self-defeating. Keep in mind that the typical supervisor of shop floor personnel is probably a graduate of the shop floor and has less than a baccalaureate-level education. For this reason, I urge those trying to introduce participatory practices into their factories to keep the processes basic and bounded by what we would all consider to be simple common sense. This leads me to the conclusion that there is only one hard-and-fast rule to follow in participatory management practice, and that's what we all recognize as the Golden Rule. To paraphrase:

Treat others as you would want them to treat you.

In my simplified view of necessary skills to learn and employ, they all stem from this industrial Golden Rule.

So, what are the skills required of the supervisor in a participatory situation? I believe they consist of the following six precepts of effective coaching:

1. Set goals for the group based on the needs of the business.
2. Provide guidelines for achieving the goals, and encourage employees to participate in selecting tactics for achieving them.

3. Help employees improve their skills.
4. Explain why certain rules need to be followed.
5. Discipline fairly and always in accordance with the known and accepted rules.
6. Measure progress in accomplishing goals, and go over reasons and ways to improve with employees.

As we see, the strategy is to get employee buy-in for all actions and plans formulated to meet the goals of the organization. This way employees willingly carry out the methods assigned to the operations, and there is no real need to order people to do their jobs. This does not mean supervisors are no longer the boss. Nor does it mean the supervisor no longer has the authority to make things happen. She still does, but participatory management aims to achieve more and does so by creating a better work atmosphere. By buy-in, we mean convincing the employee that he is part of a team and as such has a shared responsibility for the success of the team. Also, this success comes about only if he does his job in accordance with the job's set parameters. Furthermore, we want him and his colleagues to participate in setting the parameters of the job.

It is the supervisor's job to get the most out of her subordinates in such a way that they do not resent doing the company's bidding. And here, the industrial Golden Rule applies. Simply put, the supervisor should never ask employees to do anything she would not be willing to do herself. In this team there is no such thing as sacrificing some people for the benefit of all. We want everyone to pull together so all can enjoy the fruits of their collective success. We want everyone to be content with the group's success. Now let's look at the six coaching skills in more detail.

1. Set Goals for the Group Based on the Needs of the Business

Goal setting is a very complex and structured task within companies. It entails all aspects of strategic and business planning, and it is not necessary to go into a detailed explanation for our purposes. Specific goals to be achieved are assigned to all departments within an organization. In the domain of shop operations, the dominant goals are to achieve production output levels at the lowest possible cost. The supervisor will receive these goals from higher levels of management expressed in whatever terms the company traditionally uses. It is the supervisor's responsibility to translate those higher-level goals into meaningful parameters for her unit or department.

When interpreting goals, the supervisor first has to assure herself that they are doable. Not necessarily easy to achieve, but that with diligent effort they can be achieved. In a company practicing participatory management, this should be a given. If done right, developing the goals was an exercise the entire workforce participated in. So the final promulgation of those goals should be no surprise to anyone.

The supervisor then must assure that the goals are compatible with the needs of the business as explained by higher-level management. Then she must present the goals to the department's employees and show how they are compatible with those needs. She must relate how the employee team played a part in developing those goals (either formally or informally), and that now they are their goals to be achieved. She then goes to the next step.

2. Provide Guidelines for Achieving the Goals, and Encourage Employees to Participate in Selecting Tactics for Achieving Them

It is the first rule of leadership that the leader has to take the initiative in planning any course of action. Even if it is as simple as directing a subordinate to fully investigate and recommend courses of action, the initiative and the responsibility stay with the leader. This is just as true for participative management as any other style. A leader must lead.

In the preferred participative style, the leader must put forth ideas and actively solicit input from subordinates. In a shop operations environment, the supervisor normally has the experience and knowledge to pretty much know what the best course of action should be. She may not have the detailed knowledge of the nuances of each operation, but she definitely has a better overall view of the situation than any operator. Thus, participative in this sense means eliciting ideas from operators that, in effect, flesh out the plan she is already contemplating. The nature of the task is to have operators constructively critique the overall idea from their perspective, and hence strengthen the ideas at the very nuts-and-bolts level of execution. This way we gain buy-in from operators who are actually involved in real planning activities.

This type of planning session has a typical script as follows:

a. Introduce the goals to be achieved.
b. In an objective way, present a plan for achieving them. The supervisor should not present in a style that is excessively advocative of her position. Instead of saying I think we should do thus-and-such, say an approach to achieving the goal could be thus-and-such.
c. Ask for comments on the proposed procedure and for ways to improve it, always leaving the door open for alternative approaches.
d. Gain concurrence on the main approach to achieving the goal.
e. Discuss improvement techniques for specific work stations with those people directly involved, and incorporate as many ideas as possible without sacrificing results. In fact, any idea incorporated must end up with improved performance. No idea should ever be included just to placate certain factions.
f. Review what the leader believes to be consensus and then gain concurrence, but never by taking a vote. Do it simply by asking whether the group concurs, and if it looks as if it does, say so affirmatively and with a convincing tone of voice.

By following this precept, the leader maintains control, usually gets the results she wants, and has allowed the team to participate in the decision process. In fact, it often aids in making the preferred idea a better idea.

3. Help Employees Improve Their Skills

As we saw in previous discussions, training is a complex subject, and there are many ways of achieving learning among the workforce. In a participative management environment it is the supervisor's role to advocate that employees continuously improve their on-the-job skills. Again, following the dictates of this style of management, we find that the best way to gain buy-in is through encouraging and not ordering participation in training activities.

The best plan is to explain, in a low-key manner, why an employee should strive to improve his skills. The pertinent factor to point out is that gaining new skills helps the individual become more valuable to himself and to the company. This way he can gain a higher compensation level, do the job better for his production team, and help the company gain or at least maintain its competitive position. I believe appealing to the individual's self-preservation instinct by explaining personal benefits is the best way to motivate someone to want to succeed in learning programs.

4. Explain Why Certain Rules Need to Be Followed

In an autocratic system, this next step is a nonstep. The rules are there, and that's it. In a participative system we find that explaining why the rules are as stated gains a higher degree of voluntary compliance. I believe this is one reason why a participative system tends to have fewer disciplinary cases for employee malfeasance than does an autocratic environment.

Any explanation of rules needs to start with a statement that rules exist to make it easier for the company to carry out its mission. And then it must immediately reiterate that if the company succeeds, all members of the production team share in the rewards. Sharing in the rewards has to be an ongoing theme stressed over and over again at every opportunity, even if the situation is a stressful one. In fact, when once asked by one skeptical employee who was resisting following rules why he should care whether the company succeeded or not, I, in a sarcastic moment, said in reply, If the company succeeds, you get to keep your job. This blunt and nonenlightened answer was certainly true, and he understood and accepted it as valid. I would not normally recommend this answer as part of a planned participative strategy, but it worked. It was truthful and to the point. In this case the rule in question was coming to work on time to start the shift on time. I explained that we needed to do that so the company could achieve the production output the goal required. I should point out that after my sarcastic answer I recovered my composure and also said that if the company succeeds, we all succeed—in this case, through profit sharing at year-end.

5. Discipline Fairly and Always in Accordance with the Known and Accepted Rules

When explaining the work rules it is also necessary to explain the results of being caught violating them. This is akin to explaining the criminal code, but within the internal company jurisdiction. This step is absolutely mandatory, whether we are operating in an autocratic style or a participative style, or any other variant. Virtually every legal entity—state, city, etc.—requires as part of its labor laws that employees understand the work rules they are contracting to abide by when they become employed by the company. They have to know what it means under their contract if they violate those rules. Therefore, it is necessary for supervisors to inform subordinates of the rules. In fact, many companies require as part of the hiring process that all employees sign an affidavit stating that the rules have been explained to them and that they understand the rules.

Whenever an employee is charged with violating the work rules, a supervisor needs to investigate the case and document findings. This can be as simple as writing up a warning notice and giving the employee a copy, or as complex as taking statements of witnesses concerning the incident. The point is, disciplinary procedures can affect the person's entire career at the company, and in rare cases involve legal penalties (such as for stealing or purposely destroying company property). Therefore, it is necessary to gain an objective appraisal of the facts and proceed from there.

After the facts are known, should they result in a clear violation, the supervisor needs to act in accordance with the work rules' prescribed "punishment" and carry it out. This is absolutely critical. A company cannot be thought to be playing favoritism with any employee over other employees. To do this would literally destroy any team building that has occurred and do so virtually immediately. You might say this doesn't sound very participative, but I must point out that participative does not mean abdicating responsibility for taking required action, no matter how hardhanded it may appear. Let me give you an example of a disciplinary action that was hard to take but had to be taken.

At one company where I was responsible for operations management, I was confronted with an employee who had failed a drug test. The test was a standard screening for illegal drug consumption that was part of the work rules. The testing, again as part of the work rules, was done on randomly selected employees periodically and by an outside vendor. It turned out that one of our most valuable office workers tested positive. The rules required immediate suspension from the job, and the only recourse the employee had to regain his job was to enter an authorized and certified drug rehabilitation program. If the employee successfully completed the program and his counselor concurred, he could at his own request be reinstated. Well, the employee pleaded for his job. He stated he had a family to support and this was just a weekend lark and the only time he had ever done this, and asked that we suspend the rules this one time.

What do we do? My choice was either to give him another chance—after all, he was a good worker—or to actually go through with the suspension. I suspended the employee. I felt I had to make the point that this type of rule violation could not be condoned even though it hurt the company to dismiss an employee who had been such an effective team member. The decision played well with the rest of the workforce. The comments we received from employees were all generally along the lines that we were to be commended for dealing with the offense as the work rules said we would. We didn't show any favoritism toward office workers over shop floor workers, as they suspected would happen. We played fair, and the vast majority of the workforce respected us for it. This went a long way toward creating one company team focused on achieving its goals.

As a postscript, the young man we suspended went through the rehabilitation program successfully and returned to work three months later. He has been a model employee ever since and has expressed his gratitude to the company for forcing him to come to grips with a then-erupting drug problem. The company did suffer some short-term business inefficiencies, but the remaining staff pulled together to minimize the impact, and we recovered.

6. Measure Progress in Accomplishing Goals, and Go Over Reasons and Ways to Improve with Employees

When goals are set, we, as a matter of good business sense, go about implementing the programs and activities required to accomplish them. Obviously, the management of the company wants to know how we are progressing in accomplishing those goals. What's less than obvious for many managers is that the workforce also wants to know how we are collectively doing in achieving those goals. For some reason, too many managers fail to take this into consideration. Even if they do, they reject showing measurements to the workforce because they mistakenly believe it's only idle curiosity and they have no need to know.

This is not smart participative management. Of course they are curious. But contrary to this "elite" wisdom, they do need to know. If we want operators to manage their work stations to "squeeze out" the most productivity they can for every shift, then we need to let them know how they stand vis-à-vis the goal. To do otherwise is like trying to navigate a ship without a compass.

Setting goals and getting buy-in, as we've seen, is critical for business success. Measurements are part of that process. We set the plan in motion after deliberation and consideration of alternative ways of doing it. Measurements tell us if our tactics were valid, or if we need to make some adjustments. If the measurements are tracking nicely in accordance with the plan, then the need to do anything but continue as planned is eliminated. But if we are not tracking in accordance with plan, then we need to understand why. The measurements are the first bits of evidence we have and can lead to effective problem solving. Once the why is determined, it is usually possible to plan an effective solution.

The process of using measurements starts with posting the results of measurements and doing it as frequently as we can. It is a good policy to measure and post the output of every work station on a daily basis. This allows us to assess where we are in relatively short intervals so we can take corrective actions before a problem gets larger and more unwieldy.

In a participatory situation, we train the operator to both take and respond to measurements in a timely fashion. We also train the operators to discuss their results in reporting situations. There are many ways to do this, the simplest being discussions one on one or in small groups to evaluate the situation. I believe this to be a most effective method. On a daily or more frequent basis, the supervisor meets with the operators and reviews progress. They should strive to use measurements of output with noted deviations, if they occur, as the starting point. Then they should assess what current trends mean as far as gaining the goal is concerned. They should always focus on achieving goals and use these dynamic representations of progress (the measurements) as indicators of how well they are doing. Based on this information, they should once more review their plan and see whether they are abiding by it or not. They should then determine what they have to do, if anything, to give them a better chance of making the goal.

This give-and-take informal discussion leads to decisions on what to do next. If any viable plan comes up to alter strategy, the supervisor may want to write up change notices or document minor changes in a log, or do some other form of documentation. The change is then made, and the cycle is started over again. This is reminiscent of total quality management (TQM), and it should be, because that is what it is. What we have is good feedback on the validity of planning, and we're getting it in a way that involves the shop floor operators so that we maintain the buy-in and team identity.

SELF-DIRECTED WORK TEAMS

No discussion about shop operations team formation can be complete nowadays without bringing up the topic of self-directed work teams. At first glance this may seem to be the ultimate in participatory management style. It is not. It certainly is participatory, but I doubt it could be called management. Now that all the basics of shop floor team structuring have been covered, I believe we can look at self-directed work teams and see how they may or may not fit into the dynamics of effective shop management.

Let me first state that I do not believe self-directed work teams will ever become the norm in an industrial organization. A true self-directed work team, in my opinion, asks too much of the individuals who are charged with making the products. In addition to actually performing the job of producing parts, we are also asking these people to do all of the non-value-added shop operations management work a supervisor would handle in a traditional system. This to me is nonoptimal. It is like asking a successful baseball team to operate with a playing manager. Of course it has happened, and successfully from time to time (the last time being 1948, when Lou Boudreau served as the Cleveland Indians' manager and shortstop), but it is an exception rather than the rule. And I do not know of any examples where true self-directed work teams are successful.

Now that I've stated my views on the viability of self-directed work teams, let me demonstrate how they are supposed to work and why they don't work. Figure 10-4 shows the four basic organizational concepts we can use on the shop floor. I know that some people may say there are more. For example, they may say we can have subsupervisors, etc., still working from the same budget as the supervisor and therefore still part of the same organization. But that's really nothing but a variant of the group leader concept. Also, note that I've shown on the figure that the self-directed style does not work; I've done that to emphasize that embarking on such an experiment is folly. It may work for a little while, but as soon as the novelty wears off, it falls apart.

Self-directed organization needs three very important things to be successful:

1. A highly motivated workforce
2. A highly skilled workforce that understands not only the technology being applied but also how to manage it and the associated administrative functions
3. A management structure set up to cater directly to the needs of the self-directed workforce

Industrial organizations, for the most part, exhibit these traits only in very small degree. The closest they come is to item 1: it is not unusual to have highly motivated individuals on the shop floor. And in fact, participatory management techniques are aimed at producing them. But how do we achieve effective management with a self-directed work team? Note, in Figure 10-4, the description of a self-directed work team: it is a group of individuals put together to "figure out" how to do a job and then go do it. Well, I

Type	Description	Workable over sustained time?
Autocratic	Supervisor manages by assigning employees to specific tasks with little, if any, input from employees.	Yes
Participative	Supervisor manages, allowing employees to suggest alternative ways of doing specific tasks, and selects best way to proceed.	Yes
Group leader	Division of a larger shop operations unit headed by a senior operator who does some value-added work and some supervisory work. Usually these divisions (groups) can operate under both autocratic and participative regimes.	Yes
Self-directed	A group of workers given a schedule to perform and a budget, and left to their own devices to figure out how to do it, including solicitation of advice.	No

Figure 10-4. Shop floor organization styles.

contend that factories are not think tanks or psychological experiments. They have to contend with the real world and remain competitive.

Now, many authors who extol self-directed work teams will have you believe we can motivate the teams to learn what they need to learn so they can get the job done. This is plain rubbish. People have to be trained in skills and practice those skills to reach a minimal competency level before they can hope to successfully compete. We can't have a self-directed workforce muddling through complex scheduling and logistic questions at the same time they are trying to derive the optimal method for making the product most suitable for their equipment, and simultaneously determine what's a fair day's effort for each of them. Manufacturing is not a commune; it depends on well-orchestrated plans to succeed.

The second point relates to a skilled workforce. I've already shown that to be successful the skills have to be there; we cannot develop them as we go along. Indeed, even if we could do that, how could it be accomplished in a committee or communelike setting? What skills should be taught, and when? By whom? And who will resolve to go and obtain the resources to teach? Who will have the forethought to even do so? In fact, who will take it upon him- or herself to be the real responsible agent in the group? Do you see the point? There are so many skills and responsibilities that have to be assumed that a self-directed workforce of factory workers is doomed before it even starts.

The third point is having a senior management willing to support this experiment. This is the least likely to occur. Senior management is hired to assure that companies meet their goals. No senior manager is going to stand idly by and let a self-directed workforce determine the fate of the company when such organizations are inherently inefficient and lack competence to do so. The senior manager will step in and become the supervisor working in a participatory style to organize the group and minimize the chaos.

I hope this discourse puts to rest the idyllic nonsense of self-directed workforces. I believe strongly in the participative method of managing shop operations, as I've outlined in earlier portions of this chapter. I also believe we need to have persons in charge with the vested authority and responsibility to make sure targets and goals are met.

This ends my discussion of the key points in forming an effective shop operations team. Let me reiterate: an informed and knowledgeable workforce gives superior performance over traditional dictated-to and divided white- and blue-collar organizations. We need to do all we can to get everyone to participate to the limit of his or her ability in setting goals and action plans to accomplish them. We need to continuously increase the capability to perform optimally and at the same time maintain a focused discipline to perform in accordance with plan.

Creating a shop operations team requires analyzing all the skills required and then setting about to acquire them. We can do this either through recruiting or building from within, most likely a combination of both. Many organizational systems are available; however, for most situations a participative approach is best, since it allows for people to readily express their opinions and join in the planning processes. With good support documentation and technological know-how—in effect, well-thought-out what-if scenarios—it is possible to quickly form superior-performing shop floor teams. I believe the precepts I've outlined in this chapter will help in doing so.

Chapter 11

Implementing Work Station Dynamics

Implementing work station dynamics means applying the techniques described in this book. Having stated the obvious, we need to look at the practical means of doing so. The basis of work station dynamics is the use of proper engineering technologies to control the processes and systems on the factory floor. Work station dynamics is the application of these techniques by the operators in carrying out their tasks. This does not mean that operators need to be engineers to do the job. But it does mean that the processes and systems used ought to be designed by competent engineers, and in a way that the operators have no problem in carrying out their dictates.

Figure 1-1 in Chapter 1 showed all of the processes and systems that this engineering work entails, and as we can see they add up to a significant amount. From what I've stated it would appear that implementing work station dynamics is primarily an engineering development exercise. But in fact it is not. Let's look at what it is, and then go into the details of successful implementation.

The engineering work associated with work station dynamics is essentially the same as that for any manufacturing operation utilizing any management strategy. Obviously, the engineering work needs to be done correctly and robust enough to provide the required results. But getting the results is the subject matter of work station dynamics *implementation*. Work station dynamics implementation is a process for implementing management techniques that take full advantage of the engineering technologies to optimize production output. We are optimizing the systems and process information going to the work station so it performs at the highest possible level. Achieving this goal requires extensive attention to details on the part of all operators and support personnel. Work station dynamics implementation is about how we do this. It is about the process that is most effective. In this chapter we will develop that implementation process and create the groundwork for making a factory capable of producing in accordance with the plan all the time and not only some of the time.

INTRODUCTION TO SHORT INTERVAL SCHEDULING

Work station dynamics is an information sponge. Looking at Figure 1-1, we see that the inputs to the work station are mostly information-related. This means that the operator has to absorb and react to an abundance of information and there is a danger of "circuit overload." If that happens, the information necessary to do the job either is not received or is ignored, but whatever the cause, it isn't used. *Short interval scheduling (SIS)* is a systematic approach aimed at preventing circuit overloading from occurring; it allows the "dynamics" of work stations dynamics to occur. Of course, there is no guarantee that this can be successfully accomplished in all cases, but SIS does reduce the risk to a tolerable one and will result in superior shop floor performance. Let's see what SIS is all about and how it works. Then let's go through the implementation trail.

Work station dynamics is the process by which we input information to the work station so an optimal process can occur. Short interval scheduling is the major catalyst and road map to make that happen in an organized manner rather than in a random fashion. You might say SIS is to work station dynamics application as laser light is to ordinary random light. To help you understand SIS, I will develop the concept from theory through specific applications, with reference to the overall schematic diagram of work station dynamics (Figure 1-1).

The short interval scheduling I will describe here is based on my experiences as a plant manager and a consulting manager in the General Electric Company. The technique of SIS is due to many authors both within and outside of General Electric circa 1970–1987. I have had the opportunity of being involved in drafting and implementing plans that follow SIS as a member of business teams, as a consultant, and as a teacher of the process in an academic setting. I know the process very well and would like to share credit with all of those who contributed to its development. Unfortunately, there has never been a definitive book on the subject, so it is impossible to say who originated the concept of SIS, and therefore whom to give credit to. Probably no one person is the originator. By describing the process in this book, I am not taking claim of authorship of the process. What I am doing is writing it down for posterity so that the work of those countless engineers who developed the technique and worked many long days to make it work in practice will not fade away into obscurity. So, even though I am part of that group of engineers who toiled in the SIS front lines and even though I think I contributed to developing the technique, my discussion of SIS is dedicated to the General Electric engineers who made it the powerful tool it is. I trust by describing it here the process will continue to be used and developed for future generations of manufacturers.

OPERATORS' ACCOUNTABILITY AS THE PHILOSOPHY OF SHORT INTERVAL SCHEDULING

Short interval scheduling attempts to correct all the "lacks" mentioned in Figure 1-1. I will list them here for ease of reference:

Inhibitors of Successful Outputs from the Work Station

- Lack of understanding of customer needs/requirements from the process
- Lack of ability to measure output for meeting quality requirements
- Lack of understanding of output expectations
- Lack of understanding of process variables
    Equipment
    Materials
- Less than optimal training on how to operate the equipment and make the product
    Support service to the work station
    Materials
    Tools
    Schedules
    Maintenance
    Training
- Inaccurate measurements of all work station dynamics; hence, constrained corrective action plans

These lacks have formed a major part of the topics of many chapters of this book and I will not repeat all the solutions offered. I bring them up now to illustrate what SIS is, as the catalyst for making the theory of work station dynamics work.

The first awareness operators should have under the SIS process is of their responsibilities in reference to preventing the lacks from occurring. The second awareness is understanding how they should perform their tasks so the lacks do not happen. And finally, the third awareness is understanding quantity and time to do the assigned job. In total, the awareness called for by SIS is a comprehensive awareness of the Two Knows:

- Know how to make the product.
- Know how long it should take to make the product.

To help crystallize the process, I've found it useful to use the traditional "plan, do, study, act" (PDSA) process. PDSA has been used for decades by engineers to structure their approach to problem solving, and that is what I have applied it to here. I think it is the premier methodology for planning how to investigate and solve problems. Unfortunately, once more, I cannot give credit to the originator of the idea, because the identity of this person is unknown. But that doesn't make it any less true or useful.

We are cognizant of the fact that we want the operators and supervisors to be totally aware of their situation and their goals. PDSA helps us focus. The process can be outlined roughly as follows:

- ***Plan:*** *Select the action to be taken.* We know that all actions are associated with a method and a time to accomplish them. The supervisor, working in a participative mode, needs to gain concurrence for the best way to achieve the goal. The proper method has to be selected and the

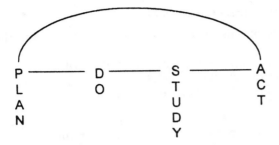

Plan: Select action to take.

DO: Complete the action.

Study: Evaluate the results.
Does the action achieve
the plan?

Act: Take steps to correct
the results. Iterate as
required

Figure 11-1. PDSA cycle.

time to accomplish it has to be verifiable. She has to assure that the operators understand all aspects of the plan and can carry it out.

- *Do: Complete the action step in all aspects.* The action step means doing the work in accordance with all aspects of the defined and understood plan. It is not sufficient to simply do the work implied by the plan; the work must also be done per the plan. To deviate will cause great uncertainty about success or failure when we try to evaluate whether we've achieved the target.
- *Study: Evaluate the results of carrying out the plan.* Does the action achieve the plan? We need to answer the question, Have we achieved the goal we set out to reach? And if not, why not? Knowing the reasons for deviation from the plan is just as important as achieving the plan. In fact, it is in many ways more important. In the world of manufacturing where many variables exist, the ability to know which ones are significant is critical to continuous success. If we are successful and don't know why, we cannot expect continuing success, because we don't understand what we did to achieve the success. It is better to fail and know precisely why so we can correct our mistakes and be suc-

cessful the next time—as we will the time after that and the time after that.

- *Act: Take steps to correct the results.* Iterate as required. This is the result of the study step. The better study we do, the fewer iterations we will require to achieve the goal we set out to accomplish in the plan step. In fact, the more diligent we are in all of the preceding steps, the more effective this final phase will be.

Thus, we can see that being aware of the needs and being fully informed is the critical first phase of SIS. In effect, we are forming a contract between the operator and the supervisor to do a job in accordance with a specified technique in a specified time. But this contract is unique. Not only are we saying what the "deliverables" are that each party agrees to, but we are willing to examine the results and take corrective actions as part of that contract. We are saying that the required end results are important, but equally important are the process and the corrective actions we may need to take to improve the process should it not yield the necessary results. In a contract law setting, failure to achieve agreed-to results would require the failed party to take corrective actions; the other parties would not care what those actions were, as long as the subsequent results were to contract requirements. With the SIS contract, both parties have an obligation to take corrective actions if the contract scope hasn't been achieved. We are literally our brothers' and sisters' keepers.

Now let's look at how the SIS process follows the PDSA steps to assure that the contract can be achieved.

SHORT INTERVAL SCHEDULING SYSTEM ELEMENTS

The PDSA cycle appears to be very straightforward and easy to apply. Of course, I believe that it is, but as with any other tool there are some "tricks of the trade" to be aware of. Let's expand PDSA for applications to SIS philosophy. Remember, our goal is to optimize work station dynamics so that we get the most productivity we possibly can out of the factory's work stations.

Figure 11-2 shows the key aspects we need to be concerned with in applying PDSA to SIS. Each block represents a segment of information we need to be aware of and prepare for. Let's discuss these segments and see how they form a plan of action—the PDSA for SIS.

Plan: Select the Action to Be Taken

Work Defined as Cycle Time Elements

On the shop floor, everything boils down to the Two Knows: know how to make the product, and know how long it should take to make the product. Work defined as cycle time elements means we understand how long it should take to do the job, the second of the Two Knows. This basic fact has

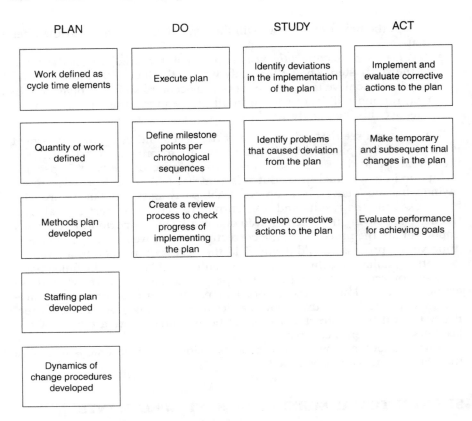

Figure 11-2. Elements of the PDSA system for short interval scheduling.

to be understood by the operators, and it becomes the key factor in productivity calculations. Understanding how much time the operator will need to do the job is also the prime basis of the contract between the operator and the supervisor (working in her capacity of representative of the company management). It is this agreed-to expectation level that allows the operator/supervisor team make SIS work.

Quantity of Work Defined

This second step of the SIS "plan" phase amplifies the time to do the job by factoring in the quantity of items to be produced. The first step defined the per piece time allowed for the operator to do the job. This step goes from per piece to job lot or number to be made during the work shift. Again, this is part of the contract of work to be done.

I should point out that a lot of this appears to be a repetition of discussions already presented in this book—in this specific case, the development of time standards. And in a sense it is, but from a different perspective. In SIS, the supervisor uses the developed time standards to set an overall acceptable time for the company and the operator to do the job. This means she is free to modify the standards within reasonable limits to suit specific circumstances. This ability to decide on the spot how closely to adhere to the engineering data is the hallmark of SIS. It is a contract to set the daily expectation rate, and I will continue to reiterate that fact. This rate varies with the current situation, and it has to be modified frequently to be in tune with the here and now. If it isn't, it's no longer a fair contract for either of the participant parties. A common example in which a rate would be modified could be a situation in which an off-standard lot of material has been accepted for use because the end results could still be satisfactory. Suppose that the factory can use a material that is toward the hard end (according to the Rockwell C hardness scale) of the specification range although still within the acceptance range. Experience may have taught the supervisor that from a practical viewpoint, the depth of cut of the lathe needs to be reduced and hence more time is needed on the machine; if the operator tried to follow the methods sheet as written, there could very well be more tool breakage, which would lead to longer downtimes and more rework or scrap.

Methods Plan Developed

Again, this appears to be a repeat of the engineering work to develop methods documentation to do the required work. However, it isn't a true repeat. It is a tailoring of the engineering methods development work for the current situation. Let's go back to the hammer manufacturing example to illustrate what is meant by taking the current situation into account.

Recall that the order for hammers required 10,000 units to be manufactured and the methods selected were based on that number. Let us now suppose the customer wanted 500 hammers immediately to use in an important trade show. The supposed correct way to make the hammers would be to follow the process as designed by the engineers. However, for this example, let's say that the fixtures for assembling the rubber grip to the handle hadn't been manufactured yet (see Figure 3-3). This means that the methods prescribed would not yet be available to follow for the entire manufacturing process. Thus, the supervisor would have to modify the method of doing that portion of the work and get concurrence from the operator on the process and the expectation rate (the contract). In the participative method, we would, of course, want the operator to agree to the procedure chosen and to be a part of the team making the choices.

What the example shows is that there could be situations where the methods chosen are not the methods designed and planned. To some, it may seem an ad hoc way to run a manufacturing operation and an excuse to vary from standard. But it's not. The purpose of SIS is to minimize all the lacks. And accepting a lack of information as to why the proposed method won't work and then suffering the consequences is not good management judgment. This is a lack that can be corrected with a focused, well-thought-out alternative method as encouraged under SIS. In looking for a suitable alternative, the supervisor need not work alone. Just the contrary: the supervisor would be within her rights to expect the engineer who developed the original methods to be a prime if not lead participant in the solution. But the operators should also be involved as much as their competency allows.

Staffing Plan Developed

In this case we are referring to the daily assignments of people in the department. The supervisor needs to assess who, among those operators available for assignment, can perform what operations. Keeping in mind the requirements placed on the department for specific output goals, the supervisor has to field the best team she can to meet those goals. Unlike a baseball game, there are no hard-and-fast rules about substitution and changes of personnel. This means the only constraints are, Can the selected operators perform per requirements, and will they? This last point is very important. In making a staffing plan, the supervisor needs to factor the mental attitudes as well as operators' capabilities. Remember, we are entering into a quasi-contract between operator and company to do the job at an agreed-to rate. That rate needs to be coincidental with needs and not something less.

Rate achievement, along with proper quality of work, is the real issue in developing a staffing plan. In making such a plan the supervisor needs to take into account whether the people will be mentally ready to produce at the proper rate. She will have to consider what motivational tactics have to be employed to assure success. She needs to work out the best method of selling the rate of work requirement to the personnel she selects to do the job. Even though the standard may strongly indicate that the required rate is sound, she still has to effectively sell it as part of her staff selection criteria.

Dynamics of Change Procedures Developed

As we can see, the entire plan phase of SIS has to do with providing for changes to predetermined methods and time standards in deference to current conditions. Therefore, the stage that ties the plan phase together is understanding the dynamics of change and getting employees to work with change, not against it.

The supervisor needs to understand that people resist change, especially in a work situation. We all feel comfortable doing jobs in a repetitive, familiar way. We resist doing them differently because we instinctively know there is a higher probability of making a mistake, and we all want to avoid that. When we ask an operator to deviate from a preengineered method of doing a job, we need to assure the operator that it's all right to do so and that it is in everyone's best interest to do so. And while we're doing this, we need to assure that operator that mistakes are forgivable. We would reason with the employee that he is not alone in being asked to change; it's all of those working as a team who need to proceed with the change as it is now planned.

This is what I mean by planning for the dynamics of change. It is simply being aware of the natural aversion to change and countering it to meet the current needs. This way the supervisor can enter into a contract with the operator that is attainable.

Do: Complete the Action Step in All Aspects

Execute Plan

After the plan stage is complete—and in many cases concurrently with formulating the plan—it is necessary to get things going right away. Shop operations cannot afford to deliberate about when or even whether to start. Time really is money, and a procrastinating team is wasting money in a big way. So quick implementation is absolutely necessary.

In many endeavors we may have the time to practice and refine plans. In shop operations, this is hardly the case. The equipment is there waiting to be used, and depreciating in value every minute whether it's idle or running. Material should be available if the MRP II system is functioning, and the operators are there collecting their hourly wages whether they're creating value or not. The clock is running; there is no recourse but to put the plan in action.

I have taught many first-time supervisors that they need to err in favor of action, always. Even if the plan is not being carried out as the supervisor would like, some action is better than no action. Making parts at a slower-than-plan pace is getting parts made. Perhaps not at the rate desired, but at least some production is being obtained. Not doing anything while we try to improve performance nets us nothing. I am always amazed at managers who think it's all right to stop, contemplate, and discuss before proceeding. It's not proper at all. The idea of shop operations management expressed through SIS is to continuously make progress, albeit at times not at a very fast pace. We make improvements as we go by analyzing data and taking corrective action. But we cannot stop producing just because we are not satisfied with the performance levels. It's like an airplane in flight: we find our position by navigation beacons or the like, and then, while we're still flying, we determine whether we're where we want to be. If not, we take corrective action. We don't land and then figure out where we are, decide what kind of course corrections are necessary, and then take off again and proceed to the destination.

In shop operations, "execute" means start at the first minute of the shift and keep going until the conclusion of the work shift. We measure as we go and take corrective actions along the way. But no matter what, we continue to strive to produce products.

Define Milestone Points per Chronological Sequences

As mentioned in the discussion of executing the plan, we continue to work no matter what; but we evaluate where we are in accordance with the plan. This is the step where we do the evaluations of the process on the fly, so to speak.

The plan spells out what we have to do and when. It also, by simple arithmetic, defines how many processes, parts, or assemblies need to have been accomplished at any point in time. Whether we are doing the job correctly can be observed simply by watching the process. We can note the deviations and instruct the operator on how to correct them, all while the process continues. This like a coach on a sports team observing the players' technique and then advising them of corrections to make to improve performance during the course of the contest.

Observing the rate of accomplishment is easy, but correcting it (if required) is a bit more subtle and indirect. Observations are a totaling up of quantitative accomplishment to the time of the observation and comparing it with the planned expected accomplishment. If the rate says we should have assembled 30 rubber sleeves to their respective handles and we have done only 18, at first it would appear that we are working at a 60% rate. But are we? We don't know until we get to the root cause of the apparent deficiency. Let's explore the example further.

In the hammer example, again, we are going to make 500 hammers, but we're not going to assemble the rubber grips to the handles strictly in accordance with the methods described in Figure 3-3. Let us suppose that we are going to assemble 10 rubber grips to their hammers per hour, or 80 per shift. That means we can devise a milestone chart of some sort to track where we are and to signal whether we're doing all right or not. Figure 11-3 is a chart we can use to do this.

We see that the chart shows in a cumulative manner the number of units that should be finished at the end of each hour. The chart is filled out by the operator to indicate how many he has actually completed at the end of the recording time, again cumulatively. The observations are a combination of operator input and supervisor notations that try to explain variances. However, perhaps the most important aspect of this tally sheet is to focus on output pace. It is a constant reminder to the operator of the informal contract he has entered into with the company to produce parts, at the proper quality level, at the rate that was agreed to.

The fact that we are only at 60% of the planned rate now has some explanation. We see reasons that may or may not be root causes, but they are a start to getting to the bottom of these variances. We will evaluate these reasons in the following sections of our PDSA discussions.

Create a Review Process to Check Progress of Implementing the Plan

Using the milestone schedule evaluation and action summary form (Figure 11-3) as the basis, the supervisor sets up a periodic review with the opera-

Department:	Hammer assembly		Date:	1/29/00
Product:	Hammer, pilot production			
Shop order no.:	1a – pilot			
Drawing no.:	123E456Pt1,Pt2			

		Production log	

Time	Plan cumulative	Actual cumulative	Observations
7:00	start	N/A	
8:00	10	4	1. Material arrived 7:20 - late
9:00	20	11	2. Hard to hold hammer to place grip over
10:00	30	18	3. Cracked 3 grips trying to spread
11:00	40		
12:00	50		
12:30	finish lunch		
1:30	60		
2:30	70		
3:30	80		
4:30	overtime		
5:30	overtime		

Actions responsible	Actions planned done	Actions actual done	Actions activity
1. supervisor	1/29/00	1/29/00	1. Arrange for inventory for next day at end of shift
2. supervisor	1/29/00	1/29/00	2. Show how to use vise with out damaging hammer
3. engineer	1/30/00		3. Dev. method of rubber stretch without cracking;
			demo. to operators at start of shift.

Instructions: Review production status every 2 hours. List results and reason for variances. List fix tasks under actions with responsibility and due date.

Figure 11-3. Milestone schedule evaluation and action list summary.

tor to discuss progress. She will also use the information from the form to establish action plan reviews with other functions. Let's see how this works.

First, the periodic review with the operator. We start with the contract. The operator has the responsibility to go about his task of performing work as agreed to. That work should yield output at the pace agreed to. The supervisor has the responsibility as the company's agent to carry out the contract from the management side. In order for the contract to be valid, the operator and supervisor need to periodically assess the state of progress. To make this happen, the SIS process proposes a face-to-face review at frequent intervals.

I have found that the best interval is every two to three hours, depending on the nature of the task. The longer the cycle time to do a job, the longer the time interval between face-to-face meetings can be. The key to the interval between meetings is whether or not a sufficient activity has occurred during that time period. For the meeting to have validity, there has to be something to review, e.g., work done that demonstrates some sort of trend.

The nature of the meeting is straightforward. The supervisor during her tour of the work stations stops to talk to the operator and review progress. She scans the form sheet (Figure 11-3) to see how many measurable units have been completed since the beginning of the shift and compares that number with the contracted quantity. If there is a significant variance, she asks why. She asks even though the operator may have made the necessary notations on the form. The operator answers the questions, and his response triggers either action or no action by the supervisor. It's as simple as that.

The second review initiated by the milestone schedule evaluation and action summary is the actions review. Note that at the bottom of the form there are actions to be taken and completed by a certain date. Their nature is determined by the reasons why the pace of performance has not been in accordance with plan. I will explain the methodology of these procedures later on. The supervisor has a responsibility to follow up on the reasons as part of the contract. The date setting is simply a mechanism for expressing priority and complexity of the action contemplated. As a rule of thumb, actions that can be accomplished within the same work day are usually within the range of the supervisor's say-so. Those that are more complex and require investigation or engineering development are assigned more time and are given to other functions to accomplish. The supervisor is responsible for reporting the need for other functions to resolve problems requiring longer cycle times. Decisions in these cases are made administratively by the supervisor's manager for all but the highest-urgency problems (like a down facility preventing work from continuing), as an outcome of a weekly meeting with supervisors not unlike a production review meeting. This meeting is a review of the week's milestone schedule evaluation and action summary, usually transcribed into a summarized form, a *short interval scheduling action log*. Such a form is shown in Figure 11-4.

The short interval action log is meant to be the mechanism for recording and measuring the efforts to correct deficiencies discovered by the supervisor during the daily multiple meetings she has with her operators. Notice that the problem concerning cracking of rubber grips has turned up on this list under quality control. It is apparent that the engineer could not satisfactorily resolve the cracking problem identified on January 29, and its investigation turned up a ductility problem with the supplied rubber. Hence, the problem is referred to quality control to resolve with the vendor.

Department: Hammer assembly				Week of: 1/23/00		
Hours worked: 252	Efficiency: 62%		Units planned: 500	Units completed: 310		% absenteeism: 10%
				Action activities		
Item no.	Assigned to	Complete by	Actual complete date	Status	Description	Comments
1	engineering	1/28/00		50%	Fabricate handle rubber grip assembly tools	Late arrival of materials
2	purchasing	1/19/00		10%	Get rubber grips in stock	Strike at supplier, need second source
3	supervisor	1/17/00	1/17/00	100%	Train operators in hammer asm. procedures	
4	supervisor	2/4/00		0%	High absenteeism last week get to root cause and correct	Possible illness factor and jury duty
5	quality control	2/3/00		25%	Review rubber grip ductility needs w/vendor; 3 cracks reported last week	
6						
7						
8						
9						
10						
11						
12						
13						
14						
15						
16						
17						
18						
19						
20						
21						
22						
23						
24						
25						

Figure 11-4. Short interval scheduling action log.

A meeting for action activities should occur weekly and be chaired by the shop operations manager. The meeting need not be long, perhaps 30 minutes. Its purpose is to highlight the problems brought to light the previous week and to resolve them quickly.

Study: Evaluate the Results of Carrying Out the Plan. Does It Achieve the Plan?

Identify Deviations in the Implementation of the Plan

In order to take effective corrective actions, we must first know what the deviations from the plan are. And they have to be factual—i.e., measured. For example knowing that we have missed a production target is not sufficient. We must also know by how much, because the *degree* of the variance, the problem, must be understood before a proper response can be made. As an illustrative analogy, suppose a person is reported to be ill. How do we treat that person? Obviously, we have to know what's wrong so a proper type of action can be prescribed. We certainly wouldn't do the same thing for a common cold as we would do for pneumonia. The same is true for manufacturing. If production is off by 50%, we would suspect machinery or process failures, or perhaps running out of materials to work with. On the other hand, if production were off by 10% we would suspect some sort of operator performance problem.

In the example illustrated in Figure 11-4, the variance is 310 units completed during the week when 500 were planned for. There are other variances shown. The department only recorded 252 hours worked. This is not divisible by 8 hours per shift to get a whole number of persons working the entire week. So we also have this variance to contend with, and perhaps it has affected the output numbers. We also see that the efficiency was only 62%. This is probably another way of stating that only 310 hammer assemblies were made during the week, but nevertheless it is a variance that needs to be evaluated. We can see that it is imperative to identify causes of variance before corrective action can be taken. This leads to the next step under the study phase of PDSA.

Identify Problems That Caused Deviation from the Plan

Using the information from Figure 11-4 or other verifiable sources, the persons assigned by the weekly meeting on the short interval scheduling action log begin the detective process of finding root causes. It is a simple fact that problems cannot be solved until we get to their root cause. As a reminder, the basic way to find root cause is similar to peeling an onion: we keep asking the questions posed by the manufacturing engineering methods development process as shown in Figure 11-5. The questions make up the traditional *work simplification pattern* that is applicable for problem solving and root cause analysis. Figure 11-5 is a copy of a work simplification pattern ruler (both sides) that I've been handing out to my employees for the past

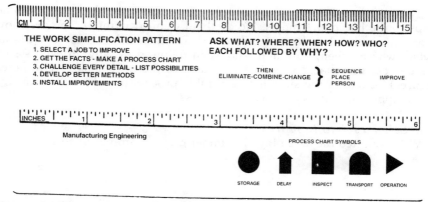

Figure 11-5. Typical manufacturing engineering work simplification pattern, as printed on the two sides of a 6-in. (15-cm) ruler.

three decades. These are the people whom I expect to be involved in problem solving and making improvements in the way we manufacture. It is a very effective method and one I recommend. The cost of making these rulers is nominal, and they are worth the expense. I also use these rulers for instructing workers on how to develop process charts so they can visualize steps in any process to find better ways of doing it. As you can see from the steps depicted on the ruler, making a process chart is part of the process of finding root cause. We shall see how that's done.

First, we need to follow the work simplification pattern by asking the questions what, where, when, how, and who. Each answer is followed by the last question, why. We keep going until there are no more follow-up questions. We can then be reasonably assured that the root cause has been determined. The procedure identifies the problem to be resolved. By knowing what the specific problem is, we can put it into specific context within its environment by constructing a process flowchart. Let's use the data from Figure 11-4 to illustrate this process.

Use of the Work Simplification Pattern in Short Interval Scheduling

The short interval scheduling action log shows two deficiencies that have to be resolved for the department to be successful. It's also realistic to think they may be related. The first item is the fact that only 310 out of 500 hammer grips were assembled onto the hammer handles, resulting in an unacceptable 62% efficiency. The second item is the 10% absenteeism rate for the week. Obviously, not having enough people available to do the job can cause lower output. But is this the main reason? Is absenteeism part of the first deficiency and not independent? Let's use the process to investigate.

The initial step is to understand the process of assembling the hammer grips to the hammer handles. We do this by constructing the process flowchart. After the flowchart is assembled, we then ask the set of question (what, where, when, how, and who, each followed by why) of each step in the process flowchart to see if it is related to the deficiencies we've noted. Figure 11-6 shows the simplified assembly process flowchart that we shall use to apply the work simplification process.

a. Select a Job to Improve
We've selected the assembly of hammer grip to hammer handle.

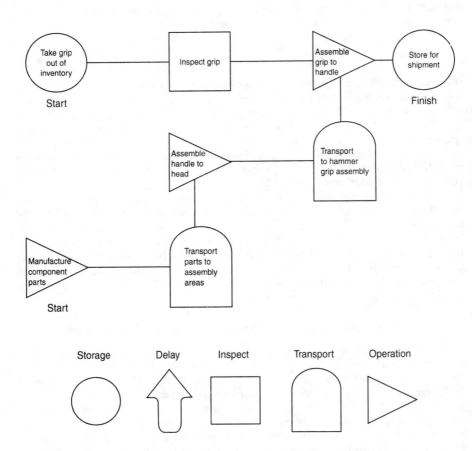

Figure 11-6 Hammer grip assembly process flowchart.

b. Get the Facts—Make a Process Chart

Process charts can be flowcharts or chronological tabular listings. I favor flowcharts so I can readily visualize parallel (concurrent) operations. That's my choice. Tables are just as correct.

We are looking for steps that may be relevant to the lack of productivity and/or the high absenteeism indicated by the action log. The pregrip to handle manufacturing and assembly steps have no apparent linkages to the problem. The grip inventory storage and inspection steps, along with the assembly step, apparently do have some relationship and need to be investigated. The short interval scheduling action log and the milestone schedule evaluation and action summary (Figures 11-3 and 11-4) have details associated with those steps of the flowchart as follows:

(Step) Take Grip Out of Inventory:

- "Material arrived 7:20"—reference to late movement of grips to work station
- "Get rubber grips in stock"—reference to low inventory status

(Step) Inspect Grip:

- "Cracked three grips trying to spread"—no reference made of a problem at inspection, and no indication of a build up of parts waiting before inspection indicating a problem to finish inspection on time

(Step) Assemble Grip to Handle:

- "Hard to hold hammer to place grip over"—reference to previous training and new training.

c. Challenge Every Detail—List Possibilities

I've found that the best way to do this is through creating an outline based on the questions what, where, when, how, and who, each followed by why. For example,

(Step) Take Grip Out of Inventory:

- "Material arrived 7:20"—reference to late movement of grips to work station

The questioning procedure could go as follows:

- *What?* What happened here that relates to the low productivity level (310 actual versus 500 planned)? Not enough inventory?
- *Why* is that significant? (Always ask the follow-up "why" question to test significance—whether the factor is relevant and not obvious.) The late arrival is significant only if it continued, which apparently isn't the case. The rate of production is 12.5 units per hour, and so lateness can account for only one-third of an hour's output.
- *Where?* Where did the incident occur? At the assembly station.

- *Why?* We don't ask why this factor might have contributed to the problem. Where the incident occurred is clearly insignificant.
- *When?* When did the incident occur? At the assembly station at the start of the shift on January 29.
- *Why?* Why is there a linkage between lack of material on January 29 and the low productivity at the time of the incident? Because there is nothing to work on for the first third of the first hour, but not thereafter. Therefore, the conclusion is that this is a minor incident.
- *How?* How did this incident happen? No material available.
- *Why?* Apparent strike at the vendor's plant caused late arrival of materials. Why is this relevant? It may be an indication of continued delivery problems. But to answer the question whether or not "Material arrived 7:20" is relevant to low productivity or high absenteeism, it most likely is not.
- *Who?* Who was responsible for late arrival? The material movers.
- *Why?* Since this is obviously not relevant to finding a cause for the low productivity or the high absenteeism, there is no need to ask why.

The conclusion to be drawn from the investigation of "Material arrived 7:20" is that it is not a significant factor in finding the cause of the low productivity. It is no factor at all in the quest to understand the high absenteeism.

Continuing our investigation of this same flowchart step, we apply the questioning procedure to the next factor:

- "Get rubber grips in stock"—reference to low inventory status

The questions yield similar if not identical results. Therefore I will not outline them here.

We would now proceed to investigate in the same way the remaining steps of the flowchart that we have targeted. Since it is not important for illustrative purposes to carry out this example any further, I will skip to the ultimate results.

From the facts given, it is apparent that the cause of low productivity is the difficulty in positioning the hammers for slipping the grip onto them without the special jigs and fixtures (described in Chapter 6), which were not ready before the start of the pilot run. Remember, the original scenario had set a production date before a need for special fixtures was discerned, so that the company had to "make do" with temporary fixtures. The fact that there was a ductility problem with some of the first grips might be a contributing factor, but since there were only three failures due to cracked grips, we can conclude that this is not a major factor at all.

The absenteeism problem cannot be resolved from any of the facts presented. I have introduced an unresolved situation into the illustration simply to point out that even though this technique is a valuable problem resolution tool, it is not capable of solving problems unless the basic cause-and-effect relationships are present. My experience has shown that absenteeism-type problems often have causes well beyond the bounds of the work situation.

Nevertheless, it is better to bat 400 than a measly 100, which is usually the case for an unstructured problem solving approach.

d. Develop Better Methods
Based on the analysis, we can reaffirm that trying to assemble the hammers without the proper fixtures is not the better method. In fact, the better method is to follow the originally developed procedure—which indeed will be done for full production when the assembly fixtures are put into service.

e. Install Improvements
This is the resultant of all the work up to this point of the analyses, conclusions and implementation plans. It is the culmination of all the efforts. In the example, we know what the resulting improvements will be. They will consist of implementing the methods previously agreed to before the pull-up in schedule forced changes.

Develop Corrective Actions to the Plan

I have purposely presented those details of the work simplification pattern that primarily illustrate a methodology for the "identifying of problem" phase of the "study" phase of PDSA, but also those that set the stage for the "corrective actions to plan" phase. I will also show later that many parts of the work simplification pattern process also apply to the "act" portion of PDSA. In fact, the work simplification pattern is the classic investigatory tool for hosts of identification and sorting processes. I've also chosen to show the entire "study" part of PDSA as a linear process. In practice, it is possible to do many steps concurrently, thus muddying the water from an explanation viewpoint, and perhaps appearing to be redundant. From a macro viewpoint this may appear to be true, and pragmatically that may be correct for some more simplistic problems. However, PDSA is a complex strategy to achieve systems optimization, and each step has its logical connection to its predecessor, so in reality there is no redundancy among the steps.

In the work simplification pattern, we have gone to great lengths to identify facts and list their potential causes so we could then structure improved ways of accomplishing the tasks, the goal being a plan for implementing the new method. In this next step of the process we look closely at the implementation plans and determine if they are capable of achieving our goals. This is analogous to saying before we sign a contract that we'd like to "sleep on it." In other words, we want to make one last evaluations before committing resources to it.

This final review may or may not result in changes: the corrective actions to the plan may consist of purposely staying with what we have. But we will look hard to see if what we've done is sufficient. The process used to determine if a corrective action to the plan is necessary is the same as for the initial steps 2 through 4 of the work simplification pattern (see Figure 11-5).

There is no step 1 because the job to improve has already been defined. Also, to be entirely correct, step 5, install improvements, is part of the approved plan and therefore should be included in this review. But we don't include it because we reserve implementing improvements for the "act" segments of PDSA.

For brevity purposes I won't go over the corrective action cycle using work simplification pattern methodologies. It is the same as the original except that most of the legwork has already been done. For every factor that is judged important to the process and a place for potential improvement, we once more ask the questions what, where, when, and how, each followed by why. The only slight nuance here is to test whether the factors are pertinent to the investigation or whether they can be superseded or dropped. The summation of these evaluations becomes the corrective actions to the plan.

Act: Use the Results of the Study to Make Improvements to the Plan

Implement and Evaluate Corrective Actions to the Plan

By now the pattern of PDSA is obvious. We create and implement a plan, determine whether it is doing as we wanted, and finally find out why there are variances so we can introduce changes that will get us back on the track we wanted to pursue originally. It is a double-check process and nothing more. In SIS this is precisely what we want to happen. We want operators to be briefed on what they have to do. We have them do it. Then, we check to see if what we wanted to happen is really happening. If not, we make the necessary midcourse corrections.

Thus, this is the second go-around for the plan, only this time, we are using the results of previous actions to modify the process to get improved results. Lots of times companies lose patience with the process and never get to this second implementation phase. This is a big mistake on their part. By not following through and making sure that the original plans are working well, they lose the ability to optimize the process, thus losing significant profitability potential. Remember, SIS is an optimization process, and to cut it off before completing the step that corrects previously discovered discrepancies is very unfortunate if not negligent.

Make Temporary and Subsequent Final Changes to the Plan

Even the second pass may need some other minor corrections, and that's what happens at the next stage. SIS is a continuously correcting process based on current performance. However, virtually all of the changes to the plan should be discovered after the first go-around if the work simplification pattern is used properly. Therefore, this step is usually not one of major changes but of very minor adjustments.

The only time we would see a need for a supervisor, on his periodic rounds, to institute major changes at this point is if there had been a major change in personnel, methods, or materials. Otherwise, the key word here is "tweaking." We are fine-focusing to get the most out of the process we possibly can.

Evaluate Performance for Achieving the Goals

The final step of the PDSA system is to evaluate the overall effectiveness of implementing a plan. We do this by tying PDSA activities into the company's overall performance measurement schemes. The basic measurement we are all interested in is, Are we making a profit, and is it as good as it can be? The shop operations aspect of that is overall operating costs versus productivity output. Put more directly: Are we making the product in sufficient quantity and at low enough cost to assure a profit that is high enough to justify the entire activity? If the answer is yes, that's fine, and we can be proud of a job we've done. If the answer is no, then we need to reconsider the entire operation from product concept to delivery to customers, to determine whether there is sufficient reason to continue.

Measurements are continuous evaluations of the company's decision to be in a particular business. They are a way of determining whether the return on investment is worth the effort or whether the company should reapply its resources. Shop operations measurements come down to quantity of product made, its costs, and its quality. These are all evaluated against targets. Sometimes these targets are set against hard-and-fast budgets, created with elaborate market forecast scenarios; sometimes they are simply desires of the company's management or owners. Whatever they are, they have to be understood by the people who have to produce the goods, and they have to be achievable. I will discuss measurements later in this chapter. I will do this after we gain an understanding of expanding the concepts of short interval scheduling by setting it within the overall manufacturing system.

USING SHORT INTERVAL SCHEDULING WITHIN THE MANUFACTURING SYSTEM

I have been writing extensively about the manufacturing system and its seven distinct steps for almost three decades. I am a firm believer that the seven steps are the linkage of all phases of manufacturing and that understanding them is the prime prerequisite for successful operations. In fact, I purposely opened this book by introducing the seven steps and their companions, the Two Knows, to signify the importance of this central philosophy of manufacturing. By direct genealogical lineage from its antecedents, work station dynamics is also governed by these rules. Therefore, it is logical to draw the conclusion that SIS works best when it is compatible with the dictates of the seven steps of the manufacturing system. This being the case, the first step in understanding why SIS has to be compatible with the manufacturing system is to briefly define that system. By doing that we shall see how

SIS makes use of the system in that it is compatible with the systems a company uses to control its business.

The manufacturing system is present and applicable whether or not a company recognizes it or not. The fact is that those that recognize the synergistic nature of the seven linked steps and actively strive to optimize the performance of those seven steps tend to be better generators of profit margins. The linkages are the information commonalities that pass from one step to the other, therefore improving the probability of performing each step optimally. In information systems terms, we call this making use of *common databases:* the same information is available to all functions at the same time, and all receive the same updates at the same time.

Perhaps a way to understand the power of this information availability and accuracy throughout a company is through an analogy in physics. We all know that laser light brings focused energy to bear at levels of magnitude thousands of times more powerful than ordinary light. Yet it is the same light, consisting of the same wavelengths of the visible spectrum. However, laser light is in resonance, as opposed to the scattering of normal light, and that's its strength. In manufacturing systems, by utilizing the common database approach we are in communications resonance between the seven steps of creating a product.

The concept of a manufacturing system is abstract but I believe easy to comprehend. Think of it as a road map for a company's information flow from step to step on how to produce a product. Every process has a start and a finish. In manufacturing systems that start is always the first step of the seven steps of the manufacturing system: obtain product specification. This is the sales/marketing/design phase. The manufacturing system for a specific company shows how the company performs the seven steps and how the seven-step sequence occurs. Often the task of a manager is to untangle the web of just how the company follows the seven steps. This is done by developing a flowchart for the flow of the information used to control the manufacturing process in accordance with the seven steps. Figure 11-7 is an example of such a flowchart for a company engaged in making a product in a job shop environment. We can think of it as the information flow system for the hammer manufacturing operation. Let's look at the various specific steps and see how they relate to the seven general steps of the manufacturing system.

1. Obtain Product Specification

The first activity in Figure 11-7 is the start of the process, "Prepare estimate for RFQ, develop preliminary BOM/route." We see that this is done by engineering. Note the "1, 2" on the upper left edge of the box. The numeral 1 indicates step 1; 2 indicates step 2. Since the box has two numbers, it indicates that steps 1 and 2 share this activity performed by engineering. (Note that the layout of the flowchart shows each step under the function that performs it.)

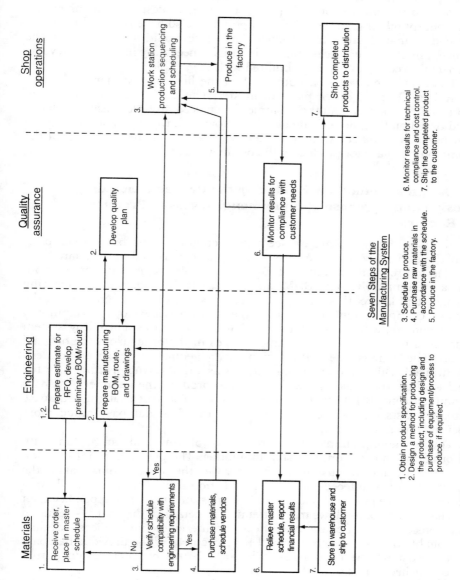

Figure 11-7. Information flow for an integrated manufacturing system.

In many job shops, business is obtained by quoting jobs, and that requires a preliminary engineering study. This preliminary engineering study becomes the first input to the common database. In this case it could have been the preliminary geometric parameters used to design the hammer and the concept bill of materials. It would probably also have specified the route needed to manufacture the product. The route would have contained the concept methods and cycle times. All of this is necessary in order to develop an accurate cost quote to be submitted with the job bid.

The next place we see a numeral 1 in the flowchart sequence is under Materials: "Receive order, place in master schedule." The quote has been sent to the customer, and the customer has placed an order based on that. I said based on that, not exactly like that. Now we have information returned but perhaps modified. Whatever the case, this is now the beginning of the common database for producing the product.

2. Design a Method for Producing the Product, Including Design and Purchase of Equipment/Process to Produce, If Required

In this specific flowchart we see three activities, done by two company functions, sharing step 2. We first see step 2 represented in the shared box related to preparing an estimate. But step 1 is also represented in developing a preliminary design, BOM, and route, which is again an engineering design step; hence, this one operation serves two of the seven steps of the manufacturing system. In this case the previously developed preliminary BOM and route has a set database that can drive the scheduling system once it is modified to include any changes in the order from the original quote. The same is true of the design for the geometric shapes and materials utilized. This original database serves as a timesaving precursor for the real working database that will be used to produce the hammer ("Prepare manufacturing BOM, route, and drawings"). The fact that this database already exists makes the work to create the final database much more focused and much faster.

This is a good example of the preciseness of work that can be done with information linked from one step to another. The preliminary information was submitted to the customer, who approved the concept, thus making the information the antecedent of the next action step. This synergy allows a more error-free process to occur because most of what will happen need not be changed. Also, it allows more attention to details of the changes required and consideration of causes and effects of different action choices (within a reasonable time frame) than would have occurred if the previous database hadn't existed. The overall result being a better product design output accomplished in less time.

The third box representing step 2, "Develop quality plan," also derives its output from the same database input as the rest of the design. In contrast to many companies that fall short in this area, we have a quality plan that is in complete synchronization with the design build plan. Therefore it is reasonable to expect we will have a quality plan that focuses on the really important aspects of the design. The ultimate outcome, of course, will be fewer defects in the manufacturing process and a better product going to the customer.

3. Schedule to Produce

The shared database information is now acted upon by the scheduling function of the company. They know how the product is to be made and the time it will take (the Two Knows) from the engineering database. They also know from the Bill of Materials the types and quantities of raw materials and parts necessary to make it with.

In our hammer example, this step 3 activity (one of two step 3 boxes) under the Materials heading, is given as "Verify schedule compatibility with engineering requirements." The information from the database (which has remained consistent, since it is a shared, common database) is used to see if the requirements can be handled by the company's manufacturing capabilities. Since it is a shared database used for each step of the manufacturing system, the chance is significantly less that the materials function will make an error and accept a job that is inappropriate for the facility. If databases were different for the different functions, then there would be a stronger possibility for the schedulers to err, thinking that the part to be made is different from the actual design requirements the engineering function will soon be presented with. Therefore, the flow as shown in Figure 11-7 could result in a wrong interpretation and the actual yes or no could be the reverse of what is really true.

If the answer asked for in the flowchart is yes when it should have been no, then the second step 3 box, "Work station production sequencing and scheduling" (a shop operations activity), will be receiving false data as input and the sequencing and scheduling could likely result in substandard product at a higher production cost. Once more, we see the value of a common database as a strong preventive of the company's reacting to false information.

It is very important to understand that if information is correct then the process will work well. The first step 3 box requires a yes/no choice. If the input information to that box is correct, then we will have correct decisions made and can proceed optimally.

Example: Let's return to the hammer manufacturing illustration once more. I have stated that common databases produce consistently higher-quality product and more of it during any given time period. Common databases make factories optimal. Referring to Figure 3-5 (the route sheet), we see a series of steps that define what work will be done at what work station to make the hammer. The most common way of creating this route sheet is for a planner (normally a person in manufacturing engineering) to review the engineering drawing and enter the geometric data and pertinent information into the MRP II database and from that create a route to be followed. There is nothing wrong with this if it's done accurately. However, my experiences have shown that over half of all processing errors occur because of errors made in this step. Common databases prevent virtually all of these errors from occurring. Let's see how.

Going back to step 1, we created a database for manufacturing the hammer to meet a customer specification. We used the data to determine the hours required to make the hammer, thus getting a labor, materials, and overhead price to do so. Sales then put on the appropriate margins, and a price was quoted to the customer. The customer awarded the company with the business for hammers, essentially as outlined in the quote. In step 2, the information received back from the customer was used to modify the original information to create drawings and instructions for the shop to make the product. If a common database existed, the original quote information was compared with the firm order and it was modified as needed. If there was no common database, then at least the same people who did the original quote engineering did the order engineering, so that in this area error potential in the conversion was reduced. If the engineers had used a common database, the potential for error would have been lessened by a factor of at least 10, since they would not have to reinput all the geometry and other parameters. Already we see where a common database could speed up the design function as well as reduce errors.

Now, traditionally the whole design package is turned over to manufacturing engineering for their work effort—to produce the methods, planning, routing, and tool and jig designs. Without a common database, they would have to reintroduce the same geometry and parameters of manufacturing into their database—again, a large opportunity for errors to be introduced. If a common database were employed, all of the geometry parameters would already exist for conversion to CNC tool paths and the parameters based selections for tooling. These parameters of design dictate materials selection and the processes shop operations will use.

For example purposes, in step 3 let us suppose no common database exists and we are in the flowchart box under Materials described as "Verify schedule compatibility with engineering requirements." It is either a yes or a no. Let's assume that manufacturing misinterpreted the information received from design engineering and thought the tolerance for machining the handle, operations 15 of Figure 3-5, was ±0.010 in. on the diameter, while actually the tolerance required was ±0.001 in. With that wrong information, they might have routed the part to an older, less capable lathe. With the error undetected, they have answered yes to the verification step indicating that they could make the part on time by using the older lathe. Time passes, and the part comes to the factory floor to be produced. The CNC program meanwhile, has independently been programmed with the correct tolerance, ±0.001 in. That program is run on the older CNC lathe, and quality problems begin to surface. The machine can't consistently hold the tolerance, so there are high scrap levels. This causes concern among the entire team. The company is late making the product, it is costing more to make, and subsequently profit is lower.

The irony of the situation is that a more accurate CNC machine exists within the factory that could easily have done the job. But since there was no common database that would have assured all functions were working off the same correct data, that machine was loaded with another product, perhaps one not needing the capability the machine possessed.

You may say that the example portrays a comedy of errors that really doesn't happen often. I would have to strongly disagree. Whenever data have to be reentered many times, probability theory teaches us that the potential for error increases significantly. Let's say the probability of doing the data input correctly is 95%. In the case of the hammer example, we had to reinput data at least three times. That means that the probability the data will still be correct at the end of the third insert is $0.95 \times 0.95 \times 0.95 = 0.857$ as compared with 0.95 if we only had to enter the data once. Which would you rather have in your factory? Of course, we can survive many such input errors and still make a profit. But think of the lost potential.

4. Purchase Raw Materials in Accordance with the Schedule

No product can be made until materials are available to manufacture it. The fourth step is to take the information about the design, as shown on the bill of materials, and determine what parts are to be made and purchased. Similarly, as shown previously, the more accurate the information is, the quicker purchasing can react and procure the right items. As in the example of the erroneous tolerance information, we can easily see what would happen if the data had been entered wrong onto the bill of materials. Suppose the answer required in the verification box was yes instead of no. We would go down the same wrong road as in the tolerance example, only this time it would be a wrong material. We see in Figure 3-6 (the indented bill of materials), the identification by drawing number of all of the parts that make up the hammer. Note that the BOM calls for 316 stainless steel. What would happen if, in reading the design engineers' inputs, the planner transposed a 4 for a 3, an easy thing to do on a keyboard? We would be buying a ferritic stainless steel instead of an austenitic stainless steel. The properties are different. Austenitic is not magnetic, and it tends to resist corrosion well (doesn't rust). The opposite is true for ferritic stainless steel. Does that make a difference in the finished product? Absolutely. The company would not have fulfilled its contract, and the customer would not have to accept it. It would mean work done without compensation, to say nothing of the bad customer relationship that would ensue. Again these things could be avoided by employing common databases.

Another thing that these previous two examples point out is that by understanding how one operation performed by one function can affect the results of another function in a future operation, we begin to see how everything is linked together. Knowledge truly is power. By knowing about these inevitable linkages, we can be consciously aware of the pitfalls ahead of us and take steps to guard against them. Obviously, without such preknowledge there is no chance of effective preactions to minimize those potential impacts.

5. Produce in the Factory

Step 5 is the shop operations phase. We are using all the information in the common database to instruct shop personnel how to make the product, what materials to use and when to do it. This is the "do" portion of plan, do, study, act, and it is driven by data generated from, or perhaps a better term is cascading from, all four previous steps.

Recall that in SIS we create bits of information to feed operators as needed. We have a contract with the operators to do work in a specific sequence and rate. Now, I think it is obvious that the information we are using as a basis for the contract is being driven and coordinated by the common database. We are not using a vague sense of intent to independently decide what that contract basis has to be.

6. Monitor Results for Technical Compliance and Cost Control

The sixth step of the manufacturing system is represented by two boxes in the flowchart of Figure 11-7. The first is a quality assurance action whereby we are verifying that the work has been done correctly and in the quantities required.

In a fully implemented computer-integrated manufacturing (CIM) system, the data for this step enter the common database via a statistical process control (SPC) program. Usually, we want operators to make the inputs, since they are the front line, so to speak, of the action activities. Who is better qualified to introduce the information into the system? No one. Again, the principle of eliminating redundancy applies. The operator does the work, so she knows what she did and can enter the information with the least amount of interpretation error. There is simply no need to risk a potential for interpretation error by giving the data to someone else to input into the common database.

This is entirely compatible with and supportive of SIS. In SIS-run factories, we are constantly reviewing progress with operators. By setting up a data collection system for the operator to use, we are simplifying this progress review process. It allows us to constantly keep score of progress and pitfalls the operator experiences and is usually more accurate than a verbal communications regime over the course of the work shift.

The second activity under step 6, "Relieve master schedule, report financial results," occurs as a by-product of the first monitoring activity of step 6 for factories that employ common databases. If we record compliance for SIS purposes, we can use the same data to update the MRP II database, which contains the dispatching database. The fact that it is integrated with all other performance measurements means that the shift dispatch reports are going to be accurate and the contract between operator and supervisor (representing the company) will remain pertinent. It means that the supervisor and operator both know what is expected with respect to original plans and modifications thereof.

This information that the operator and supervisor use is also being shared with the finance department. They are matching up hours to do the job versus planned hours, and in this manner can calculate the profit levels associated with the specific operator's work station. In CIM-based companies, this information is now real-time, and we get current activities feedback sometimes even within the shift it is occurring on, but certainly no later than the next shift. Think of how powerful a tool this is for the operator and the supervisor. They can see the effect of an action almost as soon as the action occurs. This was a fond wish of SIS proponents only few years ago, but now is becoming reality. The reason for short intervals is to be able to react quickly to detriments to quality and productivity as soon as they occur. When that happens, the detrimental effects of mistakes are greatly curtailed, and improved overall performance results. With CIM, the desire for rapid and effective response to problems is a reality, not a wish.

7. Ship the Completed Product to the Customer

We are leaving the domain of traditional SIS. The CIM system's seventh step creates accurate information for knowing what shop orders have completed the production cycle, in what quantities, and with what resolved quality problems. The supervisor/operator contract has produced results that are comparable to predetermined schedules, and since the information has been flowing on short interval time frames, the database for distribution and shipping has been upgraded more frequently, thereby becoming more accurate.

Shipping goods to customers requires constant communications with customers. Think of customers as extensions of the manufacturing process. They use the company's products to satisfy their goals, be they personal or commercial, just as the company uses raw materials and parts from vendors to satisfy its manufacturing flow needs. The customer can be thought of as another partner in the supply chain from raw material to ultimate consumer. The more frequently we have database updates, the better we can keep the supply chain fully informed so each member can make timely decisions. In

SIS we stress frequent communications updates via frequent one-on-one sessions between operator and supervisor on the shop floor. As we've shown, CIM makes it easier to accomplish this task.

MEASUREMENTS AND THEIR RELATION TO SHORT INTERVAL SCHEDULING

What kind of information do we want to be recorded? There are only two categories we can place information into for manufacturing measurements purposes. First, we want to measure whether work is done correctly or not. Second, we want to know how much product we've produced over specific periods of time. And in both cases we want to be able to compare trends against previous periods, standards, and goals.

For the first category, quality, if the work was done incorrectly we want to know why. We want to list the cause, or causes, of the problem and the frequency of the occurrence over time. We want to make Pareto charts of the causes so we can focus on the most prevalent problems first and fix them, then move on to the second group of most frequently occurring problems and fix them, and so on until all problems are corrected.

For the second category, productivity, we want to record quantity of good work accomplished versus the amount scheduled and graph it so we can discern trends. Once we see trends, we want to understand the reasons for them and see how they affect our ability to achieve the daily quotas we have collectively set for the factory.

The SIS process helps us gather data because it requires specific inquiries of how we're doing several times during a shift. The need, then, is to make sure we structure the data in a way that it is understandable and actionable by both the supervisor and the operators. Figures 11-3 and 11-4 are a result of the daily inquiries, and their purpose is to support immediate or short term corrective actions. As good as this technique is, we see that it does only a superficial job of categorizing deficiencies and really does nothing to compare trends. In fact, we would categorize these reports as tactical rather than strategical documents. But we need both kinds of documents. Short interval scheduling requires quick response. It does not set into motion strategic corrective actions as a primary motive. However, the information it produces can and does enhance the ability to get data for strategic trends analysis. Let's now look at the nature of these data collection and presentation techniques and once more demonstrate a relationship to SIS.

Pareto Method

The Pareto method is named after a pioneer industrial engineer who devised a way of ranking problems in accordance with their importance. What is important is defined by the team doing the analysis, and defining it is one of the skills the team needs to acquire. Unfortunately, determining what is or isn't of primary importance is not a skill that can be readily taught. It is difficult to do so because it depends on the entire business situation and the team's understanding of it. The only available criterion for ranking problems by importance is the team's best understanding of the situation from its own viewpoint. That viewpoint can be defined as what needs to be achieved and should be, based on what the team considers important for its company to be successful.

In Chapter 5, I introduced the Pareto method to demonstrate how it can be used to establish a "perfect quality" manufacturing scenario to support the third axiom of just-in-time (JIT). Figure 5-6 illustrated testing of a product manufacturing process to see what tasks had to be improved to achieve that perfect quality goal. We saw in the figure the use of a Pareto chart to rank problems for solution actions. In that example we were attempting to set up a method of achieving perfect quality as part of a special project and not necessarily trying to fix ongoing problems. The Pareto chart was used to make sure the most prevalent problems were attacked first so improvements of greater magnitude would occur sooner rather than later.

In the Figure 5-6 case, the data came from shop floor operations but the time of the data collection spanned two months. This made it virtually irrelevant for fixing here-and-now production problems. Shop operations can't wait two months to determine what has to be fixed. Their horizon is much shorter, typically a week. However, the technique is virtually the same when used as part of an SIS regime. In this section, I will expand upon the Pareto method to show how it can be a useful tool for supervisors and operators as well as engineers. Furthermore, we shall see how it can be used to track short-term trends as well. That information will tell us more about the nature of the problems and whether they are random or predictable.

The basic tool for Pareto analysis is the bar chart. When we use it for quality defect analysis, we group defects by reported causes and keep score over designated time periods—shift, days, weeks, etc. We then create a bar graph with the cause having the highest occurrence all the way to left, the next highest to its right, the third highest-cause category to the right of second, and so on until all of the item categories are display in descending order. We now have a good visual representation of the problems and their magnitudes. Obviously, we can see the relationship between number of failures and the various causes. Two things become evident:

1. *The chart will demonstrate the complexity and interconnectedness of failure causes.* The more causes we show, the more chance there is that we'll find compounding and mixed or matched reasons exist for events. This makes it more difficult to completely cure the problem. For corrective action analysis we need not be too fine. For example with the hammers, dividing weld cracks categories into one for those detected in the head verses another category of those in the shaft are meaningless. They're both weld cracks and it's a virtual certainty that they're caused by errors in the weld process. We don't want to be side tracked

into investigating for metallurgical abnormalities in either the head or the handle when the probability of it being true and causing the weld crack is remote.

2. *The frequency of occurrence is shown.* If there is only a gradual decrease in occurrences between the highest and the lowest, we need to look at the categories. Are they too fine, thus showing us nuances of the same cause? If so, the categories should be consolidated. Having too fine a grouping is a common mistake made in Pareto analysis.

For example if a broad cause would be operator error and we turn up "operator misreading documents," "operator setting machine wrong," "operator not measuring correctly" as independent causes, then we have too fine a cut. This is very similar to what I described above in the hammer weld crack example. Looking at all of these breakdowns, we see they are a case of the operator not knowing how to do his job, perhaps not being trained properly. Most likely the solution to all the operator error nuances would be better training for the operator.

A Pareto chart with correctly selected categories will show a definite trend downward from left to right. In fact, in many cases the 80-20 rule will be demonstrated. The rule states that approximately 80% of all problems will be represented by approximately 20% of the known causes. The approximation ranges could be large, but the rule typically holds in that a minority of the causes will yield a majority of the problems. This means that the effort the operator and supervisor team make for problem resolution should be aimed at the few causes with a high frequency of occurrence.

Figure 11-8 shows a typical Pareto bar chart used for shop operations problem analysis. The figure uses our familiar hammer manufacturing example to illustrate how data are collected and then collated and presented on the bar chart for study.

In the left-hand section of Figure 11-8, we see the raw data for problem reports for a week. The upper far left column contains descriptive language for the different problems, and the upper second column from the left shows the number of incidents. What we have here is the reporting of raw data that has to be evaluated. I'm going to explain a typical shop operations approach to using the raw data to construct a Pareto chart.

First, to every reported class of incident assign a quality control (QC) code. The code is a constant that doesn't change. The descriptions of problems will vary based on interpretation and certain facts the supervisor and operator can agree on. It is in some degree an independent investigation they conduct for each descriptive explanation of a problem. The goal of this mini-investigation is to classify the incident in accordance with a predefined code, the QC code, also explained on the left-hand side of Figure 11-8.

We use the QC code to classify each problem area incident. To the right of the incident listing, we see a tally for the week, and to the right of that we observe the classification the investigation deemed appropriate. Now, we have to organize the data in such a way that we can input them into the Pareto chart itself. This is done by counting up the number of incidents for

Weekly data				Percent of total					
Incidents	No.	QC code	no.	42%	23%	16%	12%	6%	1%
Cracked grips	22	4	30						
Spot welder misfire	8	2	29	x					
Handle machining oversize	16	3	28	x					
Head assembly misaligned	3	1	27	x					
Wrong CNC program used	1	6	26	x					
Burrs on head after assembly	4	1	25	x					
Forge machine temperature error	2	1	24	x					
Wrong material used for head	3	6	23	x					
Assembly jig doesn't work	1	5	22	x					
Handle material hardness out of spec	7	4	21	x					
Burrs on shaft after machining	2	1	20	x					
Total	69		19	x					
			18	x					
			17	x					
QC code	QC code no.	No./QC code	16	x	x				
Operator error	1	11	15	x	x				
Machine error	2	8	14	x	x				
Program error	3	16	13	x	x				
Materials error	4	29	12	x	x				
Engineering error	5	1	11	x	x	x			
Planning error	6	4	10	x	x	x			
Total	69		9	x	x	x			
			8	x	x	x	x		
			7	x	x	x	x		
			6	x	x	x	x		
			5	x	x	x	x		
			4	x	x	x	x	x	
			3	x	x	x	x	x	
			2	x	x	x	x	x	
			1	x	x	x	x	x	x
			0	x	x	x	x	x	x
			QC code	4	3	1	2	6	5

Figure 11-8. Pareto chart.

each QC code, and then entering the tallies on the Pareto chart. Let's look at an example:

QC code = 4 = materials error
Types of incidents judged materials error = 2: cracked grips (22 times), handle material hardness out of specification (7 times)
Therefore, under QC code 4 we will enter 22 + 7 = 29 on the Pareto chart.

We do similar groupings for the other five QC codes, and now we have data to create a Pareto bar chart with. Figure 11-8 shows the descending order of QC codes by rate of incidence over the past week to be 4, 3, 1, 2, 6, 5.

The Pareto bar chart itself is a distribution by frequency of occurrence along the abscissa of the graph. We see how distinctly this shows the data. Pictorially, we see that the first two QC codes of causes (one-third of the codes) account for roughly two-thirds of the data. This is not exactly the 80-20 rule, but a vivid demonstration that we should be solving these first two reasons before looking to the next reason in order of descending frequency. This approach assures we are focusing on the majority causes and not going off on a tangent. If we wasted time on the lesser reasons before the primary ones were resolved, we would not be getting much return for our effort. This is the value of Pareto analysis: a supervisor will direct her operators to use it so that she can identify problems whose resolutions are most likely to have a large positive impact.

The Pareto chart of Figure 11-8 is for one week only. This is only one set of data over a relatively short period of time. Naturally, we want to fix the problems that are occurring the most often, because they probably represent a sizable percentage of all failure costs. But are this week's biggest problems the same as last week's, and are the same problems likely to remain the biggest over the near-term future? (Let us assume that fixes take longer than a week or two to implement, so that we can even address this question.) The only way to make an educated decision is to observe trends. We can do this for a few periods with the Pareto chart. Large numbers of periods, however, would require a different kind of trend chart, as will soon become evident.

Figure 11-9 is a Pareto chart that demonstrates trends. Let's take a look. In this chart, we see multiple bars under each category. Each bar represents a production week. The trend chart is revised every week to show the latest week plus the previous weeks in descending week order. Note that the characteristic Pareto chart appearance is altered in that the bars no longer show a clean downward trend from left to right. This is so because the most current Pareto analysis is represented as the leftmost column under each category (i.e., the QC code), and so the leftmost column is the only one retaining its strict Pareto form. All other weekly data sets are rearranged so that they can be placed next to the corresponding columns for the current week. This means that if code 4 was the highest-frequency cause for the last three weeks, then the three columns for code 4 would be grouped together at the far left in each of the other weeks. But if the frequency race had a different leader from week to week, there is no telling where the code 4 columns would end up from week to week.

Let's look at what the trends are telling us. We see that materials errors have been the highest-frequency problem for the second week in a row, and were the second highest in the first of the three weeks. The data strongly indicate that the materials situation is probably the most troublesome problem and is not getting better. This is a clear call for intensified action.

For programming errors we see an erratic trend that peaked in the second week. Perhaps this has a direct relationship to the initiation of the pilot run. It is feasible to hypothesize the process is going through a debugging cycle, which is not uncommon.

Both operator error and machine errors are decreasing each week. This is a good trend and indicates that the actions taken to correct these "people" mistakes are working. You may think it strange to relate machine errors to people, but they normally are. Lots of operators are reluctant to admit mistakes and try to blame the equipment. Usually, equipment will either work

```
Number       30
of incidents 29  x
             28  x
             27  x
             26  x  y
             25  x  y
             24  x  y                       z
             23  x  y           y           z
             22  x  y           y           z
             21  x  y  z        y           z
             20  x  y  z        y           z
             19  x  y  z        y           z
             18  x  y  z        y           z
             17  x  y  z        y           z
             16  x  y  z  x  y              z
             15  x  y  z  x  y              z
             14  x  y  z  x  y              z
             13  x  y  z  x  y        y  z           z
             12  x  y  z  x  y        y  z           z
             11  x  y  z  x  y  x  y  z              z
             10  x  y  z  x  y  x  y  z     y        z
              9  x  y  z  x  y  x  y  z     y        z
              8  x  y  z  x  y  x  y  z  x  y  z
              7  x  y  z  x  y  z  x  y  z  x  y  z
              6  x  y  z  x  y  z  x  y  z  x  y  z
              5  x  y  z  x  y  z  x  y  z  x  y  z        z
              4  x  y  z  x  y  z  x  y  z  x  y  z  x     z
              3  x  y  z  x  y  z  x  y  z  x  y  z  x  y  z
              2  x  y  z  x  y  z  x  y  z  x  y  z  x  y  z
              1  x  y  z  x  y  z  x  y  z  x  y  z  x  y  z  x  y  z
              0  x  y  z  x  y  z  x  y  z  x  y  z  x  y  z  x  y  z
                 33 32 31  33 32 31  33 32 31  33 32 31  33 32 31  33 32 31
                    4         3         1         2         6         5
```

Fiscal week
QC code

QC code	No.
Operator error	1
Machine error	2
Program error	3
Materials error	4
Engineering error	5
Planning error	6

Figure 11-9. Pareto trend chart.

100% of the time or won't work. It's unusual to have intermittent failures, and they're more than likely caused by operators setting up the machines incorrectly or some other type of human interface error. I always advise my managers not to try to pin obvious operator mistakes on the operator if he resists it. Let him call it a machine error to save face. The only important factor is to assure that the situation gets corrected.

The two minor items, planning errors and engineering errors, are people errors, too. In both cases we see the incidence level is small and therefore requires only giving the group of professionals involved a simple "talking to."

Productivity Trend Charts

The second goal we need to achieve is to know how much product we've produced over specific periods of time and whether we're getting better, getting worse, or staying the same. A corollary to that would be knowing if we are achieving the stated goals. Pareto charts are good tools for examining problems and deciding what corrective actions should be taken, particularly for quality improvement actions. But they are mostly short-range and tactical correction tools. In order to evaluate how the company is performing on a strategic level, we need to have longer-range productivity comparisons. These comparisons show how the company is performing on a daily, weekly, or monthly basis from one time period to the next. These measurements fall into the category of *trend evaluations*.

By measuring productivity and comparing it in different periods, we can learn whether we are making progress in achieving goals or retrogressing. Many people think they can remember how they did last month or last year. Most can't. A few will recall incidents that caused uncharacteristic performance. But saying they can remember accurately what happened and why stretches credibility. Think how hard it is to recall what you did all day, in detail, only a few days ago. It's difficult. In manufacturing shop operations, where the same or similar products involving hundreds and possibly thousands of operations are being made day in and day out, how can people think their recall will be sufficient to know if they're getting better or worse? They can't, in any specific manner accurate enough to base decisions on. The only way to do so is by keeping trend records.

Trend measurements measure accomplishments over time. Time is always a factor and is always the denominator of the equation. We speak of *rate* of accomplishment per time period, such as hammers produced per day or week. We can also choose to measure accomplishments of subassemblies such as forged heads spot-welded to hammer handles. Quality can also be measured as a trend. Think of a quality measurement as a negative accomplishment. Quality trend analysis is used frequently for tracking operator errors and process robustness. Here the goal is definitely to create a negative trend. We want to see the frequency decrease, not increase. Trend measurements can also be thought of as scorecards to show how the manufacturing process is being accomplished over time.

Figure 11-10 shows a typical productivity trend chart that can be used to track production output over time. Here we see the specific level the company is achieving with respect to time, and by looking at previous periods we can make comparisons. I must point out, however, that the data being portrayed must be of a similar nature for any comparisons to be valid. For example, note that the figure shows a sharp decrease in output per day from February to July and then a sharp increase from August to October. At first glance this would seem to indicate that we have a falloff in productivity. That may or may not be true. We can't tell from this chart alone. All we can derive from the data is the amount of product made each month. We have know way of relating any other information. The information we do have is very

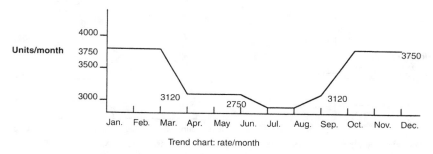

Figure 11-10. Productivity trend chart.

important. We can compare product made with the targets given to the specific shop operations units to see if they are reaching goals. Let's say that for
the month of April they are not. Let's further assume that the miss is by 25%.
Now the question is, Why? From these data alone, we have no idea. This
leads to a second type of trend chart, a rate per smallest specific integral production unit. That could be per machine tool or work station, but is most
commonly shown (for shop operations purposes) as per operator assigned to
the department.

To construct this type of chart we divide the output per time period by the
number of operators available to work. This creates a rate per operator per
time period. By comparing the value for one time period value against that
for a second time period, we can evaluate whether productivity rate
increases, decreases, or stays the same. This is nothing more than measuring
against a time standard for performance, which would usually be expressed
in units per hour per work station. This, in turn, is frequently a measurement of the operator's output, because most work stations are staffed with
only one person.

It is interesting to note in Figure 11-11 that the productivity level has
gone up over a time span in which the total output has gone down (compare Figure 11-10). What we are seeing here with these two trend charts is
a portrait of a typical factory producing a seasonal product output that is
doing what it should do. During peak season, the company increases the
labor force to meet increased demand. But it does so at a price in productivity, since the seasonal workers can't be expected to work at the same
proficiency as the full-time employees. The seasonal people are embarking
on a learning curve where their output will continuously improve over
time to eventually reach that of the full-time employee. The reason the
lower-output months have higher productivity rates is simple to see now.
During this part of the year, only full-time employees are on the payroll.
They have already traveled the course of the learning curve and are
performing the prescribed procedures according to defined methods and
order.

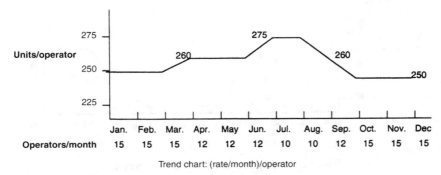

Figure 11-11. Productivity trend per operator chart.

The combination of these two types of trend charts can tell management, at a glance, how the company is performing. For this reason, they are the most popular measurement charts in use. Later in this chapter I will explain how to gather the data via the SIS process to establish these types of measurements. But first, let's look at a common variation of trend charts. While all trend measurements of productivity have the common characteristic of showing changes in time rate *with* time, there are other creative ways of showing trend charts. Figure 11-12 is an example of the most common variation. Notice in this chart that progress is shown by accumulating achievement on a bar graph with the time superimposed with time lines. This graph makes it easy to see if achievement to schedule is being maintained. This is another way of measuring rates of accomplishment.

The bar graph trend chart is a very visual presentation of status. Variations of it are used quite often in advertisement and fund raising campaigns. It fits in well with a strategy where progress is hyped to get more donations or sales. As an aside, marketing people find this style of trend chart very effective. But it definitely has its uses within the factory. It is a valid choice for certain goals related to manufacturing tracking of trends.

Looking at Figure 11-12, we see at a glance that hammer heads are on schedule, assemblies are about half a day behind schedule, and shafts are about half a day ahead of schedule. This information is instantly available without any interpretation necessary on the part of the viewer. For this reason, the style is a favorite with organizations wanting to present data in an "attention-getting" format. From the viewpoint of analysis, it doesn't offer any insights as to why the events are as shown. In Figure 11-12, there is no indication of previous-period trends or even the previous day. The bar just grows with each day's update. (Of course, we could color-code or mark each day's cumulative amount, but that would complicate the presentation and take away from the instant understanding of the present situation for which the chart is designed.) Contrasting this style with the trend charts of Figures 11-10 and 11-11, we see that the common trend charts readily show previous

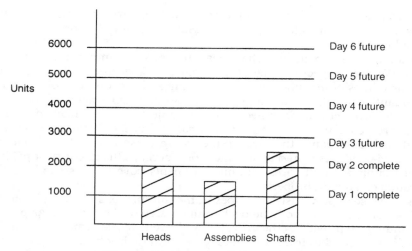

Figure 11-12. Bar graph trend chart.

history, but are not as easily interpreted for how well performance stacks up against the current period's goal.

The previous discussion points out the need to interpret any set of data presented on graphs or in any other form. For this reason it is important to try to put as much explanatory data on a trend chart as possible. With this auxiliary information, we are giving the viewer a guide to how the data should be interpreted. In Figure 11-12, days completed and future days are distinguished (again, I have to point out that there is no way on this graph to know how much progress was made each day). In Figure 11-11, the number of operators per month is shown under each month, even though this has only indirect bearing on the productivity measurement of units per operator. But this information does help explain why the trends in units per month shown on Figure 11-10 and in productivity rates per operator are opposite. The rule of thumb for trend graphs is to put as much information on them as you can without making it confusing for the viewer. By giving more information than the prime information we're trying to convey, we make it easier for the viewer to interpret the data the way we intended.

Obtaining Data for Pareto and Trend Charts

Short interval scheduling depends on data to evaluate how the contract between operator and company is being carried out. We use data to determine whether or not the operator and the supervisor are meeting the dictates of the contract, so it's not surprising that measurements to obtain the data are a large part of the SIS methodology. There are a few rules we need to teach operators in collecting data to assure accuracy of information. Let's take a look.

First, we need to define what measurements are important and what aren't. We don't expect the operator to make these decisions. These are the responsibilities of manufacturing engineering and process control engineering (quality control) and are based on the design requirements of the product. If the product is a machined or formed object, the most likely measurements are geometric, followed by material properties. If the product is a liquid such as a paint, the measurements are those that indicate that the product is within its materials specifications, perhaps the viscosity or pH levels of the fluid. In all cases, the measurements have to be something the operators can obtain properly.

As we've seen previously, the types of measurements are specified on the methods sheets and directly tie back to the design of the product. As part of the training we provide to the operator, we include measurement training. It is obvious we need to train operators to perform their jobs. It may not be as obvious, but it's just as necessary, that we need to train operators on how to measure the results of their performance. Some manufacturing cultures aren't aware of this and may even think it is the quality control department's responsibility to measure, not the operator's. I don't believe that, because SIS theory requires operators to comply with their contract. How can that happen if the operator doesn't know if she did the job right? Therefore, the operator needs to be trained how to take those measurements to determine if the job has been done correctly.

The supervisor has ultimate responsibility to assure that the operator can take the measurements properly. But in practice, the company will assign the training responsibility to the manufacturing or process control engineer. No matter who does the training, it is imperative that we recognize the primacy of the operator in taking trend measurements. The training needs to emphasize two things:

- The skills and techniques required to take the measurements
- An understanding of when the measurements should be performed

Skills and techniques are particular to the process and products. They range from the general skills of using a micrometer to titration of a chemical solution to determine percents of solutions and everything else in between, adjacent, before, and after. Some companies have operators evaluating industrial x-rays for weld repairs and making critical tolerance measurements. They also have operators qualify the validity of the measurements by keeping the instruments calibrated themselves. Thus, we see that the scope of measurements that are done by operators is not trivial but gets right to the heart of the process and product evaluations. In participative situations, particularly in SIS-managed activities, even certification of achieving the design specifications is the responsibility of the operators.

When a measurement needs to be taken is defined by the methods developed for the process. Often, especially in a participative situation, the operator is called upon to make inputs into decisions on scheduling measurement. Generally, measurements need to be taken to verify the validity of a work station setup to prove it will yield good product. Subsequently, additional measurements will be scheduled to check whether the process is still within acceptable output boundaries for proper product performance. The exact number of measurements taken will depend on the nature of the product and the specific statistical process control algorithms. The operator's input in the setup of these parameters is driven by his knowledge of the process, particularly how easy or difficult it will be to do the measuring. These inputs are factored into the measurement scenario so the best indicators of continued process viability are obtained.

We can also divide types of measurements into two categories:

- Quantity
- Attributes

Quantity measurements are used for trend charts. They are most frequently, as discussed previously, measurements of output per time period—which rightly implies they are productivity measurements. For quantity measurements, the operator counts the product or operations completed over a specific period and records them on a tally sheet or even through a bar code system. This type of measurement suits short interval scheduling techniques well, because SIS suggests reporting productivity type progress every few hours.

Attribute measurements are data points for Pareto charts. An attribute is a measurable characteristic of the product or process. An example of a product-related attribute would be a shaft diameter after machining. A process-related attribute might be the voltage and amperage of the spot welder during every weld cycle. Both of these types of attributes provide data for Pareto charts. In the former case, we could be measuring whether the diameter is within or outside the design shaft tolerance. In the latter, we could be relating weld defects via the process amperage and voltage readings. Obviously, there are quite a few characteristics that can be looked at via a Pareto chart, and our measurement scheme should also define how data should be presented.

Taking of measurements is an integral part of any control scheme. In SIS, it is the prime method of obtaining data for defining whether the contract has been complied with. But taking measurements is not as easy as saying just do it. It has to become institutionalized, as a normal part of the daily routine. And this is not an exaggeration. In order for data to be useful, they have to be comparable to previous history. Contrary to what some would say, history does have a habit of repeating itself in manufacturing. We often find ourselves doing things today that are considerably similar to what we did previously. This is especially true in job shops, because they tend to informally specialize in things they do best. For this reason it is advantageous to know how the company fared with past work in order to benefit from experience. It becomes evident, then, that information meticulously gathered in accordance with a prescribed protocol is a necessary discipline for success.

How do we instill that discipline? First, senior management need to accept the argument for continuous measurement. Second, the managers and supervisors have to determine what is important to measure and what is not. Third, the measurements have to be relatively easy to make without undue burdens on the manufacturing team. And finally, the daily routine has to be designed to allow time for measurements even though this is a non-value-added activity in a direct sense (it is very much value-added in an indirect and long-term sense).

As I've said before, the exact nature of the measurement has to be designed by the process control and manufacturing engineers based on the functionality of the product design. This means that the goal of minimizing the difficulty of measuring may have to be compromised somewhat in order to obtain the measurements the design verification requires. But the routine to be followed in obtaining the data can be made a priority of the shop floor's daily expectations. One proven successful way of incorporating the taking of measurements into the shop floor culture is by highlighting it in all stages of operator orientation. Also, a specific part of that orientation should be dedicated to the way measurements should be recorded and when they should be taken. Measurement as a component of the culture needs to be reinforced even though in an SIS environment, the periods are specifically defined; usually every two hours. The need for accuracy has to be stressed along with the need to enter data fully without omissions. The main message to be imparted is that the company takes measurements seriously. It allows production time to do so and expects all employees to do this portion of their job as well as any other.

With accurate and timely data available through appropriate measurement routines, and with operators well trained in them, a company can enjoy the fruits of this endeavor. It will find that decisions are being made with precise information, not best guess estimates. So its decisions will be an order of magnitude more effective than those of the competitor who doesn't have that advantage. This means the company can win more often than not in the competitive battles for profit. A not insignificant advantage.

The factors I've described in this chapter, and in fact the entire book, could truthfully be said to be nothing but old-fashioned common sense. And I admit to that. I also stress that common sense is a scarce commodity in many businesses today because we become so enamored with technology that we hardly ever pass judgment on its practicality. It is the macro good judgments that I've tried to champion. In business, it more important to be approximately correct than accurately wrong. By this I mean, Act on good information that may not be the most complete instead of waiting for all the information to be collected before acting. SIS helps us do that by setting targets, not based on precise time standards but on what the operator and the supervisor understand to be doable, even if it is a stretch. We do not waste time getting precisely calculated production rates before committing to a target. We can always modify a target as more information becomes available.

The message conveyed by SIS is, Take action sooner rather than later and don't worry about the so-called lack of accurate goal setting. I am often amused by the engineering student who expresses a measurement to the sixth decimal place just because his calculator has space in the display for that number of digits. If a distance to a destination is 636 miles and we are traveling at 50 miles per hour, any fractions tagged on are probably irrelevant to the real-world calculation of our arrival. The same can be said about short interval scheduling and the whole of work station dynamics. We are interested in the macro applications of engineering principles to get repetitively excellent results by doing things where the odds are always in our favor. Saying we're going to arrive at our destination in 13 hours instead of the precisely correct 12.72 hours is as accurate as we need to be. Going to the sixth decimal place of the calculator is irrelevant. We are not interested in micromanaging every step, but we are interested in doing those major tasks that will give use consistently good results. We need to get to our destination, not spend energy trying to save that additional 2.2% of total travel time.

All of work station dynamics exhibits this pragmatic philosophy. Understand what is doable and do it well. Expend some energies expanding the frontiers of knowledge, but not at the expense of sacrificing long-term profit potential. This means using pragmatic good common sense in managing the shop floor, by taking advantages of the best practices and technologies, to gain profits. But always keep in mind that a factory manager uses technology only to enhance the ability to make profits. If the technology does not contribute to achieving profits, then it has no place in the factory.

I hope this book contributes to your understanding of how to run a factory and that I've given you some useful points to ponder and apply. Try them. I know you will be delighted with the results.

Glossary

backward scheduling. *See* pull system.

basic tenets of manufacturing. The fundamental theory of manufacturing: the Two Knows (know how to make the product, know how long it should take to do so).

BOM. Bill of materials; a concise summary of sequence of manufacturing along with the materials required in the required quantities.

capability. The equipment and skills to perform a manufacturing operation in a manner that meets design requirements and at the same time can produce profits.

capacity. The measure of ability to make products to required design standards at a rate suitable to economic viability.

CNC. Computer numerical control, referring to a specific set of machines and processes controlled by computers.

concept design. Idea for a product rationalized in terms of science.

concurrent engineering. The synergistic process of doing preproduction, production, and postproduction development work at the same time.

continuous improvement. Striving for perfection by learning from previous actions and designing modifications to the process to allow for better results.

cycle time. The amount of time to start and finish an operation, a set of operations, or an entire manufacturing sequence.

estimated time standards. The amount of time to perform an operation or set of operations based on approximate times usually from observations.

flow manufacturing. Long production runs characterized by special-purpose designed machines and transfer lines to achieve high levels of output at lowest possible cost.

forward scheduling. *See* push system.

group technology. A philosophy of manufacturing that exploits the principle of sameness, in order for job shop production to approach the efficiency of flow manufacturing.

ISO 9000 certification. A formalized evaluation of a company's methodology, primarily control of documentation, to assure consistency of results. Being evaluated as acceptable by a set of examiners constitutes certification by the International Standards Organization.

job shop manufacturing. Small and sporadic production runs characterized by general-purpose designed machines and transfer lines to achieve high levels of flexibility and not necessarily at lowest possible cost.

just-in-case. A strategy for inventory control that emphasizes emergency buffer stock at strategic locations. It is usually associated with non-MRP systems.

just-in-time. JIT, a popularized version of good industrial engineering practices resulting in elimination of waste in manufacturing processes.

kanban. A basically manual pull production dispatch system pioneered by Toyota Corporation that infuses production dispatches with the philosophy of JIT; e.g., eliminate waste wherever found.

manufacturing facilities design. Specific designs for jig, fixtures, and processes necessary to implement the producibility design.

methods instruction. A detailed step—by step set of instructions on how to perform designated work at a work station.

MRP. Sometimes called little mrp, which means materials requirement planning. MRP is a computer program for determining the quantities of materials required to support scheduled production and in the sequence of receipt necessary.

MRP II. Sometimes called big mrp, which means manufacturing resources planning. MRP II is an outgrowth of MRP and is an integrated scheduling and feedback system that allocates work station time and delivery of materials in accordance with a master schedule.

Pareto method. A means of ranking problems in accordance with their frequency of occurrence, used to determine what problems to work on and in what order.

participatory management. A decision-making method based on allowing subordinates to participate in idea generation and decision analysis discussions in order to get support for the ultimate decision.

PDSA cycle. Plan, do, study, act; a technique for systematically evaluating a problem, devising a process for its solution, then implementing and evaluating results with iteration of improved plans (if necessary) until the problem is solved.

predictive maintenance. Minimizing machine and process downtime through calculations of cycle times to failure, then using these data to plan replacements of components on a scheduled basis before failure occurs.

preventive maintenance. Minimizing machine and process downtime through periodic short shutdowns to inspect components for wear and change and/or fix parts before failure occurs.

principle of sameness. The basic theoretical concept of group technology. Parts are grouped on the basis of similar geometry or processing and are produced on the same equipment in a batch mode.

principles of motion economy. An industrial engineering body of knowledge based on the physics of human body motions related to energy expenditure, a major subset of ergonomics.

process control system. A methodology for measuring the effectiveness of an organization for producing perfect products with generic corrective action steps.

process instructions. Directions to the various work stations explaining what has to be done, how to do it, and how long it should take.

producibility design. Process of customizing a design for the production source.

pull system. A scheduling system based on the set required finish date where operations cycle times are subtracted from the finish date to obtain a start date. Sometimes called backward scheduling.

push system. A scheduling technique based on starting operation on a set schedule to finish in accordance with cumulative operation cycle times. Sometimes called forward scheduling.

quality plan. A specific set of actions to ensure each step in the process of making a specific product, or subcomponent of the product, is manufactured in accordance with the design and manufacturing instructions

quality requirements. A definition of what criteria a product or service has to meet to be judged acceptable.

QFD. Quality function deployment, a methodology of matching customer needs with company requirements to determine if the company can supply those needs.

reactive maintenance. A strategy to minimize machine or process downtime by responding rapidly, similar to a fire department responding to a fire.

route sheet. A router, or document, showing the sequence of operations to be performed and the work stations or centers at which the work will be performed.

scientific time standards. A developed time requirement for performing an operation or set of operations based on the principles of motion economy.

self-directed work teams. A tactic for organizing the workforce whereby a group of workers are given the task of planning, performing, measuring results, and taking corrective action for achieving given production goals.

seven steps of the manufacturing system. The fundamental theory of control of an enterprise providing goods and or services.

short interval scheduling. A method of monitoring production to assure attainment of goals through creating an output level agreed to between operator and supervisor and identifying and correcting impediments to achieving the goal. Usually employed in time periods of less than a shift.

SMED. Single-minute exchange of dies, a process pioneered by Shiego Shingo for minimizing nonproductive time through preparing for future jobs in parallel with running current jobs. First applied to punch press operations; now used as a general philosophy for all job changeovers.

SPC. Statistical process control (sometimes known as statistical quality control, SQC), quality control accomplished via statistical methods.

time standard. An evaluated amount of time to perform an operation or set of operations.

TQM. Total quality management, a philosophy of striving for continuous improvement by measuring results of previous actions against established goals and then correcting the process to achieve better future results.

value engineering. A method of evaluating functionality of products with respect to the environment and then seeking ways to provide them at the lowest possible cost.

work simplification. An industrial engineering technique for evaluating manufacturing processes for improvement through a detailed evaluation of each step of the process.

work station. An assembly of tools and equipment, including machines and processes, where value-added manufacturing activities occur.

work station dynamics. A process of focusing direct and indirect support function inputs on the work station necessary for optimal performance.

Selected Related Readings

Allegri, Theodore H., "Advanced Manufacturing Technology," TAB Books, Blue Ridge Summit, PA, 1989.

Bertain, Leonard, "The New Turnaround: A Breakthrough for People, Profits and Change," North River Press, Croton-on-Hudson, NY, 1993.

Clausing, Don, "Total Quality Development: A Step-by-Step Guide to World-Class Concurrent Engineering," ASME Press, New York, 1994.

Creech, Bill, "The Five Pillars of TQM: How to Make Total Quality Management Work for You," Truman Talley Books/Plume, New York, 1994.

Chryssolouris, George, " Manufacturing Systems, Theory and Practice," Springer-Verlag, New York, 1992.

Dawson, Roger, "The Confident Decision Maker," William Morrow and Company, New York, 1993.

DeMarle, David J., and M. Larry Shillito, (Chap. 14, Value Engineering) "The Handbook of Industrial Engineering," 2nd ed., Gavriel Salvendy, ed., Institute of Industrial Engineers and John Wiley & Sons, New York, 1992.

Gerelle, Eric G. R., and John Stark, "Integrated Manufacturing: Strategy, Planning, and Implementation," McGraw-Hill, New York, 1988.

Gershwin, Stanley B., "Manufacturing Systems Engineering," PTR Prentice Hall, Englewood Cliffs, NJ, 1994.

Goddard, Walter E., "Just-in-Time: Surviving By Breaking Tradition," Oliver Wight Limited Publications, Essex Junction, VT, 1986.

Goldratt, Eliyahu M., "It's Not Luck," North River Press, Croton-on-Hudson, NY, 1994.

Goldratt, Eliyahu M., and Jeff Cox, "The CM: A Process of Ongoing Improvement," 2nd ed., North River Press, Croton-on-Hudson, NY, 1992.

Hall, Robert W., "Zero Inventories," Dow Jones-Irwin, Homewood, IL, 1983.

Hayes, Robert H., and Steven C. Wheelwright, "Restoring Our Competitive Edge: Competing through Manufacturing," John Wiley & Sons, New York, 1984.

Hibino, Shozo, and Gerald Nadler, "Breakthrough Thinking," Prima Publishing & Communications, Rocklin, CA, 1990.

Kanter, Rosebeth Moss, "The Change Masters," Simon & Schuster, New York, 1983.

Katzenbach, Jon R., and Douglas K. Smith, "The Wisdom of Teams: Creating the High-Performance Organization," Harvard Business School Press, Boston, 1993.

Karwowski, Waldemar, and Gavriel Salvendy, eds., "Ergonomics in Manufacturing: Raising Productivity through Workplace Improvement," Society of Manufacturing Engineers, Dearborn, MI, 1998.

Koenig, Daniel T., "Computer Integrated Manufacturing, Theory and Practice," Taylor & Francis, Washington, DC, 1990.

Koenig, Daniel T., "Introducing New Products," Mechanical Engineering Magazine, August 1997, ASME, New York.

Koenig, Daniel T., "Making It in the Competitive World," Mechanical Engineering Magazine, May 1998, ASME, New York.

Koenig, Daniel T., "Manufacturing Engineering: Principles for Optimization," 2nd ed., Taylor & Francis, Washington, DC, 1994.

Lu, David J., trans., Japan Management Association, eds., "Kanban Just-in-Time at Toyota," rev. ed., Productivity Press, Cambridge, MA, 1989.

McMullen, Thomas B., Jr., "Theory of Constraints (TOC) Management System," St. Lucie Press, Boca Raton, FL, 1998.

Miller, Stanley S., Competitive Manufacturing: Using Production as a Management Tool," Van Nostrand Reinhold, New York, 1988.

Monden, Yasuhiro, "Toyota Production System: Practical Approach to Production Management," Institute of Industrial Engineers, Norcross, GA, 1983.

Nevins, James L., and Daniel E. Whitney, eds., "Concurrent Design of Products and Processes: A Strategy for the Next Generation in Manufacturing," McGraw-Hill, New York, 1989.

Schwarz, Roger M., "The Skilled Facilitator: Practical Wisdom for Developing Effective Groups," Jossey-Bass Publishers, San Francisco, 1994.

Shingo, Shigeo, "Non-Stock Production: The Shingo System for Continuous Improvement," Productivity Press, Cambridge, MA, 1988.

Spechler, Jay W., ed., "Managing Quality in America's Most Admired Companies," Institute of Industrial Engineers, Norcross, GA, 1993.

Suzaki, Kiyoshi, "The New Manufacturing Challenge: Techniques for Continuous Improvement," Free Press, New York, 1987.

Voss, Christopher A., ed., "Manufacturing Strategy: Process and Content," Chapman & Hall, London, 1992.

Weaver, Richard G., and John D. Farrell, "Managers as Facilitators: A Practical Guide to Getting Work Done in a Changing Workplace," Berrett-Koehler Publishers, San Francisco, 1997.

Zandin, Kjell B., "MOST Work Measurement Systems," 2nd ed., Marcel Dekker, New York, 1990.

Index

skills to accomplish, 252
understanding, 250–251
Golden Rule, industrial, 276–277
Group technology (GT), 6, 331
emulating flow manufacturing,
129–132
groupings, methods for establishing,
119–128
impact of, on scheduling, 117–119
with preproduction planning, 129
relationships to cycle time
evaluations, 128–133
Group training techniques, effective,
268–274
GT, *see* Group technology

H

Hammer process instruction example,
41–53
Header for bill of materials, 51
Hierarchical–type code, 125–128
Human carriers, 170
Human interface ergonomic situations,
177

I

Indented bill of materials, 46
creating, 51–53
Industrial Golden Rule, 276–277
Informal audits, 63–64
Informal classroom sessions, 265
Inspection tours, 273–274
Inspections, 63
Inspectors, 67
Instruction routine(s)
in company, 262–274
on-the-job, 263–264
Interference time, 189–191
Internal work station line balance, 171
Inventory
managing, 219–226
on-hand, 213–215
Inventory control, role of, 211–216
Inventory databases, 224
Inventory system implementation plan
guideline, 223
ISO 9000, 61
ISO 9000 certification, 72, 331
Item inquiry file, 215
Item master database, 224

J

Jigs, 136–138
attributes of good design factored
into, 143–145
creation of, 145–146
definition of, 136
Job shop manufacturing, 119, 332
Job shops, 40
Just-in-case, 6, 108, 332
Just-in-time (JIT), 107, 332
benefits of, at work stations, 111–117
compatibility with manufacturing
resources planning system,
107–111

K

Kanban, 108–110, 332
KISS principle, 23
Knowledge levels, 180

L

Lead time evaluations, 203–209
"Learning organizations," creating,
260–262
Level number, 51
Limping machine, 228
Line managers of work stations,
operators as, 257–259
Long-term corrective action, 65
Lower control limit (LCL), 81
Lowest feasible cost, 23
Lunchtime learning, 272–273

M

Maintenance, 227
effective, planned cycle time and,
227–230
preventive, *see* Preventive
maintenance *entries*
relationship of shop operations to,
246–247
Maintenance effectiveness,
measurements of, 235–239
Maintenance methods, 230–235
Maintenance organization personnel
requirements, 245–246
Maintenance strategy, choosing,
239–243
Maintenance strategy selection matrix,
240
Man-machine chart, 177

Total quality management (TQM),
 72–76, 334
TQM (total quality management),
 72–76, 334
Training program, shop floor,
 successful, guidelines for, 262
Training shop operations team, 259–274
Transitional management practices,
 274–276
Transportation cycle time, 207
Traveler, 95
Trend charts
 bar graph, 325
 obtaining data for, 325–328
 Pareto, 320–321
 productivity, 322–325
Trend evaluations, 322
Trends, 85–86
Two Knows, 1–2

U
Unplanned downtimes, 230
Upper control limit (UCL), 81
Usage, reporting, 217–219

V
Value-added work, 116
Value engineering, 8, 334
 definition of, 149
 improving cost optimization of fixture
 design, 149–162
 process of, 150–152
 techniques of, 152–162
Value measurement, 157–162
Value ratio technique, 159, 161–162
Vehicles, 170
Vendors, relationships with, 210–211
Verb/noun process, DeMarle and
 Shillito, 154–155

W
Warehouse cycle time, 205–206
Waste(s), 11–12
 eliminating, axioms for, 111–117
 silent, 60
Work
 defined as cycle time elements,
 291–292
 quantity of, defined, 292–293

Work orders, detailed release of, 95,
 199–200
Work rules, discipline and, 279–281
Work simplification, 334
Work simplification pattern, 300–301
Work station configuration, 8, 163
 automation considerations in,
 176–178
 effect of methods of manufacturing
 on, 167–168
 people selection based on, 180
 to perform intended manufacturing
 operations, 163–195
Work station design, ergonomic factors
 in, 164–167
Work station dynamics (WSD), 1, 16,
 334
 checklist, 15
 implementing, 287–329
 lack of accurate measurements of
 activities of, 15
 overview of, 1–16
 schematic of, 2–11
Work station dynamics measurement
 schemes, 11
Work station efficiency, 99
Work station line balance, internal,
 171
Work station loading scheme, 100
Work station maintenance, 9–10
 for optimum productivity, 227–247
Work stations, 334
 benefits of JIT at, 111–117
 conceptualizing, to fit flow of
 manufacturing, 178–179
 generics of, 164–178
 inhibitors of successful outputs from,
 289
 operators as line managers of,
 257–259
 quality control at, 55–87
 scheduling, with manufacturing
 resources planning, 89–133
 selecting, 48–49
 support service to, lack of, 14
Work teams, self-directed, 282–284,
 333
Workable designs, 4
WSD, *see* Work station dynamic